GW00394170

AUTHOR'S NOTE

The main problem with writing about another country, is that the inhabitants invariably speak a different language. In my book, we encounter three different categories of Spaniard. Firstly, those with almost perfect English. Carlos the Spanish teacher, for example, and Rafi the estate agent. For them, I have reported their conversations verbatim.

Secondly, we meet those locals attempting to learn English. 'Plees we go bar of old queens thees night, take beer!' Once again, what appears in these pages, is how it came out. More or less!

Finally, we are introduced to the *Village People*. No, not six camp singers from the mid-seventies, waving their arms above their heads, to the tune of Y.M.C.A. Great song, danced to it many-a-time, at weddings. But sadly, native Americans, cops, bikers, builders, soldiers and cowboys do not feature in this volume. No, when I say *Village People*, I mean the people of the village, the neighbours, the older generation generally, who speak not a word of English. For them, I have attempted to translate, as best I can, which was not easy at times, especially at Andalucian pace, and volume!

Hopefully, all will become clear, as the book progresses. So read on, and enjoy! I hope you get as much pleasure from following our adventures, as we did 'living the dream'!

John Austin Richards, Andalucia, Spain.

PROLOGUE. EUREKA!

My 'Eureka Moment' is etched in my memory. I am in the South Island of New Zealand, sitting in a folding chair, outside my rented camper van, in a forest clearing, cup of tea in one hand, an estate agents newspaper in the other. Over the past three weeks we have gradually fallen in love with New Zealand, little seeds of ideas planted here, pieces of the jigsaw germinating there, until right here, right now, the whole jumble of dreams blossoms and falls into place. 'Look at this.' I turn to my wife Chrissie. 'You can get a detached bungalow with a good plot of land here for fifty-grand. Let's sell our place, pack in our jobs, cash in our pensions, move over here, maybe start a little business.'

'Are you serious?' she asks.

'Deadly serious' I reply. 'I am fed up with working all year just for one big holiday. We have gone as far from England as we can go, we always said we would get to New Zealand then see what happened, the girls have left home, we both hate our jobs now, I am sick of spending November to March going to work in the dark, coming home in the dark, I need sunshine, warmth, time for us.'

Chrissie laughs. 'Yeah, but you say that every year, every place we go.'

'Well this time I mean it' I reply. 'Think of all those places we passed through last week where there was nowhere to stay, nowhere to park the van. We could open a small wayside B&B, couple of pitches for camper-vans, maybe a tea garden.'

She laughs again. 'You really are serious? Come on then, what are we waiting for!'

Ten miles down the road I am filling the van with fuel, and I tell the lady behind the counter that I am thinking of moving here, and does she think we will get a visa? 'You a crook, a thief?' she asks.

'Never been caught!' I laugh.

'Well I reckon you'll be all-right then' she smiles. 'Good luck now!'

Back in the UK it's on-line visa applications, business plans and cash-flow projections. If you need to know the net profit on a cream tea in NZ dollars, I'm your man. Then reality hits home. I am not sure I can be that far away from the girls. It costs £1,000 to fly to the UK. Each. They will never be able to afford to visit us. Sorry New Zealand, you are just too far away. We need to find somewhere Ryanair flies......

So two months later we are in Andalucía, Southern Spain, the small town of Alhama de Granada. You won't find it in any guide books but it is just like a film set, largely unchanged from the time the Moors ruled this part of Spain, six hundred-odd years ago, all Moroccan arches, narrow cobbled streets, ancient stone buildings. As dusk falls we are sat outside a bar in the main square, drinking cold beers and eating free tapas of grilled prawns, watching the townsfolk emerge from their siesta. The church bells are ringing and old women, arm in arm, are strolling unhurriedly in that direction, gossiping. Old men meanwhile are walking slowly in line up and down the square, stopping to laugh and joke with other groups. Kids of all ages are playing a gigantic game of football featuring one goalpost chalked on the castle walls. Families with pushchairs are standing round, talking animatedly, each person greeted with a double-kiss. All generations together, sharing the space, enjoying the day. Quite by chance, we have found the real Spain.

An hour or so later the heat is still radiating up from the ancient flagstones, and we are eating at a pavement restaurant. People walking past are smiling and wishing us 'Buenas Noches.' An old man stops to chat, and although we speak different languages, we instinctively know what the other is saying. 'Andaluz bonita' he tells me. It certainly is my friend, it certainly is.

CHAPTER 1. TORREMOLINOS

It is after ten PM as I guide my rental car into the grounds of the Torremolinos beach-front hotel, and I am guessing that any chance of a hot meal tonight has long gone. What should have been an easy five-minute drive from Malaga airport turned into a ninety-minute nightmare on the motorway towards Seville, my head is banging, my eyes feel like I am wearing someone else's contact lenses, my stress levels are sky high, and I need two things in life; a hot shower and ten hours sleep. As I extract my Ryanair-approved hand luggage from the minuscule car boot I realise I know virtually nothing about this hotel. It could be anything from the Ritz to the Walsall Travelodge, although at less than thirty quid for the room I am guessing it is more likely to be the latter. Reception is no doubt a scruffy area with strip lighting, manned by an unmotivated Latvian who will scoff at my request for a meal, but will then try to sell me a continental breakfast in a cardboard box for £5.99. Not that I care that much. We are not here for the joys of the Costa del Sol. Shaven-headed, grey-faced lager-louts in nylon leisurewear, swigging Carling Black Label whilst watching reruns of Coronation Street and EastEnders, in between Manchester United matches on Sky TV, are of no interest for us. We are seeking the real Spain, castles and windmills, *El Cid* and *Don Quiote*, siestas and fiestas, matadors and conquistadors, bull runs, tapas, sultry-eyed senoritas, flamenco dancers and hot sunshine. Oh yes, and cheap houses. Tomorrow, after a quick walk on the beach, we are heading inland to Granada, home of the Alhambra Palace, for two nights, after which we are meeting an estate agent to check out some likely looking houses, then just touring round, searching out the true Spain, if it is still there, and providing we can find it.

We climb the four steps into reception and are immediately impressed by the décor, hacienda-style, two welcoming Spaniards behind the desk and the sound of a band playing 1970's Euro-pop in the bar. We have gate-crashed a party. Check-in is quick and efficient, the restaurant is still open, and they will phone through to reserve us a table. In our room however it is clear some mistake has been made, for this is not a room, but a suite, complete with fitted kitchen. From the balcony comes the unmistakeable sound of the Mediterranean lapping gently against a palm-fringed shore, unless they have had a lot of rain here lately and the pool has overflowed. Unlikely. I get my hot shower, but instead of the ten hours sleep I was craving just a few minutes ago, my spirits have suddenly lifted, my headache and stress have vanished, and we are raring to go.

We are greeted at the restaurant by two waiters in crisp white shirts and tight black trousers. They look a swarthy pair to me but Chrissie seems fascinated by their choice of pantaloons and almost knocks over a table as she is not looking where she is going. Menus are brought, the wine list is offered, and after some recommendations, and much arm-waving and gesticulating, choices are made. The wine arrives, it is dark, fruity and full-bodied, a bit like the wine-waiter, and my taste buds rejoice. This must be a grape the Spanish keep to themselves as I have never seen it on sale in Tesco, but Senor tight-crotch was correct- it is indeed *delicioso.* My starter arrives, a large plate of sliced tomatoes, drenched in olive oil, they are big, beefy and humming with garlic, a bit like the head waiter, and my taste buds perform hand-stands. How can something this simple taste so utterly amazing? I feel I am eating sunshine, and clearly these tomatoes have not been air-freighted from Zimbabwe, or wherever it is that British supermarkets get their tasteless vegetables from these days.

Across the room is a bar-counter, and my eyes are drawn to an unusual sight. On the top of the counter is a pig's hind leg, sticking straight up in the air, like the last desperate wave of a drowning man. It has clearly been there for some while, as the skin is the colour of John Wayne's saddle, and the toenails have been painted black, like some East-German transsexual at a Freddie Mercury reunion concert. The ankle is quite slim and it looks almost as if the pig was wearing a pair of stilettos when it died. Quite fetching really, in a perverted sort of way.

Just then a wild-eyed chef bounds from the kitchen, brandishing a knife almost two feet long, which he is crashing against a steel sharpener, as if he is about to go into battle. With me probably, as he is staring in my direction. I cannot think of anything I could possibly have done to upset him, unless he has heard that an English tourist has scored a suite for thirty quid, or maybe he still harbours a grudge about the Spanish Armada. Guilty on the first count, but the other one was a few years before I was born, although my ancestors were Cornish watermen, so maybe he has a point. He is grinding his knife so fiercely that sparks are almost flying, and I am starting to wonder exactly what is about to happen, and whether I need to make a quick exit, when he turns towards the pig's leg and starts carving, caressing the knife and shaving off wafer-thin slices. He is concentrating so hard, like a surgeon performing open-heart surgery, or a violinist playing a priceless Stradivarius, but eventually he stands up, eases the coils out of his spine, and gestures to the head waiter with his fearsome knife. My main course is ready. This is of course Jamon Iberico, Spanish ham, a whole plateful carved personally for me by a maestro. To anyone used to the watery, rectangular-shaped, pink ham they serve in Britain this stuff will come as a bit of a shock, as it is meaty, chewy, dark red in colour, but bursting with flavour, and my taste buds think they have died and gone to heaven, after performing somersaults.

At that moment the door of the restaurant bursts open and three hombres dressed in sombreros and ponchos, strumming guitars, singing, stomping, clapping (proof that men actually can multi-task), dive in. They weave their way past our table, and reserved Englishmen as I am, I applaud them politely. The Spanish customers however go wild, joining in the singing, stamping and clapping, and the noise is unbelievable. Maybe it's the wine, the tomatoes, the garlic or the ham, even the waiters bums, or possibly all of the above, but my senses are overwhelmed. I've only been in this country a couple of hours but already Spain has taken me by the hand and turned a stressed, angry Englishman into a laid-back chilled-out Continental. Something is definitely happening.

After the meal, back in the bar, the atmosphere has ramped up a couple of notches in the last few hours. The 'band' turn out to be a female vocalist together with an older bloke on a keyboard, and apart from us, they are the youngest people in here. By a long way. And the dance floor is packed. As we weave our way through the gyrating geriatrics, in search of a table, I catch snatches of German, Dutch, Scandinavian, and suddenly the penny drops. Pensioners from all over northern Europe have come down to the Costa del Sol to escape the winter, enjoy their retirements, and spend their kids inheritances. And who can blame them? They are dancing like there is no tomorrow, which for a few of them might actually be the case. Tall blond Norwegians in scary trousers are jiving with lumpy, misshapen Germans, but the undoubted star of the show is a slim woman with orange hair in a long, floaty chiffon dress. She looks as if she probably danced naked round the camp-fire at Glastonbury in about 1971, then sat down cross-legged on the grass and rolled a giant joint. She is channelling her best Pink Floyd moves, arms waving above her head as if she is in some spliff-induced trance, unlike her dance partner who either has a wooden leg, or a massive erection. He is limping round the floor like a demented jack-in-the-box, trying but failing to catch hold of orange-hair.

The song ends, old limpy stumps back to his seat, and our heroine returns with what looks like an eastern European lorry driver, dressed in skin-tight jeans, shirt unbuttoned to the navel, revealing a solid, mahogany-coloured gut, sprouting a massive bunch of snow-white chest hairs, in the middle of which nestles a gold medallion. Classy. In profile he looks like a letter 'P', and seems in real danger of toppling over. The band are playing a slow, romantic number and lorry-driver is trying to grapple orange-hair into a smooch, but she skilfully evades his amorous advances and the pair of them remain separate until the end of the dance, when he lurches back to his seat, sweating profusely.

She then casts round for another partner, our eyes meet for a split second, and she seems about to come over, then spots Chrissie glowering next to me and thinks better of it. Instead she disappears behind the pillar and re-emerges with a whiskery, white-haired man so old he might be her grandfather. It seems she has raided a nursing home as he is still wearing a pair of tartan slippers, but she guides him carefully round the floor and they get a huge round of applause as the song comes to an end.

Meanwhile we sip our *sangria* and enjoy the people-watching. This reminds me of a mid-1960's holiday camp, in fact there is little evidence that the last forty-odd years have actually happened. It's like being back in Bognor Regis, only with Germans.

On my first visit to the Gents I spot a poster in the foyer advertising a concert the following Friday by *Los Paraguayos*. Now as many people over the age of about sixty might recall, this group had a 'one-hit-wonder' in the pop charts about fifty years ago with the song 'Guantanamera'. Since that time, supporters of football clubs all over Britain with four-syllable names have adopted the song.

'One Bristol Rovers,

There's only one Bristol Rovers,

One Bristol Ro-vers,

There's only one Bristol Rovers.'

I can see them now on 'Top of the Pops', (*Los Paraguayos* I mean, not Bristol Rovers) in black-and-white of course, three (or was it four?) caballeros in ponchos and sombreros, strumming and singing. Surely they can't still be alive? They must be well into their seventies if they are. Perhaps the concert is by 'Sons of *Los Paraguayos*', or maybe a *Los Paraguayos* tribute act, but the poster just says '*Los Paraguayos.*' The thing is, there can't be more than half a dozen people alive in the world today who could actually name a single member of the original group. So what's to say this latest lot are not imposters? What's to say they are even Paraguayans? I mean, I couldn't even place Paraguay on the map. South America of course, but where? I could pick out Brazil, the big lump on the right, Argentina below that, Chile on the left, long and thin. But the rest of them? Not a clue. So as far as I am concerned, they could pick out three (or is it four?) Uruguayans. for example. and I would be none the wiser. This stuff is important, at one o'clock in the morning.

Returning to my seat I find Chrissie upending the *sangria* jug, trying to get at the fruit at the bottom. 'For heaven's sake, you can't still be hungry!' I laugh.

'I love the fruit in *sangria*' she giggles, spearing a slice of orange. 'Besides, this is part of my five-a-day!' I tell her about the forthcoming concert. 'Oh my God, are they really here next Friday?' she cries. 'We have to come and see them! I had their record! My Nan brought it back from her holiday in Benidorm!'

She is joking, right? She had that record? While I was buying discs by the Beatles, and the Stones? Is this grounds for divorce, concealing these secrets from her past? 'Tell me you're not serious, return to this pensioner's paradise? I'd rather eat my own liver.'

She hooks out a slice of apple, and slurps it down. 'Actually, I'm really enjoying it here. We have to be back in this area on Friday, for the flight on Saturday morning. So why not come back here? Go on, you know it makes sense!'

On my next visit to the Gents, my eyes alight on a scene I have never before experienced in fifty-four years on this earth. Half a dozen people are sat round a table, knitting. Not drinking, just knitting. One o'clock in the morning, crowded hotel bar, waiters busying round trying to keep up with the orders, and this lot are taking up a whole table without buying a single drink. For a few moments I am unable to process this information, although the wine, the tomatoes, the garlic, the ham and the sangria are clouding my brain. I look away. Surely it was a mirage? Surely when I turn my head back they will be gone? No, there they are, and two of them *are blokes.* Where I come from, this kind of behaviour would get you beaten-up. The four women all have this 'holier-than-thou' look on their faces, as if they are saying *'look at you lot, drinking, dancing, making fools of yourselves, whereas us, we are doing something wholesome, without the need of artificial stimulus.'* The two guys however have the boggle-eyed look of concentration on their faces, one of them is sticking out his tongue, as he 'knits one, pearls one, drops one', as my Nan used to say when she taught me to knit when I was about six, and had to do some knitting for my Wolf-Cub badge.

Returning to my table, I slide into my seat, with my hand against my mouth. 'Don't look now, but on that table in the corner, people are knitting. Germans.'

Chrissie roars with laughter. 'How do you knit a German? Lederhosen? Huge steins of beer? An oompah band?'

I shake my head, to clear the total shock to my system this first night in Andalucia has been. 'No, they're not knitting Germans, they are Germans, knitting. Blankets, by the look of it, although the blokes are doing hankies! With holes!' We are both crying with laughter.

'That'd be right' she splutters, 'blankets for the nursing home!'

Heading back to our suite, I am floating. 'You know what? I haven't had so much fun for ages' I announce. 'I came here expecting to hate the place, and look at the pair of us! Maybe, just maybe, we could come back and see *Los Paraguayos* next Friday.' As we drift off to sleep, Chrissie starts to sing, softly.

'One Leeds United,

There's only one Leeds United.....'

CHAPTER 2. JUST LOOKING.

As 'House-For-Sale' signs go, this one has to be unique. Someone has painted 'Se Vende', the Spanish equivalent, in three-feet- high black letters on the front wall of the house, followed by a phone number. Whoever buys this house, and it certainly won't be me, will have the devil's own job covering this unconventional advertising up.

Following the realisation that New Zealand was just a step too far, well ten thousand miles too far actually, I have been burning the midnight internet oil searching for the best combination of value for money, sunshine, and proximity to budget airlines. And here we are, inland Andalucia, around fifty miles north of Malaga, as the crow flies, bordered by Cordoba to the west, Granada to the east, and Jaen to the north. A land of olives. Unending olive trees, as far as the eye can see. We are out with Rafi, our Spanish estate agent, who worked in the UK for several years and therefore speaks pretty good English. We have been corresponding for the last few weeks about our requirements and budget, and somehow I had pictured her as middle-aged. Not so. She is like a model, or thinks she is. Glossy, wavy, shoulder-length black hair, which she is constantly flicking and preening, a tight white t-shirt, even tighter jeans, and red stilettos, with a smart-phone seemingly welded to her ear. Not that I am complaining mind you, but Chrissie seems to have taken an instant dislike to the woman. For some reason.

Rafi has dozens of detached rural farmhouses on her books, mostly in great condition, some with pools, all within our budget. I have selected about half a dozen we would like to see, and have printed the details from the internet.

'So which of these houses are we seeing first?' I enquire, shuffling my papers.

'Oh, none of them,' she cheerfully replies. 'One is under offer, and the rest are not suitable for you. But don't worry, I have beautiful house here for you. I am sure you love it.'

She is wrong. I hate the place, and we've only just got out of the car. A wreck, surrounded by a jungle. I feel overwhelming, crushing disappointment. All this time, all these plans, all the research, convincing Chrissie that this is a good idea. For this.

'Rafi, do you remember I said we wanted an old farmhouse in good condition, preferably with a pool, and around four thousand square metres of reasonably flat land?'

'Yes.'

'Do you recall I said I was keen on DIY, but not a builder, so the house needed to be ready to move into?'

'What is this dee eye why?'

'DIY. Do it yourself. It's what we call repairing and decorating your own house in the UK.'

'Yes.'

'Do you remember I outlined our business plan? That we wanted to let the house as holiday accommodation, on an occasional basis, maybe one week a month? And that we would put our caravan on the land, in a secluded spot, and when the guests came, we would move into the caravan, to give them privacy, but still be on hand if needed?

'Yes.'

'So why have you brought us here? This house is in very poor condition. There is not much land, and what land there is, is a hill.'

Rafi sweeps her hand through her hair, like a matador flapping a cape in front of a charging bull. 'There is land, much land, at the back of the house. Look! And the house only needs a bit of, how you say, PLC.'

'TLC' I correct her. 'Tender loving care. And where is the land? There is no garden wall. All I can see are olive trees.'

Rafi laughs. 'You English and walls. There are no walls out here, look, why would you need a wall here?' and she gestures out across the landscape. She is correct, there are no walls, hedges, fences or any obstructions of any sort. Just a never-ending sea of olive trees, stretching to the horizon. They even climb up the sides of the mountains, almost to the rocky summits.

'Sorry, but I just cannot see where the garden of this house is,' I reply. 'And for me, it needs a bit more than PLC. I mean TLC.'

She disconnects her phone from her ear and stabs it in the general direction of the jungle. 'See that big tree on the left? And the other tree on the right? Well that is the limit of your garden.' I wish she wouldn't call it 'my garden.' It is not, and never will be, 'my garden'. 'The farmer know where his olives are, and he will not bother you. He will come here maybe three times a year, to put fertiliser on the land, then in January or February he will pick up the olives, then in Spring maybe return to cut back the trees, and that is it. Yes the garden need PLC and you could put up a fence, but there is no need.'

OK, I can understand that. This is abroad, they do things differently here. If we are to assimilate, we have to accept local customs. If Rafi says we don't need a wall, then so be it.

'So how much is this house, Rafi?'

'Oh, eighty thousand Euro's.'

Hmmmm. That is exactly the same amount as our budget. Even though she has houses in better condition, with more land, with swimming pools, for the same money on her website. I detect a funny smell here, and not just the whiff of decay around this house.

'This is exciting opportunity' she continues. 'This house has been in the same family for generations. You are very lucky. The house belonged to a couple, she got up in the morning to cook the breakfast, she call her husband to come for his breakfast. He don't come so she go upstairs, and see he die in bed. So she leave the house, to live with her daughter, and not come back.'

'You mean the husband died here in this house?' Chrissie queries. 'How long ago was this?'

'Oh, twenty years' Rafi confirms, nobody live in this house for twenty years.'

Blimey, not only has she brought us to a house we didn't ask to see, somebody actually died upstairs. This day is getting worse by the minute. No wonder the place is falling down, presumably it has had no PLC for twenty years, and it didn't have any for the twenty years before that either, by the look of it. Well I suppose we might as well look inside, even though there is zero chance, less than zero chance, of us deciding to buy this.

'Are we going inside?' I enquire.

'I have no key' Rafi admits, 'but they are coming now to meet with us. *La famillia*. The family. They are very exciting that English people come to see their house, they never see English people here.

Suddenly I am gripped by panic. Spanish people are coming to meet us. And we have never met any 'real' Spanish people before. I mean, we went to Barcelona twenty years ago, but everyone there in the hotel and bars spoke English. And this trip, we have spoken to waiters, receptionists, and this useless estate agent, and they all speak English. Now obviously, if we move here, we fully expect, and want, to learn Spanish. Especially out here in the wilds. But today, right now, I know about half a dozen words.

Just then, a large car comes trundling up the country lane and pulls over outside the house. The family have arrived.

Doors fling open and out step an old woman, presumably the widow, a middle-aged woman, presumably her daughter, and a girl about eighteen, the granddaughter I imagine. The male driver, the son-in-law I am guessing, remains in the car. Rafi bounds over, and lots of 'kissing and flopping', as my mother would have described it, and excitable shouting, ensues. Then it is our turn. I would have preferred a solid British handshake, rather than this foreign malarkey, but no, cheeks are proffered, and we have to go through the whole double-kiss ritual. Actually it is lovely, we are here to learn, and if living without a garden wall, and kissing all and sundry is what it takes, bring it on.

'Benga! Bamos!' Cries Rafi. 'In we go!'

'Which one is Benga, and which one is Bamos?' I enquire, pointing at the two senior ladies who are making their way towards the house, jangling keys.

Rafi bursts out laughing. ''Benga, Bamos' means 'come on let's go!' ' she giggles.

'OK then, lets benga bamos!' I cry, even though I really have no interest in wasting everyone's time. But they are here now. Benga!

There is actually a low, falling-down garden wall in front of the house. Granny approaches, tries to open the rickety wooden gate, but it's stuck solid. 'Give it a kick!' shouts Rafi, raising a vicious-looking stiletto. 'Benga!' I shout. Blimey, this Spanish is easy. I will be fluent by nightfall. But it is hopeless, the gate is going nowhere.

'OK don't worry' Rafi continues, 'just step around and follow me.' The famillia start to rummage round in the boot of the car, leaving the three of us to 'explore'. After much heaving and pushing Rafi manages to prise the front door open, and in we go. And it's just like stepping back in time. In the hallway, coats are hanging on the rack, with shoes laid out below, just as if the occupants have nipped out for a pint of milk, and will be returning any minute. There is a thick layer of dust everywhere, but apart from that, we could be in our own episode of Doctor Who?

Into the sitting room, with wedding and communion photos on the sideboard, fireside chairs with wings, I feel like I have stepped back in time to my granny's house. I am beginning to understand now why the family have not followed us inside. Clearly, no-one has been back here for twenty years. This must be so difficult for them. The widow is no doubt reliving the day her husband passed away, the daughter likewise, losing her father.

Following Rafi into the kitchen, suddenly I receive a huge shock to the system. On the two-ring gas cooker is a frying pan, containing what is obviously the remains of a fried breakfast. A shrivelled egg, and what appears to be about three rashers of bacon. I stare at this in sheer, utter disbelief. The man's breakfast is still there. I would have imagined that the ravages of time, flies, rodents, maggots or whatever would have rotted the food away to nothing.

But no, there it is, not quite as fresh as it once was, possibly just past its sell-by date, but unmistakably a good old-fashioned fry-up. I am dumbstruck. You would have thought, wouldn't you, that having finally decided, after twenty years, to put the house on the market, that the family might have thought it a good idea to come out here and, I dunno, tidy up a bit? Maybe lose the fried egg?

I turn to face Chrissie, who appears to have turned several shades paler than when I last checked. Rafi however seems completely unperturbed, as if this kind of thing is entirely normal in the life of an Andalucian estate agent. 'Needs a bit of updating, maybe, but a good size kitchen, don't you agree?' *A good size? Is she serious?* I am desperately trying not to look round this kitchen again, in case I catch sight of the two-decade-old fry-up. I have just remembered I had egg and bacon for breakfast in our hotel this morning, and I am supremely keen not to become re-acquainted with it.

'OK, bamos arriba!' Rafi cries. 'Lets go upstairs.' She is clearly enjoying this, although I am beginning to wonder if this whole trip to Spain is just a dream, and that I will soon wake up from what is rapidly turning into a nightmare. We follow her up the stone, tiled stairs, into what appears to be the main bedroom, old iron bedstead, blanket and sheet turned back... OH MY GOD! There, in the middle of the bed, where the sheets are crumpled slightly, is where the husband died. Where his body lay is clearly visible. My hands instinctively rise to my face as I gaze in horror at this grotesque scene. I start to feel light-headed, in urgent need of fresh air. I want to push the walls away and get out of this place.

'I'm off' I croak, as my throat has suddenly gone dry. 'This house is doing my head in', and I push past Rafi and crash down the stairs, and out into the sweet, beautiful daylight.

Meanwhile the women are unloading the boot of the car. A portable CD/radio player, a number of large bottles of spring-water, and half-a-dozen large tubs of white paint. Painting? They are going to be *painting*? This house needs a good clear-out, followed by a thorough, serious clean. Two week's work, at the very least. Just the possibility that they could seriously be considering painting is unthinkable.

'Son-in-law' is standing in the shade of a tree, watching me with undisguised interest. 'Una buena casa?' he enquires. *A beautiful house? Are you kidding mate? There's a dead guy's breakfast in the kitchen. The imprint of his corpse is visible in the bed. Una buena casa my arse.*

Just then Rafi and Chrissie appear at the front door. Chrissie is now almost completely white, like she has seen a ghost. Which I suppose we almost have. 'Rafi, I have seen enough. Please thank the family, and get us the hell out of here. Now!'

At this stage of house-hunting in the UK, the next step would be to trot out the usual platitudes to the vendors. 'We love the house, but have a few more still to view....' Obviously we cannot say that here, but I do manage a 'buena casa' as we go through the same kissing ritual as we say goodbye to the women.

'You not like the house?' asks Rafi as she drives away.

'Put it this way' I reply, 'I went to Turin a few years ago, hoping to see 'The Shroud'. The church was closed or something, so I didn't get to see it, but never mind, I think I saw it today!' I'm not sure she understands my meaning, or good old British sarcasm, but I am past caring.

'OK you will love this next house' Rafi confidently predicts, 'it is a bit nearer civilisation, in a village, near a small town. The owners are not there, he has developed skin cancer working in the garden, so has to move to the north of Spain where it is not as sunny. But their English friend is staying there and she will show us round.' *Blimey, tell it like it is Rafi, why don't you?*

'So how much is this next house?'

'Oh, one hundred and twenty thousand Euros.'

I am struggling to remain calm. *What part of 'our budget is eighty, but we could go to one-hundred maximum, including all the buying costs, for something exceptional, which ticked every single box', doesn't she understand?*

'You remember I told you about our budget?' I ask, wearily.

'Yes, one-hundred, but the people have just reduced it to one-hundred and nineteen.'

Oh that's OK then, they've knocked off a grand. 'So how much are the buying costs for a house this price? I already know this information, but need to hear it from the horse's mouth, so to speak.

'About ten thousand' she confirms.

'Right, so one hundred and twenty, plus ten, makes one hundred and thirty. Even with a thousand off, it's still twenty-nine thousand too much. Do you think they will reduce it by another twenty-nine?' Sarcasm is creeping into my tone again, but this woman is starting to get severely on my nerves.

'Maybe, who knows' she answers, 'anyway, we are here now.' We are approaching a village, in a steep-sided valley. On the left, the hillside is covered in olive trees, right up to the summit, but on the right hand side the gradient is so acute that not even olives will grow. We pull up outside a pretty white cottage, on the right, and I stare in disbelief at the forty-five degree bare hillside rearing up behind it. She has done it again, completely ignored our instructions about the business plan.

'Beautiful cottage, don't you think? she chortles cheerfully.

Actually it is a very pretty cottage, but as I gaze upwards at the steep, bare, barren hillside rising up behind it, I feel a mounting sense of anger. 'So where is the garden, Rafi?'

She waves a well-manicured hand at the useless forty-five degree slope disappearing towards the summit. 'Up there.'

I am grinding my teeth. 'And the caravan?'

She looks around desperately for inspiration, then catches sight of a rough olive track snaking its way up the hillside, clearly not part of the cottage land, but close enough. 'Maybe the farmer will give you access?'

'So how far up does the garden go?'

'To the top of the hill.'

'So what is at the top of the hill?'

'Don't know.'

'Does the land extend past the top of the hill? Is there access from the other side of the hill?

'Don't know.'

'Why don't you know?'

'Because no-one has ever been up there!'

No, because you have not bothered to find out, you mean. I am clearly wasting my time asking this woman any more questions. Chrissie was correct in her original opinion, as she usually is. Whereas I was distracted by something or other..

'OK, lets go inside' she continues, tapping on the front door. It is opened by a middle-aged lady, the house-sitter no doubt. She is extremely welcoming, even though it isn't her house, and has no hesitation in showing us around, starting with the small front patio. 'It's important to have plenty of shady areas, whatever you eventually buy,' she explains. 'You are here for the sun of course, but you must realise that in high summer, you also need to get out of the sun during the day. This grape vine for instance is perfect, even if you don't like grapes, never cut a grape vine down! Perfect shade under the vines. And you need different outside areas around the house, for different times of the year. For example, the terrace at the rear of the cottage is perfect in winter, sheltered from the wind and catching most of the sun during the day.' I have learned more from her in five minutes than I have from Rafi all morning. Why couldn't this lady be our estate agent?

Inside, the cottage is a gem, and I am really frustrated that the outside land is completely unusable. Plenty of exposed wooden beams, both downstairs and upstairs, and a library area in one of the bedrooms. Outside at the back is another terrace, then climbing up the hillside we can see where the owner has started terracing the garden. He has only made two terraces however, one above the other, and I can appreciate what a monumental task this would be, digging out and levelling each step. The women disappear back inside so I resolve to walk, or rather climb, to the top of the hill to see for myself just what is up there. Maybe the cottage land extends along the top, and maybe there is another access, which we could use? After about ten paces however I am perspiring freely, but I am determined to reach the summit, but when I have made it about halfway I hear Chrissie calling me from below. 'Rafi says we have to leave now.'

'Well tell her I am climbing to the top!' I shout down, and resume my task.

I have only made it another few steps however when I hear Rafi's voice. 'Come on, we have to get back as I have another appointment now.' In disbelief, I start to climb back down, we thank the lady for her advice and walk towards Rafi's car. To be as obstinate as possible I pretend I want to see what is around the corner in the village, deliberately stalling for time, but Rafi is getting agitated so in silence I get in her car and we drive back to town.

And that was it. Our first experience of Spanish estate agents. We never heard from her again.

We collect our car from outside Rafi's office, still somewhat shell-shocked from our house-hunting experiences, and head south out of town, destination unknown, but still generally in search of the real Spain. 'Has this whole trip been a complete and utter waste of time?' ponders Chrissie, shaking her head.

I consider my reply carefully, bearing in mind this whole episode in our lives has been driven by me. 'I don't think so. OK, we are not buying either of those houses, but we have seen a lot of inland Spain, Granada, the Alhambra, we have met real local people, enjoyed the ambience. I think I could live in this country, I feel at home here, the sun shines most the time, palm trees grow, the cost of living is low...'

'Yes all right, Neil Diamond!' She giggles. 'But don't forget that song was about someone who was torn between New York and LA! But I agree, I could live here too.' She brightens visibly. 'And besides, we still have the *Los Paraguayos* concert tomorrow night to look forward to!'

CHAPTER 3. ONE YEAR LATER - ON THE MOVE!

I am dozing in our caravan. I am quite good at this, just lie flat with a cushion under my head and I am away to the land of nod. Suddenly I wake up and for a few moments cannot remember where I am. Then I glance out the window and see a forest of cars, lorries, caravans, and a huge boat. Yes we are in Dover waiting to board the ferry to Dunkirk, leaving England behind. A bloke in a yellow jacket then appears and tells us we are boarding in five minutes so can we return to our cars? We do, and twenty minutes later boarding commences. The elderly German camper-van in front wheezes into life like an arthritic smoker in a Munich beer Keller, and after the pall of black oily smoke has dispersed I steer the caravan into the bowels of the ferry.

Taking our fleeces (this is August, the end of the British summer) we head up on deck, and find a seat looking out over the rear of the ship, with a great view over the white cliffs, or it would be if it wasn't drizzling. There are many things I will miss about England, but drizzle isn't one of them. Then, and how can I be kind about this, a rather large woman comes and sits right in front of us, completely obscuring our view, and proceeds to rummage in her bag for a magazine. Why do people do this? I feel like telling her but she is bigger than me so decide to do the British thing, and keep quiet. However every cloud has a silver lining, as she is wearing Flight Socks, pulled right up her meaty calves, and sandals. I am no medical expert but have never heard of anyone developing Deep Vein Thrombosis on a ferry. Perhaps she is mad and thinks she is on a plane, maybe she was checking the magazine for the in-flight movie and the price of two-hundred Benson & Hedges, and thinks that soon a trolley dolly will come up to check her seat belt, and give her a boiled sweet. Then the boat will hurtle across the Channel and rise to thirty-thousand feet, before descending to Dunkirk, I don't know, two minutes later?

To complete the comedy of the situation her husband is a tiny thin man, and together they look like one of those couples on the seaside comic postcards you used to see. All it needs now is for a blonde with huge breasts in an impossibly tiny bikini to walk by, and for the husband to remark 'Blimey Mother, we should have had melons for tea last night!'

As the white cliffs fade into the mist and we head out across the channel, we nip inside for a coffee, and a warm up. At least we won't need fleeces where we are going, but France is only twenty miles away so the weather is unlikely to be any different on the other side, but remarkably as we roll off the boat the sun is coming out. We head carefully along the motorway past Calais, easing my way into driving on the other side of the road, then turn onto the rural French byways where you see all those Gallic signs like *Prochaine Sortie, Toutes Directions,* and *Centre Ville.* No idea what they mean, but they do seem so wonderfully , well, French.

Following the coast road towards Boulogne, we find a camp site where I practice my schoolboy French, and in the evening head out for our first Continental meal. Being pensioners however we stick to the fifteen-Euro set platter, three courses which happily do not contain anything fried in breadcrumbs, another aspect of British life I will not miss. Next day, which is the first Monday of our retirement, there is no six O' Clock alarm, no Monday morning feeling and no mad rush, just an excited and slightly scary feeling as we turn the van towards the south, and new adventures.

Retirement. Early retirement too. What will it mean? What does the future hold? Will this turn out to be a colossal mistake? The one single thing almost everyone said, when we announced our plans, was 'you are too young to retire, what will you do all day?' Well that's as maybe, but there is one sure thing I will not be doing all day, and that is working. Done my share, time to let the younger generation have a go. So can we be together constantly without killing each other? I believe so, one hundred percent, although I am sure Chrissie has had serious doubts, in the eighteen months since I sat on the folding chair outside the camper-van in New Zealand, and came up with this plan. Several times I have caught her giving me sly, sidelong glances, as if she is mentally calculating how big a hole she needs to dig, to bury my corpse. And to be fair, the plan has changed several times since then. No wonder the poor woman is looking slightly shell-shocked these days, she never knows what crazy ideas I will come up with next. First it was a B&B in New Zealand, then it was a part-time holiday let in Andalucia. And now? Well the problem was that both those plans involved selling our house in the UK. And the even bigger problem was the massive banking crash and economic recession which happened the week after we finally decided to put the house on the market, which meant that people basically stopped buying houses. And the prices dropped by tens of thousands, making selling a less attractive option.

Having tried unsuccessfully to sell the house over the past year, we are now on plan C. Which is to let the UK house and buy something cheap in Andalucia. A town house basically, there are dozens of them apparently just waiting for British people to snap up, at prices which wouldn't get you a garage in the UK. We can live on the rent, plus our small private pensions, so we no longer need to involve ourselves in the letting of the Spanish house, and can just, well, retire. Foolproof, or what?!

So here we are, towing our beloved caravan behind us, bound for a small rural camp-site about five miles inland from the Costa del Sol, where I have secured a bargain monthly 'pensioners special deal'. The site has a pool and is open all year, so we will just live there until we find a cheap house. No rush, we can scout out the area, although we do have an appointment in two week's time with an estate agent (no NOT Rafi!) in the small town of Santa Marta. Denise, the British lady who runs the agency, has dozens of properties on her books, ranging from ruins for less than ten thousand Euro's, wrecks for under fifteen, general dilapidation at less than twenty, slightly falling down for around twenty-two, but for twenty-five or thereabouts, some really quite promising ones. And it is the quite promising ones we hope to look at. No idea what this Santa Marta place is like, all I know is it has a bank, a post office, a supermarket, an outdoor swimming pool and about a hundred bars. So we won't go thirsty whilst house-hunting, that's for sure!

Six days later we are in Andalucia. Dusk is approaching as we travel the last few kilometres along the coastal motorway, then turn off along a snaking, winding mountain road, heading for the rural camp-site. Chrissie is gripping our trusty *Michelin* map, and looking decidedly apprehensive. 'I thought you said there were no big mountains round this camp site?' she complains.

'No, I said I didn't *think* there were any big ones,' I reply. 'How could I know? I cannot tell from the map. Anyway, never mind that, just let me know when we get to the turn-off, will you?' We have been on the road all day, tempers are getting frayed, and I need to get there. Soon.

Hairpin bends follow hairpin bends, until we reach the top of the mountain pass, and start down the other side. 'Oh my God, will you look at the size of those mountains in front!' she cries. She is not wrong there. About five miles across the valley, even higher rocky, barren peaks rear their heads above steep-sided valleys. Lights are coming on in the *Pueblos Blancos,* the white villages for which this region is known, and with the setting sun casting it's red and orange glow, the panorama is stunningly dramatic. And yes, quite mountainous.

Just then we spot the sign for 'Camping Rural.' We have arrived. Journey over. I steer off the road, following the sign; then, nothing! Where the hell is it? 'Oh no, look down there!' Chrissie exclaims. Sure enough, at the bottom of a precipitous, hundred-foot drop is the camp-site reception. Next to it, a small shop, and the barrier for the site itself. A few people are standing around outside reception. From up here, they resemble ants. The site seems to be built on a narrow spit of land, surrounded by steep valleys on three sides.

'Hold on tight!' I cry, and jamming the ancient Volvo into drive, we plunge down the slope, foot hard on the brake, until we arrive, shaken and stirred, outside reception. Phew. My legs feel like jelly as I slowly climb out of the car, and we both head into reception, where a middle-aged lady is sat behind the counter. I sent the site an email last week advising when we hoped to arrive, but how do I explain this? 'Me John Richards' is the best I can manage, pointing to myself. Then I spot the computer on her desk, so mimicking a typing action, 'email, pensionista especial', remembering the Spanish wording from her website. She looks at me blankly. 'Email' I repeat, jabbing my finger at her computer screen.

She calls up the site email account and sure enough there is my message, nestling in her in-box. 'AHH, Senor Reechards!' she cries. The penny finally drops. Easy, this Spanish language!

Just then a small, wiry man, about our age, dressed only in cotton shorts and flip-flops, all-over golden tan, arrives. 'I watched you coming down the hill' he announces. 'Bit of a shock, the first time! Welcome, the name's Ed.' and he holds out a leathery hand for me to shake. This is a nice touch, the site have an English manager, to deal with all the British *pensionistas,* no doubt. 'Follow me' he continues, 'I'll give you a quick tour, before it gets too dark. Leave the car, we can walk'

We follow Ed through the gate and into the site, as he keeps up his running commentary. First up is a residential caravan. 'Sadie lives there, with her cats. Lovely lady. The pool is over there look.' Next comes a proper mobile home. 'Pete and Sarah, that's their holiday bungalow, you'll meet them next week, lovely people.' Next come a pair of bungalows owned by the site apparently, for letting. 'This next one here is Dave and Sally, from Scotland, they live here full-time. Lovely couple.'

'Are there any Spanish people here, or is it Little Britain?' I query.

Ed laughs. 'This is the British end, the Spanish are at the far end. Look, here's our place, me and Celia. Look at the big pitch opposite us, you might want to go there. Very quiet, you'll like it there.'

Next is the toilet block, then we come to the caravan pitches proper. And what a shock. The Spanish caravans are so close together that some are actually touching. Huge canvas and plastic awnings have been strung up everywhere, and the whole scene resembles a third-world shanty-town. 'I know what you're thinking' whispers Ed, 'but it's the Spanish way. They love to be close together, can't stand being alone, they come at weekends, whole families, three generations, and they all want to be close, have a good old chat, a big meal, just socialise.' In one area, three vans have been arranged around three sides of a square, with a huge communal table set up on the fourth side.

'I'm surprised you allow this' I comment. 'In the UK, vans have to be three metres apart I think, in case of fire.'

Ed looks bemused. 'Me? What's it got to do with me?'

'Oh sorry,' I blunder, 'I thought you were a manager here or something.'

He laughs. 'No fear! I'm retired. Finished. Packed it all in. Finito. Terminado. I just saw you struggling with Ana in the office, and decided you needed a tour!'

I try to look contrite, in the gathering gloom. 'We are retired too!' I announce. 'Two weeks ago actually, still getting used to the feeling.'

'Hey welcome to the club!' he grins. 'I know why you're here now. It's that pensioners discount!' Sussed. We've been sussed!

We reach the end of the site and the track doubles back the same way we came, past more caravans grouped impossibly close. Soon we are out of the 'Spanish' end and back outside Ed's bungalow. 'I think you're right' I decide. 'This is a better pitch, opposite you, if you don't mind?'

'Course not, be good to have some neighbours', Ed smiles. 'But this pitch opposite you is three times the size of the ones down there' I continue. 'Won't Ana mind? Won't she want to charge us extra, for a bigger pitch? We are just retired, got to look after the old pounds now, you know!'

Ed laughs again. 'This is the beauty of being British on a Spanish camp-site. The Spanish don't want these big pitches on their own, like I told you. They want to be all in together. This is what they're like. You wait till you get to the beach. I can guarantee, if you are in a secluded spot, Spanish people will come and sit right next to you. They just can't be alone. So here, Ana can't let these pitches. So she thinks the Brits are daft, being all on their own, but she doesn't know it's what we really want!' And he taps the side of his nose, conspiratorially. 'Anyway, there's the electric hook-up, I'm off now but in the morning I'll introduce you to Celia. Good night!' And he turns and wanders back to his bungalow.

'OK, you wait here, I'll go and get the caravan,' I tell Chrissie.

'Hang on' she replies, 'I don't want to stay here, on this site.'

I could tell she wasn't happy, she had gone very quiet all of a sudden. 'What, is it Ed you don't like?'

'No of course not' she snaps. 'Ed seems very nice, very helpful. No, it's these mountains. They are brooding, menacing, it feels like they are closing in on me. And the steep valley's either side, I won't get a wink of sleep, in case the caravan runs away down the mountainside. '

I understand what she is thinking, the mountains do look a bit menacing, even though we can't actually see them in the dark, but she knows they are there. She was the same in Switzerland. 'Look, I know what you mean' I reply in a sympathetic voice, 'but the van will be perfectly safe here, the land is flat, no chance of it running away. And we'll have the legs down, and the chocks under the wheels. We can't go driving round now looking for another site, can we? Let's stay here tonight, and in the morning if you really don't like it, we can move on somewhere else. Won't take us five minutes to set up, I'll cook us a nice pasta, we still have a bottle of red left.' And I place my arm around her and give her a quick hug. 'Come on, it's all part of the adventure!'

'Adventure my eye' she shoots back, 'I know you, we are only here 'cos of that pensioners discount, you tight wad!' OK, guilty as charged. What can I say? Then she starts to laugh. 'Oh just go and get the ruddy caravan, but don't blame me if we end up at the bottom of the valley in the morning!' Phew again! It's going to be all right. I can just feel it. And my pensioners discount is secure. Result!

CHAPTER 4. HOUSE-HUNTING, PART-TWO

We are in a traffic jam in Santa Marta. Only a small one, consisting as it does of us, that is our estate agent Denise who has been showing us houses all day, and a beer lorry. The trouble is that this appears to be a one-way street, and the beer is coming down the wrong way. Added to this, a kiddies merry-go-round carousel has been erected on one side of the street, and directly opposite three blokes are wrestling with huge sheets of plywood, building what appears to be a giant coffin. Denise is clearly used to this however, and after the lorry has backed into an impossibly small gap, she steers round the mêlée and continues up the narrow, cobbled street, which is actually one of the main routes through the town, past old buildings with shutters and wrought iron balconies, up a steep hill and emerging into a large square, with gardens and fountains, and more old buildings on the perimeter.

She then heads back in the same direction from whence we came but on a different level, as Santa Marta, like many Spanish towns, is built on the side of a mountain, with the streets below each other in terraces, like a gigantic wedding cake. Eventually we can drive no further and have to park up and walk, as the streets were designed in the days when the main form of transport had four legs, two pointy ears, and went eee-aww eee-aww. This morning we saw an old fellow bringing a donkey, laden with wicker panniers, out through his front door.

This is the tenth and last house of the day, and quite frankly I have had enough, but I don't care as I have already seen the house I want to buy, a two-bed cottage in a little village twenty-five miles from here, all white with thick stone walls and small windows, a garden, and bags of Spanish character.

 As we approach this final house, I notice it is number fifty-five, the year of Chrissie's birth. Hmm could be an omen. The son arrives with the key and in we go, and it is clear that this one is a gem. Double wooden front door, typical Andalucian style,stepping down into a large hallway with beautiful marble floor, and the first room on the right is *dormitario Abuela*, granny's bedroom, again typical of this area. As we have no granny, this could be a perfect dining-room, or whatever you like. The lounge is next, again with the same marble floor, then open-plan marble stairs up to the three main bedrooms. Chrissie is delighted with the smallest bedroom, which contains an ancient sewing machine with treadle. 'Oh look, this would be perfect for my craft room!' she exclaims.

Off the lounge is a dining area with patio doors leading to an open air patio, as the house is built on a hill it is three stories at the back so the patio has fantastic views over the higgledy-piggledy roofs of the houses below, down to the town centre in the valley, then open countryside beyond. To the right is a church and bell tower with cottages clustered round, the sort of view you could never tire of.

Next comes the kitchen, 'granite worktops' says Denise, 'cheaper than Formica over here!' and the bathroom. Down stairs to the lower ground floor, there is a summer kitchen with a room next to it, both of which would make a separate annexe for visiting offspring, then a covered patio area the full width of the house with the same view across the town, and an open patio dominated by a huge grape vine, laden with dozens of huge bunches of juicy black grapes, and an old stone shed. It is not clear if the vine is holding up the shed, or vice-versa. Down a few more steps to the garden proper which is a bit of a jungle, with a fig- tree and an almond tree. The house comes with all the furniture, but hopefully not the religious artifacts and statues which are dotted around the house, and the price for all this? Just twenty-five thousand of your English pounds.

This is by far and away the best house we have seen, and it won't be for sale long as it only came on the market this week and is not even on the website yet, but I have set my heart on the cottage. Nevertheless we ask Denise for second visits on this house, and my cottage, tomorrow evening, to view them both again.

She drops us back to our hotel as we are staying in the area overnight, but before we eat we drive ourselves back to the cottage for a further look. The village is just the same, one or two grannies sat outside their houses on plastic chairs, a few old men in the square and two boys playing football, both of whom politely wish us *hola*! as we pass. It is a tiny village so only has the two bars, and yes I am utterly sold.

Next day we have more viewings with another agent, but see nothing as good with her. In the afternoon we head back to Santa Marta as we do not know it that well, and try to find fifty-five again, which proves extremely difficult as the streets are a maze and a rabbit warren all rolled into one. We know roughly where the house is but after an hour are on the point of giving up when hey presto, there it is! It is all locked and shuttered but still it is a lovely property for the money. The road outside is just wide enough for a car to pass, but walking along the cobbled lane towards town, it narrows to a footpath, then turns into ancient stone steps, through an old stone arch, and eventually into the square we saw yesterday. That explains the lack of passing traffic then!

In the evening Denise picks us up and we visit the cottage first. Sat in the lounge I make a decision, this is definitely 'The One', and to prove the point I get a chair and sit outside the front door, like an old granny. I can tell Chrissie is not one hundred percent sold, although she seems very keen. Moving on to

Santa Marta, Denise confuses us by parking in a different place, and we notice that the coffin of yesterday has morphed into an outside bar, complete with beer pumps and optics. Clearly a party is about to start in the town. The daughter arrives with the key, and by this time the jungle drums are beating as all the neighbours come out for a look, and we get many friendly smiles and *hola*'s. Chrissie clearly has her heart set on this one, she is telling Denise all her plans for the garden, and her craft-room, but I am not sure I want to be bothered with four bedrooms, a jungle, grapes and fig trees, and the only time I eat almonds is Christmas, and they are such fiddly bastards to get out the shells.

'I know what John is thinking,' Chrissie whispers to Denise, 'he doesn't want four bedrooms, a jungle, grapes and figs'. Funny how they always know what we are thinking.... Still it is a beautiful house, by far the best of the two, and being in town would be so much better being able to walk everywhere, the town centre, the squares and gardens, the supermarket, are all walking distance, whereas at the cottage it is a fifteen-minute drive into the nearest town, but the cottage is exactly what I envisaged when I first dreamed up this crazy scheme.

Just then, however, as we lean on the patio railing, gazing out across the olive fields, the sky is shot with crimson and orange in the setting sun. I adore sunsets, and this one has to be one of the best I have ever seen. Denise cannot fail to notice my amazement, and ever the consummate professional, she points out that the back of the house faces west, and that we will probably get something similar most evenings.

The classic scenario, wife likes one place and the husband the other. We tell Denise we need to sleep on it and will let her know in the morning, but as Chrissie is getting out of the car I whisper to Denise that my mind is made up.

So which one did we decide to buy? The one with the sunsets, and the view of the olives, obviously...

CHAPTER 5. BUYING A HOUSE, SPANISH-STYLE

Our Spanish lawyer, Pedro, is like no lawyer I ever came across in England. He looks like he stepped out of a gents fashion magazine, sharp, shiny suit, slicked-back hair, patent leather shoes. If I had to use one word to describe him, it would be 'dodgy.' Would I buy a second-hand watch from him outside Paddington Station? No! The one thing everyone in Britain warned us about, before we came to Spain, was to trust no-one, and to avoid buying a house which didn't actually exist. 'Be careful over there!' was the general opinion, of those supposedly in 'the know.' 'You buy a house one day, then wake up next morning to find a motorway running through your garden.' Which naturally we are keen to avoid.

I am possibly a poor judge of character, although Chrissie is as sharp as a knife, and she reckons Pedro is trustworthy. She likes him, so if she likes him, he must be OK, because many times during our married life, her judgement has proved correct. Pedro speaks excellent English and explains everything to us in great detail, several times. He has given us the land registry entries for the house we are hoping to buy, number fifty-five, including a plan of the street, the house, the terrace at the back, the garden, even the trees in the garden. Fairly comprehensive then! It also shows the owners, the father during his lifetime, and his two sons and daughter after his death. Blimey. Because we are giving Pedro power of attorney to deal with our Spanish ID cards and change the council tax and utilities on the house to our names, we have to go to the Public Notary office to sign the deed. An interpreter also has to be present by law, even though Pedro speaks better English than we do.

So off we go to the Notary, the equivalent of the Probate Office in the UK I suppose. In there are loads of people milling around, and as Spanish property tends to be held by the whole family, whole families are there, and it seems like total confusion. The person who types the Power of Attorney's is on holiday so we have to wait, but it is like a snapshot of local life in here and the time passes quickly.

Just then the door opens and in sashays a woman dressed in impossibly tight jeans, top and high heels, with designer shades and handbag. Yes it's our interpreter! The trouble is she speaks hardly any English.... Hmm. The deed is finally typed out and Pedro explains what it all means and what it covers, while the interpreter says nothing. In fact she is flicking through a glossy magazine.Then the door opens and out comes the Notary, and our jaws drop, as he is just about the handsomest man I have ever seen, and Chrissie's tongue is hanging out, as he is the living image of Nicholas Cage. Her favourite actor. He is tall for a Spaniard, slim, with dark liquid eyes, and Chrissie knocks over the chairs in his office as she is gazing at, well, his arse. 'Where do I sign!' she drools. He asks us if the interpreter has explained the deed, and we nod as both of us have lost the power of speech, then we all sign up and the meeting is over. Pedro stuffs a crisp twenty-Euro note deep in the interpreter's handbag and off she totters, She has not spoken a single word during the meeting, but she did have a great behind....

Next we go to the bank to open our account, and something odd strikes me about it but I cannot put my finger on it. The customers are all in a queue gossiping, most of them are related it appears and no one seems in a hurry, if I have to wait two minutes in my bank in the UK I have steam rising from my ears but here the pace is more relaxed. Then I realise what is missing from this bank-there is no counter, or bullet proof glass. There is just one employee, sat at a normal desk with a computer screen, and the customers come up one by one, sit down, tell him their life stories, he gives them some money and off they go.

Eventually the one employee is able to deal with our new account, but he cannot type and takes four attempts just to get 'John & Christina'. Eventually it is all done, I give him forty-Euros and I am officially Don John Austin Richards with a bank account! In the corner of the office is a pile of food blenders, gifts for opening accounts, we ask for one but it seems you need more than forty-Euros to qualify... never mind I am transferring twenty-four grand next week so maybe I will get one then?

To celebrate the purchase of our Spanish property we arrange to take all the Brits at the camp-site out to Sunday lunch at a beach-side restaurant in a little village near Malaga. You sit on long tables and the waiters come by with plates of fish, crab, lobster, squid, shouting their wares, you choose whatever you want and they charge you at the end by how many empty plates you have.

There are about a dozen waiters all hollering at the tops of their voices, and every sort of seafood done every way imaginable is brought round. It is absolute bedlam but hugely enjoyable and I cannot ever recall a Sunday lunch quite like this. There must be almost two-hundred people in here, just a huge marquee next to the sand, all large family groups all talking excitedly, as the Spanish always do, and we manage twelve plates between the seven of us in our group. Looking down the beach I spot a fishing port about a mile away, so I am guessing seafood doesn't come much fresher than this!

After the meal we all stroll along the seafront to walk off the excess, and I get talking to Pete who actually recommended this place. 'Bet you never had Sunday dinner like that, in England!,' he laughs.

'That's for sure!' I confirm, 'that was nothing like roast beef and Yorkshire pudding at the Rose and Crown!' For an instant I feel a stab of regret, a touch of homesickness, for our old way of life. Then I look around, at the beach, bathed in golden sunshine, each of us in shorts and t-shirts even though it is late October. I wipe a bead of perspiration off my forehead. Usually, at the Rose and Crown, it was raining, especially at the weekend. And besides, we can always pop in there for roast beef, next time we go back to Britain., whenever that might be. Not for a while, I am sure.

CHAPTER 6. GETTING THE KEYS, SPANISH-STYLE

I am snoozing gently by the camp-site pool when my mobile phone shatters the peace. This early-retirement business is easy. Our lives have slipped into, not a pattern exactly, but a vague shape. The morning following our arrival at this site, Chrissie declared herself happy that the mountains were not as forbidding and threatening as she had first feared. She still grips the car seats as we go round the hairpin bends, but she does feel more secure here. As is the pensioners discount. We go to the beach, we explore the surrounding towns, we stroll up to the village, where there is a weekly Spanish class in one of the bars, and like today, we lounge by the pool. We have even bought a house. We are still in holiday mode of course, although I consider we are entitled to a bit of a break, having worked since we left college, and managing to bring up two beautiful girls who are now making their own way in the world.

So who in the hell is this rudely interrupting this orgy of self-congratulation? It is Amy, my much-loved secretary from my time in the accountants office, which seems such a long time ago now, although it was only, what, just over a month?

'Johnny, it's Amy here. I've just fielded a call from the fraud department of Barclay's Bank. They were asking for you urgently. I wasn't sure if you had told them you no longer work here, so I said you were out of the office, but they need to speak to you as a matter of priority! What the hell have you been doing, over there in Sunny Spain?!'

A shiver of fear runs down my spine. I was used to dealing with banks in my job of course, usually over a long lunch, but I thought I had left all that behind. 'Did they say it was about a client?' I ask her.

'No' she replies, 'just some suspicious activity about a bank transfer, but they wouldn't give any further details. I got the impression it was personal, not about a client.'

Suddenly, the penny drops. As does my blood-pressure. 'I know what it was, we have bought a house, so I have just transferred some money to a currency exchange company. They were cheaper than the high-street banks, so I guess my lot are just getting arsey!'

Amy laughs. 'Blimey, that didn't take you long. Not one of those villas where you wake up one morning to find a motorway in your garden? Or where you get home to find the council has knocked it down?'

'Yeah yeah, very funny' I smile. 'Actually the house is about a hundred and fifty years old, in a village half-way up a mountain, with a huge stone wall around the garden. So unless they're building motorways up mountains these days, I reckon we're safe. And if the council want to knock it down, they will have to demolish the whole village!'

'I can just picture you half-way up a mountain,' she giggles. 'Mind you, when you worked here, I often wished you WERE halfway up a blooming mountain!'

'Right, that's you crossed off my guest list!' I half-joke. 'Where are you going for your holidays next year? Siberia, was it?'

We chat about the office, who is doing what to whom, then I ring off and concentrate on settling matters with my bank. Not a problem. Like I say, I am used to putting banks in their place! About the only thing I miss now I'm no longer working.

About five days later another phone call disturbs my afternoon pool-side siesta. But this call I am expecting. From our estate agent. 'Johnny, it's Denise here. I have just had a call from Pedro the lawyer. He exchanged contracts this morning at the notary, so the house is now legally yours. Congratulations!'

Chrissie is just doing a few quick lengths of the pool, so I give her a huge grin and a big thumbs up sign. 'Fantastic news Denise,' I exclaim, 'thank you so much. So when is the completion date?'

Denise chuckles. 'Today! There are not usually completion days over here!' she explains. 'The house is yours today, I have the keys, it's too late this afternoon to meet, so what if we say tomorrow at two pm, meet me in that filling station by the crossroads, on the Granada-Cordoba road?'

I know this garage, and in common with most Spanish filling stations, it has a great cafe/bar attached. Unlike the UK, where it's 'in and out as fast as you can, speak to no-one, grab a three-day-old cardboard pasty if you're really desperate', filling up here is a social event. Depending on the time of day, you might see the cycling club, the motorbike group, or even a vintage car club, the members all grouped around long tables in the bar, everyone chatting excitedly about all and sundry. Not much cycling, riding or driving going on mind you, but plenty of talking about it. And the bars always serve a wide selection of beer, wines and spirits, and food ranging from tapas to a three-course meal. Oh, and coffee of course. Forget about 'in and out as fast as you can', there is usually a group clustered round the till, everyone talking animatedly at once, buying long sticks of fresh crusty bread, browsing the free-gifts catalogue, cracking jokes. Call it ten minutes, minimum, to get served. It doesn't pay to be in a hurry in this country.

The following afternoon we arrive at the garage to find Denise already seated on a bar stool, tucking into a plate of chips. With a beer on the side. She digs into her bag and comes out with two keys, then as if by magic, a beer for me and a lemonade for Chrissie rapidly appear. 'Here you are, your first Spanish house! Salut!' Suddenly I am gripped by, not outright panic, but deep apprehension. We have finally done it. After around twenty months of planning, dreaming, and a few arguments, I am holding the keys to our overseas property.

I quickly divide the key-ring and hand one to Chrissie. 'You better have this, it was all your idea, after all!' I joke.

Denise wags a severe finger in my direction. 'No it was not!' she laughs. 'Chrissie told me all about it! It was all your idea. Going to Australia or somewhere. Then you end up here. Anyway, welcome to Spain, I know you will love the house, and the lifestyle. And tell your friends where to come, if they want a cheap bolt-hole!'

'So what about the meter readings and all that?' I ask.

Denise giggles. 'Don't worry about all that, this is Spain!'

'Yes I know we are in Spain, but surely they have things like meters, for water and electricity?'

She is still grinning. 'Pedro will have changed the names, so the water and electric will come in your names, for the next bills. Forget it, the bills will work themselves out.'

This seems a strange way to carry on to me, but Denise has done this before, she must know what she is doing, and how these things work. 'OK, you're the expert Denise. Thank you so much for all your help, I think we might pop up to the house now, just a quick look, see what's what, sort out what we need to do before we move in, cleaning and whatever. The family said they were leaving the furniture, so I hope its still there! We left ours in the UK, sold most of it, so if they've taken it away, then we will be living in our caravan a bit longer!'

Denise is still chuckling. Whether it's my worrying about electricity meters, or about us living in a caravan I cannot say, but something is amusing her. The beer, maybe? 'If they said they were leaving the furniture, then they will. I bet you will have a few surprises, actually!' and she gives me a sly wink, which I am unable to interpret.

So we head up the road to Santa Marta, park the car, and after a few wrong turnings, we arrive at the house. Our new Spanish house. Luckily, it's mid afternoon, the middle of the siesta, so the street, in fact the whole town, is deathly quiet. I unlock the door, and resisting the temptation to carry Chrissie across the threshold, we step inside. And immediately freeze. The family are still here! The house is silent, but they clearly have not left yet. All the personal possessions are still there. Brushes, combs, and make-up adorn the hall table. We creep silently into the sitting room. Photos, a clock, pictures, cushions, knick-knacks. Into the kitchen, cookware, utensils, a half-eaten bag of crisps, in the bathroom, soap, shampoo, flannels, towels. 'Hello!' I call out. *'Ola! Ola!'* Nothing. Not a sound. The house is empty, unless they are in bed, and that is not a road I want to go down.

We quietly retrace our steps, lock the front door, and retreat down the street a hundred yards or so. I whip out my phone, and call Pedro. 'Hello Pedro, Denise has just given us the key to number fifty-five, we are here now, but it seems like the family are still here. I mean, they are not actually here now, but they haven't moved out yet, everything is still here, personal possessions, everything.'

Pedro is silent for a few moments. 'Maybe they don't want these things' he replies. 'They tell me they take everything they want. The house yours now, I pay the money to Notario, so you can move in.'

I am momentarily stunned. 'Well, I am not happy to just throw their possessions out, can you please call the family and check? They might return, and be upset!'

Pedro agrees to do this, and we spend twenty uncomfortable minutes strolling round the town, before he calls back. 'Yes you are OK to move in, I call family and they have gone, they not want any of these things, they are yours.' *Oh yes, like I want an ancient electric razor full of old man's whiskers. Like we need a hairbrush clogged with old woman's grey hairs. Half a jar of marmalade? Used soap? A drawer full of grey underpants? No thank you, very much. Now I know what Denise was chuckling about.* 'Actually this is quite common,' Pedro continues,'often when families say they leave the furniture, they mean they are leaving everything. Anything you don't want, leave it in the street, someone will take it. Don't worry, enjoy your new house, I will bring deeds to you one day next week.'

We have heard about this 'just leave it in the street' business. Denise explained it to us. As the zigzag streets of the old town are so narrow, refuse bins cannot be left outside individual houses, so there are communal bins every few hundred yards, which are emptied by the council every night. And three times a month, they collect big household items, bed frames, sofas, TV's, anything really. Or that was what Denise told us. I guess this is where we find out whether or not it is true.

But where do we begin? This house is like the *Marie Celeste*, or the *Starship Enterprise* after everyone's been beamed up. What we really need to do is get some plastic sacks, or cardboard boxes, and get rid of everything we don't want, before we can start cleaning up. But we can make a start today, before we head back to the caravan. 'OK, Granny's bedroom first, as it's the first room off the hallway,' I suggest. 'What do you want to keep out of that lot in there?'

'Oh just let me think' Chrissie ponders, in a sarcastic voice. 'A bed with the headboard attached by parcel tape and string? A crappy chipboard chest of drawers? About half a dozen rickety dining chairs, every one different?' So none of it then. At that moment there is a knock at the door. I open up to find two middle-aged women, one dark one fair. The neighbours, I recognise them from the time we came to look at the house. The dark one shouts something intelligible, and the pair of them barge past me into the hallway. Chrissie gives me a severe 'what the hell did you let them in for?' look, whereas all I can do is shrug apologetically. I point towards my chest, 'John' I tell the pair, then I point at Chrissie. 'Christina.' We have picked up a few phrases and words from the Spanish lessons at the caravan, but we cannot string a sentence together yet. The dark one is doing all the talking, non-stop, at a hundred miles an hour. *'No hablo mucho Espanol'* I apologise. I don't speak much Spanish, which is an exaggeration actually. I don't speak ANY Spanish, and here we are right in the deep end. I should have spent more time studying the phrase book, rather than lazing round the camp-site pool, although 'Can I buy two return tickets to Madrid please?' and 'Where is the nearest police station?' are clearly going to be of limited use to us today.

The our new neighbours are strolling round the house, sizing up our possessions. '*Para mi*?' the dark one asks, pointing at the sofa. Can I believe this is actually happening? Is she asking for the sofa? Surely not. We have only been here less than half an hour, and haven't even been upstairs yet. 'Have you got that pocket dictionary in your bag?' I whisper to Chrissie. 'Look up '*para mi?*' and see what it means.

She has a quick flick through. 'For me' she confirms, and we stare at each other in disbelief.

'*No, para mi*' I tell the dark one, pointing to myself again. The fair one smiles apologetically, and fires off what sounds like a reprimand to her compatriot. 'What's the word for furniture?' I ask Chrissie.

Again a quick flick. '*Muebles*' she confirms.

'*No muebles*' I announce, pointing to us both. '*Caravanna, Malaga*', and I make a sleeping gesture with my head resting sideways on my hands. '*Proxima semana, Santa Marta.*' Next week. I learned that at the Spanish class the other day. I make a gesture of looking at my watch. '*Bamos Malaga*', and as gently as possible, I guide the pair towards the door. The dark one fires off another rapid barrage, from which I am only able to catch '*muebles*' and '*para mi*', then grinning wildly, they step outside and disappear from whence they came.

I gratefully close the door behind them, and stare, open-mouthed, at Chrissie. Who starts to laugh. Uncontrollably. Tears are rolling down her face, and unable to resist, I join her on the sofa, helpless with laughter. 'Can you believe that?' I splutter. 'We haven't even sat on the sofa yet, and she wants it. Did you catch their names?'

Chrissie dries her eyes with her fingers. 'I think the dark one was 'Leeee', and the blonde one 'Beeeehhh' she stammers, 'but don't quote me on that!' and off we go again. Regaining her composure, she suddenly starts patting the sofa. 'Look, this is a cover, get up a moment and let me take it off.' I dutifully rise and she starts tugging and pulling, and slowly off comes the cover to reveal a pristine unused sofa underneath. A grey floral print, not what I might have chosen, but gift horses and all that. 'Try the two armchairs, I bet they're the same' she continues, and sure enough, a bit more huffing and puffing and we have a brand new three-piece suite. 'No wonder Leeee was so keen to get her grubby little hands on it,' Chrissie chuckles, 'she knew this was brand new!'

I slump down into my brand new armchair. 'Right, get your pen out and start making a list,' I command, a smile on my face. 'Items we definitely want to keep. Number one, the three-piece suite. PARA MI!!'

CHAPTER 7. MOVING IN.

I hate Volvo's. No that's not true actually, I love my big silver tank, long and wide and low, deeply unfashionable, thirsty as an Irish builder on pay-day, but a trusty workhorse nevertheless. It even has heated seats, which admittedly might not be much use to us here, but a nice thought. No, what I hate is guiding this beast down our narrow, winding switchback of a street, door mirrors pulled in, inching along, exhaust scraping the road as we crest a particularly nasty ridge. Having a brand-new double mattress strapped to the roof does not help navigation much either. The back of the car is filled with mops, buckets, cloths and cleaning products, sweeping brushes, a dustpan, bread, milk and cereal, towels, toiletries, some clothing, bedding, and my tool box. Yes we are moving in temporarily, to get the place clean, chuck out what we don't want, get the place straight. Or straighter.

The street really has to be seen to be believed. Starting from the road below, it rears up alarmingly, then dog-legs to the left, before the exhaust-scraping crest, on the right is a gap between the cottages where a set of steep steps climb to the street above. Plunging downhill, and narrowing severely, it then passes another set of Spanish Steps hurtling down to the street below, before a particularly wicked lurch to the right and a gut-squeezing narrow uphill section, eventually widening slightly by the communal bin, where we are going to have to park, temporarily at least, as the stretch outside our house is so narrow we will not be able to open the car doors.

It is mid-morning and surprisingly the street is quiet, although there is not the remotest possibility of unloading the car without the neighbours coming out to see what is going on. The presence of a UK registered vehicle parked up will also act as a red flag, I might just as well get a megaphone and announce 'English couple in number fifty-five, please come in and help yourselves to our furniture!'

The story of our first trip to the house last week got plenty of laughs at the Spanish class in the village near the caravan-site, although Carlos, our teacher, was not surprised. 'This is what Andalucian people are like' he told us. 'they are very direct, unlike you British. If they want something, they ask. If they think you are fat, or have a big bum, or don't like your clothes, they tell you, they don't, how you say, beat the bush!' Chrissie was delighted to hear this news. Particularly the bit about big bums. 'They probably think you are having your furniture shipped from the UK,' he continued, 'so you don't want the stuff that's in the house. They are trying to be first in the queue, when you give it away.' I explained to Carlos that no, we were not shipping anything from the UK, and that we planned to keep all the furniture, apart from any rubbish, at least for the time being. 'OK I will teach you some phrases to explain this,' he said. 'What were their names, your neighbours?'

I start to laugh. 'We are not sure, but it sounded like 'Leeee', and 'Behhh'.

Carlos grins. 'Sounds like 'Loli, and Isabel' to me. Andalucian people 'eat' their words, so they only pronounce about half the word. So for instance the word 'adios' comes out like 'dio'. I can teach you some of these eaten words, also some things to say when you go out for your *paseo* in the evenings.'

'Our what?' I queried.

'*El paseo*', the evening walk around the town' he confirmed. 'You must do this, you will find the neighbours out in the street, sitting on wooden chairs, all gossiping loudly, laughing and joking. It's great, you will have a lot of fun, but do not expect to get anywhere quickly', he leaned in and whispered. 'Actually I think you are very brave. There are so many British people here on the Costa, and they don't really get to experience real Spanish life, but where you are going you will have the true Andalucian spirit.'

Amazingly, we manage to untie the mattress from the roof of the tank, manhandle it into the house, and then return for the rest of our stuff, without attracting an audience. The house still looks like the Marie Celeste and the Starship Enterprise all rolled into one, although now we have a plan worked out. Chrissie will start clearing Granny's bedroom of the crappy chest and the rickety chairs, while I shift the old mattress out to the bin, then dismantle Granny's bed. Simple! I drag the old mattress downstairs, out through the front door, and prop it up against the front wall of the house. 'Let me untie the headboard a minute, before you get started,' I tell Chrissie, and brandishing my trusty Stanley knife, I set about cutting through the string and sellotape holding the bed together. It takes about three swipes of the blade, 'timber!' I shout and the whole contraption collapses into an ungainly pile, with a mighty crash. And a cloud of dust. Chrissie starts sneezing, and between us we are making enough noise to alert the whole town to our arrival. I won't need the megaphone after all.

'Right' I splutter, trying not to cough, opening the front door and sticking my head out. 'I'll just whip the headboard and the mattress down to the bi... I don't believe it! The mattress is gone! How did that happen? It was only there thirty seconds! Nobody came past the window, there was nobody in the street when I put it out!'

'What are you talking about?' Chrissie exclaims, in disbelief, sticking her head out, 'of course it's still there, you idiot. OH MY GOD! Where did it go?' Where did it go indeed. Perhaps it was beamed up, like the previous occupants of this house. 'When Pedro said the stuff would get taken, I didn't think he meant in less than a minute,' she giggles, 'but it saves you dragging it to the bin. Put the headboard out and see what happens.'

So I do, and we wait inside the hallway to see if we can catch the collector in the act. Just then there is a tap on the door, I open it to reveal a tall Moroccan man standing on the doorstep. He is smiling widely. 'Greeting!' he whispers, in broken English. 'You have bed *quadro*, frame of bed, I have plees?' We beckon him inside, he seems really friendly and utterly charming, and we instinctively like him. 'My name Ahmed, thing you no like, in casa, I have plees, tree cheeldren, and womans!'

I smile brightly at Ahmed. 'OK, we only come today, must sort things,' I explain, gesturing at the stuff scattered around the house, like a church jumble-sale, 'but things we no want, for you!' and I point to him.

'Gracias my friend! You good man. I see you good man, and good womans also!'

I hand him the bed-end, complete with bits of sellotape still attached, then drag the frame out into the street. It is an ancient steel specimen, with diamond-pattern springs, and looks like it might have come direct from Florence Nightingale's hospital.

'Where your house?' I ask.

'Plees, thees way' he replies and points down the street. He gathers up the headboard and end, I grasp the frame, and Englishman and Moroccan stagger down a Spanish street carrying items which, quite frankly, are only fit for scrap. Still, one man's rubbish is another man's treasure, and I am glad he can make use of it. We reach his front door and he beckons me inside, to find his 'tree cheeldrens and womans' waiting, with a plate of what looks like cous-cous and vegetables. 'My friend, plees, for you' he smiles, handing me the plate. I am of course extremely unwilling to take his food as I am sure his family needs it more than me, but refusing would be ungracious so I shake him warmly by the hand and accept the offering.

It is an extremely touching moment, and I feel moved as I trudge back up the street, to hear a commotion coming from inside our house. Oh no, Loli and Isabel have paid us a visit. Chrissie is looking extremely harassed and shoots me a 'why are you never around when you are wanted?' look. Loli is talking nineteen to the dozen, and is pointing to various items she is keen to relieve us of, so, taking a deep breath, I recite the Spanish phrase Carlos taught me. 'Loli, we do not have any furniture here in Spain, so we are keeping most of it, but anything we don't need, you can have.' Chrissie gives me another warning glare, and mouths the word 'Ahmed?' Oh no, what have I done? I have promised both Ahmed and Loli our surplus items. Sadly, Carlos didn't teach me how to dig myself out of a big hole, so now it is back to sign language, and bluffing.

Chrissie has already taken down all the ornaments and nick-knacks from around the ground floor, and placed them in cardboard boxes by the front door. There is a cancer charity shop in one of the little seaside towns near the caravan, and we have already decided that some of our unwanted items can go there. She has also shifted the six rickety dining chairs ready to go to the bin, which I take to mean we will not be sitting in the street chatting away to the neighbours, of an evening. We have a lovely patio at the back of the house, looking out to the olive fields, and I am planning spending my evenings there, watching the sun go down.

Loli is not keen on the chairs for some reason, although she has already grabbed a box of nick-knacks and is sorting through. 'No, those are for charity' I tell her, another Carlos phrase, although I cannot remember the Spanish word for 'charity.'

Loli looks at me blankly. *'Para mi?*

'Look up 'Charity' in your dictionary' I ask Chrissie.

She flicks through, *'caridad'* she replies.

'Para caridad, cancer'. Loli still has no idea what I am talking about. So I decide to go off message and deviate from Carlos' phrases. 'Look up the word for 'poor'' I ask Chrissie.

More flicking. 'Pobre'.

I point at the box. *'OK, caridad, para cancer, para los pobres.'* There. What do you think of that? My first Spanish phrase, not a long one, almost certainly not correct grammar, but I am proud of it.

'Oh bugger the poor!' Loli chuckles, or words to that effect, ' this lot is para mi!' What can we say? By British standards, her behaviour is, putting it mildly, appalling, but as Carlos warned us, people here are very direct. We have come to live among them, so who are we to judge, to impose our standards?

Just then Chrissie emerges from Granny's bedroom with a large 1970's transistor radio, covered in dust. I plug it in, not expecting it to work, but to my amazement it crackles into life, and a loud blast of pop music fills the room. *'Musica!'* shouts Loli, and the pair of them start dancing, with Isabel is clapping along to the beat. This is quite unlike any moving-in day I have ever experienced, but we really do need to crack on if we are to get the place at least partly liveable before nightfall. So I decide to play Loli at her own game. Unplugging the radio, I roll up the cable and place the whole greasy appliance in her box. I then grab two of the rickety dining chairs, and thrust them in her direction. *'Regalo para ti!'* I cry, present for you. She throws her head back and roars with laughter, like some manic pirate, with her missing front tooth. She opens the front door, throws one of the chairs into the street, steps outside and proceeds to stamp on the chair legs, snapping the wood, like some demented savage, kicking and crushing until the legs and back of the chair are completely smashed. Chrissie and I are open-mouthed in sheer utter amazement. Isabel is grinning as a fugitive chair leg goes rolling down the street, but Loli is not finished yet. She reaches into the box, grabs the radio, and gives it the same treatment, stomping until the plastic smashes and splinters of electrical bits fly off in all directions. This is so utterly bizarre that we start to laugh, if she didn't want the radio and the chair she only had to say 'no thank you', and I start to wonder that maybe Loli is mentally unstable, perhaps her medication has worn off, and I make a note to ensure we securely lock our doors and windows tonight. Possibly that is why we got the house at such a good price, perhaps the locals knew it would be like living next to a madhouse, and wouldn't touch it with a bargepole. Maybe the woman howls at the moon once a month, who knows? We certainly don't, although we might be about to find out.

Then, incredibly, having committed this orgy of destruction, she steps back inside our house, leaving the fragments of the chair and radio lying in the road. I have no choice but to gather up the debris, and carry it down to the bin, before someone trips over it and tries to sue us, if that stuff happens here. I can just imagine a headline on one of those ambulance chasing websites. 'Been to Spain? Tripped over bits of a broken chair? Slipped on pieces of smashed audio equipment? No-win no-fee! Contact Rip-Off Solicitors today!'

Back in our house Loli is banging on nineteen to the dozen, even though it should be obvious that our grasp of Spanish is basic, at best. At least Isabel, when she can get a word in edgeways, speaks slowly and clearly. Chrissie gives me a 'don't leave me with this mad woman again!' kind of look, although I can see her relaxing, and I feel a strange sense of contentment. Our house is a complete mess, our neighbour is a complete lunatic, but this is why we came here. Not I hasten to add for mess and lunatics, but to experience life overseas, although if all the neighbours turn out to be the same, heaven help us.

Amid Loli's machine-gun delivery I can make out the word *'cortina.'* Now the only cortina I know is the Ford Cortina from the 1960's, I almost bought one once, a '66 model, white with green stripes, although it turned out to be a Lotus model and third party, fire and theft was beyond my means. Got an Anglia instead, the 1200cc model mind you, white with green stripes, bit of a babe-magnet I felt, until the exhaust fell off and the fumes seeped up through the rusty holes in the floor. *'Cortina?'* I ask Loli.

'Yes, cortinas' she replies, tugging at the curtains in the hallway. *'Para mi?'* Ah-ha, 'cortina' is 'curtains' in Spanish. The Ford Curtains, what a joke! That is a one-up on my old mate Mart, who had a Cortina and always felt himself superior to us Anglia drivers. Until I 'borrowed' his Cortina one night using my Anglia key, and abandoned it outside the local police station. As you do.

As far as I am concerned, Loli can have the curtains, of which there are many in this house. Behind the front door, across the hallway, at the bottom of the stairs, and bizarrely, across the glass patio door, thereby blocking out most of the natural light coming into the back of the house, and obscuring our wonderful view. We came here primarily for the weather, the sunshine and the light, and I am damned if I am shutting it out. I raise my eyebrows at Chrissie in a 'what do you think?' gesture, and she nods in agreement. Give Loli the bloody curtains and hope she goes away.

'Si, son para ti' I tell our crazy neighbour, which I hope means 'yes you can have them.' More or less.

'Oi?' Loli asks. What does she mean, oi? A thank-you would have been nice, not ruddy oi. I am not a dog. I frown at the ungrateful woman. *'Oi?'* she

repeats. *'Loonie.'* Oi loonie, what the hell is this? I have just given the woman a room full of curtains, and she is calling me a loonie? Pots and kettles, Mrs.

Suddenly Chrissie comes to the rescue. She claims to have studied Spanish at school, although has conveniently forgotten most of it since. The only phrase she can remember is *'Mi casa su casa'* which apparently means 'my house is your house', which is absolutely the last thing we want to be telling this pair. 'Do you remember Carlos told us they do not pronounce the letter 'H' in Spanish? I reckon she is saying 'hoy', which means 'today.''

'So what about the loonie bit then. The only loonie here today is her', I comment.

Chrissie giggles, while Loli and Isabel stare at the pair of us speaking in a foreign language. 'Again, do you recall Carlos saying how Andalucian people eat the ends of the words? I think she is saying, 'today, Monday.' Lunes is the word for Monday.'

I turn to Loli, grabbing hold of the nearest curtain. *'Hoy? Cortina?'* I ask.

'Si, para mi, hoy' she confirms. Absolutely fantastic. She wants them today, although why the rush? The curtains are going nowhere. I thought I might have a leisurely unhooking session maybe tomorrow, then the big hand-over. Still, I suppose it will get the cursed curtains out of the way, so balancing on a rickety dining chair, and gritting my teeth, I reach up and start unhooking the *cortinas*. 'And the *supportes*' Loli cries. What? She wants the ruddy curtain poles as well? Giving her a severe stare, followed by a grin, I climb down, extract a screwdriver from my toolbox, and remove the pole. I suppose if we are not having curtains, we don't need the poles. Soon, there is a large pile of curtains, which Isabel folds meticulously, brushing off the dust as she goes. If they are having the curtains and the poles, they might as well have our dust too. *Gratis.* Stands to reason.

Loli casts her eye around the room. *'Bassos? Bassos para mi?'* I have no idea what a bassos is, whether we have one, or where it might be found. I am assuming we have one somewhere, and I suspect Loli knows that we do, but other than that I haven't a clue. Time to get my Spanish into gear again. Carlos taught us four sentences he felt might be useful to us in many situations. 'I am sorry.' 'I don't know.' 'We are from England,' and 'I don't understand.' I decide to use all of them together, apart from the England bit. She knows that already. *'Bassos'* she replies unhelpfully. *Yes I just told you I don't know what a bloody bassos is.*

Once again, dictionary-woman comes to the rescue. 'Carlos told us that the Spanish pronounce the letter 'V' like a 'B'' she reminds me. 'I think she is saying *'vasos'*. 'Glasses.' I turn to the hall table and pick up my glasses, and slip them on. Both our neighbours burst into hysterical laughter. *What? These are my glasses, for heaven's sake.* Loli walks across the sitting room, where a massive 1970's lounge unit covering the entire wall stands. MFI sold something similarly hideous, although to be fair the one we have just acquired with this house is in an attractive dark shade, it looks like real wood veneer too, not just plastic covered chipboard. Chrissie has already stripped the unit of its ornaments, but there are glass doors, cupboards, drawers and shelves on the thing, which we have not yet explored. Out of sight, out of mind. Emptying it will be a job for another day. Or apparently not. Loli pulls down a large folding shelf to reveal a cocktail cabinet filled to the brim with glasses. Drinking glasses. *Vasos.* We both stare at this in utter amazement. There are enough glasses here to stock a pub. Brandy glasses, three different sizes of wine glass, sherry glasses, champagne flutes of different sizes. No pint beer glasses mind you, but still an impressive display. I walk over and fling open the glass doors, and the cupboards, revealing even more *vasos* of every conceivable style. Good quality stuff too, everything matches, with a leaf-style motif engraved on each one. Were these people alcoholics? Was this actually a pub at one time? Seriously, I worked in a busy city-centre bar in my Ford Anglia days and I don't think they had this many drinking receptacles.

Chrissie comes over and starts counting. 'There are a dozen glasses of each design' she confirms. 'There must be well over a hundred glasses here.' This is truly beyond belief. Where did one old Spanish couple get this collection from, and why would you need twelve of each style? You would be pushed to get twelve people in this room, and even if you did, and they were all drinking, surely some would be on the champagne, or cava, a few would fancy a sherry, or a wine, the blokes on the beer. Twelve brandy glasses? Come on! I mean, I like a drink as much as anyone, but this is just so far over the top. I glance at Chrissie, and mouth 'fifty-fifty?'

She nods in agreement, so I reach into the cocktail cabinet and start dividing the collection in half. *'Para ti, para mi'* I confirm, and almost before the words are out of my mouth, Isabel appears with a large cardboard box and some newspaper, and the pair start boxing up half of our glass collection. Incredible. Utterly, utterly incredible.

Right, having furnished Loli's house for her, she can do something for me. In our kitchen is a large rectangular cooker, very much like an Aga, only made from cheaper metal rather than cast-iron, but still an impressive piece of kit. It has a lid which folds down over the hobs, an oven below, and clearly it runs on gas, but I cannot find the gas tap anywhere in the house so have no idea how to switch it on. Also there is an ancient water heater on the kitchen wall, with an aperture for a pilot light, so again it must run off the gas, but how? I beckon her into the kitchen, and point at our appliances. *'Butano!'* she cries, and opens a little door on the side of the cooker to reveal a gas cylinder. Butane. Just like our caravan, only this cylinder is about three feet high, much bigger than a caravan equivalent. Suddenly the penny drops, I have seen these cylinders piled up in filling stations. But do we have to go to the filling station every time we run out of gas? Loli reaches into the cooker and drags out the cylinder, still attached to a rubber hose. She flicks a switch on the regulator, pulls out a lighter, and tries to light the hob. Nothing. She lifts the cylinder, gives it a shake, and cackles with laughter. Yes, I understand. Empty. She points to the cooker, then the water heater, and finally the gas cylinder. I get it, the one cylinder supplies both appliances, which means unless I drive to the filling station, we are not having a shower or anything hot to eat today.

Isabel injects some sense to the proceedings. *'Manana, el butanero biene'* she informs us, and grabbing the empty cylinder, she takes it out through the front door and places it on our doorstep. I glance at Chrissie. We are developing some kind of telepathy with this Spanish translation.

More flicking. *'El butanero,'* she confirms. 'The gas-man.' Ah, so that's what happens, we leave our empty cylinder out, and a gas-man comes by, presumably in an extremely small gas lorry, and supplies us, although what the practicalities are and what it costs, we have yet to discover.

Meanwhile Loli is gathering up her boxes, and the pair of them, having presumably got everything they came for, are preparing to take their leave. Out the door they go, Chrissie gratefully closes it behind them then rests her head on the wood and mimics beating it against the wood. We flop down on the sofa and the pair of us start laughing. 'Well, I don't know about you' I giggle to my wife, 'but I fancy a nice cold shower, followed by something cold to eat!'

'Best of luck with that!' she grins, 'I'm off to the pub!' Just then there is a loud knock on the door. *Oh for heaven's sake, who is this now? Can't these people leave us alone?* I consider ignoring it but the knocking gets louder. I drag myself to the door, to find Loli standing there, clutching a large bag of fruit, and a bunch of flowers. She hollers something on the lines of 'thanks for everything', cackles her best pirate laugh, then vanishes inside her house. What a lovely thought, we only gave her stuff we didn't want after all. Saved us taking it to the bin, although what we are going to do about Ahmed, I have no idea. 'Don't worry' Chrissie reassures me, 'there's plenty here, we can nip down his house when it's quiet.'

So a quick rest, then a cold water freshen-up, and we are ready to start our first *el paseo*. We can hear voices outside, I don't know quite what to expect, but grabbing Chrissie by the hand I fling open the front door and we step briskly into the street, to be greeted by a small sea of faces. Loli and Isabel we recognise, plus an older lady, and a man with a massive stomach. He steps forward and pats me on the back, like he is congratulating a racehorse in the winner's enclosure. 'Fernando' he informs me, gripping me warmly by the hand,'brother of these,' and he sweeps his arm in the general direction of Loli and Isabel. The older woman clearly has hip or knee problems as she limps painfully across to us. 'Mercedes' she smiles. 'Abuela.' Now I know this word, it means 'grandmother', although to whom she is the granny is unclear. Fernando and Isabel are clearly brother and sister, the likeness is uncanny, he said Loli was his sister, but quite where Mercedes comes in, is impossible to say. Something for another day, I am starving. I point to my stomach, then in the general direction of town. *'Comer?'* shouts Mercedes. If you say so

Mercedes, no idea what it means, but I nod my head enthusiastically, and we head off down the street, Loli still barking commands, so Chrissie pats me affectionately on the belly, which gets a laugh, and more comments, although whether they are saying 'fat English bastard' or 'what a slim handsome man he is!' I cannot begin to imagine.

On the way down the street, we get stopped about half a dozen times, clearly everyone has heard that British people have moved in, and are keen to make our acquaintance, unless of course they are joining the queue for our unwanted household items. Eventually however we make it to the steps, and the steep descent towards the centre of this crazy town, passing various little shops, and about half a dozen bars.

Carlos was correct. Whole families, grandparents, parents and children are strolling around, of course the weather helps but thinking about the UK at the end of October, who would be out and about at 8pm? Dog walkers certainly, people going to the pub say, but everyone actually going somewhere or doing something. Here, nobody is *doing* anything. They are just enjoying the evening, and I have to say I find it enchanting.

Directly in front of us is a large, elaborately decorated and tiled old building, standing in its own, well-manicured grounds, with palm trees. Anywhere with palm trees is OK with me. It is clearly a public building of some sort, and as it still appears to be open, even though it is gone eight pm, we walk in through the gate. *'Casa de Cultura'* states the sign, and we climb the steps and enter the ground floor. A huge immaculately and ornately designed room featuring a stone sculpture greets us, old men reading newspapers seated on one side, a mother-and -toddler group on the other, and a big wide staircase leading up to the next floor, marked 'Biblioteca.' 'Ooh look,' whispers Chrissie, an avid reader, as we both are, 'a library. Come on, let's have a look.' *Now it might seem pretentious to claim that our future lives in this town hung on that very moment, but our future lives in this town did actually hang on that very moment, although clearly we didn't know it then. As we climbed the stairs, everything we would become, everything we would eventually do in this town, were beckoning us inside, bidding us to follow.*

At the top of the stairs is a reception desk, behind which is a blonde, smiley woman, who looks at us as if her prayers have been answered. 'Welcome' she laughs, 'my name Maria, this is library, you holiday, or you live here Santa Marta?' We confirm that we have moved here today, after much gesticulating. I think. Maria's smile grows wider. 'Here in library, we haff Espaniss and Eengliss classes of conversation, peoples Espaniss speak Eengliss, and peoples Eengliss speak Espaniss. Problems for us no are mucho peoples Eengliss here in Santa Marta. You Eengliss? You come classes tomorrow in the morning eleffen hours plees?' This is just what we are looking for, a chance to learn Spanish, so we tell Maria we would be delighted to come to her classes at eleven in the morning. I think.

Just along the road is a pub. I need to eat. Soon. And a beer would be nice, after what has been a fairly momentous day. We take our seats, a waiter appears, and two ice-cold beers arrive, together with a free tapas, in rapid order. On the table is a menu, although on a chalk-board above the bar is a daily special list. I know a few of the words for beef, pork and lamb, but I am attracted by a dish called 'lomo con tomate'. 'What sort of an animal is a lomo?' I ask Chrissie.

'Dunno, I left the dictionary at home' she confesses. 'I know a 'lobo' is a wolf, perhaps it's a misprint?'

'Oh yeah,' I reply, with more than a hint of sarcasm. 'Wolf is a well-known Spanish delicacy. Wolf tapas, chorizo of wolf, Iberico wolf ham.'

'Well they eat horse in France,' she snaps, 'you had dog and snake in Vietnam, so why not wolf here?'

Why not indeed? 'Right, decision made, I am having the wolf, but shall I have it well-done, medium, or howling, and what do you fancy?' It's been a long day, and we are feeling light-headed.

'Anything but the wolf!' Chrissie giggles, 'it might repeat on me. Just get me the fish, fangs very much.' Our meals arrive, mine is medallions of pork, about twenty on a huge plate, with garlicky, oily, sliced tomatoes. Sensational, but obviously not wolf. *Because wolf tastes like chicken, right?*

I wake next morning to the sound of scuffling, scratching and tapping. My senses are instantly alert, as I am scared of certain creatures which scuffle and scratch. Scuffle scuffle, scratch, tap, scratch, scuffle. It seems to be coming from the direction of the bedroom window, so after peering down to the floor in the half-light to check for anything which shouldn't be there, I tiptoe across to the window. There it is again, scuffle scuffle. The two interior shutters are closed so I gingerly pull one back, dreading finding any creatures with twitchy noses, beady eyes, and long tails, looking in at me. Suddenly there is a scuffling sound behind me, and, my senses on overtime, I jump and turn, only to find Chrissie sitting up in bed. 'What the hell are you doing?' she demands.

'There is something outside, scratching and shuffling,' I whisper, throwing open the shutter.

'Don't be ridiculous,' she counters, 'what can possibly be out there?'

'Shh' I reply. 'Listen, there it is!'

She cocks her head and sure enough, there is the rustling, scuffling sound again. 'That's someone sweeping, you great lummox!' she cries.

'Well it sounded like a rat outside the window to me, listen, rustle rustle. I reckon we have rodents.'

'Well for Pete's sake, open the window, see what it is, then come back to bed, you're enough to drive a girl to drink.' Chrissie is not big on sympathy first thing in the morning.

'Oh yeah, it's OK for you, tucked up in bed, telling me to stick my head out the window. What if there's a rat on the wall, lurking below the window sill, waiting for me to poke my nose out? I'd look great wouldn't I, with a dirty great rodent hanging off my hooter?'

Chrissie angrily flings back the sheets and stamps across the room. 'Get out the way, you big girl, let me have a look' and she wrenches open the window and shoves her head out. 'Look, told you it was someone sweeping. It's Isabel.'

I poke my head out, and sure enough Isabel is sweeping the street, not just a quick brush down, but a stone-by-stone meticulous, thorough going-over. Who does she think is coming, the Queen of Sheba? I check the time on my phone. Seven o' bloody clock in the morning, Jeez, what is wrong with the woman?

Heart still racing, I flop back into bed and eventually drift off to sleep, only to be woken again by a car horn beeping, followed by women shouting. What in God's name is going on now? The sun is slanting through the shutters, and a quick check of my phone reveals it to be almost nine-thirty. We have overslept, if such a thing is possible when you're retired. Again I open the shutters, and satisfied that no rodents could possibly be waiting outside, with all this noise going on, I poke my head out, to be greeted by a perfect Spanish scene. A baker's van is parked almost directly below our window, I can see down into it where sacks of fresh crusty bread are piled, one on top the other. The smell wafting up is divine, and I am immediately reminded that it's breakfast time. The baker himself is passing out loaves from the back of the van, and two women in house-coats and slippers are handing over money, and greeting each other at maximum volume. 'Come and see this' I tell my wife, 'the bread-man is here.'

She wanders over and pops her head out. 'Oh. My. God! It's James Dean in a bread van!' she pants.

I whip my head out again, I must have missed the James Dean bit. 'Oh yeah, a decidedly middle-aged James Dean' I protest, with just a hint of jealousy. Chrissie is not listening however, she is hurriedly throwing on a t-shirt and shorts. 'Where are you going, we don't want any bread do we?'

'Who cares!' she cries, almost running down the stairs, 'I want to check out his buns!'

'I don't think he has buns' I inform her, 'only crusty bre...YOU DIRTY COW! You are talking about his man-buns! Come back here at once!' My words have no effect, peering out the window I see Chrissie joining the other simpering women crowding round the bread van.

I lie back on the bed and reflect on the vagaries of life. I wouldn't mind a job like that, driving round town, doling out bread to an adoring clientele. Not as James Dean of course, but I can do a passing impersonation of James Bond. Or James Bond's dad at least. Not the original Bond, Sean Connery, but the new one, what's his name, Daniel something? I have the fair hair, mostly grey these days admittedly, the blue eyes, and most importantly, a dinner suit, complete with bow tie. I could get a little white van, attach a sign 'Bread by Bond, or maybe 'Bond's Buns', don my suit and drive about dispensing bread to drooling women. That would, as Del-Boy Trotter might have said, 'knock 'em bandy.'

On the other hand, I am not sure I would want Loli, Isabel or Mercedes to be knocked bandy. Maybe at the other end of the street it's like the set of 'Baywatch', with bronzed, bouncing, bikini-clad beauties parading around, although somehow I doubt it. And someone actually has to bake the bread, load it into the sacks, and pile it into the van. I bet old James Dean gets up around three am every day, whereas here I am lolling around in bed at half-nine.

Chrissie comes back inside, closes the front door and jogs upstairs, brandishing a two-foot long length of crusty bread. Her eyes are sparkling, her cheeks are flushed, and she is panting. 'Look at the size of this,' she crows, 'best fifteen-bob I ever spent!' I regard the admittedly impressive loaf with casual interest. '*Barra de Pan*' she continues.

'So his name is not James Dean after all?' I ask. 'Barry what is he called?'

She waves the bread above her head. 'You idiot, *barra de pan* is what this is called. The baker is Jose. Jose with the sexy eyes.'

Who cares? He might have beautiful eyes, but he also has a bigger gut than me. I could easily put him out of business with 'Bond's Buns', but I don't think I will. Let him have the three o'clock starts, and the adulation of a hundred house-coated women. I'm all right where I am!

CHAPTER 8. THE GAS-MAN COMETH

Beep, beep, beep beep beep, beep beep! For pity's sake, who is this now? Is there no peace in this country? We've just had a fruit and veg man with a megaphone, shouting about his potatoes and tomatoes, his juicy plums, the length of his bananas, and his ripe melons, all at fantastic prices. Now, we have a vehicle continuously honking, coming along the street.

I unlock the front door and pop my head out, then I curse loudly, as disappearing round the bend is a little truck, laden with gas bottles. 'Well so much for Isabel saying the gas-man would call,' I complain. 'I thought she said if we left the gas bottle on the step, he would knock on the door?' I turn to hide my annoyance, then spot Chrissie coming out of Granny's bedroom, carrying an empty gas bottle. Our empty gas bottle. The very gas bottle Isabel placed on our step yesterday. 'What are you doing with that?' I enquire politely.

'I got it in last night' she confesses, 'I was worried about it.'

I start to seethe. This gas is, to use modern terminology, doing my bloody head in. Why can't it simply come out of a pipe, like it does in civilised countries? My conversation takes a somewhat sarcastic tone. 'Worried about it? Did you think it might be lonely out there on the doorstep? Were you concerned it might be scared of the dark? We need to get this gas sorted, unless we want to eat in the pub until Kingdom Come. I need a shower, WE need showers, we are stinking. And you are worried about the gas bottles welfare. Next you will be starting a gas-bottle support group.'

My wife gives me her full-on glare. 'I beg your pardon, I am not stinking. It is you who is stinking. I am perfectly clean, thank you very much. You know what they say about the fox and his hole? Well you smell like the fox, and his hole.'

How do they do that, women? Twist the story, so that it is always us in the wrong? In over thirty years of marriage, I doubt I have won one single argument. Suddenly my mood brightens. 'Hang on a minute, this street is a dead-end. He must be going to turn at the top somewhere, and will be coming back very soon. Give me the bottle, I will wait here and catch him on the way down.' Chrissie hands me the empty canister, sniffs the air, turns up her nose, utters an exaggerated 'phew!' and turns away. Women. Chalk another one up to the fairer sex.

I feel a bit of a lemon standing in the empty street clutching a gas canister, so I place it on our step and start to follow the gas-man. Maybe I can catch him up by the turn, and ask him to call at number fifty-five. I can still hear the honking in the distance, then suddenly the sound seems to change direction, and gradually grows fainter. The street by our house is the only flat part, it turns to the left, dog-legs to the right then climbs steeply, before levelling out at the point where it becomes a set of steps, descending to the road below. I puff my way up the hill, then stare in amazement, as the gas man has simply vanished. This is not possible, where has he gone? In front of me are the steps, clearly he hasn't gone down there, but where? There is simply no explanation, has he been beamed up? I stand there scratching my head, when suddenly I notice a tiny street forking to the right, at an acute angle up the hill. If our street is the zig, this little thoroughfare must be the zag. Amazing, we have only been up here once, but I didn't notice it. Mind you, to access the zag must take about a nine-point turn, but that is the only possible solution to the case of the vanishing vendor of gas. I decide to follow this new route, in places narrower than our road, until it meets with the street above, and turns back on itself and rears up again. Amazing. Not for the first time, or the last, I am in awe of the ancient builders who constructed a village on the side of a mountain.

I return home and spot Isabel waiting by our doorstep. *'El butanero'* I laugh, and wave my arm to signify that the fugitive gas seller has departed without leaving us any. Isabel giggles. *'Gasolinera?'* I ask her, pointing to myself, in an attempt to enquire whether I need to go to the filling station, or maybe even convert the house to all-electric and have done with this charade.

Isabel waves a finger in my direction indicating that I leave the gas bottle on the step, although quite when we might expect to be graced by another visit from a purveyor of propane is impossible for me to tell. Maybe gas-men are like buses, another one will be along in a minute, although really I have no idea, and mentally decide that we will be eating in the pub again tonight. And continuing to pong. Sorry, I will continue to pong, Chrissie will no doubt retain her unique fragrance.

I head back inside and relate the whole sorry tale. 'Well of course there is a way-out at the top of the street', states my wife, the one who failed geography 'O' Level and always reads a map upside-down. 'Where else did you think Jose-

Sexy-Eyes went this morning? He didn't come back down the street, I can tell you that for nothing!

I have had just about enough of these delivery persons. Sexy eyes or not. 'Right, grab your bag, lets go out for a drive.' The car is still where we left it yesterday, so now I have to somehow negotiate the rest of the street and the nine-point turn. I gingerly edge my way up the steep hill, and approaching the zig-zag bit I stop and let Chrissie out, to guide me around the bend. One of the advantages of driving a £350 car is that I am not too worried about scrapes and dents, in fact I am more concerned about demolishing one of these rickety old cottages. The Volvo has solid rubber bumpers, inside of which must be steel girders, as I hit a wall in England a few months ago, causing zero damage to the car, but terminal as far as the wall was concerned. The last thing I need here is to introduce myself to our new neighbours by appearing in my car in their front room. I wrench the car round to the right, then backwards, steering in the opposite direction. Turn three gets me a bit closer to a right angle, but just then a one-eyed old man emerges from the house I am in danger of demolishing, and starts shouting. I have no idea what he is talking about, and I really need all my concentration to be focused on my steering, so I smile politely and ignore him. Turns four and five are completed successfully, although my arms are starting to ache, as is my head, because 'one-eye' is still rattling on.

'He's telling you to reverse' Chrissie explains.

'Well tell him to f...' I reply, continuing with turns six and seven. This is really starting to look like something now. The car is almost round the zigzag, although it takes another two turns before I am clear, and able to continue our journey. Chrissie hops into the car, I give one-eye a big grin and a cheerful 'gracias', and we pull away along the zag. 'Remind me never, ever, to bring this car up here again' I state emphatically. 'If I do, you have my permission to shoot me.'

We are not out of the woods yet however, as there are more dog-legs, big-dippers and gut-squeezing sections to negotiate, and I am seriously considering contacting Walt Disney World and suggesting a new ride for thrill seekers. 'Drive a Volvo through Santa Marta.' The name probably needs a bit of work, it hardly compares with 'Big Thunder Mountain', but I am sure it would be a roar-away success.

Eventually the old part of town gives way to the newer part, where there are normal sized streets, and pavements, and wiping the perspiration from my forehead, I begin to relax. We head out of town on a back-road, winding through the olive fields, passing mountains and dry river beds, until we reach the town of Almorate. We have been here before, it is where the Nicolas Cage-lookalike notary has his office where we signed up for the house, and where our lawyer Pedro is also based. 'Look!' cries Chrissie as we approach the town centre, 'a British shop. I wonder what they sell there?'

I glance across and sure enough, a shop front decorated with a Union Jack paint-job stands proudly next to a rather nondescript Spanish bar. Intrigued, we park up and approach the shop, wending our way through about four Brits smoking outside, and enter the emporium, which resembles a small warehouse. A middle-aged woman spots us and comes over. 'Hello, my name is Julie, are you new here?' We confirm that we have indeed just arrived in this neck of the woods. 'Well we have everything here to make your new life in Spain complete' boasts Julie. 'Here is a cafe, look, you can get a proper cuppa, with PG Tips. There is the computer area, you can rent a computer for a Euro per hour, or bring your own and use the Wi-Fi for fifty cents. That bloke there is my husband Bob, he can sort you out with a Sky TV package so you can watch all your favourite British programmes. The Spanish lady there is Ana, she does translation of documents and anything you can't understand, ten Euros an hour, very cheap, and over there is the shop section where you can get all your favourite English food, Fray Bentos steak and kidney pies, Jaffa Cakes, HP sauce, Findus crispy pancakes, all that sort of stuff.'

I do my best to look interested, but honestly? We tried three different Spanish supermarkets when we were staying at the caravan site and each one sold their own perfectly good teabags. The library in Santa Marta has free computers and Wi-Fi. I have never watched Sky TV and hopefully never will, the librarian in Santa Marta said she would be happy to help us with any paperwork, and I would rather eat my own liver than a snake and pygmy pie. Mind you, I could murder a Jaffa Cake.

'See that chap by the front door?' Julie continues, 'that is Paul, and his wife is Lucy, they live in Santa Marta. Go over and say hello, I am sure they would like to meet you.' Over by the door is a well-built man with a florid complexion. Either he has been spending too long in the sun, or he has a heart condition. He has a shock of fair hair, swept back across his head. A dead ringer for Donald Trump. Next to him, almost obscured by his bulk, is a petite, dark-haired woman. Lucy I presume. We stroll across and I offer my hand. 'Paul? I am John, this is Chrissie, we have just moved to Santa Marta.'

He takes my hand, looks me up and down, then turns to Lucy. 'More bloody Brits moving into the town' he half-chuckles. Charming. Then he softens his stance slightly. 'What are you doing about your TV?' he asks. 'I have a Sky dish for sale if you want one, fifty Euros.'

What can I say to that? I decide to be frank. 'I honestly haven't thought about TV, we have more important things to worry about, getting the house straight, but I fundamentally disagree with Sky, or any pay-TV. I thought we might watch some Spanish telly, help us pick up the language, there is an ancient TV which came with the house, although I haven't plucked up the courage to switch it on yet!'

Paul looks me up and down again as if he is unable to grasp the concept of someone not having TV as their number-one priority. Lucy seems much kinder than her boorish husband. 'Which street are you living in? She enquires.

'Calle Castillo, Castle Street' Chrissie informs her.

'Oh that's the next street to us, isn't it Paul?' she smiles. 'We must get together sometime.'

I always get carried away in these situations. 'So why don't you come to us on Saturday?' I suggest. 'You'll have to accept us as we are, a bit up in the air at the moment, but we inherited about a hundred different glasses with the house, so they need christening, so to speak!'

Lucy professes herself delighted to visit us, we make the arrangements for Saturday night, then we head outside to continue exploring the town. As soon as we are clear of the smoking Brits, Chrissie gives me the full glaring treatment. 'Whatever did you do that for?' she growls. 'Inviting someone like that over to our house.'

I decide to play the innocent. 'Someone like what? A red-faced Londoner you mean? Or Donald Trump's double?'

She is not seeing the funny side however. 'Don't try to be clever, you know full-well what I mean. That Paul. He's a pig. Did you see how he was looking at you? And our house is a mess, we don't even have any gas, how can we possibly get it straight before Saturday? You are impossible sometimes.'

OK innocent didn't work, so I decide to try conciliatory. 'Don't worry, it's only Tuesday, we have plenty of time, and anyway, we said we had only just moved in, they won't notice if the house is a bit of a mess. OK, Paul was a bit brusque, but that's just his way. And Lucy was very nice I thought.'

Chrissie is not consoled by my soothing words however. 'Lucy will notice if the house is a mess, she's a woman. It's OK for you blokes, you will just sit around drinking, but Lucy will want the grand tour, and the place looks like a bomb-site.'

Suddenly I am gripped by panic. 'Oh no, what have I done? I have just thought of something really important.'

'What, what's important?' she asks, with concern.

I put my face in my hands. 'What an idiot I am, I didn't realise, I simply forgot, I could kick myself sometimes.'

Chrissie is starting to panic, 'What is it, you're scaring me now. Tell me, tell me.'

I rub my hand across my face. 'You mentioned us blokes drinking' I continue. 'I have just remembered, we have no beer glasses!'

Back in Santa Marta, still nursing a painful arm, we leave the car in a side-street where the old town meets the new. Approaching the house, Chrissie suddenly starts cursing. 'I can't believe it! Someone has stolen the gas bottle from our front door step.'

I stare in disbelief. Some thieving oik has indeed made off with our empty canister. 'Why would anyone do that?' I exclaim. Surely an empty has no value? Does someone have a grudge against us? As far as I know, we are on good terms with everyone we have met. This is indeed a sad moment, and has taken the shine off our arrival in this town. I just cannot believe that someone has done this to us.

We have only been in the house about two minutes when there is a knock on the door. Isabel. She beckons me to follow her, and there, standing in her hallway, is a brand-new sealed gas cylinder. Never in the history of bottled gas can one man have been so glad to have caught sight of a canister of butane. 'Come on!' she laughs, pointing the way to our house, Loli appears and the three of us, me staggering under the weight of our precious cargo, form a ragged procession to our kitchen. Loli then takes charge, opening the door of the Spanish Aga, coupling up the regulator, heaving the cylinder into its place, and closing the door. Then, grabbing the lighter from the worktop, she turns on a tap, sparks the lighter, and after a few feeble splutters the hob lights manfully up, to cheers from the four of us.

'*Cuanto, el butano*?' I enquire to Isabel. How much? I really have no idea what to expect. Back in the UK, a canister of caravan gas was the best part of £15, but the little blue container was only about the quarter the size of it's Spanish equivalent. So £60 or thereabouts, seventy Euros? No idea.

'*Diez-con-vente*' replies our neighbour.

I turn to my Spanish translator, 'Ten Euros and twenty cents' Chrissie confirms.

Nine quid, are you serious? Loli spots my confusion, grabs my palm and traces the figure ten, *diez* she confirms, and then sketches a twenty, 'vente centimos.' Unbelievable. I quickly fish eleven Euros out of my wallet, and wave my hand, to signify I don't need the change. Then I point to the boiler on the kitchen wall. It has two dials, one is clearly a temperature setting, the other has several settings including a lightning bolt, which I assume is the ignition setting, and there's also a button to push, but how the thing fires up I cannot imagine. Loli walks over, cranks the button a couple of times, then explodes into a torrent of abuse, directed, I hope, at the boiler, rather than me. Among her words I catch *antigua* which I assume means 'antique', and *nuevo*, which I know is 'new'. The two sisters then turn their backs on our antique appliance, and with a wave, leave us in peace.

OK, progress of a sort, we can now cook some food, providing we can get the boiler to actually fire up, although this will entail going out to buy some ingredients, as we have nothing in the house, which I guess means another night in the pub. Retirement can be a real bugger at times. I am however looking forward to cooking some traditional Spanish meals. For a retirement gift, Chrissie gave me a *Rick Stein* Spanish recipe book, as throughout our married life I always complained that I could be a fantastic, imaginative chef, if only I had the time. Now I have the time, so I have to start putting my boasting into practice. I have already identified half a dozen dishes I am keen to attempt, so with this happy thought I decide to retire to the patio, recipe book in hand, and compile a list of things we need to buy. The best laid plans etc.

Suddenly there is a loud knock on the door. I raise my eyes to the heavens and silently curse. Why can't these people leave us alone? I open the door to reveal a short, stocky old man, glasses, flat cap, the living image of one of the Tetley Tea Folk. The old one, the foreman, Gaffer was it? Behind him is a skinny woman in a sleeveless crimpline dress, white trainers, and a white baseball hat. 'Ey oop!' cries gaffer, 'ah knew tha' were English, tha's left tha' blind oop!' I am not known for my razor sharp detective qualities, but it's a fairly safe bet that people from the north of England have paid us a visit. And Gaffer is correct, we have left our blinds up. As well as the interior shutters, our windows also come with exterior roll-up blinds, operated by a ropey length of string. The Spanish all keep their blinds down, possibly venturing to raise them maybe six inches at sundown, whereas us fugitives from rainy England are damned if we are shutting out all that glorious sunshine. 'Ah saw tha' bloody great Volvo, an' said to t'missus there were English people 'ere. We lives in the street aboove, Keith's the name, t'missus is Diane, get t'kettle on lad!'

I grit my teeth and step backwards, gesturing to our visitors to come inside. 'You must excuse the mess, we only moved in yesterday, but we do have some tea bags. Tetley I think. We brought them from England.' Chrissie almost chokes with laughter, she knows how my mind works and has also made the 'Gaffer' connection. 'Sorry, John and Christine' I apologise. 'It's been a busy couple of days.'

Gaffer is looking around, until his eyes come to rest on our ancient TV. 'By gaw lad, tha's got theesen a reet antique telly! Me an' Di, we got oursen's a sixty inch, Sky TV package, inter-web, the bloody works. Be tha' gettin' Sky TV?' *What is it with these Brits and their Sky TV? Is that the only source of conversation in this town?* I repeat more or less the narrative about TV I gave Paul not two hours since.

Diane then spots the Rick Stein book resting on the coffee table. 'Ee, look at that bloody soft, soothern Jessie! We don't eat that foreign muck!' 'Nay lad' Gaffer interrupts, 'meat-an'-two-veg man me, allus was an' allus will be!'

'Speaking of which' I smile, 'we need to get some supplies in. Which shops do you recommend?'

Diane looks about to respond but Gaffer speaks over her. He is the Gaffer after all. 'Two supermarkets are best, lad, Dee and Donna. There are two Dee's, big Dee and little Dee. Little Dee is in town, big Dee is on the poly-wotsit. Donna is in town an' all, but they're dearer than the Dee.' *Well that was as clear as mud.* Gaffer hasn't finished yet however. 'I got a card from the Dee tha' knaws,' and he delves into his wallet and pulls out a supermarket club-card, bearing the legend *Dia*.

I stifle a chuckle. 'Is that pronounced *Dia*?' I ask.

'Gawd knaws lad' he replies, grinning, 'we can't speak the bloody lingo. Tell thee what thaw, there's naw need ta bother with learnin't. I can ask for a beer, like, tha's all tha' needs.'

'OK so those are the supermarkets,' I continue, 'but what about fruit and veg, the butchers, fishmongers, shops like that. Which ones do you recommend?'

Gaffer looks as if he is struggling with the concept of fruit and veg. 'Nay lad, we don't use shops, they are full of old Spanish women, all gabbling away, an' we can't ask for the stuff anyway. In the Dee tha' just pick it off the shelf, and pay. No need to speak the lingo see,' and he taps his nose. 'Naw flies on me, lad, naw flies on me! Then once a month we goes t' Iceland, in Fuengerola, they sells all the British pies, sausages, biscuits, tea-bags, steak, English steak lad, not foreign 'oss-meat tha' knaws!'

'Were you two ever on TV?' I chuckle. He has that twinkle in his eye, and his mouth has a way of curling up at the corners, as if he has either just cracked a joke, or is thinking about the next one. Yet his wife meanwhile is deadpan, and I cannot work out if it is a double-act routine they have perfected, of if this is their usual dispositions. Whatever, they are highly entertaining, a stark contrast to the the first couple.

Diane roars with laughter. 'Well I were on Miss World, tha' knaws, an' ee were on Crimewatch!'

'What did you do, Keith? Are you a desperate fugitive?' Chrissie grins.

'Nowt, lass!' he bellows. 'I were innocent! I were caught ridin' me bike through t'woods, an they accused me o' bein' a psycho-path!' The four of us are groaning, and laughing all at the same time. But what an entertaining pair.

'Well speaking of horses, as we were a few minutes ago' I grin, 'we have to gallop to town, to get some groceries in, but we are having a little get-together on Saturday night, maybe you would like to pop in for a drink? Paul and Lucy are coming, do you know them?'

'Ee, that bloody soft soothern Jessie?' asks Diane. 'Like that Yankee feller off the telly? Wassisname? 'You're fired!' We watches it on Sky. Trunk?'

'You mean Donald Trump?' I ask her. 'I suppose Paul does bear a passing resemblance. So is that a yes, or a no for Saturday?'

'Too bloody right lad!' Gaffer confirms. 'Us'll be there, if there's beer goin!'

I can feel Chrissie's glare burning two holes in the side of my head, but what the heck? In for a penny and all that. With that they bid us farewell, and once again the house falls quiet. But not for long. 'I can't believe you sometimes' Chrissie storms. 'The house is a complete tip, and you go and invite two couples round here for drinks. And you haven't bought any beer glasses yet!'

What can I say? 'OK, but we need to get to know these people' I protest. 'And these two seemed really nice, I thought you would like to meet a few of the girls, make some friends, go for a coffee with them. I can handle the blokes, chat about guy stuff, repairing motorbikes, United's defence, I was only thinking of you, really!'

'Thinking of me my eye!' my wife splutters. 'You just want an excuse to get rat-arsed.' Enough said. I have been sussed again.

The curly perm and the mullet must rank amongst the worst-ever hairstyles. Especially on men. Yet here we are, the second decade of the twenty-first century, and two examples of these hairy disasters are seated in our lounge. Pete and Dave, two British builders, together with Denise, our estate agent, who recommended these clowns. Our house has two immediate problems. Firstly, we need to get the ancient gas boiler to work, and second, there is a leak at the back of the toilet bowl. We have the old-fashioned cistern on the wall above the toilet, complete with lead pipe supplying the flush, which has a small leak. Nothing major, but it needs sorting. I could quite possibly mend this myself, if I knew where to buy the materials. The cistern is actually in good condition, and so retro, and we would like to keep it. I enjoy pulling the chain, but getting my feet wet is not part of the deal. Hence Dick and Dom, sorry Pete and Dave. Like a cross between the 1978 England football team, and a glam-rock tribute band. Pete regards the gas boiler. 'It's effed mate' is his professional opinion.

In the meantime Dave casts his eye over our toilet. 'Can't fix that, like trying to nail a jelly to a wall' he opines. 'get a new one, close-coupled, sorted.'

Chrissie meanwhile has asked Pete to have a look at our inherited washing machine, the electrical wiring on which, to say the very least, is unconventional, featuring as it does copious amounts of parcel tape. The cable takes a circuitous route from the plug socket, travelling upwards to what can only be described as a drunkards knitting basket, before disappearing behind the washing machine in a truly scary fashion. I have simply refused to get involved with this death-trap, on the grounds that as someone who once wired an electric cooker with thirteen-amp cable, and almost blew up the entire street, I am completely unqualified to make a decision on whether or not we should use it. Pete studies the venerable appliance. 'It's a washing machine' he firmly states.

'Yes, but what do you think?' Chrissie continues.

Pete looks at his watch. 'It's six o'clock, that's what I think, it's Friday, the pubs are open. You get the materials, the new boiler, the new toilet, and we'll come and fit them. Give us a shout.'

And with that, the three of them depart and hurry away down the street. Unbelievable. The reason we called for help is that we don't know where to buy these items, having only been in this town for a few days. 'Don't worry' I tell Chrissie, who is still open-mouthed in astonishment, 'we have Paul and Gaffer coming tomorrow, I am sure they will know where we can go for help. Dick and Dom can go to hell.'

The night of the party arrives and our kitchen worktop is groaning under the weight of the food. We have prepared small tapas plates, Spanish ham, about four different types of chorizo, olives, crusty bread from old sexy-eyes (of course), three different cheeses, my speciality Rick Stein tortilla, tomatoes and much more. We have enough beer and wine to bathe in, which soon proves just as well. First to arrive are Paul and Lucy, bearing litre-sized bottles of San Miguel. I have only bought the own-brand stuff from Dee, sorry Dia, as to me, being a real-ale man, lager is lager. The Dee stuff tastes perfectly good to me, and at 4.8% is a fair bit stronger, and at around 30p a pint, considerably cheaper, than its British equivalent. 'Forgot to tell you' cries Paul, 'I only drink San Miguel, can't stand that supermarket crap!' I smile sweetly, whilst gritting my teeth, an action it seems likely I will need to perfect when dealing with this bloke. Anyway, he's brought two litres, surely enough for him? Gaffer and I can drink the Dee lager. Not so. I carefully pour him a San Miguel into one of our newly acquired pint glasses, and he calmly pours it down his throat, without swallowing, then holds out the glass for another.

'Blimey mate, you worked up a thirst, walking down from the next street.'

He chuckles, and Lucy simpers. 'I likes me beer, but only San Miguel mind!' Chrissie meanwhile fixes Lucy a glass of wine while I head back into the kitchen, but this time pour about a third of a pint of Paul's favourite, topping the rest up from my supply. He takes the glass and sips this one. 'Great stuff this San Miguel, so much better than the supermarket rubbish.' I can't help a wry chuckle to myself. *OK sunshine, you've been sussed!*

Just then another knock at the door, I open it to find Gaffer and Diane, plus two other couples. 'Now then!' laughs Gaffer, 'look who I found wandrin' round t' town. Jimmy and Jenny, from Scotland, SEE YOU JIMMY! And Jason and Sadie, from gawd knows!' Jimmy seems to be about twenty years older than Jenny, a slim blonde about our age. I assume they are a couple as they are holding hands, although you never know these days. Jason and Sadie meanwhile look as if they have just stepped off the set of The Addams Family, they must be the palest people I have seen in this country, where a glowing suntan is the norm amongst most ex-pats. They are also dressed mainly in black, which heightens their spooky appearance. They remind me of a pair of bats, who will possibly flap their wings, swoop into the air and hang upside-down from the light fittings. 'Well come on in, and welcome' I smile, although I am seriously wondering if we will have enough to drink now. Maybe they are all teetotal, and not very hungry, although somehow I doubt it.

'Ohh look, San Miguel!' cries Jason, 'my favourite.'

'Get your bloody hands off my beer Jase,' cries Paul, 'you can have the supermarket crap. There's a fridge full of it out there.' *Now how did he know that?* Everyone then crowds out on the terrace, while Chrissie and I dispense drinks to our latest arrivals.

'Ach look at the sunset Jimmy' coos Jenny, 'why don't we get sunsets like that at our house?'

He looks at me and rolls his eyes. 'Cos our wee hoose faces north, that's why.'

'And they have a garden too!' Jenny wails, 'why can't we have a garden?'

'Well we think we have a garden,' I smile, 'but we can't get down there at the moment, as the wall has fallen down, and buried the path. We are planning to start digging next week!'

'Why did the wall fall down?' Jenny persists.

I am starting to come to the conclusion that she is possibly not the sharpest tool in the box. 'I'm not sure, it was like that when we bought the house, it looks like next door have shovelled all their earth and stones onto our side.'

Jenny digests this news for a moment. 'Why did they do that?' She asks.

Jimmy has suddenly had enough, 'Ach will ye no shut up woman? Drink yer wine!' and he turns to me with the briefest shake of his head.

Meanwhile Chrissie is trying to round up the women for a grand tour of the house, but just then there is yet another knock on the door. I open it to find a small, wiry man, just a bit older than me maybe, carrying a litre of Donna lager. 'I was told to look for the 'ouse with the shutters up' he laughs, 'an this is the only one! 'Ow ya doin', Derek's the name, Del-Boy to me mates!' and shoving the beer under his arm, he extends a hand.

'Now then Del' shouts Gaffer, 'you found us then, yer Cockney barn-cake!'

I turn to Gaffer. 'How many more people have you invited, or is this it?!'

Gaffer chuckles, 'Nobbut a few friends, lad!'

Del quickly pours himself a beer and we all head out to the terrace. 'Right everyone' I announce, 'the beer and white wine are in the fridge, the red is on the worktop, you all have glasses so just help yourselves, OK? Food in the dining room. When it's gone, it's gone!'

'But 'ands off me San Miguel!' growls Paul.

Chrissie gathers up the girls and they head upstairs, so I corral the fellows and head downstairs. The house is three storey at the back, on account of being built on the side of a mountain, so the garden is accessed downstairs, through what the estate agent called the 'summer kitchen.' Outside the back door is a rough patio area, covered by the kitchen extension above. The problem is that the area is a horrible slope, impossible to sit on due to the angle. 'I want to level this area' I announce to the guys, 'make a covered patio area, for the winter maybe, or if it rains, but I'm not sure how to go about it yet.'

'Easy!' pipes up Del-Boy. 'Build a block wall at the front, and at the side, fill it with hardcore, and tile over the top. I was a builder in England, I can 'elp you wiv it.'

'Only one problem there' I protest, 'I don't have any hardcore!'

Del shakes his head at the assembled throng. He is really playing to the crowd now. He slips his arm round my shoulder. 'Oh yes you do sunshine, oh yes you do.' And he gives me a little wink, and a squeeze. I am baffled. I know what hardcore looks like, and I am 100% certain I have none.

'Oh no I don't, sunshine' I grin.

Del shakes his head, then steps away and heads in the direction of the garden. Then he stops dramatically, throws his arms in the air, 'oh my God, look at that bloody great pile of hardcore!' The garden wall! The collapsed garden wall, reduced to a huge pile of rocks, stones and soil. The pile of rocks, stone and soil which we had not the faintest idea what to do with. Hardcore, for our new patio! Everyone bursts out laughing, and I grip Del by the hand and pump it firmly, gazing into his eyes like a lovesick puppy.

'Del an' me are buildin' a patio at the back of our place next week' announces Gaffer. 'Come an' 'elp oos, mixin', carryin', fetchin', two mornings, mebbe three, an' you can 'ave the leftover sand, cement and blocks. Got a job-lot of tiles an' all, should be plenty left for this job 'ere.' *Looks like I have next week sorted, then.*

The summer kitchen is the most original part of the house, with exposed beamed ceilings, whitewashed stone walls, and a huge walk-in fireplace. 'See you got your Spanish heating system sorted' Jason grins.

'Yes, beautiful fireplace, isn't it, just a shame it's down here, and not in the sitting room' I reply.

'No, not the fireplace, the Spanish heating system, I mean' he says, deadpan. What is he talking about? There is no other heating system, as far as I am aware. He can see my confusion, and clearly knows something I don't. He taps a table which is standing in the corner. It is a curious piece of furniture, an ordinary rustic circular wooden table, maybe four feet in diameter, but with a strange arrangement at the bottom of the legs, where a circular wooden shelf has been fitted, maybe a foot off the ground, but with a large hole cut in it. It is a perfectly round hole, so clearly done by the manufacturer, but why I have no idea. As a footrest, the shelf is useless, with the large hole in it. 'This is your Spanish heating system' explains Jason.

'What, chop it up and chuck it in the fireplace?' I laugh. 'Come on, we have all had a drink, but how can a table be a heating system?' The other blokes are all laughing at me now, clearly they are all in on the secret, but I actually wish Jason was hanging from a light-fitting. I will personally hang him from one, unless he puts me out of my misery.

He does. 'What the Spanish do is put a circular ash-pan in the hole, fill it with vine clippings, or twigs, charcoal, or similar, light it up, and it gives off heat. Then they cover the table with a huge blanket, the family all sit around the table, grab a bit of blanket each, pull it round them, the heat rises and they stay warm' he explains. 'The ash-pan is called a brassiere.'

'Och, it's called a 'brasero', ye eejit!' cries Jimmy.

Right, I have had enough of this. 'OK, I will personally eject anyone else who tries to kid me that the Spanish use a table and vine clippings as a heating system!' I laugh.

Del is crying with laughter. 'They really do, mate' he splutters, 'but these days the braseros are electric. You will see them in the window of the ferreteria, the ironmongers.'

Come to think of it, I have seen these curious-looking circular electrical devises in the ironmongers' window. I wondered what they were for. 'But what about the smoke, in the old days, before electric?'

Del is wiping the tears from his eyes. 'Have you heard the old people here clearing their throats?' We certainly have. In Britain, I used to love waking in the mornings to the Dawn Chorus of birdsong. Here, the sunrise is greeted by a symphony of hawking, gobbing and flobbing. And that's just the women. A Spanish man clearing his pipes just has to be heard to be believed, like a sty-full of pigs followed by a clap of thunder.

We head back up to the ground floor, still chuckling, and out onto the kitchen patio. 'I don't suppose anyone knows how to fire up these gas boilers?' I enquire.

'Meat an' drink, lad! cries Gaffer, 'meat an' drink. There's nowt I can't fettle,' and he turns towards our ancient appliance. 'Blooody 'ell, it's antique, but I bet five pints I can get 'er runnin'!'

'Get that pile o' crap running and you deserve ten pints' laughs Jimmy, so Gaffer, thus challenged, presses the dial marked with a lightning bolt, and holds it down. He waits a few seconds then starts pushing the other button. A loud cranking sound emits from the boiler, but nothing happens, so he repeats the procedure, and hey presto, the pilot light comes on, to raucous cheers from the guys. 'Just leave it a few seconds, let t' pilot light warm oop, then turn on t' 'ot tap', he instructs. I am starting to get excited. Maybe, just maybe, we will have some hot water. And trust me on this, I need some. 'OK' grins Gaffer, 'fire 'er opp. Turn t' tap on, lad.' I walk over to the sink, turn the hot tap full on, there is a horrible gurgling, spitting noise, and suddenly rusty water starts flowing, and the boiler fires into life. Cue even louder cheers, just as the ladies are returning from their tour.

'We have hot water!' I announce, 'give that man five pints!'

Jason then returns from the bathroom. 'Got a little leak there' he announces, 'you need Peggy.'

'Peggy who, and where does she live?' I ask. Maybe there is a lady-plumber somewhere here.

Jason laughs, 'Peggy's not a person, it's a sticky mastic, like silicone but much thicker. It's called Peggy here.'

This is just the information we need. 'So where do you buy this Peggy?' I enquire.

'In the Ferry,' replies Jason, 'the Ferry Terry!'

'Ye dafty pie-can!' cries Gaffer, 'your bloody Spanish is worse than mine. He means the ferreteria, t' hardware shop, down in the little square.'

And so the evening continues. The drinks flow, the food is consumed, and it's stupid o'clock before the last of our guests have finally staggered home. We decide to leave the clearing-up until tomorrow, and as I drift off to sleep I reflect on the evening, which seems to have been an unqualified success, with reservations. Which makes it a qualified success possibly, who knows, at this time of night. There was copious use of the F-word, the C-word made an appearance, even the N and P-words had an outing. Racism, homophobia and misogyny all shared the limelight, and at times it was like being back in the 1960's. OK, so none of us are whiter than white, but surely these views have no place in these more enlightened times? Paul in particular seemed to be oblivious to the sensibilities of others, and once again it seems Chrissie's initial assessment was the correct one. I don't imagine we will be inviting him around again.

On the other hand, some of the banter was excellent, particularly the interplay between Del-Boy and Jimmy, who appear to have a cabaret act sketched out between them. Someone said tonight, I forget who, that Spain today reminded them of Britain fifty years ago. I assumed they were referring to the little individual shops, the almost complete absence of chain stores, the two-hour lunch break, and the fact that Sunday is a true day of rest. Suddenly, I am gripped by a disturbing thought. What if he was actually referring to the prevalence of the 'Alf Garnet' mentality among the ex-pats? Time will tell I imagine. On Monday, I have to get down the Ferry for some Peggy. No hang on, Monday morning I am building a patio with Del and Gaffer. Complicated business, this retirement game.

CHAPTER 9. THE ENGLISHMAN, THE COLUMBIAN AND THE MOROCCAN.

To many people, a Colombian would conjure up images of a gun-running, drug-smuggling, terrorist desperado, but in the case of Paolo, nothing could be further from the truth. He is a foreign language teacher living in London, and has bought a run down cottage for use in the holidays just a few doors from Lucy and Paul, which is where we met him at a dinner. Following our house-warming party, Lucy asked us round to their house for a meal, and in the spirit of neighbourliness, we decided to accept. In fact we have become good friends with Lucy, she has accompanied us to the library for conversation classes, to the cafe, and even on one of our walks in the countryside around the town. The problem of course is Paul. Everyone is naturally entitled to their views, but we are not willing to socialise with people who believe that racist and sexist ranting constitutes a conversation. This is not why we came here, and we are not prepared to engage with these opinions. Maybe Paul was in a bad mood when he came to our house two weeks ago and I am prepared to give him the benefit of the doubt for now, but any more of it and he is history.

Paolo paid about £15,000 for a three storey cottage with four bedrooms and a small garden, but there was a lot of work needed and the electrics had been condemned by the electric board who were refusing to re-connect him until it had been sorted. He was looking for a competent DIY person to help him out for a week getting it sorted, but in the absence of such a person I volunteered my services, so after negotiating a daily rate I found myself gainfully employed for the first time in three months.

Paul had suggested meeting up at his house so I duly arrive around nine-fifteen in case there is any chance of a cuppa before getting down to work, to find the TV on, and Paul slumped on the sofa watching the Jeremy Kyle show. I am not really sure what to do next. There is no sign of Paolo, he was supposed to be meeting us here, but as his cottage is currently uninhabitable, he is staying in the local hotel. I am sure he will be along soon, so in the meantime I sit in an armchair, and wait. When I decided to retire, little did I know that in just a few months I would be sitting down watching daytime TV with a homophobic racist. 'I can't believe you are actually watching this stuff', I observe. 'Isn't it a bit, you know, chavvy?'

Lucy arrives with the tea, 'Oh I know, it's awful, but Paul likes it.' Enough said.

Heading up to Paolo's cottage, our first job is to turn on the water, and the second job is to turn it off again *mucho rapido* as a tidal wave is coming down the steps from the garden, so Paul rushes off for a blow-lamp and solder while I investigate the source of the leak. With that fixed we turn it on again only to find a leak in the bathroom so I spend the next half-hour with my head inside the toilet cistern, not a great start to the morning!

After this Paolo and I spend the day stripping old plaster and flaking paint from the first floor bedroom walls and ceilings, prior to me filling the cracks with flexible filler then plastering over. Late afternoon the Spanish electricians arrive to quote for the re-wiring, Paolo's native language is Spanish of course, albeit Latin American Spanish, so he can converse easily with them, I can follow some of it and hear the phrase 'seven hundred euros' which I feel is a very good price for all that work, until Paolo informs me that we have to cut out all the channels in the walls ourselves, and plaster in the plastic trunking which will hold the actual electric cables. The electricians will then thread the cables through and connect up all the sockets and switches, do the testing and sign it all off. Do I think I can cut out all the channels in the walls? I assure him it will all be OK, even though I don't have a disc cutter, or angle-grinder or whatever you call it, and have never actually used one before......

After a restless, sleepless night, dreaming of severed limbs, I arrive for work next day, and decide to forego the cuppa and the Jeremy Kyle Show, and wait outside Paolo's for him to arrive, which he duly does, pulling goggles and a face mask from the boot of his car, and he has also acquired an angle grinder from somewhere. The electricians have drawn pencil marks on the walls where the cables have to go, plus the square holes for switches and plug sockets, so off we go with this highly dirty, dusty and downright dangerous task, with the disc spinning inches from my face and the plaster and stone raining down on my head, and I soon resemble a giant mutant panda covered with white plaster dust, apart from two circles round my eyes and mouth. Spaniards have a fascination with construction work of any sort and before long a small gathering of old men has assembled out in the street, no doubt attracted by all the noise and dust, and as I have to take frequent breaks to get the dust out of my ears and have a drink, they are rewarded for their patience by the sight of this crazy English ghostly apparition.

Paolo is coming along behind with hammer and chisel to tap out the channel for the cables. Work progresses well and by the end of the day we are across the lounge and into the kitchen. The assembly of Spaniards outside has steadily grown and now there are about half a dozen of them, and as I look out the window I see an old woman hobbling up the street to get a better look. As I emerge from the house I give a wave and say 'Trabajo muy duro' very hard work, but there is a collective drawing in of breath and several cries of 'Sangria, sangria'. What are they on about sangria for, I need a bath and a cup of tea! Plus a beer tonight. 'Sangria', they keep saying, 'su cabeza'. My head? What are they talking about? Suddenly it dawns on me, sangre is the word for blood.

They are not offering me a red wine-based drink with fruit in it, I am bleeding from somewhere, my head probably. I look in the window at my reflection and see that I have a jagged wound where a piece of flying stone must have hit me, the blood has run down the side of my face and matted and congealed in the white of the plaster. I am a grotesque sight, like some monster from Dr Who in about 1976, or a spooky apparition in the ghost train at the end of the pier, some of the men are laughing but the women look truly horrified, so I mumble something about a bath again and hurry off home. My house is only in the next street but this is the time when the siesta has ended and people come into the streets to gossip with their neighbours, so I get many strange looks and a few comments about *sangre*, before I thankfully sink into a hot bath, and yes I do have that beer in the evening.........

Next morning as I arrive at Paolo's I notice two chairs placed in the street opposite the house. Clearly a big crowd is expected today, but there are obviously no Germans about as nobody has placed a beach towel on a chair.... Progress is good today, across the kitchen towards what was originally the back wall of the house until the bathroom extension was built, me cutting and Paolo chopping out, until lunchtime when he has to go off to a meeting with his lawyer, leaving me doing the cutting and the chopping. All goes well until I start cutting down the back wall from the ceiling, I have gone about a foot when I realise the cutter is going through easier than usual, and I am being showered with red dust instead of stone. Bricks!! It doesn't take a genius to work out that a two-hundred year old house will not have brick walls, particularly these modern hollow ones which are only 2 inches thick. Hmmmm.... I stop the channelling and decide to cut out the rectangle for the cooker point, and once again encounter bricks, and can get my hand inside the wall where I can feel the original stone wall behind it. Someone in the recent past has built a free-standing brick wall in front of the original stone, but has not tied it in so it is just asking to fall down if I cut any more channels in it. I go to get Paul to have a look, and tell him I reckon we should run the cables outside the wall in plastic casing, it will not be pretty but later we could attach wooden battens to the wall, tack plasterboard on and plaster or tile it, but we cannot cut any more channels. We cannot run the cables between the walls as there isn't room. Mine is the only solution. Definitely. I think. I am not a builder, but this is common sense.

Paul doesn't agree, he reckons I (note he says 'I') could cut one channel at a time, feed the plastic trunking into the channel, then plaster over with the magic Spanish plaster called *yesso* which sets like rock in about 3 minutes. I am not having it however, the wall will fall down for sure if we muck about with it any more. Paolo then arrives back so we put our views to him, and to my annoyance he seems to be siding with Paul. I tell them again that the wall will collapse, and that I am going outside while they decide what they want to do. A sizeable collection of Spaniards has assembled, some new faces from yesterday, and I am just trying to remember what the words for 'bricks' and 'idiots' are when there is an almighty crash and a huge grey cloud comes billowing out the front door. The Spaniards all rush forward but nothing can be seen in the choking dust for a few minutes, but eventually I go inside to be greeted by a scene of utter devastation. Paul is standing there with a hammer in one hand and a look of horror on his face, and Paolo appears to be crying, although it might be the dust in his eyes. On the ground is a big pile of Spanish bricks. I completely lose my rag. 'I EFFING TOLD YOU THAT EFFING WALL WOULD FALL DOWN IF YOU EFFED ABOUT WITH IT' I shout, and storm out the house, almost scattering a few Spaniards on the way. I am so annoyed I can hardly speak, the locals probably didn't understand my burst of Anglo Saxon, but I am sure they got the gist of it.........

Eventually Paul comes out, minus the hammer, and, without glancing in my direction, simply slopes off home. Paolo appears, still wiping his eyes, 'Sorry John' he says, 'you were right. What shall we do now?' I am still livid at my advice being ignored. 'Lock the door, eff-off back to England, and forget all about it' I tell him. I am still cross. 'Phone 'DIY SOS' and see if Nick Knowles will come over and sort it out' I suggest. He looks at me with his big puppy-dog eyes. I offer an olive branch. 'We could try Mohammed' I say.

'What, find a local mosque and convert to Islam? he asks.

'No, Mohammed the Moroccan builder' I tell him. 'This job is now beyond my skills, but Mohammed has all the proper tools and about three blokes working for him. He can sort this mess out for you.'

I first met Mohammed a few days ago when he was doing some work in our street for Ahmed, Mohammed has lived in Spain half his life and speaks

Spanish fluently, but talks slowly and clearly and I can understand most of what he is saying. He has two favourite phrases, *Proxima Semana* and *Muy bien*, 'next week' and 'very good'. Luckily I have his number in my phone, as he had insisted I take it 'in case of emergencies', so a quick call and he promises to come over right away as he is just off for lunch. Ten minutes later an elderly moped comes phutting up the street and Mohammed appears, he looks at the pile of bricks, '*Madre Mia*', but says he can rebuild the wall and re-plaster, no problem. Paolo is worried he might take months and asks when he can start? *Proxima Semana* replies Mohammed, '*Muy bien*'.

So this basically ends my period of employment, it was great fun while it lasted, I earned some money which I can use for my new garden wall, and it got me going after a few retired, inactive weeks.

A few evenings later Chrissie and I are out for a drink and we spot Mohammed in a bar. He sees us and gestures for us to come in, he wants to buy us a drink, in fact he want to buy us drinks all night, as a thank you for getting him the work. Paolo has found some more money from somewhere and has asked Mohammed to completely re-plaster the two upstairs floors, I didn't think Muslims were supposed to drink alcohol but this particular Mohammed seems to have no such inhibitions. And so the beers flow!

A bit later Mohammed's wife and daughter come into the bar,his wife is Spanish and sells lottery tickets in town, Spaniards are lottery mad and the sellers go round the cafes and bars night and day selling tickets. It is quite usual to see kids in bars here, in the UK I used to get sniffy about kids in pubs but here it seems so natural, if mum and dad go out they take the kids with them, and often granny as well, so it is very common to see three generations out on a walk or having a drink or meal in a bar. Miriam the daughter is about eight, and Mohammed says she is learning English and will we help her with her homework? Quick as a flash Miriam gets her English text book out of her bag, it is full of pictures and she turns to the section on farm animals and asks us to pronounce the words. After a few glasses of *San Miguel* I can do better than that, I can do the sounds as well, so I find myself in a bar in this crazy town on the side of an Andalucian mountain grunting, bleating, mooing, braying and barking, Miriam is laughing, Mohammed is laughing, Antonio the bar owner is laughing as he hands me a plate of prawns, in fact the whole bar is laughing. Truly, you could not make this stuff up.

Chrissie turns to me, 'you are enjoying this, aren't you?' she asks.

'What, mooing or drinking?' I laugh.

'You know what I mean' she giggles. 'The teaching. We could do this, you know. Think of all the kids in this town who are learning English, there is bound to be a market for native English speakers.'

I rub the cut on my head I got in Paolo's, which is starting to itch as it heals. 'Well it certainly beats cutting out walls!' I smile. 'But how do we get started? I agree, there must be a huge potential for English conversation, and we have seen those English academies in town, but how do we get an introduction?'

Chrissie ponders this for a moment. 'Remember that girl who came to the conversation class last week, Paloma was her name I think? She told me her father had a small academy, maths and English classes as far as I remember. I will mention it to her when I see her next, you never know.' I smile as Miriam shows me a picture of a goat. Try as I might, I cannot make a goaty sound, unless I start singing 'The Three Billy Goats Gruff,' and I doubt whether Antonio would be too pleased at that. Actually, perhaps I could suggest a karaoke night to him, once a month in the bar. Everyone does 'I will Survive', that is old hat, but I bet 'The Three Billy Goats Gruff'' would go down a storm.

Yes, I am rather enjoying the teaching!

CHAPTER 10. WARDROBES AND DOG-FOOD SACKS

I am perched precariously on a Spanish roof, hanging on for grim death, frozen with fear. I am unable to move forwards, backwards or side to side, in case I dislodge any more of this dilapidated structure, which by rights should be condemned, demolished, and turned into something useful, like a car park. Already this morning several large lumps of masonry have been sent crashing into the room below, with a sickening thud. Above me, clambering effortlessly over the ridge like one of those little monkeys you see in the zoo, is my new best friend, Derek, (call me Del, everyone does), a wiry, chirpy little Cockney, ten-and-a half stone fully clothed, whereas I, almost half as heavy again, am the original china-shop bull.

What the hell am I doing here?

A few evenings ago, in the bar, it all seemed so easy. 'Wonder if you could do me a little favour mate?' enquired Del, slipping an arm across my shoulder. 'Got a little 'ole on me roof, they forecast a drop o' rain next week and I wanna getta tarpaulin acrost it 'afore it does. Won't take more 'n half a hour.'

I should have told him the truth, that I am terrified of heights. I should have said I had a dental appointment that day, or a note from my mother. *Please excuse Johnny from mending roofs today as he has been suffering from a bilious attack.* But no. With a couple of beers nestling comfortably in the pit of my stomach, it felt good to play the hero, riding to the rescue of Derek's roof on my white charger.

Later that evening, at home, my wife Chrissie went ballistic. 'Why did you agree to that? Call him back now and tell him you can't do it.'

'I can't, I've promised,' I complain.

'Well call him back and un-promise' she firmly states. 'You know that house is falling down, you've said so yourself. You can see the cracks in the walls, what must the roof be like? Its too dangerous, I don't want you doing it.'

'You know I am fascinated by these ancient roofs' I protest. 'I want to find out how they build them.'

Chrissie comprehensively dismisses my argument. 'If you want to find out how to build a roof I will buy you a set of Lego. You are supposed to be retired. It's too dangerous. Tell him I said you can't do it if you like, but I don't want you going up on that roof.'

There are times when a man needs to put his foot down. 'Look, it's perfectly safe. He has a scaffolding at the back of the house apparently, so there's no climbing ladders. It will only take half an hour, I have promised him and I am not going back on my word.'

She narrows her eyes and fixes me with a glare. 'Right. Have it your own way' she hisses. 'But I tell you this. If you fall off that roof and break your back, don't come running to me.'

I am dying to point out the physical impossibility of her last statement. But like all men, I know when a woman needs to have the last word.

Actually, I am fascinated by these roofs, and spend hours just gazing out over the jumble of terracotta from the various vantage points of my new home-town of Santa Marta, Andalucia, Southern Spain. Built on the side of a mountain, the narrow cobbled streets zigzag their way ever upwards. The little white cottages look as if some giant hand has spilled a box of sugar cubes into a higgledy-piggledy pile. Throw in a couple of church towers, a ruined city wall and an ancient castle, with the mountain looming above, the whole scene looks impossibly picturesque.

Up close and personal however is a different story. For a start, I had thought these half-round tiles would be cemented down. Not so. If you stand on them, they shift. Put your weight in the wrong place, and they crack alarmingly, like someone firing a starting pistol in your ear. And if you sit on them, as I am right now, they dig you painfully in the backside. In fact, so painfully am I being dug in the backside it feels like I am on a lost weekend in some sleazy eastern European 'pink' venue.

And this 'little 'ole' described by Del looks more like a gaping chasm to me. It must be six feet across, and several roof beams, or 'tree trunks' as we would describe them in the UK, are exposed to the elements. The room below, which I assume at some stage might have been a bedroom, now resembles a war zone. Directly below me is what might once have been a double bed, but is now a grotesque collection of rubble, broken tiles, bricks, stones, earth and bizarrely, bamboo canes. A clump of weeds is sprouting optimistically from the pile, which appears to have taken on a life of its own.

In one corner of the room is a dismantled wardrobe, the pieces of which have been thrown into an ungainly pile. Doors, sides, backs, tops bottoms and legs.

In fact it looks like a number of different wardrobes, as the pieces very in size, and range in wood shades from teak to mahogany.

In another corner is a collection of plastic dog-food sacks, big ones, 20 kilos or thereabouts, each one depicting a happy, healthy golden retriever, mouth open, tongue lolling in a big doggy grin. I have no idea what he is laughing at. Me, probably.

Meanwhile the sun is beating down mercilessly, and the top of my head, devoid as it is of anything resembling 'hair', is starting to burn, as are my arms and the back of my neck. To say I am 'glowing' or even 'perspiring' would be the understatement of the century. I am sweating like a horse. In fact I am sweating like a stable-full of horses at Aintree after the Grand National.

My eyes are full of grit, and my hands, unaccustomed as they are to this type of work, are cut and bleeding from various knocks and bangs on the climb up to this accursed ruin.

What the hell am I doing here?

My thoughts drift back fondly to my previous life, in the accountants office, where I spent over twenty-five pleasant if largely uneventful years. Nobody ever dug me in the backside, painfully or otherwise, that's for damn sure. A nice comfy chair to sit on, a big wide desk to lean on, a window with a view of some trees to look at, educated, qualified, professional colleagues to talk to, tea and coffee to drink, an hour for lunch, six weeks holiday, BUPA, a pension scheme, a hugely fulfilling client list, and most importantly, a monthly pay-cheque. And to think I gave all that up to take early retirement and come here to do this. I must have been insane. For the first time since we arrived here several weeks ago, I am starting to think I have made a monumental, catastrophic mistake.

Suddenly, my reverie is rudely shattered. 'Oi, I didn't invite you up 'ere to look at the bladdy view! Get on the end of this tarpaulin, will ya?'

In that instant, my fear of heights is banished, never to return. In a move which would surely have impressed any British Olympic Gymnastic team selectors who just happened to be watching, I lift myself up on my arms, pivot my body, tuck my legs under and swivel round so I am kneeling up, looking down into the hole. 'I am not looking at the view,' I inform him, in a slow, deliberate voice, keeping my gaze firmly on the damaged roof. 'I am working out how we can repair the damage permanently. I was watching some blokes repair one just the other day' I continue, still not looking at my new friend. 'They sell giant bricks here, about a yard long, a foot wide and a couple of inches thick. We square off the hole, then use the bricks to span the beams, mortar them into place, giving a good solid base. Then we use plastic/PVC sheeting, again they must sell it somewhere here, to make the whole thing waterproof. Then we replace the tiles, they sell reproduction ones that look aged. There you go. Job done. Boof!'

And only then do I turn my head and look Del square in the eye.

His face is a picture, he is grinning from ear to ear, and scrambles down the roof to place his hand round my shoulder. Then his mood changes. He looks as if he is about to cry.

'Would you really do that for me? Come and help me like that? Be fantastic if you would. It's me neumatics, see. I got the neumatics in the backs of me legs. Means I can't climb up and down like I used to. I'm all right once I'm up here, but the mixing of the mortar, carrying it up, bringing up the bricks and the tiles, I just can't do it no more.' He pauses for breath, while he wipes away a tear. Or a piece of grit. 'An' I can't get nobody to 'elp me. The Spanish won't get out of bed for less than fifty euros, and even then they wanna sleep all afternoon. And the English what are 'ere are too old, or too drunk, or prob'ly both, to wanna bovver.'

He turns and sits on the tiles next to me, then winces painfully, and shifts his position. 'Jeez, reminds me of a night out I 'ad in saaf London in 1973,' he grimaces, laughing, whilst massaging his backside. Reaching into his jeans pocket, he produces a battered packet of tobacco, from which he extracts a cigarette paper and proceeds to break off a few meagre strands, rolling the thinnest fag I have ever seen, about the thickness of a knitting needle. Reaching behind him across the roof, he produces a cylindrical blow-lamp, flicks the switch several times, and a sheet of flame about six inches long shoots out, narrowly missing the peak of his cap. Boggle-eyed, he draws luxuriously on the smoke, then descends into a fit of coughing, sending a shower of spittle high into the sunlit sky. As I say, the accountants office was nothing like this.

'Blimey Del' I protest. 'They sell lighters in the bazaar, ten for a Euro or something.'

He turns all serious. 'Yes but this 'uge cylinder of gas was only two Euros. It will last me about a year. You're the bladdy accountant, work it out!'

'No you work it out' I tell him in my best 'Financial Advisor' voice. 'One of these days you will ignite your face, doing that. Consider the cost of plastic surgery.'

Del roars with laughter. 'Well at least with plastic surgery I might stand a chance of getting myself a bladdy woman!' *Can't argue with that, Del. Can't argue with that.*

'Anyway mate' he continues, patting me on the shoulder, 'what you said about the repairs to the roof was spot on. That's exactly the way I would normally do it. Fing is though, I already got the materials.' *Strange, I didn't notice any yard-long bricks piled up anywhere, whilst climbing up the scaffolding this morning. Must have missed them, what with my scuffed knuckles and all.*

Del spots my confusion. 'There they are, look,' he points, nodding into the room below.

Now its my turn to laugh. 'Yeah right, pull the other one. Best of luck sticking that rubble back together. Hope you have lots of super-glue!'

'Nah, not the rubble, ya pillock!' he chuckles. 'There, look,' pointing into the corner, where the ungainly pile of wardrobe pieces lies.

We have all heard the expression 'a jaw-dropping moment.' Well my jaw does precisely that. It drops. In disbelief. 'What? Eh? Uh? Um?' I am gabbling, like a gibbering idiot. Is he seriously proposing to repair a roof using bits of wardrobe?

'Fink about it mate, you're the accountant,' Del persists. 'These wardrobes was free, good solid wood that is. We can saw them to size, and screw them down to the beams, do just as good a job as the bricks.'

I am unable to speak. My jaw is still disconnected from the rest of my body. Gradually, I regain control of my facial muscles, and the power of speech. 'Right. OK. But what about the mirrors on the wardrobe doors? Are you having mirrors on the ceiling? Like the Eagles song *Hotel California*?'

Del cackles like a banshee. 'Well you can check out any time you like, but you can never leave!' We are both roaring with laughter now, and simultaneously start to sing *Welcome to the Hotel California!* Clearly some male bonding is taking place here.

I glance down into the bedroom and spot the dog-food sacks. 'Yeah, and you're going to tell me now that you are using these sacks in place of the PVC sheeting!' Del's face is impassive. 'Oh no! You ARE using these sacks. Tell me you're not using these sacks.'

Del is nodding his head. He IS using the sacks. 'Fink about it mate...'

OK OK I get the message. The sacks were free. 'So what are you using for tiles?' I query. 'The foil cartons from Chinese take-aways? Empty paint tins? Raindrops on roses and whiskers on kittens?' We are both doubled up again.

'Well these are a few of my favourite fings' he chuckles. 'Especially Chinese take-aways. Nah mate, I got 'undreds of tiles on the patio, originals like. So we got all the bits, 'ow does next Tuesday suit you to come and gimme a 'and?' *Can't wait, Del, can't wait.*

'Seriously though mate,' he continues. 'There's plenty of this work about if you fancy it. I'm always getting asked to do jobs, but I gotta turn most of 'em down, 'cos of me neumatics. But if you could give me a 'and, we could do 'em togevver. Earn ourselves a few bob, like. Just a few mornin's a week, nuffin too strenuous. I will learn you all the tricks, bricklaying, plastering, you ain't just gonna be mixing. And maybe you can learn me all about accounts, 'ow to sort out me finances an' all that.'

I gaze across the rickety old cottages and out towards the sea of olive groves surrounding the town. Half an hour ago I would have seriously preferred to have spent a month in a sleazy European pink venue, than another second on one of these ancient structures. Now however, bizarrely, I find the prospect strangely enticing. 'What, come and work for you, helping you out, you mean?' I enquire.

'Yeah, I s'pose. Why not?' Del replies.

Hmm, actually I've been an employee all my working life. If I am having a complete change of direction, I might as well go the whole hog and become a partner. 'What I would prefer is to share everything, like a partnership' I inform him. I propose a percentage split, not quite fifty-fifty, as Del is more experienced after all, but not far off. He needs me, 'cos of his neumatics, after all.

'Sounds good mate!' he confirms, and spitting on his palm, holds it out in my direction. *Oh. My. God. I thought they only did that in films.* In my previous existence, I would recommend that new business partners speak to a solicitor and get a partnership deed drawn up. Still, my life has taken on this crazy new course. In for a penny and all that. My throat is so dry I can barely conjure up enough spittle to lick a postage stamp, but I make a fair attempt and we grip our phlegm-encrusted hands.

Walking home later, I reflect on what has without doubt been a potentially a life-changing morning. For the first time in over a quarter of a century I have been offered a job. And for the first time in my life, I have been offered a job when I wasn't actually looking for one. I have a spring in my step, a new purpose, a fresh direction. And like Del says, a few bob.

Entering my house, Chrissie is overjoyed to see me. 'Thank heavens you are safe' she cries. 'I have been so worried all morning, thinking of you up on that crappy roof.' And she flings her arms around my neck. Then recoils in horror. 'What is that terrible stench? It's you! You reek of that house! Please take off your stinky clothes and let me chuck them in the bin. You won't be needing them again. Promise me you will never go up on any more roofs.'

I am silent for a few seconds. 'Sit down will you?' I ask. 'I have something to tell you…'

CHAPTER 11. MEET THE DOGS

'When do you want to start on your roof then?' I am standing in the street outside Del's house, he is inside talking to me through his stable-style front door. Actually 'stable' is a rather apt way of describing the smell wafting through the half opened door, emanating largely, though not entirely, from his collection of approximately eight dogs of varying sizes. I say approximately eight, as even Del is not entirely sure how many canines he has at any given time, given that he regularly finds strays tied to his front door. The local Spanish population seem to regard this soft-hearted Englishman as a repository for unwanted bow-wows. Imagine a bus station full of wet tramps, a cage full of damp lions at London zoo, and the gents toilet under the main grandstand at Twickenham on the Monday morning after an England-Wales rugby international, and you are not even close. My eyes are watering and I am trying to gulp some fresh air on this baking hot afternoon, but I seem to be losing the battle. After several fruitless attempts to patch up his roof, Del has finally decided to go the whole hog and strip the lot off and start again. The problem is that the house was originally two knocked into one, the roof is not a simple 'A' shape, more like an 'N' or an 'M', and there were quite a few effs up there too, I remember. The roof is on several different levels, with hip walls joining each level, in fact there are more dodgy hip joints up there than a coach load of pensioners on a day trip to Eastbourne.

'No rush mate' he replies, 'I need to order the timber, and the gordo, I reckon I need about five sacks.' 'Gordo' is the thick waterproof white mortar they sell here, it comes in large sacks in powder form, you simply mix it with water to the required consistency, trowel it on and then in about half an hour you can go over it with a wet brush or sponge to get the finish you want.

'You had about five sacks of gordo' I remind him, 'you were using them as a coffee table in the lounge last time I was here.'

He gives me a hunted look, 'Yeah well I don't have them now.'

I refuse to give up. Has the crafty Cockney been doing a bit of private work, and if so, where? Clearly not on his own house, as the cracked and peeling façade is just the same as on my last visit. 'What, been doing a bit of work yourself have you? Five sacks is a lot of gordo.'

He runs his hands across his face. 'What happened was, Harley, the big dog, chewed the ends of the sacks, so of course it all spilled out over the floor. Then he pissed on it. I had gone down town to pay a few bills, get a bit of shopping, so I was gone a few hours, and by then the mortar had set rock hard. The other boy dogs must have peed on top of Harley's pee, so there was a huge solid yellow puddle in the sitting room, they had walked it through into the other room as well, climbed onto the furniture, they all had stiff white and yellow booties on their feet and one of them had sat in it, as it was all over his arse.' I have been fighting an increasingly losing battle to stop myself from laughing while the tale unfolds, but the thought of a dog with a gordoed arse sets me off, and soon I am crying with laughter. 'It's all right for you' shouts Del in mock anger, 'you have never had to pick gordo off a dogs nuts, have you?' He is correct, I have learned many skills since moving to Spain, but removing white mortar from a canine's testicles is not one of them.

'How did you know it was Harley wot did it?' I enquire, wiping tears from my cheeks.

'Because it's always him that does the damage' Del replies, 'and besides, he had white powder all over his nose and lips. He looked like he'd been on a night out with Keith Richards, snorting cocaine.' I have to steady myself against the outside wall. 'It gets worse,' he continues. 'One of them had a crap in the middle of the puddle too, it was like a stiff Mister Whippy ice cream cone standing up on the floor.'

I am shaking with laughter. 'What did you do with the Whippy statue? I ask him.

'What do you think I did with it, I scraped it up with the rest of the mess and stuck it in the bin at the end of the street. Three black plastic sacks full of solid yellow mortar, and I only managed to salvage about half a sack of Gordo.'

'Well you missed a trick there' I say, tears running down my face. 'That designer bloke off the TV, that programme 'Changing Rooms' what's his name, Laurence Llewellyn-Boner? He could have sold the Mister Whippy as a new Spanish design feature, 'Andalucian Abstract Art, each piece unique.' They would pay a lot of money for that in London. Imagine some posh woman with one on her mantelpiece?'

Del is rocking with laughter now. 'Or' he splutters, 'what about that chef off the telly with the bald head, the one who does the snail porridge, Heston Blooming-Tool, he could have turned the Mister Whippy into "Baked Andalucian Alaska', would have gone down a storm in his restaurant!'

'Not sure you're thinking clearly about that mate' I respond, 'you can't actually give people crap to eat.'

'Why the hell not' he shouts, 'you been to that American fried chicken place lately?' He has a point I suppose.

'Anyway, when did all this happen?' I ask.

'Two days ago' he replies. 'I spent most of yesterday scraping the floors, and the sofa. Hopefully I've got rid of most of the smell.' He catches the look on my face. 'What?' he shouts. 'What's that look for?' I mention the tramps, the lions and the rugby supporters. He puts his head in his hands. 'The thing is' he continues, pointing to the bridge of his nose, 'I broke me nose in school playing rugby when I was about thirteen, so I have very little sense of smell.'

That explains a lot. That explains a hell of a lot!

CHAPTER 12. MANOLO'S UNDERWEAR.

You know sometimes when you have a small incident or accident, and everything seems to happen in slow motion, like a Hollywood movie, only there is nothing you can do about it? Well here I am sat on a roof, about ten feet away from me is my mate Del, whose roof it is, and we have stripped off the tiles and placed them in neat little piles all around us. Ancient Spanish roofs fascinate me, I love looking at them, from our patio or from various viewpoints around the town, I spend ages just gazing at them and the colours of the tiles, from brown to cream to terracotta, and I have given up my weekend to learn about their construction, and to earn a few pesetas along the way, before our new 'partnership' begins in earnest.

The roof timbers are tree trunks about a foot thick, and they lay bamboo canes cross-ways on the beams, put mortar on top of the canes and bed the tiles on the mortar. The tiles are made from terracotta shaped like a half round, about eighteen inches long, and they are laid one row face down and the next face up, which more or less keeps out any rain which might fall. Over time the whole roof becomes porous so we are replacing the mortar and relaying the tiles, which should do for another fifty years or so. Unless some stupid English idiot gets in the way of course....

The view from up here is pretty spectacular, behind us is our mountain , its granite outcrops and ruined castle on the summit towering above us. In a pen behind the house a matted Alsatian is sharing the space with a huge white turkey-cock, who is bigger than the Alsatian, and I know who I would back in the event of it all kicking off...In front of us are the roofs of the town and the cemetery on the hillside opposite, and I remark to Del that if we fell off the roof we would roll down the hill into the cemetery, to save them the bother of burying us. He doesn't find this funny for some reason...The street in front of the house is so narrow that we cannot see down into it, but we know it is there as we can hear children playing and people walking past. We can however see into Manolo's patio opposite, where his wife has hung out her washing on a clothes airer.

Del has spent most of his adult life smoking and drinking, and is suffering from 'neumatics' in the legs, so he just sits on the roof, while I nip down to his patio below and mix up the mortar, lift it onto the scaffolding, climb up the scaffolding, lift the mortar onto the roof, climb up on the roof, sit down on the tiles and haul the bucket of mortar across so that he can spread it on the canes, and refit the tiles, which I have to pass him. 'Not working too hard you lazy cockney bastard' I chuckle, as I haul the umpteenth bucket up to the roof. He hurls abuse in reply, as us roofers tend to do, and I pause in the heat to admire the view for a second or two. Or a minute or two. Then, to my horror, the bucket of gordo begins to slide, slowly slowly, down the roof. There is nothing whatsoever I can do as it is already out of my reach, but surely it will catch on one of the piles of tiles and stop? Not a bit of it, just like Maradonna waltzing through the English defence in the 1986 World Cup, the bucket and the gordo slalom gracefully round all the tiles and head uncontrollably towards the edge of the roof, and then disappear. Del shouts 'Whoa' like he is trying to control a runaway pony, but to no avail and after what seems to be an age, we hear the sickening thud as it hits the street below. As I watch, three huge gloops of gordo rise into the air and drop onto Manolo's patio, one scoring a direct hit on his underpants.

'Quick!' yells Del, panic spreading across his face, 'we have to clean the street up as I don't have a permit for this work.' Now he tells me. You are supposed to get a two-Euro permit from the Town Hall for work of this nature, or face a fine if they catch you, so we climb down the scaffolding and out into the street, and while we do this an elderly Spaniard on an even older moped comes chugging up the hill and steers his way through the white gloop which is clinging to just about every possible surface, not to mention Manolo's pants. Del is now moving with a speed which belies his sixty-a-day habit and produces buckets of water and a brush, and we quickly set to sweeping and washing the narrow cobbled street, and removing the white tyre trail. Soon all evidence is gone, and remarkably for Spain, not a single neighbour has come out to see what is going on, no old men on plastic chairs, or old women sweeping the streets in their pink housecoats and curlers. We have even managed to salvage most of the gordo which can be mixed with a bit more water and used again. We seem to have got away with it.

Back on the roof we can now afford to see the funny side and start to chuckle. 'Did you see that great flop of mortar land on Manolo's keks?' I splutter. 'I reckon that tomorrow he will put them on, walk down the bar for a drink in his battered straw hat, then at the bar will feel something digging into his arse. Rooting around with a meaty finger, he will extract the foreign body and exclaim in an indignant voice, 'Some bastard has put gordo in my pants!' 'Well what about the moped rider?' cries Del, 'he almost had a bucket of plop on his head, imagine him riding along covered in white mortar!' We are both laughing uncontrollably now, tears are streaming down our faces, and looking behind I see the Alsatian with his mouth open and tongue out, for all the world like he is smiling, even the turkey is grinning it seems.

Like I say, I love Spanish roofs!

CHAPTER 13. WHO LET THE MOUSE OUT?

Dereeek! Donde estas?

I am on Del's roof, as arranged last week, when we hear a commotion in the narrow street below. As Del is up the top by the ridge, and I am on the bit above the street, I gingerly peer over the edge, and get quite a shock. A young man is standing below, mid-twenties, wearing a red satin shirt unbuttoned to the navel, exposing about an acre of tanned, muscled chest, tight black trousers, dark liquid eyes framed by eyelashes the length of which any woman would be proud of, and hair styled and combed into the quiff favoured by many young Spaniards. He looks like a matador on his way to the bullfight. We have been visited by a sex-god.

'Oo the ell is it now' asks Del.

'Some bloke who looks like a bull-fighter' I reply.

'Does he have a big willy?' comes the response.

'How the hell would I know', I shout back, 'you are not paying me enough to look at his willy. But yeah. Probably.'

'Sounds like Raul, the scrap metal man. Tell him we will be down in a minute' laughs my colleague. So I peer over the edge, and averting my gaze from his groin area, I inform Raul that we will be down shortly.

So we edge across the roof to the scaffolding tower that is a permanent fixture on Del's sun terrace, climb down the tower, in through the spare bedroom, down the stairs past a large plank of wood wedging the back door shut holding back the pack of eight or nine dogs in the yard, through the kitchen, through the sitting room and out into the street to the waiting Raul. A more unlikely looking scrap metal man I have yet to see but Del greets him with handshakes and back-slaps, while I make do with eye contact and a smile. 'I have an old washing machine for you' Del informs him, and we head back inside the kitchen. Sure enough, an old machine of indeterminate vintage is standing forlornly in the corner. 'Give us a hand with this' he asks me, easier said than done as getting a grip on the grease-encrusted carcass proves difficult, but eventually we manhandle the filthy contraption into the street.

'Perfecto, una lavadora!' cries Raul, 'my brother will be here in a few minutes with the van.'

'Tell you what, mate, there's an old microwave in the kitchen,' Del remembers, 'grab it for us will you?' So back inside I venture and sure enough, I spot what possibly might have been described as a microwave oven, in an earlier century. Luckily I have a strong stomach, but stifle the urge to gag as I grasp the fat-splattered appliance and deposit it in the street next to the washing machine. This part of town is starting to resemble a scrap-yard. Raul looks delighted and performs a few steps around his new acquisitions, like a matador pacing around a bull.

Just then two Moroccan men come round the corner, Rashid and Mohammed. Rashid has on the traditional three-quarter-length garment, with hairy legs and sandals visible below, Mohammed has the same but with trousers as well. *'Una lavadora!'* shouts Rashid, 'can I have it?'

'No, its mine' replies Raul, but undeterred, Rashid bends down and opens the door of the machine, carefully checking the interior like he is in John Lewis' electrical department. 'Does it work OK?' he asks nobody in particular.

'Hombre' shouts Raul with a look normally reserved for two tons of charging flesh, 'I told you, it is mine.'

Before the exchange can become even more deadly however, and old woman appears from the opposite direction. Granny Abuela. She is less than five feet tall, with wrinkled leathery skin, and is completely bandy. In fact she doesn't so much walk, as rock from side to side, and watching her approach is making me feel decidedly seasick. She spots the washing machine, *'Una lavadora!'* she cries, 'can I have it?' Honestly, what is wrong with these people that they want something which would probably be rejected by a Bangladeshi sweat-shop? Before Raul can reply however she starts screaming, *'Miras, un raton, un raton!* Look, a mouse! Five pairs of eyes follow her gaze and, sure enough, strolling casually along the street is a mouse, quite a large one in fact. A daddy mouse out for his morning forage. Now had this been a rat I would have been climbing the wall, but I am just about OK with mice. Rashid however grabs the hem of his cloak and clamps it firmly round his legs, but the most spectacular reaction comes from Raul. He jumps back with a look of absolute terror. Thirty seconds ago he was strutting about fending off imaginary bulls, now he is hiding behind the washing machine as the mouse approaches. Actually you have to wonder what Mr Mouse makes of the scene, confronted as he is by two Englishmen, two Spaniards, two Moroccans and two repulsive domestic appliances. From here, the mouse has two options for his daily meander. Fork right, down the narrow cobbled street and he would come to *Plaza de la*

Constitution, the main square of the town, with several bars, grocers shops and a fruit market, ideal foraging territory. Or keeping straight on, past Del's, he would arrive at the house of Jimmy the Scotsman, known in these parts as 'See You Jimmy.' He is renowned for his strong cheese and wine, which he gets from a *wee mon* in the next village, not to mention his collection of malt whisky. Decisions decisions for Senor Mouse.

It seems however that our vermin friend has decided to pay Jimmy's cheese supply a visit, but there is just one problem. I am standing in the way. And I reek. No seriously, I really am humming. As well as gently roasting away on the roof all week, so that my work clothes have taken on a pungent aroma all of their own, earlier this morning Del had asked me to clear the rubble from the spare bedroom, which had fallen through when we replaced the roof a few days ago. This involved loading the rubble into a large rubber bucket and carrying it through Del's bedroom, out through his patio doors, across a concrete bridge above his lower garden and onto a raised area at the top of the garden, below where a huge turkey lives. One day this will be a Jacuzzi patio, but for now it is a rubble dump complete with a selection of dog crap in various stages of decomposition, most of which I had managed to step in whilst heaving the rubble down. Del had come along to check the progress and had caught me scraping my trainers on the side of the bridge. 'I didn't tell you to walk bloody crap through the house' he shouted, rather like Michael Caine in 'The Italian Job.'

'Well its your bloody crap' I replied, 'look' its all stuck in the tread of my trainers, its gonna take me ages to get it out.'

So the mouse approaches me, gets to within about two feet of my trainers, and stops. I swear he twitches his nose, takes a lungful, then turns and heads back the other way. Truly I smell bad enough to repel rodents. Now the problem is that Granny Abuela has moved back against the wall, so that the mouse is now heading straight for her. She starts screaming again and hopping about, performing a passable impression of Michael Flatley in *Lord of the Dance,* although thankfully without the shaved, oiled torso. Seeing this, the mouse turns again, heading for Del's front door, whereupon there is a loud crash and one of his dogs, it looks like Harley's son 'Squirt', thrusts his head through the double doors, spots the mouse, and tries to bark, but traps his neck in the doors and instead of a loud 'woof', emits a strangled 'wiff.' Our mousey friend has clearly had enough by now so he turns again and runs straight under the washing machine. We are all expecting him to emerge the other side, but no, he stays out of sight. Abuela takes the opportunity to hobble away up the street, Rashid lets go of his cloak, smooths it down and with a hasty *adios* heads off with Mohammed, leaving Raul looking forlornly at his washing machine, which now contains a mouse. Keeping his feet well back he leans forward and gives the machine a gentle tap, then jumps quickly back. Nothing. Another louder tap. No mouse. So he reaches forward with a leg and gives the side a hefty kick, but still our rodent friend refuses to budge. So Raul then gets hold of the top of the machine, and with a heave he pushes it onto its side, sending it crashing down on the cobbles in a cloud of flaking rusty particles. But still the mouse remains hidden. 'OK, good luck Raul' cries Del, as we head back up onto the roof, leaving the quivering Spaniard with his pile of scrap.

Back up on the roof I take a peek down, and see Raul still standing there like a frightened old woman, giving the machine an occasional kick as he tries in vain to dislodge his unwelcome guest. Del and I then carry on with our work and I forget completely about Raul, but about an hour later I look down again and see that the machine, the microwave and Raul have disappeared, the only evidence that all this actually took place being a pile of rusty metal in the middle of the street.

Oh yes, just one further thing to report. Raul's appendage? Nothing special actually. About average, I thought......

CHAPTER 14. MEET STUMPY, AND THE OCTOPUS

When the sun goes down here, the lizards come out to play, and you often see them climbing walls, presumably looking for food after spending the day sheltering from the sun. It never ceases to amaze me how they can cling to a vertical surface, although whether they have tiny claws, or suckers on their feet I have no idea, my name not being David or Attenborough. We have one who lives in or around our vines, called 'Stumpy' on account of him having no tail. Now whether he lost it in a fight, left it in a bar somewhere, or was born that way, I cannot say, but most evenings we see him climbing the wall above the ancient stone shed where I keep my wood, known over here as 'El Woodshed'. Now it so happened that last week I scraped that very wall, as part of our ongoing crusade against peeling paint and flaking masonry, a battle I am glad to say is at long last going our way. When we bought this place I honestly thought I would be re-plastering for the rest of my life, but as I sit here on our new patio 'El Sombrero' I have a vista of blinding white walls and not a flaky bit in sight. Mind you, down the steps further into the garden, is a different matter...

Anyway, seeing old Stumpy on the wall I suddenly realise he will not know that all his former footholds have been scraped away, and quickly shout a warning, 'Look out Stumpy!', only to see him at that very moment fall off the wall onto the woodshed roof. It is only a drop of about three feet, but when you are a little six inch lizard that must be quite a distance, and I fear that he might possibly be on his way to Lizard heaven. We rush to the edge of the patio, and are so relieved to see after a few minutes that he is resuming his climb, albeit a lot slower than previously, and he manages to stagger to the edge of the wall and disappears onto our neighbour's patio. I imagine him limping home that night and saying to Mrs Stumpy 'That stupid English bastard has scraped the wall off and I fell on my backside' and her saying 'Huh, likely story, you have been in the bar again, you stink of booze, and now your tea is in the dog', if lizards keep dogs, you know what I mean.

But since that night, we have not seen him. Whether he now finds a different way home, or whether he quietly died of his injuries, but every night as the sun goes down my eyes are glued to that bit of wall, in vain. I have been tramping all over the woodshed roof with buckets of plaster so there has been a lot of trauma in Stumpy's former stumping ground, so my hope is that he might come back soon, but you know that tonight at sunset I will be keeping an eye out for our little bit of Spanish wildlife.

The back of the house is three-storey, and getting up to re-plaster that has been quite an experience. I told Loli I needed to borrow a ladder to get up there, and a long one at that. 'Just paint it with a brush on a long handle' she said. 'Lean out of the window for the upstairs bits.' So I told her I needed to scrape the old paint and plaster off. 'Put the scraper on the long handle' she said. So I said I needed to re-plaster the walls. 'Why?' she replied. The thing is, the Spanish do not see the point of wasting time on outside walls, as they spend most of their day indoors, especially during the summer heat. Looking at our neighbours' gardens, they cultivate them, early in the morning and late at night, they water them at the same times, but they never actually just sit in them. They spend the afternoon indoors with the shutters down and curtains pulled, and the lights on. Of course, when you are born in the sun and the heat you just want to hide from it, but us Northern Europeans who have come over here to escape the cold and the rain, certainly aren't gonna sit indoors. I am spending time creating lots of places to sit outside, sunny and shady, and I am damn well not going to look at peeling paint and flaking plaster. But this re-plastering work takes ages, especially as I am still learning the ropes, whereas splashing on a bit of whitewash is much easier.

This was brought home to us a few weeks ago. We were woken at about eight AM by the sound of shed doors being unlocked, tools being cleaned off, and tins being opened, and by the time we had got up Fernando was in the garden, with his long handled brush, painting lime-wash on his garden walls. Any flaky stuff he was just knocking off with the other end of the handle and just painting over it, and by the time we had finished breakfast he had whitewashed his entire garden walls. 'Painting over the cracks' is exactly what he was doing, and I know for certain that the next time it rains the stuff will start washing off again, and that next year he will have to do it all over again. The thing is he is probably quite prepared to spend a couple of hours once a year doing this job, and if it washes off over the winter what the hell?

'Fernando has a ladder, would you like to borrow it?' enquires Loli. I express my gratitude and tell her I would indeed like the loan of said ladder, for about a week maybe. 'A week?' cries my neighbour. 'A week? Fernando painted the whole garden in just two hours.' Gritting my teeth I explain that these walls are part of the house, rather than just garden walls, so I want to scrape and re-plaster everything. 'OK, tomorrow morning at eight? she confirms, then disappears back inside her house.

So now I have to break the news to Chrissie. 'We have to put the alarm on for half-seven, tomorrow morning,' I advise her.

'The alarm?' she cries in mock horror. 'The alarm? We don't have an alarm clock! You made a big thing of throwing our alarm clock away when we retired, along with your work suit. You swore you would never again wear a suit, or set an alarm clock, remember?.' This is true. The church bells in the town square are silent during the night, starting up again at eight in the morning, and we are usually wakened by their melodic pealing, followed by a leisurely breakfast on the patio, which means we are generally ready to face the day by nine-thirty. This is one aspect of retirement I feel I have earned.

'Anyway' she continues, 'you don't need me to get up just to collect a ladder, do you? You can get up at seven-forty-five, get the ladder, leave it in the garden, then bring me breakfast in bed!'

I chuckle at her suggestion. 'OK, coffee, toast and orange juice, providing you help me with the re-plastering,' I smile. 'I got neumatics in me legs, see, so I can't climb up an' down ladders' I continue, in my best Cockney accent. 'You can mix the mortar, carry it up to the bathroom, then hand it out the window to me.'

Chrissie sniffs. 'On your bike sunshine, I will get my own breakfast thank you very much!'

'But seriously, what are we going to do about the alarm?' I ask.

Chrissie ponders this for a moment. 'What about our mobile phones?' she suggests, 'are there alarms on them?' No idea, we are old-school when it comes to mobiles, retaining our ancient clam-shell devices, not having succumbed to the smart-phone revolution of the past few years. I have a quick fiddle, and sure enough an alarm function is revealed. It appears we, or rather I, will be getting an early start tomorrow morning, for the first time in almost four months.

I wake during the night to a strange sound. It is pitch dark and feels like it might be around three o'clock, so it's unlikely to be Isabel sweeping, but what is it? Like a tapping and rushing sound all in one. Alert to the possibility of vermin trying to gain entrance, I quietly slip out of bed and tiptoe to the window, and gently ease back the internal wooden shutter to reveal drops of water on the windowpane. It is raining! This is the first rain we have had since we moved to Santa Marta, virtually every morning we have risen to bright sunshine, and I have almost forgotten what it is to be cold and wet. 'What on earth are you doing now?' groans Chrissie.

'It's raining!' I inform her. 'Look, come and see.'

'No ruddy fear, I've seen rain before' she complains, 'for heaven's sake stop wandering about and get back into bed, so I can get some sleep.'

The problem is, I am now wide awake, and as this is the first rain we have experienced in this house, I am not sure how water-tight our roof is. Having spent days sorting out Del's roof, over the past few weeks, I am more than slightly concerned. I don't however want to worry Chrissie, 'I am just going to check that the back bedroom windows, and the patio doors, are closed' I whisper. 'You go back to sleep, I won't be long.' I tiptoe into the second bedroom, and sure enough the window is wide open, as is the one in the third bedroom, which Chrissie has commandeered as her craft room. I close them both, listening carefully for tell-tale drips, of which thankfully there are none, then pad silently downstairs and close the patio door, before returning to bed.

Some hours later I wake to the sound of my phone ringing. Who the hell is this, at this hour? It is still dark outside, and in my half-asleep state I grope around on my bedside table, knocking the phone onto the floor in the process. 'For pity's sake, can't a girl get any sleep around here?' complains my wife.

I am now scrabbling around on the floor trying to locate the still-ringing mobile, which eventually I find, and open. 'Hello? Hello?' Nobody there. 'Hello?' Bastards, what are these idiots playing at?

'You blithering idiot' Chrissie hisses, through gritted teeth, 'it's the bloody alarm. Turn it off, get up, go and get the cursed ladder off Fernando, then get the coffee on!' Easier said than done, my sweetness. I am jabbing just about every button on the phone but can I get the pigging alarm to stop? No I can't. Chrissie sits bolt upright, snatches the phone out of my hand, and with one press, the irritating ringing ceases. 'Right, bugger off will you?' she half chuckles. 'Toast, coffee, orange juice, quick as you like!'

I quickly get dressed, set the coffee-maker going, then stick my head out the front door. It is still raining, although not heavily, but I am going to need a coat. And something a bit more substantial on my feet than plimsolls. Problem. We are simply not prepared for rain. Having spent the last four months living in tee-shirts, shorts and flip-flops, I am not sure where my wet weather gear is, or even if I have any. I vaguely recall, in a different lifetime, packing some jeans, fleeces, leather boots and a raincoat into the caravan when we left the UK, but did we bring them to Santa Marta, or are they still in the caravan, which is fifty miles away on the rural camping site? Obviously we knew it would eventually rain here, but we have been enjoying the sunshine so much, and have not given it a minute's thought. I debate going back upstairs and asking Chrissie if she knows where said items are, but the prospect of another tongue-lashing is sufficient deterrent. Oh what the hell, I am only going next door, I am British for heaven's sake, it's only a bit of rain.

I slip out the front door and knock on Loli's. After about thirty seconds she sticks her head out. *'Que?'* Has she forgotten about the ladder? Did she even tell Fernando I am coming for it? 'Fernando's ladder?' I remind her. 'You said to call at eight o'clock?'

She cackles loudly, pointing up at the sky. 'Neighbour, it's raining, Fernando will not come out in the rain. Tomorrow it will not rain, come tomorrow, same time! And where is your coat?'

Smiling my best smile, but inwardly seething, 'I am from England' I remind her. 'This is normal weather for us!'

She cackles again, like a demented witch. 'Not here it isn't!', and with that she retracts her head and closes the door. I head back to our house, lock the door, run upstairs and slip back to bed.

'That was quick' Chrissie murmurs, half asleep. 'Everything OK? I didn't hear the clanging of ladders!'

I start to growl. 'Grrrr. No it's not bloody well OK. The chicken-livered Spaniard is frightened of a bit of rain. I have to go through this whole charade again tomorrow.'

'OH FOR PITY'S SAKE' she explodes. 'Why don't you get down the hardware shop and buy a damn ladder, like I told you in the first place, instead of this mucking around?'

'Have you seen the price of ladders?' I cry. 'They want thirty Euros for a pair of steps. A ladder is around a hundred. A short one is no good, I want the longest one I can get!'

Chrissie giggles. 'My feelings entirely! A short one is no good whatsoever! I've been telling you that for years!'

'Yeah well, you get what you're, given, and think yourself lucky!' I reply, in mock anger, 'and for that you're getting your own coffee. And toast.'

Just before lunchtime there is a knock on the door. Gaffer, and Diane. 'Get tha coat lad!' he cries. 'it's Friday. Fish Friday' Tha's heard of Fish Friday in Wetherspoon's, now tha'll see Fish Friday in Santa Marta, in t' boos station!'

I have no idea what he is talking about. 'Come in a minute' I say, glancing at Chrissie, 'we have a bit of a problem with the rain. We don't have any umbrellas here. We've been caught on the hop slightly.'

Chrissie looks at me with a 'what are you talking about you idiot?' look on her face. 'Yes we do' she contradicts, 'we have that big National Trust umbrella in the back of the Volvo.'

Diane snorts in derision. 'Tha big soft Soothern middle-class jessies! A Volvo, an' a National Trust brolly!'

'Oh no no no!' I smile, 'the Volvo is over twenty years old, and the umbrella is on 'long-term loan' from the National Trust! You know, when you visit a stately home and they lend you an umbrella at the ticket office if it's raining? We forgot to return it, so next time we drive back to the UK, we will do. Probably!'

'A stately home?' cries Diane, 'ye Soothern jessies! Tha don't get lent brollies at Blackpool Pleasure Beach!'

No you probably don't, Diane, you probably don't.

'We got brollies at 'ome, f' ye Soothern jessies, I'll joost pop back an' fetch two' laughs Gaffer, and off he goes.

'What about raincoats?' I ask Chrissie, 'did we bring them up from the caravan, or are they still there?'

She rolls her eyes in that 'do you actually live in this house?' fashion. 'Yes, your waxed jacket is upstairs, in your half of the wardrobe. Men!'

'A wax jacket?' Diane splutters. 'Tha great Soothern middle-class jessie. I bet tha's got a blooody Barbour.'

'NO! I interrupt, 'it's not a Barbour! It's just an ordinary, a very ordinary, waxed jacket, from Tesco or somewhere like that. Poundland maybe. But it's definitely not a Barbour!' and to prove it I bound upstairs, root around in the wardrobe, locate said garment and hurry back down, just as gaffer returns with two folding umbrellas.

'Tha's got thessen a Barbour!' he cries. 'Woss wrong wi' a donkey jacket, lad?'

I make a huge show of turning the coat inside-out to expose the label, and thrust it under Diane's nose. 'There you are , proof, one-hundred percent proof, it's not a Barb.. oh hell, it IS a Barbour! Where did that come from?' and I glance beseechingly at my wife.

'My Dad gave it to you, don't you remember, for walking the dog?' she confirms.

'What sort o' dog did y'ave?' Gaffer enquires.

'A golden retriever, called Nelson' I tell him. 'He died last year sadly.'

'A golden-blooody retriever?' echoes Diane. 'Woss wrong wi' a whippet, tha' Soothern jessies!'

'Anyway, we now have umbrellas, and raincoats' I chuckle, 'all I need are some boots. Did we bring my leather Clarks boots from the caravan?'

Chrissie grits her teeth. 'Under the wardrobe. Honestly. Men!'

'Clarks? Clarks?' Diane shouts, 'we go t' Shoe Zone! Tha's a reet pair o' Soothern middle-class jessies. A Volvo, the National Trust, stately-blooody 'omes, wax-blooody Barbours, Clarks boots an' a golden-blooody retriever!'

We are all laughing now. 'Well I'm very sorry I wasn't born in a dark satanic mill either!' I apologise, 'and I've never been anywhere near a coal-mine. Now, are we going out, or are there any other aspects of our former lives you wish to ridicule?'

'Get thee-sens ready lad!' cries Gaffer, 'I'm so 'ungry I could eat a scabby 'oss between two slices o' fried bread!'

'Is that with dripping, or without?' Chrissie laughs.

So I don my Barbour and Clarks boots, together with jeans and a long-sleeve shirt, none of which have seen the light of day for months, and gathering up our borrowed umbrellas we slither down the wet cobblestones towards the bus station, in the centre of the new part of town. It is rather a large bus station, considering the size of Santa Marta, with about a dozen bays, a waiting room, a small ticket office, one bus daily to Malaga, and a cafe/bar. 'Coom on lad' Gaffer instructs. 'Into t'bar, get thee-sens a seat, I'll do t'orderin'. I have to admit that my previous experience of bus station cafes has been entirely negative, places to be avoided at all costs, and absolutely the last place I would have imagined spending a wet Friday lunchtime, not being a fan of watery, overpriced coffee, and tramps. But this place is a gem. Large picture windows overlooking the town centre, a long bar crowded with locals, walls covered with oil paintings depicting local scenes, plenty of tables and chairs, and at the back, a silver service restaurant with tables covered by crisp white linen. In a bus station. It could actually be the bar of a decent three-star hotel. A waiter approaches with our beers, then disappears around the back of the bar. 'Watch this, lad!' chuckles Gaffer, 'tha's in fer a surprise. T'tapas is all seafood on Fridays, tha gets what thees given like, but tis blooody amazin'. An' of course, it costs nowt!'

Sure enough, the waiter reappears carrying four small plates, which he sets down on the table. Chrissie recoils in disgust. 'Oh my God, get that away from me, I'm not eating that!' Each plate contains char-grilled baby octopus, small tentacles part-blackened, covered in olive oil and finely chopped garlic.

Diane likewise expresses her displeasure. 'I ant eatin' blooody octopus, me!' she complains, 'last time we was 'ere we 'ad prawns!'

Gaffer guffaws loudly. 'All the more for thee an' me lad! Get thee laffin gear round that!' I need no further encouragement. Seizing a fork, I spear a tentacle and take a bite, which sends my senses reeling. Heaven has descended to Santa Marta bus station. Rarely have I tasted anything so utterly sensational, Chrissie and Diane are grimacing but Gaffer and I are chewing madly and are in raptures. Truly, if this were a Michelin-starred restaurant, better-tasting food would be unlikely to appear. I am rolling my eyes and making appreciative groaning noises.

'Don't think you are coming anywhere near me tonight, after eating that!' Chrissie giggles.

'An' no blooody nookie for thee an'all!' Diane informs her husband.

'Do I look blooody bothered?' Gaffer replies, gimme that other plate!' He is wolfing down his tentacles like a man possessed, taking alternate slurps of his beer, tearing savagely at his food like a pack of hyenas. A final gulp of his drink, he then rubs his mouth with the back of his hand, slumps back in his chair, and belches appreciatively. 'By gaw, that were blooody greet! Coom on lad, finish tha' octopussy, sup tha' ale, let's all have another one!'

And so the afternoon passes. More seafood tapas appears, fat juicy prawns, anchovies on crusty bread, pieces of salt cod. I have to keep reminding myself we are in a bus station, and if anyone had suggested when we retired that we would be spending a wet Friday afternoon in this manner I would have called them crazy. It's past four PM by the time we finally stagger home, the sun has returned, and dressed in a coat and boots I am gently perspiring, climbing the steep cobbled hill up to the old part of town.

Later that evening we switch on the TV to catch the local news bulletin. We do this from time to time as it helps with our Spanish, and we usually have some idea what the presenters are talking about, by looking at the accompanying film footage. Tonight the lead story is the rain. 'It rained today in Andalucia, for the first time since April, and we can go live to Alonso in Seville. What is happening in Seville, Alonzo?'

'Well it was raining earlier, but it has stopped now' confirms Alonzo. Bit of a non-story then.

The anchor is struggling what to say next. 'Was it heavy rain there in Seville, Alonzo?'

'Not really, it only rained for about two hours' comes the reply.

'OK we can now go live to Ana in Malaga. What's it like in Malaga, Ana?'

A glamorous, mini-skirted blonde totters into view, 'It was raining here, but it has stopped now' she pouts.

'So was it a lot of rain?' gabbles the anchor, clearly starting to panic, as presumably he has a set amount of time to fill on what was little more than a shower.

'No not much, it cleared up by lunchtime' she confirms, and the camera pans to some people enjoying an evening stroll on the promenade, not a rain cloud in sight.

The anchor is sweating now, with the last throw of the dice. 'Over now to Granada, where we can speak to Francisco, what is happening in Granada, Francisco?' You can see the guy praying for a biblical deluge in Granada.

'Well it was raining this morning, it has stopped now, but I did speak to these men earlier' confirms Francisco, and the footage switches to about five old men standing on a small bridge, looking down into what amounts to little more than a brook. A raging torrent it is not. Francisco interviews each grizzled countryman in turn, but their accents are so thick we can barely understand one word in ten.

Suddenly Chrissie jumps up irritably and switches off the TV, 'oh to hell with this' she cries, 'we are learning damn-all Spanish from that rubbish. 'It was raining but it's stopped now.' When are we ever going to use that in conversation? There was more news value in you and Gaffer gobbling up that disgusting octopus! 'Over we go to Santa Marta bus station where two fat Englishmen are chewing away on a plate of garlicky tentacles. Can you smell them in Seville, Alonso! And what about Ana in Malaga, do you fancy jumping into bed with either of this stinky pair, you old tart?' Chrissie is not keen on glamorous blondes, for some unknown reason.

I am laughing as I pour myself a glass of wine. 'I am going out on the patio' I smile, 'are you coming?'

'Only if you stand down-wind of me!' she giggles. 'But at least there's no chance of any rats trying to sneak in through the bedroom window tonight! Any self-respecting rat will be a hundred miles away by now!'

'Yes but there's no chance of you being bitten by a vampire, either' I point out, 'see what a great husband I am to you, protecting you from Dracula!'

'Actually I would prefer Dracula to sleeping with you,' she snorts, 'why don't you take a blanket and go and sleep in El Woodshed?'

'I'll tell you why I can't sleep in El Woodshed' I grin, 'because if I do, the garlic-infused aroma will surely scare old Stumpy away, for evermore, and you know how much you want him to come back. Sorry, but you are stuck with me!'

For once, Chrissie has no answer. It seems as if I have the final word, for the first time!

CHAPTER 15. MEET UNCLE BOB.

OK I admit it. I am scared of rats. Always have been, ever since one ran across my foot in the Wolf-Cub HQ in the early 1960's. I still have the occasional flash-back, and every time I have anything to do with drains, it's the same. I expect a furry creature with whiskers, beady eyes and a twitchy nose to pop his head out. Occasionally, there are stories in the papers about someone finding a rat in their toilet bowl, which is why I always invest in a heavy, wooden toilet seat, on the assumption that a rodent would be unable to lift the lid. Unless he was the size of a cat, in which case he would be unable to slide around the 'U' bend in the first place. So I reckon I am fairly safe, although to this day I always whistle when entering a bathroom, to give any local vermin the chance to run back down the pipe. Truly, this is the stuff of nightmares.

And now, almost fifty years later, we have one stuck in the waste pipe of the bidet in our bathroom. For several weeks now a lurid green gunge has been seeping out of the bottom of the bidet, over the bathroom floor, I have been putting it off but it is getting worse and would be a huge embarrassment if we had friends round. A rat must have crawled up the pipe, got stuck, died, and is now slowly dissolving over my porcelain. And it is my job as man of the house to get it out.

But this is the 21st Century after all so in the spirit of being a 'New Man' I decide to confess my fears to Chrissie in the hope that she might grab a shifting spanner and do the job herself. Fat chance. She laughs. 'How can a rat have crawled up there? The pipe is only two inches wide.' *Ah yes but rats can do that can't they? I read it somewhere once. There's even an expression about it, 'like a rat up a drainpipe.' And it gets worse. If I get the waste pipe undone, and extract the creature with a pair of pliers (I can hardly push it back down the pipe as it will cause a blockage) there might be some more lurking down there which will come running out the pipe. With me lying there on the bathroom floor, spanner in hand, unable to escape, right in their path.* The nightmare continues.

Chrissie laughs again. 'What, do you think there is a family of them down there? Uncle Bob has got stuck and the family go to look for him, get stuck behind him and cannot turn back? For God's sake don't be such a baby. I will do the job myself if you are that much of a coward.'

OK I have had enough of being a Twenty-First Century New Man. I thrust the knife in. Hard. 'Well either it's a rat, or a snake' I tell her. She is petrified of snakes, cannot even look at one on TV. And two of our friends have had snakes in their Spanish houses in the last few weeks. Metre-long ones.

'Well if there is a snake down there I will run all the way to Madrid!' comes the panicked reply. *Ah well, nice try, but it looks as if I will have to do the job after all.*

I put it off another couple of days until the green stain gets even worse, and then decide to do it the next day, Saturday. Definitely. Friday night I drift into a restless, nightmare-tinged sleep, where rats are popping up everywhere in the bathroom, the size of pigs. Saturday morning comes round all too soon and I down three mugs of black coffee, and a huge fried breakfast, to sustain me, even though the chances of being reacquainted with it later in the morning are all too real. Grabbing all the tools I think I need, and leaving the bathroom and kitchen patio doors open to give any fugitive vermin an escape route, I position myself on the bathroom floor with my head wedged between the bidet and the wall, with just enough room to squeeze my arms round to work.

The first task is to cut away about ten feet of plastic electrical tape wound around the joint. Don't ask me. I had no idea that electrical tape had waterproofing qualities.... With the tape removed I get a good look at the joint, the threaded drainpipe from the bidet, two large brass nuts, old copper pipes, a perished rubber seal, and a load of brown fur stuck to the outside of the waste pipe. I recoil as I spot the fur, bashing my head painfully on the underside of the bidet and unleashing a stream of oaths. Almost gagging, feeling the fried breakfast about to put in a reappearance, I scramble to my feet, exit the bathroom at a run, and gratefully find solace on the patio, where I breathe in fresh restorative air, and wait for my heart-rate to return to something like normal.

'What the hell are you doing now? exclaims Chrissie, who I have placed on standby, just in case. In case of what I have no idea, but just in case.

'FUR!' I cry, 'there is fur around the pipe. Brown fur, mousy brown fur!. There is definitely a rat stuck in the pipe!'

'Rubbish, rats are black, aren't they?' she laughs. 'You great big kid! As Diane would say, tha' blooody great Soothern Jessie!'

'Black, brown, who knows what colour Spanish rats are?' I shout. 'They could be pink with green spots for all I care. But I am telling you, there is fur on the outside of that bloody pipe. And I am going nowhere near it!'

Chrissie starts to laugh. 'On the outside? Did you say on the outside? For God's sake get a grip. Think about it, if Uncle Bob, or indeed Hissing Sid, are in the pipe, they will be inside, not outside.'

Suddenly I realise what a silly boy I have been. It is an old fibre washer of course. A mousey-brown fibre washer. Easy enough to mistake for a rodent, in the circumstances. Returning to the bathroom and resuming my former position, I get a spanner on each nut and gently tug on them but the silver waste thing in the bidet is turning and the nuts will not unscrew. I call Chrissie, 'stick a large screwdriver in the drain and hold it tight.' She dutifully arrives but I notice from my vantage point under the bidet that she is wearing running shoes....and she closes the toilet lid..... 'Oh yes, not so brave now, are you?' I laugh. This time the nuts undo and gradually I can pull the waste drainpipe out of the bidet, noticing a load of bright blue crystals stuck inside the pipe. Strange. I suddenly get a flashback to my Chemistry 'O' Level exam forty-odd years ago, and so evidently does Chrissie, and she didn't even do chemistry at school. 'Domestic science' they used to call it. Science for girls. Cooking and sewing.

'Have you been putting *Agua Fuerte* down the bidet?' she asks, accusingly. *Agua Fuerte*, literally 'Strong Water', is a mild acid they sell here to remove lime scale and unblock sinks etc. Acid, alkali, copper, brass, steel, blue and green crystals..... I suddenly realise what an idiot I have been. There never was an Uncle Bob. I just didn't rinse that blasted Agua Fuerte away..... The rubber seal was leaking and the chemical reaction just seeped out. The electrical tape didn't do much of a job either. I will take a long time to live this one down. It should have been me doing domestic science at school, for all the good chemistry did, although to be fair, Mr Ferguson never envisaged a scenario like this in his science lab, all those years ago.

And by the way, I failed 'O' Level Chemistry......................

CHAPTER 16. COMETH THE SAND

It is just past half-four on a baking hot afternoon and the street outside is silent. People are indoors having their siesta and will be for another hour at least, after which they will emerge with wooden chairs to sit in the street and gossip with neighbours or passers-by. Just then the chug-chug of an ancient diesel engine heralds the approach of my building materials, we can hear the dumper truck well before we can see it, but soon it comes wheezing into view in a haze of exhaust fumes and pulls up outside the house. I cannot yet see the driver for the smoke, but he cuts the engine and after a few seconds Diego becomes visible, or 'Dirty Diego the Dumper Driver' to give him his full title. He nods a friendly greeting then eases his considerable stomach from behind the wheel, climbs down to street level, rearranges his groin with a pleasurable scratch, clears his throat spectacularly and gobs majestically behind the truck. Unloading can now begin.

We have ordered bricks, three bags of cement and a load of sand, I get the bricks off the truck and Chrissie helps with the first bag of cement which Diego hands her, managing to grope both her breasts in the process. She copes effortlessly with this, no doubt it has happened before but if a grubby old Spaniard grabbed my tits I would drop the cement right on his toes, I can tell you.

With bricks and cement unloaded, Diego disappears behind the truck and pulls a lever, and our load of sand tips off the dumper into the street causing a huge dust cloud like a sandstorm in the Sahara, I almost expect to see Omar Sharif riding a white horse emerge from the choking cloud but sadly it is Diego still. With a wave and a cheery *'Adios'* and another rummage in his trousers, he climbs back onto the truck and fires the reluctant conveyance into life, disappearing into the fumes and back the way he came. Silence reigns again.

Then the hard work begins. Because the old town is built on the side of a mountain, the bottom of our garden is probably thirty feet below street level, so we have no rear access, meaning that all the materials have to be carried down through the house to the garden. In through the front door, down eight stairs to the summer kitchen, out through the back door, past our new patios *El Sombrero* and *El Rincon*, down two more steps under the vines (where the next patio is going) out onto the open area past the El Woodshed then down another eight steps to the two animal sheds on the next level of the garden.

The first shed lost its roof when an idiot knocked the beam down a week or so ago, but the next one has a roof of sorts so that is where the sand is going. And what a load of sand it is. It covers the whole width of the street, so no one can get past, OK this is not the M5 but there are occasional cars coming up, which is why I have chosen what is hopefully the quietest part of the day for the delivery.

So Chrissie shovels it into two large rubber buckets and brings it to the top of the stairs and I do the carrying. While I lug one bucket down to the garden, she is refilling the other so I have a continuous supply to hump down, but it is so hot that after each load I have to drink about a pint of water and the pile does not seem to be getting any smaller.

Then the neighbours decide to come out for a look, Loli and Isabel, the two sisters next door who are great fun and always interested in what the crazy English are up to, they emerge with sweeping brushes to clear the dust off the street and houses and I am becoming exhausted with all the carrying. After about forty-five minutes of constant shovelling and carrying the pile has almost disappeared, and I am just about out on my feet. The sisters get buckets of water and start washing down the road, and soon it looks as good as new.

Suddenly, another front door opens, and Granny Mercedes comes stumping along. 'What are you doing, neighbour? She cries. I open my mouth to reply but my throat is so dry I am momentarily unable to speak.

Not a problem, with Loli on the scene. 'Neighbour has had sand delivered' bellows Loli, and we have been sweeping up. La Cristina has been shovelling, we were all working very hard. **Weren't we, neighbour?**' she cries, pointedly. I nod in agreement, then nip into the kitchen and get them all a choc-ice from the fridge, which I hand out one by one. Loli snatches hers from my hand. 'Neighbour, Mercedes has done no work, why does she get an ice-cream?' she complains, winking at me and cackling at the same time.

'I am the boss!' laughs Mercedes, 'I have come to see that you have cleared up properly!' and she glances round as if conducting an inspection. I place my hands on my hips and glare at Loli in mock anger, then pop back inside again and return with the whole box of remaining choc-ices and hand them to the sisters. I bow in gratitude, and we all start laughing hysterically. I am surrounded by women eating choc-ices and gabbling away about what a good neighbour I am, or I think that was the gist of it.... Most of our conversations with the locals end up in laughter. The choc-ices were only about a Euro for a box of ten, dog chocolate really, I was glad to see the back of them. But if they think we are good neighbours, that is the main thing.

One thing is for certain; I never experienced a pantomime like this having building materials delivered in the UK. But our lives are all the richer for it.

CHAPTER 17. MEET THE IRISHMAN

I am sitting in the main square of Santa Marta on a red leather-look sofa, cradling a beer in my hand. Next to me on said sofa is a mad Irishman, Declan, who is also nursing an alcoholic beverage. The old men lounging round the square are not taking any notice of us, as if this behaviour is quite normal, but passers by are laughing and joking 'that looks like a great place for a beer' or 'have a great siesta', but equally they could be saying 'you look like a pair of tossers', my Spanish is not that good yet. When I planned my life in this crazy country I did not envisage sitting on a sofa in the middle of town, outside a bar, but the sun is beating down and there are far worse places to spend a Tuesday afternoon in early November.

Declan only moved here a few weeks ago, like the rest of us he has bought a cheap old house on a narrow street with flaky paint and dodgy wiring, but he is only using his as a holiday home as he is still gainfully employed in Ireland. He is full of natural charm and wit, or should that be charm and bull, he could entertain a room full of people all night long, all delivered in that soft Irish brogue. He has a Mexican girlfriend living in Madrid, who is coming for a visit this weekend, and he is worried there is nothing for her to sit on at his house, not that he has much sitting in mind when she arrives....

Now one of the best things about this country is the attitude to recycling. Basically anything you no longer need you simply leave in the street, and someone will more than likely take it away. We do not have individual refuse bins to leave outside the house, as the streets are too narrow, so there are small communal bins in the wider parts of the streets, which are emptied every night by the council. Any large items like beds, wardrobes, sofas, anything at all, is left by the bins and collected every ten days, if it has not already been taken by someone who needs it. Obviously a lot of the stuff is broken and of no use, but you would be surprised what people will get rid of. We found a sun-lounger a few weeks ago, simply took off the canvas cover, washed it and hey presto it has pride of place on the patio.

Earlier today and we are chatting to Declan at the library, where he has temporarily joined the Spanish/English conversation class for the duration of his holiday, when along comes Lucy, who has managed to give her oppressive husband Paul the slip for a couple of hours. 'There is a lovely red leatherette sofa outside our house!' she laughs. 'Great condition, no idea why someone has left it out.'

Quick as a flash Declan expresses an interest. 'Ah fer sure, I need a sofa, like, can yer man sit on it like, while Johnny and I run up there and pick it up?' he asks Lucy.

'OK, I will call Paul, tell him to stay by the sofa, but you'll need to be quick, as he's going out in half-an-hour' she confirms. She whips out her mobile, dials, then explains to her husband that he needs to sit on said sofa for ten minutes, while Declan and I pop back there. A stream of oaths is audible over the airways, before Lucy rings off.

'Was that a yes or a no?' I laugh. Lucy looks a bit sheepish, as it's clear we all heard her husband swearing at her.

'It was a yes, but he's going out so could you, er, get a move on?'

'Ah yer grand' cries Declan, no doubt picturing a sofa-based encounter with his girlfriend this weekend, 'come on Jonny, I'll make it worth yer while, like!' and he gives me a big wink, and digs me in the ribs with his elbow. So back up the steep cobbled streets we trudge, and sure enough, there is Paul perched uncomfortably on the sofa, in the street outside his house.

'Took yer bloody time, din'cha?' he grumbles, seeing us approaching.

'What are you moaning about?' I ask, with just a trace of humour, 'you'd only be inside watching Jeremy Kyle, or one of the other chav programmes you like. At least you're out here in the sunshine.' Give this bloke the same as he gives out, is my motto from now on. And like most bullies, if you stand up to them, they back down.

'Well you're right there, I need to top up me tan!' he laughs.

So Declan grabs one end of the sofa, I catch hold of the other, and we hoist the beast onto our shoulders and stagger away up the street. After fifty yards or so I am perspiring heavily, and my back is breaking. 'Drop it down for a minute' I tell the Irishman, 'we have plenty of time, your girlfriend isn't coming until Friday!' We both slump into the upholstery for a well-earned rest.

'Ah ye know, this is a grand piece of furniture,' cries Declan, surveying his acquisition. 'A three-seater, too, plenty of room to get jiggy, on Friday evening!'

The thought of Declan getting jiggy is more than I wish to contemplate, especially as I seem to be doing most of the work. 'Right, too much information, and you get at the back now!' I tell him. So off we trudge, another hundred yards or so, and soon we are approaching the main square, from which it is only a short hop to Declan's cottage. Outside the cafe/bar we pause for another rest, and I flop gratefully onto the sofa. 'Right, mines a beer!' I laugh, 'in you go.'

'No need' giggles the Irishman, 'Antonio's coming out to us!', and sure enough, all eyes in the bar are glued to the sight of two foreigners slumped in a red leatherette sofa in the street outside.

'Welcome to my beer garden, gentlemen!' chuckles Antonio, 'what will it be?'

'Ah two bottles of yer finest, landlord!' Declan declares, 'Star of Galicia, none of that Malaga rubbish!' He feels he can discern a certain nutty quality in the beer from the north of Spain, which is not present in rival brands. And I have to say, I don't disagree. The beers duly arrive, together with a tapas plate of chorizo, and by gaw, as gaffer might have said, it went down a blooody treat!

The first beer barely touches the sides, but here comes Antonio with two more, plus a plate of potato salad. Suddenly there is a shout, 'Jonneee!' and who should be approaching but Mohammed, the Moroccan builder. He is laughing fit to burst, Declan and I shift apart and Mohammed slots in between us. A beer arrives for him, and there we are, an Englishman, a Moroccan and an Irishman, sitting on a sofa which was left out for the bin-men this very morning, in the main square of a little Spanish town, quaffing *cervezas* and nibbling tapas.

'Ah sure, they'll niver believe this, when I get back to Waterford next week!' laughs Declan.

'I can't believe it!' I concur, 'and I am actually sat here!'

CHAPTER 18. MEET ALICIA

At the English/Spanish conversation class at the library, Alicia, a lady of a certain age, has an urgent question for me. 'Jonneee, you come my house, weeth you free-end?'

I'm not sure how to respond to this request. Blonde, divorced, crazy-but-lovable Alicia dresses thirty years too young, today she is in high heels, fishnet tights, a mini skirt and low cut blouse, like a Parisian hooker. Or I should add, what I have been told a Parisian hooker might look like. Apparently. She always arrives late, and usually sits next to me. I gaze into Alicia's eyes. I cannot glance down as there is around an acre of bosom nestling provocatively inside her blouse, and several yards of stockinged thigh on show, and it is getting very hot all of a sudden in the library. And my free-end? I am not sure if I have a free-end, or any sort of end come to that. Or if I do have one, is it free, especially as far as Alicia is concerned? Particularly with my wife, whose red-hot glare I can feel wafting across the table, sitting opposite me.

'Free-end?' I venture.

'Yeees, you free-end. How you say, Dereeek? You free-end.'

I exhale gratefully. She needs some building work doing. I hope. 'My friend Derek? You would like me to come to your house with my friend Derek? Is there a problem with your house?'

'Yeees. I 'ave no water, my peeps they broke-ed. You look my peeps? Roof. Water. Yees. My roof, ees water, rainings, ees ver bad.' I nip outside and phone Del, and we arrange to call the following day to look at Alicia's peeps. Her village is about ten miles from Santa Marta, along a winding road through the olive fields. At eleven in the morning there is just one old woman in the street carrying a crusty loaf in her bag and not another soul around, and the only car on the road is us, yet a policeman is on traffic duty in the village square. We find Alicia's house, and discover she does indeed have broke-ed peeps, and rainings in her roof. Del is leaning out the third floor window surveying the offending lean-to roof below when Alicia calls me. 'Jonneee, plees you come my bedroom, you look my crack.'

I stifle a guffaw and hear a loud thump, followed by the muffled sound of English swearing. I follow our prospective client to her bedroom and indeed there is a large fissure in the wall. 'Not a problem' I hastily affirm, 'we can get some mortar in there', before gratefully escaping her bedroom and returning rapidly to Del, who is rubbing the back of his head.

He works out a price, gives Alicia the bad news and we head back to the car, whereupon my business partner bursts into uncontrollable laughter. 'Jonneee' he giggles, in a passable impersonation of Alicia. 'You come my bedroom plees, you look my crack!'

'Yeah yeah yeah, you heard that I suppose' I venture, sheepishly.'

'Heard it? he shouts, 'I was laughing so bloody much I hit my head on the window lintel. But it was worth it! It will be a long time before you live that one down sunshine! Oh my God, lets stop for a coffee.' So we pull into the village bar and order refreshments. 'So tell me Jonneee, did you look at her crack? Wait till I tell Chrissie!' And he keeps it up for the entire journey back to town. And then proceeds to tell everyone. The following evening I bump into See-

You-Jimmy. 'I hear you are the new expert at filling divorcees cracks!' he cries, digging me in the ribs. Yeah yeah yeah.

We have a wonderful group for the conversation classes, we have become firm friends and Chrissie and I have been invited to each of their houses, meeting their families, drinks in the bar, family meals, and so on. This is exactly what we were hoping for when we came to inland Andalucia, although never in our wildest dreams did we imagine it would happen this quickly, or this successfully. Juan, another member of the group who is not here today, took us to the local GP surgery last week to get us registered, and to obtain our Spanish health cards, which actually arrived this morning. This gave me particular satisfaction, as several other Brits, naming no names, but one of them began with 'P' and ended 'aul', complained that it took them two years of bureaucratic wrangling to obtain them, whereas for us, by engaging with the local community, and trying to learn the language and customs, making Spanish friends, it took less than ten days.

Today the theme of the class is local cuisine, and we have to describe a typical delicacy of our region of Britain. As we are from the West Country, I am attempting to describe a Cornish pasty, which is not unlike a Spanish *empanada*, although a pasty comes with a thick pastry crimping down one side, which tradition had it that tin miners, when eating the thing, would grip by the crimping to avoid getting poisonous minerals into their digestive systems. The Spanish version on the other hand is usually baked on a huge tray and cut into portions, and not as far as I know, eaten by tin-miners. So nothing like a pasty then. Why didn't I describe fish n chips? My language skills are still extremely basic of course, so I decide to mimic eating a pasty by holding it up to my mouth, and for good measure I make chomping and slurping noises, and lick my lips to signify I have enjoyed my pasty very much. The Spanish dissolve into laughter, which is not quite what I was expecting, whereupon Jose leans across to me, wiping his eyes, and splutters 'John, you have just told us you enjoy eating penis!' My embarrassment is acute, and I start waving my arms about to signify that I have mispronounced a word, although I think, no I pray, that they realise that.

The following day is Halloween, and we bump into Juan in town. 'I cannot talk much time' he apologises, 'I go to cemetery, die my haunt.' OK, what is going on here? Is he taking part in some Halloween festival, with his friends possibly, dressing as ghosts or ghouls, running round the cemetery, scaring the bejaysus out of each other? The problem is, its eleven o'clock in the morning, its not dark for another seven hours, so why is he in a hurry? Being late for things is a Spanish speciality, in fact I don't think there is a phrase in the Spanish language for 'I can't stop, I am late already.' They are always late, and nothing ever starts on time. Last week we went to a concert in the local theatre, which was advertised to start at ten in the evening. We duly arrived a few minutes early, being British of course and never late for anything. Everyone was standing around chatting, with no sign that a concert was actually taking place, no evidence that anyone had a clue what time it actually was, or that they were remotely bothered. So we just did what everyone else was doing, wandered into the theatre bar, ordered some food and a bottle of sherry, and set about eating and drinking. The concert eventually started at eleven-fifteen.

So why is Juan in a hurry? I frown at him to signify that his English is not making perfect sense. 'You are going to the cemetery now?' I ask.

'*Si*, yees, I am go cemetery.'

OK, got that bit right. 'It's Halloween today' I continue.

'Yees, Halloween this day! Today.'

Right, we are on the same wavelength. 'So you are going to the cemetery now, to do some haunting?'

He looks at me in total confusion. 'What this haunting? Sorree, I no understand haunting.'

I smile gently to signify there is no problem. 'You told me you are going to haunt in the cemetery?' and to illustrate the point I flap my hands next to my head. 'Whoooo!' He looks at me as if I have taken total leave of my senses. I blunder onwards. 'Halloween? Whoooo! Boooo! Ahhhh!' and again I do my best to imitate a ghost, and a perfectly good attempt I must say, given that I am not in possession of a white sheet.

Suddenly the Spanish penny drops. 'No sorree, Halloween no, yesterday, die my haunt. The sister of my mother. My haunt. She die.'

I stifle a smile, about the 'haunt' bit, not his aunt dying, obviously. Chrissie has to turn away, for the same reason. 'So your aunt died yesterday? The word is aunt. A.U.N.T. Pronounced *ahhnt*. To haunt is what a ghost does. Whoooo! I am sorry to hear your aunt is dead.'

Juan smiles. 'I sorree, my Eengliss ver bad. Is OK, my haunt she with Cassoo.' Right, total confusion again. Is she dead, or with this Cassoo character? Whoever he might be. I turn to my Spanish translator, with a 'what the hell is he on about?' expression.

'Jesus' Chrissie replies. 'He is saying his haunt, sorry aunt, is with Jesus now.'

Of course, I should have realised, although learning Spanish vocabulary is made doubly difficult by the Spanish themselves refusing to pronounce the endings of many words, especially those ending in the letter 'S'. 'Did you say she died yesterday?' I query.

'Yees, she die yesterday' he confirms.

'And the funeral is today? I continue.

'Yees, is tradition here in Espain, sometime if she die in morning, is possible funeral the same day, but if she die in afternoon, funeral is next day. Is this not tradition in Eengland?'

Chrissie takes over. 'No, in Britain it takes maybe ten days to arrange the funeral, maybe two weeks.'

Juan smiles, 'You strange, you Eengliss, but I must to go, I no want be late for my own funeral! You teach me this last week, remember?' I do remember, we were talking at the conversation group about Spanish people being late for everything, and I explained the sentence about being late for your own funeral. I didn't mean it literally of course, although it feels good that my teaching is sinking in. Didn't make a scrap of difference of course. They are still late for everything!

CHAPTER 19. FORK HANDLES!

'I need some plastic wood to fill that hole in the bathroom door,' I announce, 'do you fancy coming down the hardware shop, *La Ferreteria,* for a stroll?' Chrissie looks up from her book, in which she has been engrossed all morning, whereas I, having rid the bathroom of the horrible gunge which turned out to be unrelated to rodents, have been turning my attention to a spot of decorating in there.

'Wow, you certainly know how to show a girl a good time!' comes the sarcastic reply. 'Let me think. Sat here with a nice cuppa? Or a trip down the *ferreteria*? Um, can I let you know?'

I consider telling her she needs the exercise, but decide against it. 'You know how we said that we never know what is going to happen next in this country?' I giggle, 'well get your coat, come on, let's live dangerously!'

My wife regards me through narrowed eyes. She sighs dramatically. 'There are times, you know, when I wish you were back at work. Come on then, there'll be no peace until you've had your walk,' and still muttering, she reluctantly puts down her book and heads for the front door.

Out in the street we encounter our neighbours, Loli and Isabel. 'Off for a walk, neighbour?' cries Loli. *Well honestly, what can you say to that?* Actually I cannot tell her the truth as I am not sure of the Spanish for 'plastic wood', and the last thing I need is a long debate about it, because judging by some of the house repairs we have encountered so far, she will probably suggest we just stick a bit of packing tape in the hole, and paint over it.

'Yes, just a little walk' I lie.

'Where are you going?' she replies. Sometimes I think the Spanish Inquisition actually took place in Santa Marta, with Loli, or one of her ancestors, as chief Inquisitor. But at least we are happy the locals engage with us, and they seem genuinely interested in what the crazy English are up to.

'Not sure, maybe the shops, maybe the cafe' I smile, and we head off down the cobbled street.

Entering the ferreteria is like stepping back fifty years. The sign over the door reads 'Hijo de Antonio Molina'. That means 'son of Tony Mills!' laughs Chrissie, as our eyes adjust to the gloom inside. Leaning on the counter we can just about make out an old man, and behind it another, middle-aged chap, son of Tony presumably. I glance around in amazement. Fans of the BBC series 'The Two Ronnies' would immediately recognise this place from the 'Fork Handles' sketch, but with even less floor space. We pick our way past enamel buckets, coils of wire, plastic hosepipe, bird cages, walking sticks, work boots, I duck my head under a bunch of dog leads hanging from the ceiling, slalom round a display of vicious-looking hunting knives in a glass case, past a pile of rat-traps, and arrive at the battered wooden counter. B&Q this is not.

'Buenas dias' smiles son of Tony, 'what can I get you?'

For a split second I am tempted to reply 'Got any 'ose?' Now the Spanish for plastic is *plastico*, and for wood is *madera*. 'I am looking for madera plastico' I tell him.

'Madera plastica? he replies, emphasising the 'a' on the end of plastica. *OK, if you want to split hairs, I can never get used to this male/female business in foreign languages, wood is clearly female, which quite possibly explains why I like working with it so much...* 'Madera plastica?' he repeats. I nod my head, and he disappears into the depths of the shop, past rows of old wooden shelves and drawers, from floor to ceiling, exactly as the 'Two Ronnies' sketch. I can hear him bumping around, and eventually he returns, carrying a six-foot length of imitation wood, the sort of stuff you might stick on the walls of a 1970's pub, in a vain attempt to make it look like an Elizabethan coaching inn. He swings it round, almost decapitating the old man, very nearly bringing down a stack of china plates, and leans the plank against the counter. 'Madera plastica' he smiles.

The urge to burst out laughing is so strong and I can almost feel Chrissie choking next to me. 'No' I tell him, in my best Spanish Ronnie Barker voice. 'Plastic wood!' and I mime squeezing a tube and applying the contents to a crack in the wooden counter.

Son of Tony eyes me malevolently. 'Ma-see-zha!' he cries. 'Ma-see-zha de madera! and he snatches up the plank and returns it from whence it came.

Luckily the old man steps niftily back like a prize-fighter evading a left hook, then cackles with laughter, tapping the side of his head. 'loco!'

Son of Tony returns, looking weary from his exertions. 'So do you have any Ma-see-zha?' I enquire.

He waves a meaty finger in my direction, 'no, for Ma-see-zha you must go to *La Drogueria*', and he points back up the street. I thank him for his time and we both weave our way out of the shop, gratefully gulping fresh air and almost crying with laughter.

'Fork handles, handles for forks!' I giggle.

'Got any peas?' Chrissie chokes. '

'Can you believe, a hardware shop not selling plastic wood?' I splutter, 'so now we have to go to this drogueria place.' *Drogue* is Spanish for drugs, so I am guessing the drogueria is a drug-store, even though, as far as I know, they do not sell medicine. There are pharmacies dotted around the town selling prescription and over-the-counter remedies, so the purpose of the drug-store, and why they allegedly sell plastic wood, is beyond me.

The shop window of the drogueria place is a curious affair, featuring as it does perfumes, hair-dye and after-shave, plus large family-size boxes of washing powder, bearing the names *Elena* and *Dixan.* 'I used to go to school with her' Chrissie announces.

'School with who?' I ask, puzzled.

'Elaine Dixon' my wife replies, 'stroppy cow she was!'

Still giggling, we enter the drug store to be confronted behind the counter by a woman in possibly the tightest pair of jeans I have ever seen. Remarkable material, denim. She appears oblivious to our appearance however, tapping away as she is on her smart-phone. Chrissie digs me painfully in the ribs, 'eyes back off their stalks, please' she hisses.

Just then an older man appears, and I perform a double-take, as he is the living image of son-of-Tony. Brother-of-son-of-Tony at the very least, although it could actually be the same bloke. Maybe there is a secret passage between the two shops. 'Buenas dias, what can I get you?' he enquires.

'Do you have Ma-see-zha?' I ask. He disappears into the space behind the counter, and I take the opportunity to glance around the shop, stepping back and almost knocking over a stack of five-litre tins of paint. 'Blimey, I didn't notice those there' I grin.

'Oh I wonder why that was?' whispers my wife pointedly. 'Maybe you had your mind on OTHER THINGS!'

'Yes, Ma-see-zha!' I smile, innocently. 'What a peculiar shop, after-shave, emulsion and Elaine Dixon!' I am tempted to mention the amazing, stretchy qualities of denim, but decide against it. Brother-of-son-of-Tony returns clutching a box of white powder-filler, the stuff you mix with water and poke into cracks in the wall. I smile my best apologetic smile. 'Sorry, Ma-see-zha for wood'.

He narrows his eyes. *'Que tinta?' Tinta? Tint? Shade? He is asking me what shade of plastic wood I want. Finally, we are getting somewhere.*

'Natural?' I reply. I am going to paint over it, but I don't want it too dark.

'Pino?' he suggests. *Pino? Pine?*

'Perfecto!' I exclaim, and he disappears again, this time to return with the holy grail, a plastic tube of wood filler. Finally, after three-quarters of an hour, I have what I set out to buy. Almost. I still need sandpaper. I have no idea what 'sandpaper' is in Spanish, but I know that sand is *'arena'*, and paper is *'papel.'* Do you have papel de arena?'

'Que?' he responds, so I mime sanding down the counter, which unfortunately is glass, but I think he gets the message. My miming skills are coming in useful since we moved to this country. Maybe those hours in drama class at school were not a complete waste of time, after all. 'Lee-Ho!' he exclaims, which in an instant takes me back over forty years to sailing lessons in the Sea-Scouts. 'Lee-Ho' was what you were supposed to shout when turning a corner in a sailing boat, to avoid the huge pole on the bottom of the sail cracking the heads of my crew-mates. Usually however I forgot this particular command, which made me about as popular as Captain Bligh, whenever I was skippering. Mutiny on the river Tamar.

So what does a maritime term have to do with sandpaper? 'Lee-Ho?' I echo.

'Papel de lee-ho' replies Brother-of-son-of-Tony.

'OK, so do you have any papel de lee-ho?' I query.

He waves a meaty finger in my direction, 'No, for this you must go to La Ferreteria' and he points the way, back down the street. I am speechless. We have just come from the ferrete-bloody-ria. Plastic wood filler needs to be sanded down, it doesn't come out of the tube smooth. The filler and the sandpaper go together like love and marriage, like a horse and carriage, as the song says. So why in the name of all things holy does one shop sell one item, and another shop sell the other. This makes no sense at all, but sadly my language skills are not quite up to telling Brother-of-son-of-Tony this, so I smile between gritted teeth, pay the man for the Ma-see-zha, and after a last furtive glance at denim-girl we head off to pay our second visit of the morning to son of Tony Mills.

'Did you see the make-up that woman was wearing?' comments Chrissie, 'you had a job to see where the make-up ended, and the woman began! And she was far too old to be wearing those jeans, and her bum was far too big, didn't you think?'

I make vague noises. 'I can't honestly say I noticed her make-up' is all I can think to say, which earns me my second whack of the morning.

'No, and we all know why that was, don't we?' my wife complains, 'and besides, she looked a bit rough to me, she would chew you up and spit you out!' Frankly, I can think of worse ways to die, but decide to keep that to myself.

'So back to Mr Four-Candles then' Chrissie chuckles. 'I can't wait to see the look on his face, when we walk in again!' We slalom our way into the shop, to find the old man still leaning against the counter, and son-of-Tony still behind it, as if the pair of them have been suspended in time while we've been away. I dig my hand in my pocket and wave the tube triumphantly in the air, 'Ma-see-zha!' I announce. 'Do you have any lee-ho?'

He grimaces, like a bulldog swallowing a lemon, and disappears into the depth of the shop again, returning with a multi-pack of square sheets of sandpaper. Wrong again. The problem is, I don't know the Spanish for electric sander, so utilise my drama techniques once again, mimicking sanding his wooden counter. 'Wrrrrrrrrr.'

The old man gets it first. 'Lee-ho-Dora!' he shouts. Well we didn't have girls in the Sea Scouts, especially ones called Dora, but I am guessing a sander is a lee-ho-dora?

'Si' I smile, as son-of-Tony snatches up the sandpaper, disappears into his cavern again, this time emerging with rectangular-shaped pack of sander paper. Correct size, but sadly wrong grade. He has brought coarse, whereas ideally I need something finer, although once again, my language skills have come up short. I turn to Chrissie, 'how do I ask for fine-grade?

She rolls her eyes. 'Well strangely enough, my 'O' Level Spanish course didn't teach us how to ask for sandpaper, forty years ago' she whispers, unhelpfully.

Son-of-Tony has picked up on my comment however. 'Mas fina?' he asks. *Fina? Fine?* I nod my head hopefully, and once again he waddles into the back of the shop, returning with what appears to be the correct grade. Finally, after a tiring hour, I appear to have everything I need.

'I am sorry' I smile, 'I only speak a little Spanish.'

The old man cackles with laughter, 'don't worry, he speaks no English!', and suddenly we are all laughing.

Son of Tony leans forward conspiratorially, his face a mask of concentration. 'Veel-ee-am Sack-es-pea-are-ay' he cries triumphantly. 'Es Ingles, no?'

English? Is he kidding? Now it is my turn to be slightly superior. 'Que?' I really have not the slightest clue what he is talking about.

'Sack-es-pea-are-ay' he repeats. 'Amigos, Romanos y compatriotas!' *Friends, Romans.. SHAKESPEARE! He is saying William Shakespeare!* In Spanish, like other Latin languages, you pronounce every single letter in a word. 'Sack-es-pea-are-ay' must be how they pronounce it. Chrissie has cottoned on too, and the four of us are laughing again.

'William Shakes-peare' I gently correct him, praying he doesn't want me to translate 'Alas poor Yorik!' into Spanish.

I pay him for the lee-ho and, still chuckling, we wind our way out of the shop. 'There you go' I tell my wife, pointedly, 'you could be stuck at home now, instead you have learned some new Spanish words, and re-visited a 1970's classic sitcom, in my opinion second only to the Morecambe and Wise 'Grieg Piano Concerto' sketch in the list of all-time great British comedy. What more could a girl want, eh?'

Chrissie snorts in derision. 'Oh yeah, Ma-see-zha, lee-ho and Sack-es-pea-are-ay. They will come in really handy in general conversation, won't they? What this girl wants is an espresso, the Spanish for which is 'espresso.' Come on, last one in the cafe pays!' Which is always me, of course.

Stuck to the window of the cafe is a glossy poster advertising the upcoming fiesta of St Cecilia, the patron saint of musicians, apparently. The poster is entirely in Spanish but we are able, between us, to decipher most of it, and it appears that this coming Friday evening there is a mass in St Mary's church at eight PM, followed by what is described as a 'solemn procession.' There then follows a description of the route the procession will take, which means little to us as we still refer to the streets by their physical features, hence 'Bank Street', 'Tree Street', 'Heart-Attack Hill', 'Gasoline Alley' and 'That Street With The Chinese Restaurant'. But we know where St Mary's Church is, and be there we will. This sounds like exactly the type of event we were hoping to see when we moved here, although what form the procession might take, who is in it, how long it might take and any other details, are not shown. There is however a photo of a statue, St Cecilia I assume, although how big she is we cannot tell, she might be life-size, or a foot tall. All part of our journey of discovery, and we are suddenly energised and looking forward to Friday evening.

At that moment who should walk into the cafe, catching us red-handed, reading the poster? Diane, and Gaffer. 'Now then!' he cries, 'what tha readin' lad?' He studies the text carefully, 'can't understand a blooody word o' that, summat t'do wi' Jimmy Jesus, ah reckon! There's his mum, look, or his auntie!'

I can feel Chrissie tensing up. 'There is a procession on Friday evening, St Cecilia' I inform him.

'Seen one procession, seen 'em all,' Diane groans.

'So I take it you won't be going in that case' Chrissie replies, a hint of steel in her voice.

'Nay lass' Gaffer hastily adds, 'don't say that, of course we'll coom wi' ye!' *Strange that, I don't recall asking them to accompany us.* 'What time do it start? he adds, 'this blooody poster tells thee nowt!'

'It tells you nowt, because you can't read Spanish' she giggles, 'but the mass starts at eight, and the procession is after that. But listen carefully' she continues, wagging her finger in mock seriousness. 'We haven't seen one of these processions yet, so we don't want it turning into a massive drinking session! We would quite like to watch the spectacle without having to waft away beer fumes!

Gaffer regards her innocently, as if the thought had never crossed his mind. 'Reet lad, gi' us a knock on yer way oop t' church, half-eight like, an' we'll have time for suppin' ale in t' bar before yon Jimmy Jesus cooms out. OOH SORRY! I meant maybe a coffee!' And he turns to me, and winks.

Walking home from the cafe, clutching my Ma-see-zha and lee-ho, Chrissie is somewhat cross. 'If he starts making idiotic remarks on Friday night, and ruins it for us, I swear I will kill him. And why on earth did you tell him about the procession? He can't read the poster, you could have told him anything. If you'd said it was a kiddies colouring competition, or a bouncy castle, he would have been none the wiser!'

I find the idea of a St Cecilia bouncy castle faintly ridiculous, but I start laughing nevertheless. 'The poster says 'Santa Cecilia'' I protest, 'of course he's going to know it's a procession.'

'Rubbish' snaps my wife, 'he probably thinks Santa Cecilia is Mrs Santa Claus! I'm telling you, if he ruins Friday night, you are in the doghouse.'

The church of St Mary's, or *Santa Maria de la Encarnacion* to use the official title, stands proudly in the main *plaza* of the town, a square roughly the size of a football pitch, surrounded by grand old buildings, some slightly falling down, as seems to be the norm in this part of Spain, ornate facades and intricate wrought iron echoing their faded glory. Mind you, if I had stood in the blistering heat of summer for several hundred years, I too might not be in pristine condition. The centre of the square is given over to flowering shrubs, orange and palm trees, inhabited by a chattering of parakeets and other songbirds, who bicker and squabble constantly. Anywhere with parrots and palm trees is all right with me. There is only one slight problem on this, the night of the supposed procession; the church appears to be closed, and no-one is here. Groups of people are congregated under the trees, gossiping, old men are strolling round the square, and a bunch of kids are kicking a ball around, using fallen oranges as goalposts. None of them however resemble church-goers.

'Tha's got t'wrong night!' Gaffer howls, 'booger this, less go t'pub.'

I have been given strictest instructions for just this scenario. 'No, we are OK for the moment' I inform him, 'you go on if you want a drink, we'll wait here for the church to open. This is definitely the correct night.'

Gaffer scowls, 'Well ah'm not standing 'ere like a lemon, coomin' for a sup, Di?'

His wife regards him disinterestedly, 'Nay, ah'll bide 'ere wi' Chrissie 'n John.'

So off toddles Gaffer, across the square, much to the relief of Diane. This will also give us a chance to have a decent chat with her for a change, as Gaffer tends to dominate the conversation. Sadly, two minutes later he is back. 'Blooody pub's packed, wi' trumpets, cornets, a twiltin' gert tuba an' a blooody bass drum! T' band are inside, suppin' ale, drownin' their guts. Ah can't blooody well get in!'

'Well at least that proves we have the right date' Chrissie smiles 'and I think I can hear noises coming from inside the church. Maybe something's about to happen.' Sure enough, the massive iron-clad doors of St Mary's are gradually opening, straining on their rusty hinges, and the congregation start to emerge in disorderly fashion, some just standing in the doorway chatting, others trying to push their way past, most brandishing huge candles about a yard long, which thankfully have not yet been lit. Glancing behind us, members of the band are casually strolling across the square clutching their instruments, some tapping smart-phones, some smoking, mingling with the crowd spilling from the church, in one huge disorganised huddle.

'Blooody Spanish couldn't organise a piss-up in t' brewery!' he laughs, 'Jimmy Jesus'll be 'ere in a minute, look at this blooody rabble!'

Doing our best to ignore him, our attention is suddenly drawn to the ringing of a hand-bell inside the church, two beats of the bass drum call the band to order, the congregation fans out into two columns either side of the cobbled street, candles are hurriedly ignited and within about thirty seconds, the parade is ready for the off. The band strike up a jaunty tune, a priest appears as if by magic followed by two small boys swinging an incense burner, clouds of pungent smoke billowing amongst the crowd, and a fusillade of rockets assault the night sky, causing a flock of birds to rise angrily from the trees and swoop off over the bell-tower, almost inducing heart-attacks among the four watching Britons. And everyone else judging by the gasps emanating from the crowd. It appears we are coming under fire, from an unseen enemy. The smoke from the apparent barrage of gunfire merges with the clouds of incense and for a few seconds my eyes are stinging and I am unable to see more than a few feet in front of me, when suddenly, with more ringing of the hand-bell, the fog clears and there, in the doorway of Santa Maria, is a huge wooden plinth, carried by maybe twenty men, and mounted proudly on top, the statue of Santa Cecilia.

The church bells start ringing, another barrage of rockets fizzes across the square, the parakeets continue their outraged squawking, the band are in full flow and the crowd starts to shout and cheer. Chrissie is wiping tears from her eyes, whether from the cordite, incense, parrot-droppings or pure emotion I cannot say, but I have a huge lump in my throat and the hairs on the back of my neck are working overtime.

The plinth is maybe six feet wide, twelve feet long, supported by two wooden beams running fore and aft, squashed underneath which are the carriers. They inch their way out of the church door, preceded by a little old man walking backwards, hands resting on the framework, shouting instructions to the now heavily perspiring crew. The whole structure clears the archway of the church door, then with more shouted instructions, begins to turn to face down the street, whereupon the old man rings the bell, and the plinth is gently lowered on to metal legs which appear from underneath, the bearers straighten their backs, un-kink their spines, rub their shoulders and grin widely, milking the applause from the crowd.

Up close, we are able to admire the intricately carved wooden frame, inlaid with inscribed silver panels. On each corner are ornamental silver lamps with fluted glass shades, inside which are spluttering candles, fanned by the breeze. Santa Cecilia herself stands maybe four feet high, either carved wood or plaster, dressed in a dark red and blue cloak, halo of flowers in her hair, and carrying a small harp. Many in the crowd are openly moved by the spectacle, a woman near me is in tears and most are making the sign of the cross. The old man then rings the bell once, the carriers resume their positions, another ring and they take the strain, then two further chimes and they hoist the plinth onto their shoulders, and move off slowly down the street, followed by the straggle of the congregation, and finally, the band.

'Reet lad, Jimmy Jesus has gone, less get in t'pub, afore this crowd!' cries Gaffer.

As before, however, I have been primed for this scenario. 'No, we are going to follow the procession for a while' I inform him. 'You come with us if you like, otherwise we'll catch you up in the bar later.'

Gaffer splutters. 'What, walk down t'blooody 'ill? Wi' my legs? Booger that! We'll see thee in t'social club!'

The procession has only made it to the corner of the *plaza*, as they pause for a rest every fifty yards or so, so we slip past and take up position further down t'blooody 'ill. We are totally enchanted. Away from the main square, the narrow cobbled streets and little white cottages are the perfect backdrop to the plinth, illuminated by the candles of the followers, and it takes little imagination to picture this scene being enacted decades, or maybe centuries, ago. And somehow we feel part of it. We receive many smiles and greetings from the followers and onlookers as we pass by, they can tell we are not

Spanish of course but they seem genuinely pleased that we are taking an interest in their customs and traditions. I had been slightly apprehensive about this, recalling a May-Day celebration in Cornwall years ago when many of the locals seemed openly hostile to visitors, but not here.

All too soon, the parade winds its way back up towards the square, then pauses in front of the church doors, where another barrage of pyrotechnics announces the homecoming of Santa Cecilia. Amid the smoke the doors creak open, and gradually the plinth disappears from view. One final crescendo from the band, another peal of bells, and it is all over. The crowd are milling around outside the church, the band reach for cigarettes and smart-phones, the parakeets return to their perches among the palm trees, and feeling slightly light-headed, we head back across the square towards home.

'What do you want to do about Gaffer and Diane?' Chrissie smiles, 'we could put our heads around the social club door, if you like, or leave them there, and say we forgot!'

I am feeling mellow, 'Nay lass! Me throat's reet dry! Let's go t'poob!'

Inside t'poob are two people only, Gaffer and the barmaid, a tiny woman in her mid-thirties maybe. 'T'missus 'ave gone 'ome, by gaw!' slurs our friend, clearly the worse for drink. 'Coom an' meet Lara! Dos beers, Lara!'

The barmaid looks relieved to see us, particularly another woman, although she appears about ready to close up, if only she could get rid of her troublesome customer, who is now slumped against the bar, leering at her. I raise my palm and shake my head imperceptibility, indicating that we are not staying. Gaffer meanwhile staggers to the end of the counter and lunges at the diminutive barmaid, grabbing her round the shoulders, and tries to plant a wet slobbery kiss on the side of her head, which she expertly evades, although she is clearly distressed. I have seen enough. I start to make a move then instantly freeze. I am about six inches taller than him, three stone heavier, not to mention ten years younger. If I make a grab at him, he might turn nasty, and the situation could deteriorate rapidly. Chrissie senses my indecision and chooses the feminine, and clearly correct, option, taking Gaffer's hand in hers. 'Come on Keith, Lara wants to close up, let's get you home, eh?' And he changes from a drunken oaf to a little lamb, like switching on a light-bulb.

Waving an exaggerated goodbye to the relieved barmaid, he follows Chrissie meekly to the door, still clutching her hand, while I mouth a silent 'sorry, goodnight' to Lara, and follow the pair out into the street.

Approaching Gaffer's house, past the zigzag bend, down the steep slope, still hand in hand with my wife, he suddenly stumbles and is about to crash to the cobblestones, Chrissie is unable to hold him but luckily I make a wild grab round his waist and just about manage to prevent him hitting the deck, although the pair of us crash unceremoniously against his front door, setting off an almighty cacophony of barking from his dogs. Diane flings open the door angrily, and stares disbelievingly at her errant husband. 'THA BLOOODY DRUNKEN BASTARD' she bellows, in a voice like a pipe organ, which can surely be heard in Malaga. 'GET THEESEN 'ERE, NOW' and she steps back allowing her inebriated spouse to topple across the threshold, where he crashes sickeningly to the tiled floor. She looks out at the pair of us. 'I swear one day I will kill t' useless piece of shite!' she hollers, banging the door in our faces. As we walk slowly back towards our house, Diane's voice continues to reverberate down the street. 'GET ON T'BLOOODY COUCH, THA EFFING TOSSER!'

We reach our front door, Chrissie fumbles for her key, then turns to me, deadpan. 'Where do you think you are going?'

I narrow my eyes, uncomprehending, 'inside of course. I need a relaxing glass of wine, after all that excitement!'

She slowly shakes her head, 'oh no you're not! I told you, any trouble from him, and you are in the doghouse. Off you go, woof woof!'

I burst out laughing, 'we don't have a dog! And this is half my house!' She regards me with mock disdain, 'well your half is the downstairs half,' hardly able to keep a straight face, 'get on t'blooody couch, tha eff...'

She is thankfully unable to complete her sentence, as I have her in a massive, enveloping bear-hug....

CHAPTER 20. NATIVITY

I love Nativity scenes. Always have, ever since I was selected to be one of the Three Wise Men in my junior school play. *Myrrh* I was, and had to deliver the following immortal line to Alan Reed, sorry, *Gold*; 'You say you too have followed this same star?'

To which Alan replied 'For many months, through many countries, I have followed this same star.' Whether Paul Hayman, *Frankincense*, had a line is sadly lost in the mists of time. And then to our own children's Nativity plays, many years later. The beauty of the story, the innocence of the children, were somehow life-affirming. Years ago, when Chrissie and I were first married, I bought a set of Nativity figures, a couple of inches high, and made a wooden stable, complete with a genuine thatched roof. Then more recently, on holiday in Kenya, we bought a hand-carved set of wooden figures from a beach-seller, each piece about six inches high, complete with animals. Sadly, both these sets are currently languishing in boxes in the attic of our house in the UK, together with our much-prized Christmas tree decorations collected from various countries around the world. These and our other personal possessions will be shipped over some time in the future, if we decide to stay here, but for this year we have no Christmas tree, decorations or Nativity scenes.

Quite by chance, the theme at the conversation group at the library the following day is 'Christmas in My Country', and I am attempting in my schoolboy Spanish to explain my love of Christmas, and Nativity scenes in particular. 'You must to go the chur and look the Belen,' explains Rafi, 'it is ver beautiful.'

'Go where, and look at what?' I query. I really have no idea what she is suggesting we do.

'The chur' she continues, 'near you house is chur, is two chur, Santa Maria, and San Raphael. Inside this chur is village Belen, is ver big, ver beautiful.'

The penny drops, partially. 'You mean a church? The word is church, C.H.U.R.C.H. In English you cannot eat the letters! You must pronounce the whole word. Chur-ch. The Spaniards round the table all start practising, chur ch, chur-ch.

'Very good!' I smile, 'now, what is in these two churches?' Rafi has exhausted her vocabulary so Pati takes over.

'Is Belen' she confirms, 'where Cassoo he was born.' I have been caught out with this before, Cassoo is how the Spanish pronounce Jesus.

'Jesus was born in Bethlehem, we call it Bethlehem in English.' Chrissie explains. 'So there are model villages in the churches?' It appears there are, although no-one is able to elaborate further. They know what they mean, we think we have an idea what they mean, but the only way to find out precisely is to go and see for ourselves.

So that evening, we set off in search of Belen. The first chur we encounter is that of San Raphael, a huge stone convent-style building. We really have little idea what to expect, I imagine there will be a fairly standard Nativity scene, with a stable, the Holy Family, maybe three kings, a few shepherds, possibly a sheep or two. It is quite dark inside and it takes my eyes a few seconds to adjust to the lack of light, the altar is in front of us but of a Nativity, there is no sign.

Suddenly, Chrissie gasps, and touches my arm. 'Look!' She whispers, 'in the corner. Look!' I follow her gaze and in front of us is a whole village, maybe twelve feet wide, by the same deep, laid out on three levels. Simply breathtaking, at the highest level is a Roman fort, with centurions and a leader who I assume is King Herod. Each figure is around a foot or so high, and the attention to detail is incredible. Next are the three wise men, riding camels, then the path descends to the middle level, past houses and market stalls, each with fruit and veg on sale, a bakery with a display of bread and cakes, a fishmonger, a forge with horses and a blacksmith, farm carts carrying various produce, a market garden with vegetables growing in the soil, geese, chickens and turkeys, dogs and cats, a field of pigs with a butchers stall. The path then drops to the lower level, crossing a bridge with running water, where a group of shepherds are huddled round a flock of sheep, and a camp-fire which actually appears to be alight. Finally is the stable, with the Holy Family clustered around the sleeping baby. We are both entranced. In my life I have never seen anything remotely like this, and the whole effect is spellbinding.

Different angles reveal even more detail, a haberdashery stall with bales of material, a windmill with sacks of flour, a herd of cattle with farm workers.

Tearing ourselves away, and vowing to return the following week, we head to the next church, Santa Maria. Now we know what we are looking for, their Belen is easy to spot, in pride of place on the far side of the building. The same basic details of course, but a completely different layout, different figures, maybe not as big as San Raphael but equally as impressive.

We emerge into the evening air, slightly breathless, and utterly enchanted. 'There is another ancient church at the bottom of the hill, near the fountain' Chrissie reminds me,'let's check that out, see if they have one too.' So down the steep cobbled street we amble, to the chur of San Francisco, which appears to be about to close, although the priest welcomes us and bids us enter. We immediately spot their Belen, in pride of place at the far end of the building, and I shake my head in wonder. Instead of different levels like the first two, this one slopes steeply for it's entire length, a mountain stream cascading down the middle, with the Roman fort at the top, then the village laid out either side. Kings, shepherds and townsfolk are making their way down the steep mountain tracks to the stable and manger at the bottom, but the most incredible feature is the lighting, which is constantly changing, to mirror day and night. From moonlit darkness, through the grey light of dawn, the full sunshine of the daylight hours, the orange glow of sunset, and back to night-time, illuminated by the guiding star. Truly unbelievable. The priest comes up behind us. 'Estupendo' I whisper, and he beams with pride, and shakes us warmly by the hand.

'Well, which one do you think was the best?' Chrissie asks, as we depart the church.

'Well, it's not a competition' I reply, 'but..'

'Ah but it is a competition' she interrupts, 'look at this leaflet. I picked it up inside, there are three categories of prizes, churches and other religious establishments, shops and offices, and private individuals. And here on the back, look, is a map of the various entrants. Tomorrow and the rest of this week we can visit the others.'

I study the leaflet, all written in Spanish of course, and in particular the map. 'There is a private house in the street below ours, we can visit that one on the way home. It says they stay open until nine each evening. Shall we do that?'

So homewards we head, turning into the street below. Approaching the house, a small crowd has gathered outside, several of whom are holding glasses and nibbling biscuits. A middle-aged lady spots us, 'come, come' she smiles, and ushers us inside the tiny cottage. Sat in one corner are an elderly couple, they look to be in their eighties at least, very frail but bursting with vitality. 'My parents' she announces, 'and here is the Belen.'

In the other corner is a table-top Bethlehem, much smaller figures of course but everything is present, the buildings clearly home-made but a perfect depiction of the Nativity. 'My parents have been married almost sixty years, and my father made the stable when they were first married.' I am choking up, and I can see that Chrissie is wiping away a tear. 'I speak little Spanish, but I want to say that your Belen is beautiful!' I tell them. 'We have just been to San Francisco, and yours is better!'

The old lady launches into a dialogue about how the pair of them have always loved Nativity scenes and how her husband made the stable, most of which I am able to follow, more or less. The daughter then arrives with two glasses full of a clear liquid, and a plate of large home-made biscuits. 'Annie and Roscoe, Thomas' she announces, gesturing us to help ourselves. We do, I take a sip of the drink and the top of my head almost blows off. Firewater! What is this vicious stuff? Tears come to my eyes and the back of my throat is ablaze, I hastily take a bite of the biscuit to try to drown the aniseed taste, but my eyeballs are stinging and I am in imminent danger of self-combusting.

Chrissie meanwhile seems unaffected, she is sipping the drink and nibbling the biscuit, 'Oh this is nice!' she purrs.

'Well have mine, for God's sake' I whisper throatily, 'before I actually die!'

Eventually we make our escape, having offered profuse thanks to our hosts, and we wend our way, unsteadily in my case, back home. 'They had very English-sounding names, Annie and Roscoe Thomas' I point out, 'well maybe not Roscoe, but Annie Thomas sounds very British. And what the hell was that fiery brew? Tasted a bit like Pernod to me. My innards are burning!'

Chrissie chuckles. 'Well I thought it was lovely, we must try to find out what it was, and if you can buy it anywhere. I wouldn't mind a bottle for Christmas! Tell you what, though, I'm looking forward to visiting the rest of the Belens!'

A couple of days later we are at the library again, and are relaying details of our Belen-visiting evening. 'For me, the best Nativity scene, the most emotional, was at the house of a lovely old couple, Annie and Roscoe Thomas' I explain. They have been married almost sixty years and have open-house each evening. They even gave us a drink and a biscuit!'

I can see mouths twitching around the table. 'They give you anise drink, and big round biscuit?' giggles Jose.

'Yes!' Chrissie replies, 'lovely it was, I want some for Christmas, what is it called?'

The Spaniards are now in fits of laughter, Jose in particular has tears running down his face. 'Annie and Roscoe Thomas are not their names' he splutters. 'Annie' is *Anise*, it made from botanical planta, is ver traditional in Andalucia in Chreesmas. And 'Roscoe' is *Roscon*, biscuit made in *casa* house of the persons. And 'Thomas' is *tomas*, it mean 'you take'. So these person they say you, *anise y roscon, tomas!* 'Take anise and roscon!' and he dissolves into laughter.

I glance at Chrissie, who is also wiping tears from her eyes. 'I told you Annie Thomas was not her name!' I chuckle. 'You are supposed to have the Spanish 'O' Level around here!'

She is still drying her eyes. 'Well I only got grade 'C', and it was forty-odd years ago!' she confesses.

'Did you see shitting gypsy?' asks Pili.

I stare at her in disbelief. Did she actually say that? 'Pardon?' I ask.

'Shitting gypsy, did you see shitting gypsy, at Belen?'

I am dumbfounded. Pili, indeed all the Spaniards at the conversation group, is well educated, and the last person I would suspect of racist sympathies.

Besides, gypsies are a part of Spanish culture, especially here in Andalucia. Flamenco dance and music is derived in part from gypsy culture, and I am unsure how to reply. My mother had a ready response for these situations, 'We are all God's children', and I decide not to mince my words. 'Estamos todos los hijos de Dios' I state, which might or might not be the precise translation, but it will do.

Pili looks aghast. 'No no no! she cries, 'I am not be, how you say, *racista*, I mean is tradition to have figure of shitting gypsy in Belen. Is from Catalonia, always in Belen there is figure of gypsy, take shit.'

Jose takes over the explanation. 'It is tradition here to have figure of gypsy, he hide in Belen, like this.' And he stands, then squats down, mimicking someone having a poo. 'Is called *caganer*, some years they have famous person having caka, one year was Barack Obama, one year Princess Kate, one year your queen, the Pope, Michael Jackson, they all have caka in Belen.'

Juan Carlos meanwhile is tapping away on his smart-phone, and produces a photo of a crouching figure, backside exposed, a brown, curled pile of faeces beneath him. As a joke it is possibly hugely amusing, depending on your sense of humour I suppose, but in a religious scene depicting the birth of Christ? Appalling, although not for the first time we have to remind ourselves we are in someone else's country, these are their customs, and if they wish to portray the Pope defecating behind the manger, who are we to criticise?

I turn to Pili, 'I am sorry, I thought you were being disrespectful.'

She laughs, 'No don't worry, is a very strange tradition, a lot of Spanish people don't like. You no have shitting gypsy in England?'

Now it's my turn to laugh. 'We don't have Belens in Britain, or I have never seen one. We have the Holy Family, kings, shepherds, but not a whole village, I have never seen anything like this, and I think it is wonderful. I wish we could have one in our house!' Chrissie nods her agreement.

'Oh but you can!' cries Juan Carlos, 'they sell these figures, sheeps, wises men, how you say, the house where live donkey?'

'A stable' giggles Chrissie, 'where do they sell these things?'

Suddenly the Spanish are all talking at once, a not unusual occurrence. 'Bazaar Chineses' shouts Jose.

'Multibuys' Rafi suggests.

Actually Multibuys gets several votes, the general consensus being they have more choice. 'Is this place Multibuys an English shop, by any chance?' I ask.

Rafi laughs, 'no, they are Espaniss people, but they use Eengliss name, they think they more sophistication! This ver popular here, use Eengliss words. This why Espaniss people want learn Eengliss!'

Chrissie turns to me, 'well I know where we will be going this evening!' she giggles.

So for our evening *paseo* we head to Multibuys, having been given the relevant directions. We don't need the whole Bethlehem village, if we can get a holy family, three wises men, some sheeps and a house where live donkey, we will be happy. The shop turns out to be double-fronted, and straight away we can see we are in for a treat. Half the floor space has been given over to Nativity items, a true Aladdin's cave of stables, inns, Roman forts, market stalls, windmills, wells, as well as every type of figure, from the Holy Family, wise men, angels, Roman centurions, and assorted villagers, camels, sheep, pigs, goats, cats and dogs, and bizarrely, peacocks and storks. Plus the infamous caganer. 'So it was true' laughs Chrissie, 'the renowned shitting gypsy!' The only figures which appear to be missing are shepherds.

'And look at the prices!' I whisper in amazement. Most of the buildings are one Euro, the Holy Family two Euros, as are the wise men, and the villagers are five for a Euro.

'Blimey, we could get a whole Belen for about a tenner!' laughs Chrissie.

'Well why not?' I ask. 'I have a sheet of chipboard in El Woodshed, about six by three, to use as a base, there are two old bedside cabinets in the spare room, we could stand the board on those, and hey presto, we have the basis for a great display. We could even enter the competition! The only thing is, I have to make the stable myself, it's a tradition!'

My wife looks puzzled, 'what tradition?'

'You remember' I remind her, 'the original Nativity, when we got married, I made the stable for that, so I shall make this one, for our first Spanish nativity!'

She bursts out laughing. 'What, in 1977? That is hardly a tradition! Plus you were moaning about how much work you and Del have on at the moment. Just buy one, they are only a Euro!'

I shake my head decisively, 'no, it's only a few bits of rustic wood, won't take me half-an-hour, well an hour max.'

Chrissie sighs. 'That means it will be ready by Easter, I know you, it will have dovetail mitres, spigots, twisty bits, whatever you call it. You will be sawing, drilling, planing, and swearing, well into the New Year. You will have saw-cuts on your fingers, splinters, glue in your hair. Then you will have to varnish it, or paint, and by the time it's finished, the three kings will have gone home!'

'Right! That does it!' I snort, in mock anger. 'I will knock up a house where live donkey, before you can say 'shitting gypsy! Just choose the figures you want, and let's get out of here. I have some sawing to do!'

So we choose the basic Nativity, minus the shepherds of course, a few buildings, the Roman fort and a couple of centurions. More can be added when I have made the stable, and we can see what space there is left for peacocks and storks. A couple of evenings later Chrissie is out for a Christmas drink with the Spanish girls from the conversation class, so I am trolling round the Chinese bazaars, of which there are three in town, searching in vain for shepherds, of which there are none. We have sheep in our village, which is taking shape nicely, although the stable still needs a bit of work... Our woolly creatures need someone to tend them however, and I am getting increasingly desperate. Whoever heard of a Nativity without shepherds? Suddenly, in the final bazaar, I unearth a set of three shepherdesses. They look quite cute to me, and being a New Man and all that, I see no reason why our lambs cannot be guarded by girls. This appears to be the last set, so I am tempted to buy them, but I suppose I had better check with the boss, given that I am still in the dog-house for failing to complete the stable.... So I send her a message asking her to meet me when she has finished. Sure enough, half-an-hour later she arrives, looking slightly the worse for wear.

'Anneee!' she giggles, 'they gave me Anneee!' and digs me playfully in the ribs.

Oh no, not the local fire-water! 'Right, listen up, if you can' I laugh, 'I have found a set of three shepherdesses, the last set in the entire town, so I suggest we get them.'

She tries to focus her eyes. 'Shepherdesses? I am not having shepherdesses! They will be up all night chatting, gossiping, bitching about who has the biggest bum, about the dress the other one was wearing. The sheep will all escape too, and we will have to draft in some men-shepherds to get them all back!'

So much for sisterly solidarity. 'Well at least come in the shop and have a look at them' I suggest, 'I think they are quite pretty, and none of them have big bums!' So she follows me into the bazaar, where I carefully unpack the figures from their box.

She gives them a sidelong glance, 'well I'm not having that one there, she looks pregnant to me, she must have been sleeping with the Roman centurions, I am not having that tart in my Nativity! And that other one, she looks like a right stroppy mare. No, it's men-shepherds or nothing.' I decide not to argue. She's been on the anneee, after all. 'Besides,' she hisses through gritted teeth, 'we don't have a stable yet, DO WE?'

The following evening, our village is really starting to take shape. We have some foil paper with moons and stars which we have pinned to the wall to mimic a moonlit evening in Bethlehem, and the base is covered by Christmas paper depicting a snowy village scene, and the whole thing looks really rather good, for a first effort. There are some areas to fill in, we need a few more people and animals, and a small group of shepherds wouldn't go amiss, and the stable is still not yet complete, due to delays with dovetail mitres, spigots and twisty bits. And a deep slice on my thumb. Otherwise, it looks pretty damn good.

Suddenly there is a knock on the door. 'If that's the neighbours, don't let them in,' Chrissie whispers,' they know we are building something but I don't want them seeing the Belen until it's finis….'

'Good evening Loli and Isabel!' I cry, opening the door wide, 'come and see our Belen!' Our neighbours crowd into the hall, I can feel Chrissie's eyes burning holes in the back of my skull, but I don't care, I have a surprise up my sleeve.

'Neighbour, how clever!' cries Isabel.

'Beautiful!' shouts Loli, 'but you have no shepherds, or stable! You can't have a Belen without shepherds, or a stable!'

I smile brightly at my crazy neighbour. 'There are no shepherds for sale in Santa Marta!' I explain. 'Shepherdesses, but Chrissie doesn't want women in our Belen!'

My wife meanwhile mimics gossiping women. 'Bla bla bla, bla bla! *Culo grande*!' Big bum. Our neighbours burst out laughing.

'Spanish shepherdesses!' I add 'BLA BLA BLA BLA BLAAAAAA!'

Just then another knock comes at the door, I open it to discover Gaffer and Diane. 'Now then lad!' he cries, pushing past me.

'Oh do come in, Diane' I announce, only half joking, to his wife.

Gaffer then spots our neighbours, 'Ola' he shouts, thereby exhausting his Spanish conversation skills. Loli and Isabel are not keen on Gaffer, they think he is a drunkard, which just might be a fair approximation of the truth. He spots our Belen, which is actually impossible to miss. 'Blooody 'ell, is that a Nativity, or Manchester Piccadilly?'

Diane meanwhile is studying our figures in detail. 'Tha's got no shepherds, nor no stable! Oop north we allus 'ave t' stable. Jesus were born in stable. Well 'e were in Bradford, any'ow.'

Gaffer guffaws, 'Jesus weren't born in Bradford, tha' dafty pie-can, 'e were born in Jerusalem!'

I turn to our Spanish neighbours. 'He said we have no shepherds or stable' I explain. 'Just a moment, please', and I nip into the dining room, and emerge with three sheep-tenders, which I hand to Chrissie. 'Present for you, men-shepherds, let's hope they don't stay up all night talking about sex and football!' She is delighted, and places them next to their flock, if four lambs can be so described. Then I pop back into the dining room, and re-emerge with my *piece de resistance*, a home-made stable, a simple, rustic structure, not a dovetail mitre, a spigot or a twisty bit in sight.

'*Que chulo*!' cries Loli. 'Did you make that yourself?'

I hand the structure to Chrissie, 'you swine!' she laughs, you really had me going there! It's beautiful, I can't believe you made it in secret. So what about the huge gash on your thumb?'

Now it's my turn to chuckle. I have a length of electrical tape wrapped around the end of my digit, which I carefully pick off to reveal no wound whatsoever. 'There you are, no saw cuts, no splinters, no glue in my hair, no dovetail mitres or spigots, just one super-deluxe stable, delivered on time and under budget!'

'Don't knaw why tha bothered, lad, they sell stables in t' Chinese bazaar for coople o' Euros' Gaffer laughs. 'Blooody waste o' time if ye ask me, I said, blooody waste o' time.' *Yes but nobody's asking you, Gaffer, are they?*

I turn to Loli and Isabel, 'he said you can buy stables in the bazaar for two Euros.'

Now Loli has told us she is barely able to read or write, but she is an avid crafter, able to turn her hand to embroidery, needlework, knitting, painting, you name it, all to near-professional standard. Last week she gave Chrissie a hand-painted tile featuring the Real Madrid football club crest. She snorts in derision at Gaffers comment, 'tell him he is a drunken idiot!' she cackles, 'your stable is very clever!' and the two sisters edge towards the door, and after some cheerful *adios*, they disappear next door.

'What the 'ell did she say?' asks Gaffer, 'I can't understand a blooody word o' Spanish, tha knaws!' *That's probably just as well, Gaffer, probably just as well!* 'Oh she just agreed with you' I lie, and can see Chrissie almost stuffing her knuckles into her mouth.

'Ooh by the way, what ye doin' f' Christmas? Diane asks, just as the pair of them are preparing to leave. 'Ye can coom to oos, we got a gollopin' gert turkey, all the trimmin's like, stoofin', Paxo tha knaws, gravy, real gravy, Bisto tha knaws, Christmas cake, mince pies, all from Iceland tha knaws, Del-Boy is coomin', we're 'avin karaoke, watch Corrie, an' that Soothern poncey lot EastEnders, it'll be grand! Mek a change for ye t'watch English telly, like, on a decent size telly, 'stead o' that blooody antique Spanish telly.' This is the longest speech I can recall Diane ever making, during which I have been frantically considering how best to reply. Pete and Sarah with the holiday bungalow at the campsite had talked about coming over, and suggested getting together with Ed and Celia, although nothing has been finalised yet.

Chrissie comes to my rescue. 'Where did you get a turkey, and Paxo, Bisto, mince pies and Christmas cake round here?' she enquires, clearly playing for time.

Gaffer taps the side of his nose. 'We fetched it from England, in t'van. We got a camper van, fetched it all over last summer, two 'undred tins o' baked beans tha knaws, all oos English food.'

My head is starting to spin. 'So you have a camper van, which you stocked with a turkey, all the trimmings, baked beans and all the rest, and you drove it to Spain last summer? So didn't the turkey, you know, go off in the heat on the journey? What did it take to drive down, three days, four days?'

Gaffer taps his nose again. 'T'turkey was in t'fridge, in t'van, lad. Iss in t'freezer in kitchen, now, like. Baked beans iss still in t'van, well most of 'em!' he laughs, patting his stomach. 'Some on 'em's in 'ere!'

'So where is this camper van now?' I enquire.

'Parked oop, edge of town, side o' t'road.' Gaffer winks, as if conveying some State secret. The penny finally drops, we have seen a crappy 1970's UK-registered camper, painted in a fetching shade of beige, seemingly abandoned on a piece of waste land. Gaffer's baked bean store!

'But they sell baked beans here, in the supermarkets' I point out.

'Oh aye!' bellows Diane, 'blooody Heinz, a Euro a tin! Owers were Cost-co, what were it Keith, 22p a tin?'

Gaffer splutters, 'nay, 21p, think on that lad, not a blooody Euro, 21p a tin!' *Yes and I bet they are cheap-tasting rubbish with thin, watery tomato sauce.*

'Anyway', I continue, deciding to discuss it further with Chrissie, before committing ourselves, 'we have half-promised to go to the caravan for Christmas, our friends with a holiday bungalow there are coming over, and have asked us to join them.' Diane's face actually falls, she looks genuinely disappointed. 'But only half-promised' I hastily add, 'we haven't actually heard if they are still coming, obviously we'd prefer to stay here, but you understand we need to check with them before we know what we are doing.' I am trying to catch my wife's eye but she is studiously looking the other way, leaving me to blunder on alone.

'S'all reet lad, give oos a shout, noo 'urry like, there's two week yet t'Christmas' chuckles Gaffer, and the pair of them head to the door.

'Not a clue!' I protest to Chrissie, when we are finally alone. 'Not a nod, not a wink, not a shake of the head, nothing! Thanks very much, allowing me to dig myself into a big hole!'

'On the contrary' my wife replies, 'I was enjoying hearing about your Christmas in the caravan, are you having turkey with all the trimmings? Mince pies? Pudding, brandy butter, chocolate log? Am I invited?'

I start to laugh, 'well I'll tell you what we're not having, blooody Cost-co baked blooody beans, that's what!'

Chrissie puts her head in her hands, starts running her fingers through her hair. 'Actually, I don't think I can face it' she whispers.

'Oh I think it will be fine' I reassure her, 'Del will be there, we can all have a laugh, Corrie is only half an hour, EastEnders the same, I can do my Elvis impersonations on the karaoke, we can all have a sing-song!'

She looks up, deadpan, 'it's none of those things I can't face, even though the thought of you singing is truly awful, but the horrifying prospect, having seen Gaffer chewing that octopus in the bus station the other week, is watching him gnawing away on a turkey leg!'

We are both laughing now. 'OK' I smile, 'what if I tell Diane we are coming, but only if Gaffer has turkey breast! Would that be in order for you?'

Chrissie is still giggling, 'not really, because you know what he's like, it will be 'OOOH I LOOVE A BIT O' BREAST, ME! I'M A REET BREAST MAN THA KNAWS!'

'Well we can hardly say we will come only if Gaffer agrees not to make any sexist remarks about his food now, can we?' I chuckle.

Chrissie is still laughing, 'Of course we can go, as you say it will be great fun, but I want you to promise me one thing.'

I am serious all of a sudden. 'What one thing?'

My wife looks me straight in the eye. 'I need you to promise that, under no circumstances, will you perform Elvis impersonations!'

'Fair enough, I can agree to that' I grin. *Besides, I do a fairly mean Elton John….*

CHAPTER 21. APPLE PIE, ANYONE?

It is Saturday afternoon, I am in Del's sitting room, and we are planning our work for the coming week. Several jobs have arrived at once and we are wondering how we can fit them all in before Christmas. Suddenly, a vile stench seeps into the room through the open door to the kitchen, a smell so horrendous that my eyes start to water and I have the overwhelming urge to retch. Del sees my reaction and quickly qualifies the situation. 'It wasn't me, it was the dogs.'

Yeah right, everyone blames the dog, although this sulphurous gas is so bad I doubt it could have come from a human being. Even Del. 'God, you won't believe the night I had last night' he continues, rubbing his hands wearily across his furrowed brow. 'Yesterday afternoon I caught the two big 'uns, Harley and Suzy, in the yard fighting over a dead carcass. It must have been a goat as the bones were huge.' His house backs on to the mountain, some of which is so steep that only the herds of goats can walk there, followed by wizened old shepherds accompanied by their mangy old dogs. 'I reckon there was a dead goat which got flung into my yard, or perhaps one got in by accident and they killed it, anyway there were bits of flesh everywhere, the little 'uns came out trying to grab bits (he has five smaller dogs and two puppies,) and it was absolute bloody mayhem. Eventually I managed to get the bones and other bits off them but not before they had eaten most of it. Then in the middle of the night one of the big 'uns barged into the bedroom and puked all over the duvet, it was pitch dark and I am slipping about covered in puke, I got the light on and found they had crapped all over the house in just about every room, there was crap and puke everywhere, and I have only just finished cleaning it all up. And they have all been farting all morning too. I tell you, I have had just about enough.' He looks at me pleadingly. 'You don't fancy a puppy do you?'

We rapidly finalise our plans and I hurriedly make my way outside and gulp a huge lungful of sweet, fresh, mountain air. As I am heading off he calls me back. 'Wait, I have a present for you' he shouts and disappears inside the house, reappearing with a plastic carrier bag. 'I have baked you an apple crumble.' Inside the bag is a pie dish containing the crumble, I stammer my thanks and say that it will go nicely with a cup of tea when I get home, although the thought of eating something which has been in that house is more than I can begin to imagine.

I head off up the street and meet up with Chrissie, who has been waiting patiently by the natural mountain spring-water fountain, as she cannot bear to hear two blokes banging on about cement and bricks and tiles any longer. I show her the crumble. 'Well best of luck with that, sunshine!' she laughs. 'You are on your own there!' Yes, quite.

We continue our walk round the far side of the mountain and descend back into town down the hairpin bends, me still carrying the bag containing the crumble. As we reach the outskirts of town I hear a scuffling behind me, Chrissie screams in fright and I turn to see two huge dogs about three feet behind us. I jump in fright and my heart skips several beats, until I realise that luckily the dogs are inside a wire fence, but they certainly gave me a scare and Chrissie is holding her head and shaking. 'It's that bloody crumble they can smell' she shouts. 'For God's sake give it to them.'

I open the bag, pull out the crumble, and am about to scoop it out of the dish and hurl it over the fence when I am overwhelmed by shame and guilt. 'I cannot do it' I tell her. 'He baked it especially for me. I have to eat it, I really do.'

'Well if you get the raging craps don't blame me' she continues. 'Don't come to me looking for sympathy.'

I put the pie back in the bag and look over at the dogs, who are sitting patiently inside the fence. One of them even raises a paw. 'Sorry guys' I tell them. 'This is for me.'

And I have to say, despite its somewhat dubious provenance, the pie was absolutely delicious. Worthy of a five-star restaurant. If you are ever in this part of the world, call in for a slice. Just avoid the puke, and you will be fine.

So Monday morning and Del and I are on yet another roof. The roof in question belongs to our friends Tony and Jo, we fitted a wood-burner for them last week and Tony mentioned that their roof was leaking. Closer inspection revealed a lot of broken mortar on the roof ridge and gullies, so Del and John to the rescue! I am on the single storey kitchen roof with my mixing platform (an old door) surrounded by bags of thick white waterproof mortar 'Gordo', several buckets of water and a collection of trowels, while Del is up on the top of the roof as he is lighter and nimbler than me, plus a better plasterer. Every now and then he shouts down and lowers his bucket on a rope, which I fill with Gordo and he hauls it back up. Consequently I have periods with little to do but admire the view, although I do notice a large crack in the mortar in the wall near where I am sitting, so I get the trowel and fill the crack, then re-render an area about 4 feet long. 'Oi' comes a shout from above, and I look up to see Del peering over the edge, 'stop bloody doing free work!'

'This isn't free work, you Cockney toss' I yell back, 'it's a free sample. When Tony sees how good this looks, we might get the contract for re-rendering the whole house. So eff off back up and get on with your work.' His reply is thankfully carried away on the breeze….

I get back to admiring the view, something I seem to have spent half my life doing, and what a view it is. The cottage is in a small hamlet of around ten houses, completely surrounded by olive trees which stretch away down the valley to the mountains in the distance. The olive harvest is in full swing and I can hear the gentle buzz of the machine the pickers use to shake the trees, then the thwack of their long sticks against the branches to dislodge the last remaining olives. It is the sound of Andalucía in the winter. So intent am I on the view that I fail to see the half-filled bucket of Gordo flying through the air, which strikes me painfully on the side of my head and shoulder, before bouncing off the roof in front of me and disappearing into the garden. I unleash a string of abuse at Del, including questions on the validity of his parent's marriage, and his sexual orientation. 'Sorry mate!' he laughs, 'it just slipped from my grasp.'

A likely story. Another couple of inches to the right and the bucket would have hit me square on the head, probably knocking me off balance and off the roof. I text Kelly, my former colleague back in the UK, asking for my old job back, although I am not really serious. Yet.

Next day we are back at Tony & Jo's again having won the contract to completely re-render the back and the two sides of the cottage, so impressed were they by my free sample. A fact of which I constantly remind my colleague, over the course of the morning....

Our first job is to dismantle a rickety old lean-to pigsty so we can gain access to the back corner of the house, Del is balanced precariously on the roof of the sty removing the old tiles, and I am inside pulling down the canes and old mortar which support the tiles. Suddenly, there is an ominous cracking sound,my colleague shouts something resembling 'OH F*CK' and a large wooden beam and lump of plaster drop onto my shoulder. The other shoulder I might add, well at least I have a complete set of bruised shoulders now. I have bits of plaster and dust all over my head and I stumble over the rubble and out into the fresh air, looking for someone to whom I can administer a good kicking, but Del is still clinging to the remains of the roof. 'Quick' he shouts, 'the whole bloody lot is gonna come down, get hold of my legs.' I position myself under him and he wraps his legs around my neck. Now, there are plenty of people on the internet who would pay a lot of money to have this done to them, but having a man's crotch around my face is not my idea of a good time, so I quickly grab his torso and half-lift, half-drag him clear of the roof, and he shimmies down my body to the ground. He pinches my cheek with his fingers, 'I didn't know you cared, darling' he whispers, and we both dissolve into laughter.

With the pigsty out of the way I can begin poking cement in the cracks and holes in the back wall, a process known in the trade as 'poking cement in the cracks and holes.' I can also get a closer look at a curious foot-square hole in the top of the 1960's lean-to kitchen wall, which Tony and Jo are puzzled about. It cannot be an air vent as there is no corresponding hole inside the kitchen, so up the ladder I climb, the first human to view inside the hole for around fifty years. What I see when I get my face level with the hole is a huge shock, as the cavity is about two feet wide and filled to the top with fresh earth and straw

A couple of months ago, Tony & Jo had an infestation of mice, caused in part to Tony's habit of bringing back meaty tapas from the bar, to feed to his dogs. One night he forgot and left the tapas in his bag, and next morning a hole had been gnawed in the bag, and the tapas was gone, to be replaced by a family of mice. Another reason might just been due to their peculiar back door, known in the trade as 'a plastic sheet.' Manuel the village carpenter has been promising to call and measure up for a new wooden door, but every time they ask him when he is coming he replies mañana. Spain is not the place to live if you want things done in a hurry. They were unable to put poison or bated traps down because of the dogs, and the humane traps proved useless, until one night Mother Nature intervened. Jo woke to find a three-foot long snake in her kitchen, and no mice, some of whom were presumably inside the snake. Then the thing just slithered away, but no one knew where. So is my nest where the snake lives? Are the mice in there? Or maybe larger vermin, like Uncle Bob and his family perhaps? Whoever lives there, they will not be too chuffed to have a fat Englishman poking his face in their front door, and quite frankly I am not that keen on having my features rearranged by the present tenant of the hole. Plus I am fifteen feet up a ladder, with a bucket of cement. To be honest I am spilling most of it on the ground, as it is very difficult to stuff the cracks and holes whilst simultaneously looking out for mice, snakes or rats.

'Try getting some in the holes.' shouts Del.

'Yeah easy for you mate,' I reply, in less than a friendly tone, 'what if something peers out of this hole and bites me?'

'Stuff some bricks in the hole then' he shouts.

'Hang on then' I reply, sarcastically, 'I'll just check my pockets and see if I have any bricks. Left pocket, mobile phone, right pocket, pack of Polo's, back pockets, nothing. Nope, I am fresh out of bricks up here.'

'Well bloody catch these then!' he shouts, and soon several large bricks get thrown up at me, which I catch like a line of slip fielders at Lord's, mortar up, and stuff into the hole, double quick. Back on the ground I try to text Kelly again, but I am shaking too much. Accountancy was never like this.

The next day we have filled all the holes and cracks and are ready to start applying a lovely thick white coat of Gordo. On one side of the house is a car port so we have erected one level of the scaffold tower inside the car port, with just a bit sticking out into the road so we can climb up onto the roof, where we have placed scaffold planks to take the weight of the ladders. The car port is uneven and sloping so the whole structure is a bit shaky, but its the best we can do. If Health and Safety happen to pass by we will probably be closed down, but in this isolated corner of Andalucia, unlikely. Del is up the ladder applying the Gordo and I am down below mixing it, it is hard work up and down the tower all day and by mid-afternoon I am just about exhausted. As I climb down the tower, for hopefully the last time today, I place my weight wrong, too far to one side, and the whole tower shifts alarmingly and I find myself slipping off. In desperation I grab the roof of the carport with one hand and the tower with the other, wrestling with all my strength to keep the whole structure upright, before gravity takes over and I fall in an ungainly heap on the ground. Del is up the ladder laughing hysterically, having seen the whole thing. 'You looked just like a rabbit caught in the headlights' he shouts down. 'Why didn't you just jump, you were only three foot off the ground?' Well instinct is to hang on of course, but I am too shaken to argue. I drag my aching body up and find a seat in the garden. I text Kim again, 'PLEASE get me my old job back.' The reply comes all too soon. 'The boss says he doesn't employ foreigners!'

The old man across the road has seen the whole charade and comes into the garden waving his walking stick, and carrying a basket of fruit. Persimmons, big and red and juicy, but he calls them *Kakas.* He shows me how to eat them, biting the top off and sucking out the sweet flesh inside. They taste like nectar, especially after the day I've had.

Del comes down off the ladder, rubs his hands through my hair, although whether this is a gesture of affection, or he is just cleaning the mortar off his fingers, I cannot say. 'Come on old son' he whispers. 'It's Christmas Eve, time we went for a pint.'

Blimey, I had forgotten it's Christmas tomorrow. Not even wrapped my presents yet. 'We're supposed to be going to Midnight Mass tonight' I announce.

'What time does that start?' asks Del.

'Twelve O'clock' I reply….'OK very funny! Look, it's been a long day, all right?' Tony and Jo, who have joined us outside, are laughing, Del is laughing, even the old man across the street is laughing. I grab another *kaka.* The olive pickers are packing up their gear, the sun is setting across the mountains, I feel a strange glow in my battered body. Nah, the old boss can stick his job. I look Del straight in the eye.' Right, pub, you're buying. Last one there is a pansy!'

CHAPTER 22. IT'S CHRISTMAAAAAS!

The week before Christmas, feeling in need of a rousing chorus of 'O Come All Ye Faithful', I ask our friend Juan if there is such thing as a Christmas Carol concert here. 'Yees' he replies, 'carol-ees at Chreesmas, for thees you must go to thee cock mass.' No, me neither. 'Thee cock mass' he continues, 'ees at middle night, on how you say, Chreesmas eeef.' *OK, sounds like Midnight Mass to me, but what is the cock business?* 'Thee cock, he crowd' he explains. 'He crowd three times. He sing.'

'You mean he crowed?' I ask.

'Yees, doodle doodle doooo!' comes the answer.

'A crowd is a group of people' I explain, 'like at a football match. The noise a cock makes is a crow.'

'I think crow is big black bird?' he queries.

'Yes, a crow is a big black bird' I confirm, but the song of the cockerel is the crow.

'Madre mia' he replies, 'Eengliss is ver complicated!'

Anyway' I continue, 'I thought the cock crowed three times at Easter, not Christmas?'

Juan Carlos laughs. 'Yees he did crowd at Easter, but you know thees ees Espain, we always late!' Enough said.

Chreesmas Eeef in Santa Marta dawned rather breezy, it clearly strengthened during the day, so much so that by evening it is blowing a gale. Must be the effect of the huge mountain behind the town, as one minute all can be calm, and the next huge gusts are whistling down the streets. Yet strangely enough, where Del and I were working, ten miles down the road in Tony and Jo's village, there was barely a ripple. Our whole house feels like a giant hand is trying to push it over, and up the street the banging of window blinds and shutters is almost deafening. Strong winds here present two problems not usually encountered back in the UK. Firstly, many of the old houses are painted with a lime-based whitewash, which is quick and cheap to apply but cracks and blisters in the summer heat, and come the first gale of the winter it literally blows off the walls and lands in broken white piles in the streets, gritty white particles gusting everywhere and liable to get in eyes and over clothes. Secondly, a prickly weed about a foot tall grows in the crevices of many of the ancient roofs during the winter, it dies back in Spring, bakes to a crisp in the summer, and again come the winter gales it blows around everywhere, sometimes forming football-sized tumble-weeds which get under feet and tangle in trouser legs.

As middle-night approaches, after a restorative hot-bath following my exertions on Tony and Jo's cottage earlier today, we head up to the church, where we are meeting Declan the mad Irishman, who has clearly been partaking of the Christmas spirit. As he approaches he looks as if he has a nasty case of dandruff. 'Sure will ye look at me coat?' he hollers, breathing beer fumes in my face. ''Tis like a feckin snowstorm up me street, that bleddy plaster blowin' every damn where. And look out fer those bastards' he bellows, as a particularly viscous-looking tumble-weed comes hurtling towards us. 'I got one of those feckers caught in me trousers, they're a divil to shift so they are , cut me fingers to feckin ribbons. I need a nice sit-down in church, so I do.' Indeed.

Inside the church is the usual collection of little old ladies, a couple of old farmers gossiping about the olive crop, but a surprising number of younger people, including, in the seats in front of us, two teenage girls and their mother. One of the girls is wearing a mini-skirt, the other has a lacy dress which is completely see-through, and the mother has skin-tight jeans. 'Sure will ye look at that?' whispers Declan, digging me in the ribs, pointing to the pew in front, 'I almost forgot me Sacraments!' The gale is still howling and the ancient doors of the church, twenty feet high and ten feet wide, are rattling and banging and it will be a miracle if we can hear the priest, and looking around I cannot see hymn books or carol sheets, or indeed an organist. There is however a collection of flamenco singers grouped to one side of the altar, complete with guitarist and a bloke with what looks suspiciously like a wooden drawer from a dressing table. The priest and his assistant appear and we are off, he is talking about shepherds, a star, angels, Mary and Joseph, and I can just about make out what he is saying over the din from outside, then the flamenco group start up, they are very good but there is no sign of 'Silent Night' or 'While Shepherds Watched', and we do not get to join in. Maybe later perhaps.

At one side of the altar is a stone arch, with iron bars across forming what looks like a cage, and from time to time the priest walks over to the bars and appears to be putting something through, like a keeper feeding the lions at the zoo. Due to the angle I cannot see what or who is behind the bars, clearly something or someone is in there, surely it cannot be a person, being kept in a cage, but whatever it is must be fairly tall as he is putting the stuff through at chest height. If it is an animal, it is a big one. The flamenco group strike up again, then the priest resumes and this time he approaches the bars and opens a gate, then steps smartly back to let whatever it is out. At this moment I have absolutely no idea what is going to emerge from the cage, and involuntarily slouch down in my seat in case whatever it is proves dangerous, so imagine my complete amazement when a diminutive middle-aged nun comes shuffling out and stands at the lectern. She begins speaking but the howling of the wind and the banging of the doors completely block out her tiny voice, and incredibly, the flamenco guitarist starts tuning up while she is speaking.

Late-comers are still arriving, causing viscous blasts of gale to roar through the doors, and one in particular causes Declan's head to snap to attention. It is a woman in black high-heeled leather thigh boots, complete with tight shiny leggings. She sashays down the aisle and with an expert flick of a buttock she turns in to the row of seats opposite the now extremely wide-awake Irishman. She looks as if she is on her way to a pole-dancing club but has just popped in for a spot of absolution beforehand, and for a moment I am unsure whether she is about to start twerking, which would certainly be an improvement on the entertainment so far this evening, but sadly with a heave of her cleavage she slides into her seat, whips out a smart-phone and logs onto Facebook. 'Ah bejaysus I fergot me phone' sighs Julius, displaying a surprising command of social networking terminology, 'I could have become her 'friend', and given her a huge 'like'. *Maybe that's what they meant by cock-mass?'*

Dragging our eyes back to the altar, the nun has now vanished, and the flamenco group have struck up again. 'All we need now is a bottle of sherry and a tapas' sighs Declan, tapping his foot to the beat.

'Well hang on, here it comes look' I reply, and sure enough the assistant steps forth with a large pitcher of wine which the priest hastily grabs, and before you can say 'free booze anyone?' a queue has formed in the aisle. 'You going up?' I ask the Irishman.

'Sure, that stuff is weak as old maids water!' he replies, but just then the two teenage girls get up and totter on their stilettos to the back of the queue. 'On second thoughts, me ole throat is gettin' a bit dry' he croaks, and displaying a rare turn of speed gets behind them in the line. The priest dispenses a small measure of wine to each in turn, then takes a huge gulp for himself and hands the pitcher back to the assistant, who whispers something behind his hand. The priest then empties the remains of the pitcher into his own glass and downs the lot in one, licks his lips and turns unsteadily back to the lectern. 'Ah will ye look at that tight ole beggar, he only gave me a sip' complains Declan, returning to his seat.

'He probably smelled you coming!' I laugh.

The service is drawing to a close. The priest asks us all to stand and shake the hands of those around us, Declan gazes lustfully across at the lap-dancer but she is wisely still engrossed on her phone, but at least he gets a smile from the teenage girls, and their mum, then after one more flamenco song we all file outside into the gale. It is Christmas Day. 'Ah, I'm not sure whether to stroll downhill into town and have a few, or head up to the square for one' says the notoriously indecisive Irishman. Just then the pole dancer comes clip-clopping down the steps of the church and turns uphill towards the square. Declan turns as if attached by a wire. 'Right I'll see ye tomorrow' he calls out, stumbling across the cobbles in her wake.

'Brush that dandruff off your coat, mind!' I reply, 'Merry Christmas!' But my words are swept away on the wind..........

Christmas Day proper dawns bright and sunny with not a hint of a breeze, and after a leisurely breakfast and the opening of our presents, we turn out thoughts to the main task of the morning, taking Diane and Gaffer's two dogs for a walk, thereby enabling our friends to prepare for the Christmas party. If I had to choose one word to describe their house, it would be 'chaotic'. Nothing is ever put away, so whenever we call in for a cuppa, we have to negotiate piles of laundry, TV remote controls, laptops, games consoles, half a dozen chargers all tied in knots, light-bulbs, batteries, computer mice, bags of sweets, and a huge tabby cat by the name of 'Blackie'. The dining room is even worse, featuring as it does a table covered permanently by a desktop computer and printer, boxes of pills, bank statements, fruit, framed photos awaiting hanging on the wall, and a Mexican sombrero. Getting the house ready for a lunch for five will be a monumental task, which is why we are planning a walk around the mountain with the dogs, which should take us several hours at least, after which we can hopefully tuck into the turkey, Paxo and Bisto which made the epic trip from England, last summer, in t'camper van. Hopefully however there will be no Cost-Co baked beans.

Their two canines are an odd pair, to say the least. The elder dog is a brown roly-poly mongrel known as 'Jess', who accompanied our friends from England. The other is a Spanish hunting dog, a huge golden beast resembling a cross between a lion and a tractor, a present from Del-Boy, out of his last unplanned litter, and going by the name of 'THA BASTARD', or 'Dougal' for short. Tha Bastard, sorry, Dougal, gets the blame for every mishap which befalls the household, of which there is at least one most days, seemingly. Gaffer and Diane are in the habit of nipping to the bar most lunchtimes, 'only for half-a-ower tha knaws', but which usually extends to half a day, during which time havoc is caused to their soft furnishings and house contents. Chewed mail, a raided food cupboard, soggy laundry, the cat cowering alarmingly on top of a dresser, a shredded pack of toilet rolls and a faeces-encrusted sombrero, all featured during the last fortnight. Suspicion rests strongly with Dougal, although hard evidence has proved elusive, particularly given that Gaffer and Diane usually arrive home three sheets to the wind, to find both dogs curled up companionably on the sofa.

So it is with some trepidation that we approach their house this morning, particularly as I have drawn the short straw in volunteering to lead Dougal around the mountain, although I am expecting to be greeted by the comforting aroma of roasting turkey wafting gently through the front door. Gaffer answers our knock, 'coom in lad, 'appy Christmas, bit of a crisis like, Di forgot to get t'turkey out t'fridge last night, so she's just runnin' it under t'tap.'

An indignant bellowing emanates from the kitchen, 'tha lyin' bastard, you forgot t'turkey, you said you were doin' t'bird, an' t'stoofin'. Never mind, it's just a bit icy in t'middle, twill thaw out in a minute.' Now I am not a food hygiene expert, but I was under the impression that frozen food, particularly poultry, had to thaw naturally, although I have what could be described as a 'robust constitution', so a drop of food poisoning is unlikely to trouble me too much. Besides, I could do with losing a few pounds... Luckily, Chrissie has already declined the turkey, on the grounds she doesn't eat meat, and has been promised a salmon cutlet instead. Hopefully that will not be under the tap with the turkey...

'Reet lad, fetch thesen a beer from t'fridge' offers Gaffer.

'Bit early for me just yet, thanks' I reply, 'we'll get the dogs out from under your feet. Where are the leads?' *Good question. I might as well have asked for the proverbial needle...*

'WHERE'S T'BLOOODY LEADS, DI? Bellows Gaffer.

'OW T'BLOOODY 'ELL SHOULD I KNOW' comes the not unexpected reply from the kitchen, I'M THAWIN' T'BLOOODY TURKEY!'

Gaffer starts frantically casting round the dining room, behind the computer, under the electric bills, inside the sombrero, he rummages among the pill boxes, all in vain. Muttering under his breath, he moves to the sitting room, where the laundry, the chargers, laptops, consols, mice, and the cat, are all unceremoniously turned over, before he gives up. 'Booogered if I knaw, lad' he sighs, rubbing his hand across his face. At that moment, as if stage managed, Dougal appears in the doorway with what looks suspiciously like two soggy dog leads dangling from his jowls. 'THA BASTARD!' Gaffer cries, 'see wot I mean? Yon dog'll be the death o' me!'

'A-Blooody-men t' that!' laughs Diane, emerging from the kitchen. 'T'turkey's all soft now, get stuffin', an' get this blooody 'ouse tidied, else we'll still be 'ere Good-Blooody-Friday!' Gaffer wrestles the leads from Dougal's jaws, wipes about a foot of drool on what looks suspiciously like one of Diane's freshly-laundered blouses from the clothes pile, winks at me conspiratorily, then carefully re-folds the blouse and replaces it in the pile.

'There ye go, lad, get them blooody 'ounds walked, then get theesens back 'ere for a reet slap-up Christmas! *As Diane might have said, A-blooody-men t'that!*

Leaving the rarefied atmosphere of the cottage, we head up the street, Dougal and Jess in tow. I have mixed feelings about this, as we have not walked a dog since our faithful retriever, Nelson, sadly died last year, and it seems strange at first. Up the deserted, narrow cobbled street, past the social club, across the plaza and on to the edge of town, where the road begins its tortuous ascent through the olive groves. It soon becomes clear that of the two hounds, Dougal is by far the better behaved, whereas Jess is proving a complete nightmare, pulling and straining on her lead, so much so that Chrissie can barely hold her back. 'Here, do me a favour?' she pleads, 'swap over, will you?'

I start to chuckle, 'hang on a minute, who said they didn't want to walk 'that Dougal'? Who asked for the little dog? Who wanted the girly bow-wow?'

My wife snorts, 'yeah, well I was wrong, OK? Just give me your dog, right now!'

I am really laughing, 'blimey, you're actually admitting you're wrong for once. It must be Christmas!'

Dodging what would have been a painful blow, we swap dogs and immediately I have my arm socket almost ripped out. For a little roly-poly mongrel, she ain't half strong, and I take off theatrically, before hauling my charge back to heel. 'Ah stuff this' I decide, 'she can go off the lead, there is nothing about, I'm damned if I'm having my arms torn off, even if we are getting a reet slap-up Christmas!' We are now on the 'wild' side of the mountain, one of our favourite walks, craggy peaks stretching to the horizon, a seemingly impenetrable barrier as far as the eye can see. Patchworks of olive trees line the steep-sided foothills, giving way to Mediterranean scrub-land, and not for the first time we marvel at the ingenuity of the farmers who presumably somehow manage to harvest their crop despite the acute gradients.

In a country dominated by olives, livestock farming is rare although there are smallholdings dotted around, and one such is ahead of us now. A sheep-farm in fact, albeit the strangest such enterprise I have ever seen, containing not a single blade of grass. There must be over a hundred sheep rooting around on the bare earth, their diet consisting of olive-tree clippings, and a pile of onions. The 'barn' is a precarious structure, built entirely from corrugated tin sheets, bed frames and what looks suspiciously like the front end of a Citroen 2CV. Still, the creatures seem happy enough, lambs gambolling between the ewes, clambering over the onions, the occasional ram regarding us disinterestedly, chewing contentedly on the olive branches. I have reined in Jess to prevent her squeezing her portly frame between the bed and the 2CV and causing mayhem, whereas Dougal seems entirely unconcerned by the woolly vista, preferring to cock his leg against a wooden pallet which is performing sterling service as a makeshift gate. 'I wonder what the meat tastes like, with a diet of olive leaves and onions?' I giggle.

'Better than that turkey you are about to eat!' laughs Chrissie, 'but can you imagine what their breath smells like?'

We have now reached the mountain pass and begin the steep ziz-zag descent back into town, where I again unleash Jess to avoid an untimely crash to earth on the gravelly surface of the road. Soon we are tapping on Gaffer's front door, he opens up and is immediately engulfed by his canines, who curiously appear to have missed him. 'GET OOPSTAIRS, THA BASTARD!' he cries, 'thee an' all, Jess', giving her a playful kick up the rear. The comforting aroma of a reet slap-up Christmas pervades the air, and entering the cottage I perform a rapid double-take; the house has been transformed, everything tidied away, dining table laid for five places , sitting room cleared, and curiously, the place seems to have doubled in size. Only the cat remains from this morning's devastation. Sitting in one of the armchairs is a small man in a beige-coloured suit, and it takes my eyes several seconds to adjust to the plethora of coloured Christmas lights which have been strung up over every available surface, and to recognise my business partner, Derek. 'Good God, look at you!' I cry. He is barely recognisable from the tramp-like, cement-encrusted specimen with whom I earn my pocket-money. He has shaved, bathed, and raided his wardrobe, sporting a cream silk shirt, a 'western-style' double-breasted waistcoat, a red bootlace tie and a pair of highly polished winkle-picker tan boots. A whiff of 'Old Spice' drifts across the room.

'Not God, but close!' laughs Del. 'And look at you! Last time I saw you, yesterday, you were flat on yer arse under a scaffolding with yer face in a bucket of mortar!' He steps forward and embraces Chrissie, ''Ello me darlln', and plants a wet slobbery kiss on her cheek.

'Blimey Del' she laughs, 'you're worse than Dougal! But don't you scrub up well!'

Laughing, Gaffer quickly produces glasses of beer and we relax in the miraculous space which has been created on their sofa and armchairs. 'Don't get comfy, dinner'll be ready in a minute' he advises, 'grab a seat round t'table, there's plenty o' room!'

'What did you do with all your, er, things, Keith?' I enquire.

'He booonged it in t'downstairs bedroom!' chuckles Diane, appearing from the kitchen. Ah yes, I'd forgotten the room next to the dining area, which doubles as a guest room apparently. Gaffer throws open the door, and there, in a massive disorganised pile on the bed, and all over the floor, are the items which occupied the rest of the house this very morning. Diane is correct. He did indeed just booong it in.

'Reet, get tha laffin' gear round this, lass!' laughs Gaffer, banging down a large plate bearing a huge mound of food in front of Chrissie. She stares in disbelief. Not only is there enough to satisfy a heavyweight boxer, it is all just piled in an ungainly heap, roast and boiled potatoes, sprouts, green beans, carrots and stuffing, all covered in a thick, brown, glutinous liquid which might or might not be gravy. Of the alleged salmon cutlet, there is no sign. As we gaze at the thick morass, a fugitive sprout makes a vain bid for freedom, rolling across the snowy white table-cloth, leaving a hideous brown trail in its wake.

'THA CLUMSY BASTARD!' cries Diane, 'LOOK WOT THA DONE TO ME TABLE CLOTH. FIVE BLOOODY MINUTES THAT BEEN ON T'TABLE.' Gaffer looks sheepish as he returns from the kitchen bearing two more plates, all piled high but this time with the addition of chipolatas wrapped in bacon, and about five thick slices of turkey each. This time he manages to spill what might be gravy onto the table just in front of Del, who has to scrape his chair back rapidly to avoid a nasty stain in the groin area of his spotless attire.

'Blimey mate' I laugh at my colleague, 'he almost got the bullseye then! You nearly had a brown gusset!'

'A bit like you did yesterday, hanging off that bladdy scaffolding!' chortles Del, you shoulda seen 'im Keef, rolling round on the floor like a bladdy girl, he only fell about a foot, but youda thought it was Mount Everest!'

'Tha blooody soft soothern jessie!' laughs Diane, plonking two more plates on the table, both equally mountainous, without spilling a drop. The pair of them sit down, Gaffer grabs his cutlery and is about to tear savagely at his brown mound, when I hold up my hand.

'Hold on, shouldn't somebody say Grace?' I enquire, keeping a straight face.

'Aye, for wot tha's got, think thee blooody sen grateful!' he laughs, spearing a chipolata and almost swallowing it whole.

Chrissie regards her thick morass with suspicion. 'Did you say I have a salmon cutlet, Diane?' she enquires of her host.

'Aye lass' confirms Gaffer, 'it's underneath, like. Tha's got t'eat a bit fust.' I know what my wife is thinking, *'why is there never a dog around when you need one?'* and *'where's the nearest plant-pot?'* And possibly *'how can I get rid of two-thirds of this pile without causing offence?'* One thing is for certain, she has never eaten salmon with gravy before.

'Actually Diane, you've given me far too much, can I have a small plate please, maybe you can save some of this for later?'

'Nay lass, just shovel it across here' splutters Gaffer, his mouth full of half-chewed turkey, and he lifts his plate towards her. 'Just scrape it off, like. I'm so 'ungry, I could eat a greasy 'oss between two mattresses.'

'That's a normal meal up north, innit?' Del cackles, 'greasy 'orses? An' I'm surprised to find cutlery 'ere, I thought you ate with your fingers in Yorkshire!'

'An' wot d'ye eat in that blooody Lunnon, then?' chokes Diane, 'Jellied eels? Pie an' licker? Whelks? Oranges an' lemons an' the bells of St Clements?'

Del adopts a deep theatrical voice, 'I do not know, cos I'm the great bell of Bow!'

And so the meal continues, plenty of north-south banter, some good old-fashioned sexism, five Brits enjoying a traditional Christmas lunch on the side of a mountain in southern Spain. But my abiding memory will surely be the sight of Chrissie eventually unearthing her salmon cutlet, scraping off the congealing grey-brown liquid from the grease-encrusted fish, cutting off a slice and rolling her eyes ecstatically to heaven as it slips down. Unless she is gagging as she swallows, who knows? Either way, she deserves an Oscar. 'Leave t'pots lad' cries Diane, as I volunteer for washing-up duties, 'stick telly on our Keef, Top of the Pops is on BBC 2, the old one from t' seventies, like, let's all have a blooody good sing-song!' And she sinks slowly into her armchair, 'reet, that's me done, I ain't movin' again till New Year!'

Gaffer meanwhile is scrabbling round like a drunken, headless chicken, 'where t'blooody 'ell is t' remote control, for t' telly? I knew just where it were to, before you tidied up!' He staggers unsteadily into the bedroom, from where the occasional strangled oath can be heard.

'DON'T MAKE A BLOOODY MESS IN THERE' Diane bellows, rising aggressively to her feet and charging into the room. 'Get out, tha gert lerrup, good job tha dick's tied on!' She turns towards Chrissie, and winks. 'Not that ee's much good wi' it!' She returns with the remote and slaps it into his hand, flopping once more into her armchair. 'Reet, I AIN'T blooody movin' again!'

Gaffer switches on the gigantic TV, flicks through a few channels, and suddenly a youthful Tony Blackburn is introducing an equally young-looking Slade, all dressed in the height of 1970's fashion. 'Blimey, look at them strides!' laughs Del, 'I 'ad a pair of them once.'

'Looks like you're still wearing them !' Chrissie giggles, 'talk about Saturday Night Fever!'

Del digs her playfully in the ribs, 'every nights a Saturday night, in my 'ouse, nah what I mean!'

'Yeah, which is why you always look like death on a Monday morning!' I chuckle.

Gaffer meanwhile is still lurching round the room. 'Ang on, I can't see boooger-all. Knaw where me glasses is, our Di?' His wife catapults up and storms menacingly into the bedroom, returning seconds later with his spectacles, which she opens and slaps painfully onto his face, one arm narrowly missing an eye, the other digging him in the ear.

Meanwhile, 'Wizard' are cavorting across the stage of the *Top of the Pops* studio 'And I wish it could be Christmas every day..' 'Only a blooody man could've written that shite!' Diane snorts, derisively. 'He wouldn't want Christmas every blooody day if he had to defrost t' turkey under t' tap!'

'So how often would you want Christmas then, Diane?' I smile. 'Every other day? Once a week? Quarterly?'

'Blooody never!' she cries, 'I 'ate blooody Christmas, me. Tis all work, ain't that reet, Chrissie?'

My wife adopts her most sisterly face, 'yes, but surely you had some exciting presents, Diane? What did Keith get you?'

'NOWT!' our friend growls, 'he didn't buy me bloody nowt!'

Del bursts out laughing. 'You mean, tight-fisted northern bastard!' he hollers, 'after all this wonderful woman does fer you, an' you ain't bought 'er nuffin'. May the fleas of a thousand camels invade yer arse....'

'Well tha's where you're wrong, lad!', Gaffer interrupts, 'o' course I got me darlin' wife summat, even though she just poked me blooody ear out!', and he scrabbles to his feet and lurches into the hallway, then clumps loudly upstairs, where a cacophony of barking greets his arrival in the bedroom.

'I 'ope 'ee ain't got me jewellery again' Diane complains, burying her head in her hands, 'ee allus buys me jewellery, an' 'ee got terrible taste. I got dozens o' blooody ear-rings, an' I don't want no more!'

More barking and shouting are heard from above before Gaffer appears in the doorway, glasses still askew, clutching a paper bag, on which is emblazoned the unmistakeable logo of the local jewellers. 'Here ye are, merry blooody Christmas!' he cries, tossing the gift into Diane's lap. His wife regards her present unenthusiastically. 'Go on then, open it up, you know you love surprises!' he urges. 'Cost me eighty blooody Euros, that did.'

Diane raises the crumpled bag in thumb and forefinger, 'but it's not a surprise, is it?'

Gaffer does his best to look offended. 'Course it's a surprise, you don't know what t' ell I got tha'!'

She unfolds the mangled wrapping, 'ooh look! Santa Marta Joyeria. Every boooger knaws what 'joyeria' means, even I knaw what it means, we walk past the blooody place every day. ISS THE BLOOODY JEWELLERS SHOP. YE COULDN'T EVEN BE BOTHERED TO WRAP ME BLOOODY PRESENT!'

Del is in stitches, 'you mean, tight fisted northern bastard! Not wrapping your wife's present!' he splutters.

Gaffer looks grievously wounded, 'EIGHTY BLOOODY EUROS THA KNAWS! he hollers, 'EIGHTY BLOOODY EUROS, AN' SHE'S BLOOODY MOANIN' ABOUT A BIT O' BLOOODY PAPER!'

I wipe the tears from my eyes, 'go on Diane, open it up, we are all agog!' I giggle.

'Ye might be a-blooody-gog, but I'm not a-blooody-gog. Iss ear-rings. I got more blooody ear-rings than t' Queen', and she delves into the bag and brings forth a small box, containing, as predicted, a pair of ear-rings, blingy Pandora-style, perfect for a teenage girl, but for a woman of a certain age?

Chrissie struggles to sound sympathetic, 'oh they're lovely, Di. They really suit your hair colour. Hold them up to your ears, look John, didn't Keith choose well?' She might as well be flogging a dead horse.

'I'll look like a reet slapper in these, ye useless twot, did ye keep t' receipt?' Suddenly I feel overwhelmingly sorry for Gaffer. He might well be a useless twot, but he is a well-meaning useless twot. He tried his best, and failed. There but for the Grace of God...

Del however is merciless. 'Ya useless northern twot!' he cries, tears rolling down his cheeks, his arm around Gaffer's shoulders, their faces almost touching. 'You Effed up again! But never mind, pour me a large glass of that single-malt ya got 'idden away, an' I'll forgive ya!'

My ears prick up. 'Single malt? Did someone mention single malt? Perfect for half-past three on a Christmas Day. And look, it's coming up to half-three!'

Gaffer brightens considerably. 'Oh aye, I forgot the Glen-mangy, See-You Jimmy give it me, I bin savin' it for a special occasion! Where's the Glen-mangy, Di?'

His wife scowls unhelpfully, 'in t' blooody dog, for all I care. Ow should I knaw?'

Suddenly there is a loud knock at the door. 'Oooo the blooody 'ell is that?' cries Diane, 'tell 'em t' boooger off. Its Christmas Day, an' there's no room in t' blooody inn!'

Gaffer staggers to the front door, returning with Jason and Sadie, who seem to be wearing exactly the same clothes they were when they turned up at our house-warming, six weeks ago. Black t-shirts and jeans.

'Bladdy 'ell Jase, you made an effort fer Christmas! You look like one of them goffs!' giggles Del.

Jason regards his little mate with disdain, 'well at least I didn't come as a Cockney spiv, did I? Where did you park your three-wheeler van?' The pair of them embrace, and suddenly we are all standing, hugging, kissing and handshaking. There is one major problem however. Well two problems actually. First, I still haven't acquired my glass of Glen-mangy, and secondly, where are the new arrivals going to sit? Chrissie is wedged between Del and me on the sofa, Gaffer and Diane have claimed the two armchairs, although our host has disappeared upstairs again, banging and crashing amid more raucous barking, before suddenly appearing with a pair of stripy deck-chairs.

'Bladdy 'ell Keef' cries Del, 'what time does the Punch an' Judy show begin? An' where's me candy floss?'

'Toffee apples!' I chuckle.

'Chips!' Chrissie smiles, 'and can I go on the donkeys please?'

Gaffer meanwhile is struggling, and failing, to erect one of the chairs. 'Ye useless twot!' cackles his wife, 'ee can't even put oop a blooody deck-chair!'

I take it from him, Jason grabs the other, when suddenly I spot something engraved on the wooden frame, in large capital letters. *B.U.D.C.* 'Hang on a moment' I advise Jason, raising my hand, 'these are stolen property, look, Brighton Urban District Council?'

'Tha blooody soft sooothern pansy!' Diane roars, 'iss not blooody Brighton, iss Blackpool!'

'Aye tha's reet lad' Gaffer confirms, 'Blackpool, tha knaws.'

I am trying desperately to keep a straight face, 'OK, let's get this straight, you went to Blackpool, stole two deck-chairs from the sea-front, then drove them all the way to Spain in your camper-van, together with a turkey, stuffing and about a million tins of baked-beans?'

Gaffer is nodding vigorously, 'too blooody reet, lad!' he confirms, 'well there is a blooody war on, tha knaws.'

I glance at my fellow guests, who all appear equally mystified. *A war?* 'A war, Keith?' I venture, ' which war would this be?'

Gaffer looks astounded at my ignorance, 'the war, tha knaws, we're at war with t' bastards!'

I rub my hand across my furrowed brow, 'and which bastards would these be? Bastards in general, or do you have specific bastards in mind?'

Gaffer is incredulous, 't' bastards on t' wrong side of t' Pennines!'

Del is doubled up with laughter, 'what, the Welsh, you mean?' Geography was never his strong point.

'Tha dozy sooothern Cockney twot!' Diane hoots, 'Lancashire! We're at war wi' blooody Lancashire! Tha knaws nowt!' Everyone takes a few seconds to process this latest nugget.

'OK' I continue somewhat nervously, unsure where this latest twist in the conversation is heading, 'so you and Keith are at war with Lancashire, is this a full-scale conflict, or are you just a little bit cross with them?'

Diane erupts indignantly, 'not just me an' 'im, all on us, tha dafty pie-can! Yorkshire, tha knaws! Yorkshire's at war wi' blooody Lancashire! Never 'eard o' t' War o' t' Roses?'

Everyone else bellows with laughter, but with a supreme effort I keep a straight face. 'I have some bad news for you Diane, that was over five-hundred years ago, and your lot lost! Richard the Third was defeated by Henry Tudor at Bosworth Field!'

Del is wiping tears from his eyes, 'I 'ad a Richard the Third in a field once!' he announces, 'ad to wipe me jacksie on a dock leaf!'

That is it, I am now crying with laughter, but Gaffer doesn't share the joke. 'Nay lad, tha's where you're wrong, see. A peace treaty 'as never bin signed, tha knaws! Officially, we're still at war wi' t' bastards. Teachers learned us that in school.'

Jason slumps back in his deck-chair, 'so you are maintaining a guerilla campaign against Lancashire, by, I don't know, going across the Pennines and nicking their deck-chairs?' he splutters.

'Blooody reet lad!' Diane confirms, 'an' iss not just deck-chairs, them knifes an' forks what we just 'ad oos dinner wi', we nicked them from that hotel in Preston, weren't it our Keef? An' the salt n' pepper set, where did that come from, Southport, weren't it?'

Del has meanwhile produced a large hanky from his jacket and is mopping his face, 'Bladdy lunatics, the lot of ya! Didn't they build a wall up there somewhere, keep you mad northern bastards out? That Roman fella, wass 'is name? Adrian-somebody?'

'Nay lad' Gaffer corrects my colleague, 'that were t' tossers, t' Jocks. Adrian built 'is wall to keep t' tossers oot!'

I fix our host with a stare, even though I can guess the true drift of his statement, 'that's a rather sweeping generalisation, Keith, some of my best friends are Scots, you can't call them 'tossers' in the twenty-first century, you know.'

Gaffer does his best to look apologetic, 'nay lad, I don't mean t' Jocks are tossers, I mean they are tossers, they go round oop there tossing blooody gert trees an' eatin' porridge, an' Adrian didn't want 'em coming t' England, chuckin' blooody gert trees round t' place. Imagine that in Leeds, lad, a load o' Jocks tossin' trees round 'Eadingley. What would Sir Geoffrey Boycott o' said aboot that, lad!'

I smile broadly at our host, 'well maybe if you'd had some tossers at Bosworth Field, you wouldn't have lost the War of the Roses! And speaking of wars, WHERE'S MY GLASS OF BLOOODY GLEN-BLOOODY-MANGY?

Sadie meanwhile is carrying a Christmas present, a rectangular-shaped object, maybe two feet by eighteen inches, and about an inch thick, clearly a photograph or a painting, which she hands to Diane. 'Here you go, just a little something for you both, Merry Christmas!' Diane stands and gives her guest a hug, then starts tearing the wrapping paper, to reveal a 3D image of a female religious figure, a head-and-shoulders shot, surrounded by a cheap plastic frame, a hideous, tasteless offering, maybe a booby-prize from a fairground, and certainly something no right-thinking person would have on their wall.

'Jesus blooody Christ!' cries Gaffer.

'No, not Jesus' laughs Del, clutching his sides, 'I reckon that's his Mum! 'an look, she's winking at you, Keef! The rest of us stare in disbelief, but Del is correct, the eyes and lips of the image are moving, in the light.

Gaffer is clearly having trouble focusing. 'She just told me to eff-off!' he laughs, 'look our Di, move t'picture again. There! She's winking at me, then telling me to eff-off! Chuck t' blooody thing in t' bedroom, and fer Christ's sake find t' Glen-blooody-mangy , shooot this whingin' sooothern bastard oop!'

Afternoon turns into evening, we sing along to Top of the Pops, then Karaoke, we watch EastEnders and Coronation Street, Diane speaks to her daughter on Skype, and we all join in a drunken rendition of 'White Christmas' across the internet. Meanwhile the beer is stored in the fridge, and Gaffer has told everyone to simply help themselves, and it on one such visit to replenish my glass that I stumble across a figure lying almost prone on the kitchen floor. I step back in shock to discover Jason, on all-fours, with his head in the oven, stuffing turkey into his mouth. 'Blimey mate' I whisper, 'don't let Keith or Diane catch you stealing their grub, they told us they were making bubble and squeak with the leftover veggies, for Boxing Day, and they expect that turkey to last them until the end of the week.'

'Well it's all right for you' he splutters, blowing turkey crumbs over the cooker, 'you've had lunch. I'm starving!' I am puzzled, Gaffer and Diane are generous hosts, so why didn't they invite Jason and Sadie to lunch. 'They did' he confirms, 'but it was too early for us, we don't get up until around four in the afternoon, and they said one o'clock. So we couldn't make it.' I am not sure how to reply to this, the first time we met the pair of them I felt they looked as if they hadn't seen the light of day for weeks, and this confirms it. Maybe they have some medical condition, a daylight allergy possibly, in which case living in the blinding sunshine of Spain is possibly not the best lifestyle choice. But this is not the time or the place for such a discussion, particularly as my new friend is now attacking the chipolatas, grabbing a couple of sprouts on the way past, then digging his fingers into the bowl of cold stuffing. I grab my beer and return to the action, where a boyish-looking Elton John, sporting all his own hair, is inviting us to 'Step into Christmas'.

'I stepped on a Richard-the-Third once, in a field!' cackles Del.

Suddenly, there comes an almighty commotion from the kitchen. 'THA BLOOODY GREEDY SOOOTHERN BASTARD, THAT WERE MY BOOOBLE AN' SQUEAK FER BOXIN'-BLOOODY-DAY! AN' GET THA BLOOODY 'ANDS OFF ME SAUSAGES!' Oh no, it looks like Jason has been rumbled. He comes into the room, looking decidedly sheepish, with an apoplectic-looking Diane standing menacingly behind him, brandishing a carving-knife. 'I went int' kitchen to cut t' Christmas cake an' choccy log, an' found this twot wi' 'is 'ead in t' blooody oven, stooofin' 'is blooody face wi' oos turkey!' She prods his behind with the tip of the knife, 'bend over, I'm gonna cut yer balls off, an feed 'em t' ower Jess!' and she breaks into a huge grin, giving the rest of us a sly wink.

'I wouldn't bovver girl,' laughs Del, 'ee's like Adolf 'Itler! 'Ee only got one!'

'And quite how do you know this, Del?' laughs Chrissie, 'is there something you want to confess today?'

I hold up my hands, 'can you leave any confessions until the New Year please Del, I'm going to be stuck up that scaffolding outside Tony and Jo's the day after tomorrow, and I don't want to be worrying about you creeping up behind me!'

'Or fillin' tha' crack wi' mortar, lad! chuckles Gaffer.

Diane reappears in the doorway balancing plates loaded with Christmas cake, 'never mind that, ye blooody soft sooothern poofs!' she cries, 'oo's fer a nice slice o' Fuengerola cake, from Iceland. Get tha' laffin gear round this!'

'I'd prefer some Iceland cake from Fuengerola, if you have any,' I smile, 'but if not…'

Diane still has the knife tucked under her arm, and she fixes me with a look. 'Right, Fuengerola cake it is, then!' giggles Chrissie, taking the plates from her host and distributing them round the room. 'But none for Jason, is that right Diane?'

For the last few weeks many of the clothes shops in town have had bright red underwear on display in their windows, tight briefs for men, lacy thongs and panties for the ladies. 'Ees tradition here give red interior clothes to you loves-ones, at Chreesmas' Juan had informed us at the library conversation group. 'Ees how you say, much sexy!' Indeed.

On the way back home that day, we again paused to admire one particular shop-window arrangement of much sexy interior clothes. 'Not sure about these little thongs on some of the huge Spanish back-sides you see in this town' giggled Chrissie, 'but how about we get Keith a pair of those pants, and give them to him on Christmas night, at the party, for a joke?'

I almost choked, 'Well thanks so much for that! There's an image which will surely come back to haunt me, in the middle of the night. Gaffer in a pair of skin-tight red briefs. Ugggghhh!'

Chrissie chucked again, 'Well don't worry if you don't fancy it, I just thought it would be a laugh, that's all.'

'Fancy it?' I spluttered, 'fancy it? Would you like to re-phrase that? If you mean would I think it a good idea, for a joke, then yes. But please, never again, in my lifetime, use the term 'fancy it' in conjunction with Gaffer in a pair of pants!'

So here we are, Christmas night, everyone the worse for drink, some more than others, and none more than Gaffer. I give my wife a nod and she reaches for her bag, produces our little gift and standing in front of our near-comatose host, places into his lap. 'Just a little something from us Keith' she smiles, 'and hopefully it will give Diane a nice surprise, too!'

Gaffer springs to attention, clutches a reluctant Chrissie in a huge bear-hug, then lurches towards me and wrings my hand, his face an inch from mine. 'Tha should'nta, lad' he belches, 'yer blooody nice people, fer soootherners!' and he starts carefully unwrapping his gift, but unable to focus, tosses it to his wife. 'Can't find me blooody glasses, lass, open this f' oos?'

His wife regards him without affection, 'they're on yer 'ead!' she chuckles, tearing open our present to reveal the bright red interior clothes, emblazoned with a Santa Claus and the logo *Feliz Navidad*. The whole room erupts. Del and Jason are crying for a modelling session, Sadie has her head buried in her hands , and Diane, for once, has lost the power of speech.

Meanwhile I start to sing, a throwback to my rugby-playing days, thirty-odd years ago. 'Get 'em down, you Zulu warrior, get 'em down, you Zulu chief, chief, chief!' And so he does, dropping his trousers in an instant, kicking off his slippers and struggling drunkenly to shed his trousers which are tangled round his ankles.

'Christ, no!' wails Diane, 'not 'ere,' and grappling her inebriated spouse in a head-lock, manhandles him towards the bedroom, kicking open the door which flies back on it's hinges, and throwing him inside. She emerges, rearranging her clothing, grinning widely, 'blooody drunken bastard!'

'Ya bladdy spoilsport!' cackles Del, 'we wanted to see 'is ole man!'

'Nay lad, tha didn't! she replies, 'besides, ye'd need a blooody microscope t' see it from ower there!'

'Point of order!' I cry, recalling the post-match rugby club, 'put it to the vote! All those in favour of a display of Keith's crown jewels say 'aye!' The men are unanimous, including a drunken shout from inside the bedroom. 'And those against cry 'nay!' There are only three female dissenters of course. 'The 'Ayes' have it! I chortle, 'this House calls upon Keith Braithwaite to display his wedding tackle, although in my position as Mr Speaker, and in consideration of the delicate nature of the Ladies here present, I am prepared to allow the display to be contained within a pair of Christmas briefs!'

And with that, the bedroom door catapults back, and there is Gaffer, clad solely in our Christmas present, apart from a sock which remains stubbornly clinging to one foot. And he starts to gyrate, one hand raised in the air, the other clutching his genitalia in what I assume he considers an alluring manner. 'Sex bomb, sex bomb, I'm a sex bomb!'

Del and Jason are roaring with laughter, Chrissie and Sadie have their heads buried in their hands, but Diane is decidedly unamused. 'THA BLOOODY DRUNKEN BASTARD' she yells, 'YE SHOW ME OOP, ALLUS YE SHOW ME OOP', and she charges across the room and shoulder-charges him back into the bedroom, where for a split-second in time he stands motionless, before slowly toppling backwards onto the bed with a sickening crash, sending a computer screen tumbling to the floor. Gaffer seems completely out cold, but his wife remains unconcerned. 'Leave t' drunken bastard there!' she hollers, 'if he's booosted t' computer, this'll be t' last blooody Christmas 'ee 'as!' As she slams the door, I get a fleeting glimpse of our comatose, red-brief clad friend, with the portrait of the Virgin Mary lying askew against the headboard. And I swear she is winking.

It's time to go home. 'Thank you so much Diane for a wonderful day' Chrissie enthuses, 'but are you sure Keith will be OK?'

'Oo blooody cares!' she laughs. 'Serve t' bastard right if 'ee dies. 'Ee's gonna die in t' mornin', anyroad, if me computer's booost. Get theesen 'ome, lass, don't worry about oos. If I need John t' dig oop t' patio in t' mornin', to bury t' bastard, I'll give thee a knock.'

'Double time tomorrow, mind, Diane' I remind her. 'It's Boxing Day, don't forget!'

As we head out the front door, she plants a big wet kiss on my lips. 'Worth ev'ry blooody penny, lad! Ev'ry blooody penny!'

CHAPTER 23. (SPANISH) BOXING DAY

On Boxing Day morning we receive a text from Teri, one of the Spanish ladies at the conversation class. 'Please we meet this day at seven and half in afternoon, at bar of old queens, I show you my fathers.'

'Hip-hip-hooray!' cries Chrissie, punching the air. 'A Spanish Boxing Day! Sanity! Local culture!

I regard my wife uneasily. It was rather a heavy day yesterday, and my constitution is in recovery mode. 'Sanity? From Spanish people? Has that salmon with gravy left you feeling unbalanced? Didn't you enjoy your 'reet slap-up blooody Christmas, lass?!'

'Of course I did!' she giggles, 'but today we will spend some time with the locals, see what Boxing Day is like in this country. Is it a public holiday?Are there hordes of people queuing at this very moment outside the shops? Are the shops even open today? Are there sales?

'Who cares?' I grunt, 'and sanity? That message from Teri is totally insane! Seven and half in afternoon? Old queens bar? Her fathers? You'd get more sense from Gaffer!'

Chrissie is laughing now, clearly having benefited from restricting her consumption of alcohol yesterday, whereas I resemble the original sore-headed bear. 'Well let's de-construct the message. Seven and half in afternoon is clearly seven-thirty this evening. You know the Spanish don't have a word for 'evening.' And bar of old queens is that cafe *Reina Sofia*. She was a Spanish queen many years ago.'

'OK I agree all that' I confirm, 'but her fathers? How many fathers does she have?' I run by hands across my face, trying to force my befuddled brain into some sort of action. 'Maybe she has a step-father? Maybe she meets her original dad and her step-dad on Boxing Day? Or what about this? Maybe her mum underwent gender realignment. Maybe she has two dads now. Perhaps the old queens bar is actually a bar for, you know, old queens. Who knows? Just text her back and say we'll meet her half-seven in *Cafe Reina*, then stand well clear of the kitchen. I'm about to raid the fridge for sausages, eggs, bacon and mushrooms. Fried bread. Black coffee. I'm in severe need of a fry-up!'

Now it's Chrissie's turn to grunt. 'Fat pig! Why don't you go up Gaffer's and ask if he'll sell you a tin of Cost-Co baked beans as well. Only twenty-five pence a tin, tha knaws!'

I smile serenely at my dearest. The thought of a full-English has perked me up. 'Now don't be ridiculous, you know I'm a *Branston* man! Besides, I don't want to be greedy, do I? Sausage, egg, bacon, mushrooms, fried bread and black coffee is enough for this man's Spanish Boxing Day! Now take cover, I'm going in!'

At seven and half in the afternoon we head to the bar of old queens to meet with Teri and her fathers. Possibly. The town is crowded with families on their evening *paseo,* the shops all appear to be open, although there do not seem to be any sales events in progress, which as far as I am concerned can only be a good thing. *Cafe Reina Sofia* is packed to the gunwales but we manage to squeeze our way inside and wedge ourselves up against the bar. Two beers and a plate of *chorizo* appear as if by magic, and I rub my hands with glee. Chrissie doesn't eat meat. 'Oh isn't that great' she complains, 'you get all the tapas again.'

'Well you can have all the horse's collars, if you like!' I suggest. *Chorizo* is often served with a savoury biscuit shaped exactly like an equine harness, although they are admittedly rather dry to eat on their own. But at least I offered. Chrissie huffs in disgust and turns her head away, so I expertly roll a slice of Spanish sausage around a horse's collar and pop the whole thing into my mouth. I roll my eyes appreciatively, as I digest the salty aperitif. 'Mmmmm, you don't get this in the Rose and Crown, do you?!'

'Fat pig, and don't talk with your mouth full' my wife hisses, 'I'm surprised you have any room left, after that damned great breakfast this morning. And never mind the tapas, keep an eye out for Teri, I can't see a thing from down here!.' This is true. She is only five feet tall, whereas I have another foot in elevation and can see over the heads of the crowd, although Teri is similarly vertically challenged and whether I will spot her in the throng is doubtful. Maybe her fathers will be six-footers, although somehow I doubt it.

Suddenly I feel a tug on my sleeve from behind, I spin round and there is our Spanish friend, with a man and a woman standing next to her. Most definitely a man and a woman, one-hundred percent guaranteed. Absolutely a mum and a dad. The man is a little over five feet tall, tubby, balding, our age, possibly a year or two younger, the lady is petite, dark, and the image of Teri. No Adam's apple, tell-tale stubble, or meaty hands. So where this 'fathers' business came from, heaven only knows. 'How did you get in here?' I smile, 'I've been looking out for you!'

'Ahh we are small Espaness peoples!' Terri laughs, 'ees easy for us! Plees, thees are my fathers, Pedro and Inma.' We all hug and double kiss, professing ourselves *encanto*, pleased to meet you, although I restrict myself to a firm British handshake as far as Pedro is concerned. I'm not hugging another man, on a Boxing Day, especially on a first date, as it were. Pedro gabbles something at the barman and miraculously a table appears, a space is cleared and five chairs are produced. 'We ees drink *rioja* this night, will you take *rioja* weeth us plees? Teri enquires. Indeed we will. Never turn down a glass of *rioja* over the Christmas, is my motto. Five huge goldfish bowls of ruby-coloured wine appear, together with plates of cheese, potato salad and black pudding, accompanied by the obligatory horse's collars.

'Now Teri' Chrissie smiles, 'your mother is Inma, and your father is Pedro. So what is the collective word for them together?'

'Fathers' our friend confirms, 'together they my fathers.'

My wife gently shakes her head. 'Parents'.

'HODER!' cries Teri. 'I know this word, 'parents', but always I forget. In Espain, mother is *madre,* father is *padre*, and parents is *padres'* and she slaps her hand against her head.

'So imagine our confusion this morning, with your text' Chrissie continues. 'Meet my fathers. We thought maybe you had two fathers!'

Teri bursts out laughing, and quickly explains to her mother in a burst of staccato Spanish how we thought she was a bloke. The three of them are now in fits, Pedro has tears running down his face as he accuses his wife of being a man.

'My Eengliss is ver bad!' Teri continues, drying her eyes on a tissue, 'and I want ask you to speak me in Eengliss, two times a week in morning plees. I must to practice my Eengliss, I you understand perfect, it will be Eengliss classes good for me! Ees good for you?'

'I am sorry but I cannot, as I have my building work some mornings' I explain, glancing at Chrissie, who is smiling and nodding her head imperceptibility. 'But I know a lady who can maybe help you!'

'Who thees lady?' Plees tell me name of thees lady,' our friend pleads.

Chrissie grins, savouring the moment. 'Me!'

Teri whoops with delight, 'I so 'appy, I so 'appy! You speak me in Eengliss!' and to prove her gratitude she springs from her chair, darts around the table and plants two kisses on my wife's cheeks. Another staccato burst to her parents and there are smiles all round the table. Our new student subsides into her chair, then becomes slightly more serious. 'Plees, how much cost thees classes of Eengliss?'

To be honest we have no idea how much the various English academies around the town cost, but we do know a British woman who does one-to-one conversation more or less full-time, and we also know how much she charges. Chrissie suggests the same figure, which admittedly will never make us millionaires, but is still worth our while. Or should I say, worth Chrissie's while.

'Oh this ees perfect for me!' Teri cries, which immediately leads me to conclude we have under-priced, although to be honest building up a network of Spanish friends and contacts is more important. 'Can we start the next Toos-day?' She can indeed.

Cue another round of *rioja*, which after the vast quantity of beer I consumed yesterday is proving easier to digest. Just what the Spanish doctor ordered.

Teri has another question. 'Plees, are you angry?'

'Angry?' Chrissie queries, somewhat perplexed.

'Si, yees, you maybe are angry?'

It's my turn to frown. 'Why would we be angry? We are very happy!'

Teri looks puzzled, then checks her watch. 'Ees eight and half in afternoon, which time you eat? I think maybe you angry?'

'Hungry!' cries Chrissie. 'Angry is grrrrrr!' and she pulls her best angry face. 'Hungry is Oooo!' rubbing her stomach, and doing her best to look in need of sustenance.

'HODER!' cries our new pupil, 'hungry, I know thees word! I sorree! My Eengliss is ver bad! I need you Cristina! Plees don't be angry me!' and again she slaps her hand across her head. Another rapid-fire burst to her fathers, and we are all laughing again. Most of our conversations with the locals seem to end up this way.

'So, are you HUNGRY?' our new student smiles. 'We go to *La Cantina*, we like you go with us plees. We go *La Cantina* this night?'

Chrissie and I have an expression for just this scenario, based on our experiences so far with the locals. *Expect the unexpected.* We don't have any particular plans for eating tonight, in fact as my system is still in shock after yesterday I had thought we might just have a sandwich. But what the hell, the unexpected has occurred, so why not? Mind you, I have no idea what *La Cantina* is, where it might be or what they sell there. A staff canteen possibly? Who knows? Whatever it turns out to be, I have little doubt it will serve excellent food at ludicrously low prices. After all, the bus station here gives away octopus, if you buy a beer.

I glance at Chrissie, who is grinning. 'Of course I am hungry!' I enthuse. '*Siempre*! Always!' Inma and Pedro are laughing again as we all get up to leave, the Spaniards donning winter coats and scarves, even though to us Brits the weather is positively balmy.

'Er, what about paying?' Chrissie puzzles, as we seem to be heading for the door without a by-your-leave.

I dip my hand inside my jacket, fishing for my wallet, but Pedro grabs my arm firmly. '*Preemo. Cow-seen*' he informs me, pointing to himself, then to the barman/manager. *Oh well that's all right then!* I have absolutely no idea what is going on.

Terri takes over the narrative. 'Thees man here, *el heffe,* ees cow-seen of my fathers.' OK, that clears it up nicely. We have not seen a single cow since we came to Spain, on account of there being no fields, and barely a blade of grass. There is a small patch in the park, but barely enough to keep a rabbit happy, let alone a herd of cows. In desperation I turn to the alleged Spanish-speaking half of our partnership, raising my eyebrows in an 'am I paying for these drinks or what?' kind of expression. My wife shrugs helplessly. Clearly the phrase *preemo cow-seen* was not part of the 1969 Spanish GCE syllabus.

Teri is aware she is making no sense. 'Preemo, cow-seen, my fathers, she have brother, she brother she have childrens, thees childrens is preemo, cow-seen.' I still have my hand on my wallet and quite honestly I am so confused I would prefer just to give *el heffe* fifteen euros, or whatever ten glasses of *rioja* cost, and get on with the rest of my life.

'COUSIN!' cries Chrissie, suddenly. 'You mean cousin! The child of your father's brother is your cousin. A cow is moooooo!'

Teri slaps her head again. 'HODER! Sorree, I know thees word, coo-sin, in Espanees we pronounce cow-seen. Eengliss words ver difficult!' and she proceeds to explain to her fathers in yet another rapid burst of her native tongue, featuring the word 'moooooo!' Inma and Pedro have to sit back down, they are laughing uncontrollably, and Inma puts her forefingers up on each side of her head, in the classic horn gesture. *'Ole, el toro!'* Indeed.

'So what about this heff man, and can I pay for the drinks, please?' I enquire, of no-one in particular.

'No is necessary pay for drink here in bar old queens' Teri confirms, 'my fathers he do work for he cow-seen SORREE COO-SIN! We drinking *gratis* in bar old queens! Bamos, we go *La Cantina,* I 'ope you ver angry. Sorree! HUNGRY! Hoder!'

We weave our way through the crowd and I manage a quick aside with Chrissie. 'You're going to have your work cut out, teaching her English! Best of luck with that! I think I'll stick with Del, on his roof!'

'What, teaching Del English?' my wife giggles. 'Teri has much better English than him!' Actually, this is true.

We follow our Spanish friends along the street, then up a side alley where we have never been, in search of this elusive canteen. I am beginning to wonder what might be on the menu, chips with everything I am guessing, maybe a flop of depressing-looking mash. Pie, sausages, battered cod? Then again, this is Spain, and you know what they say, *expect the unexpected...*

Suddenly the sound of people having a good time reaches our ears, although from precisely where is impossible to determine. There is simply nothing visible which might be a place of entertainment, or sustenance. No signs, no lights, just a general hubbub which is getting louder by the second. 'Here La Cantina' Teri announces, pointing to what appears to be a deserted shop-front, with curtains across the windows, and a door to one side. 'Plees, thees way', and she pushes open the door to reveal what is undoubtedly a Mexican restaurant, all red, green and white paint, sombreros hanging from the ceilings, the sound of guitar music strumming wildly from the speakers, about ten tables pushed together and what seems at first like about five hundred people all shouting at once. The tables are groaning under the weight of the food, huge jugs of wine are being passed around, dark-eyed *señoritas* are weaving expertly through the crowd, some of whom are standing, posing with sombreros, taking selfies, while others are seated around the tables, all crowded together, handing round plates, laughing, joking, hugging and doing Spanish things generally. Absolute bedlam, and I am immediately reminded of an equivalent British restaurant scene, couples seated at individual tables, the low murmur of conversation, emotions under control, upper lips completely rigid.

Inma puts her fingers to her head again. 'Moooooo!' she smiles, pointing to a middle-aged man weaving his way through the throng towards us. Oh no, another cow-seen? Surely not.

'El heffe here is coo-sin of my father' explains Teri.

'Another cousin?' laughs her new English teacher, 'how many cousins does your father have?'

Teri shrugs, 'no idea! In thees town are much relatives. Ees normal, in Espain!'

Which is all well and good, but there is absolutely nowhere to sit here, and nothing to sit on. Unless we stand at the bar, we are going hungry tonight. And I am starting to feel a bit peckish, bearing in mind my last major intake of grub, albeit of mammoth proportions, was about twelve hours ago. Suddenly however, *expect the unexpected* comes into play again. There is a cry from across the room and here is Paloma, another of the young ladies from the library conversation class, standing and waving. Behind her are an older man and woman, her fathers possibly, and we are swept up on a tidal wave of Spaniards all rushing across the room, where much kissing and hugging is in evidence. I double-kiss Rosa, Paloma's mother, but again escape with a handshake for Eduardo, her father, once again declaring ourselves *encanto. El Heffe* somehow manages to squeeze five chairs into a space where maybe one might fit, at a push, in a British restaurant, and we are in. Utterly beyond belief. Somewhat breathlessly, I smile at Chrissie who is wedged between Teri and Paloma, whereas I have ended up on the fathers side of the table, although there is little time to compare notes as a bottle of *Corona* is shoved into my hand, and a plate of *quesadillas* appears from nowhere.

'Paloma!' cries Teri, 'Cristina agree me teach Eengliss. I ver 'appy, classes of conversation with she. Two times week in mornings, Toos-day, and Tours-day!'

Paloma is delighted for her friend, although before she can get a word out Eduardo jumps in. 'Are you two teachers?' he enquires hopefully, in excellent English. 'I have a small academy in town here, and I am looking for one or two native speakers to help out. It's only a small academy for the moment, but English is so popular here, the Government has just passed a law that university students must have an English qualification, so I anticipate a huge demand. The problem is the few British people I have seen here in Santa Marta have, how shall I say this, not a good command of English!'

I smile at this observation. Clearly he has met Gaffer and Diane. 'We are not teachers as such, but we both originally had Civil Service jobs in the UK, and I worked in the Accountancy profession for thirty years, so we have a good command of the language.'

Eduardo seems delighted at this news. 'Paloma has already told me about you from the library, and how patient you both are with the Spanish people there.

Could you come to the academy next week and we can have a talk? I am thinking maybe a couple of evenings per week? Would this be good for you?'

Indeed it is, and to celebrate the fact a plate of *tacos* arrives, followed closely by a dish of *nachos* and some *tortillas*. The waitress seems to have something on her mind, however. 'Plees excuse' she ventures, timidly, 'I listen you speak Eengliss, I want maybe you speak Eengliss me, I must to practice Eengliss, I een university Granada and must to study examins, plees you speak me the day Wed-day in the morning?'

Eduardo digs me in the ribs, 'You see? I told you it was crazy for English.'

This is rather awkward however. Here I am sitting next to a man I have only known for half an hour, who runs a fledgling academy, who has just offered us a job, and now we are being asked to cut him from the equation, and pinch a potential customer. 'Well, my friend here has an academy' I reply, as kindly as I can, 'maybe it is better you speak to him?'

Eduardo seems completely relaxed however, but does address the waitress in their native tongue, of which I am able to catch her reply of 'only Wednesday mornings.' 'No don't worry' our potential employer replies, 'she can only do Wednesdays, we are full that day at the moment, so it's best she speaks to you, especially for the time being. When her exam approaches, we can maybe fit her in for specific exam practice.'

So we exchange phone numbers with Estefania, and agree to meet on Wednesday for a brief chat, to make the various arrangements. Some Boxing Day this is turning out to be!

And so the evening flows, and the unexpected has happened again. Plates of food are passed round, I get to sample the local *tequila*, we all have our photos taken with the sombreros, but sadly, all too soon, the evening is drawing to a close. I hug Eduardo and Pedro, double-kiss the ladies, and Estefania takes a group photo, as we all get up to leave. 'Er, what about paying?' Chrissie enquires, for the second time tonight.

Once again I reach for my wallet, but this time Inma grips my arm. 'Es chocolate del loro!' she giggles. Now I know this word, *loro*. It means 'parrot', and I know this because a beautiful African Grey lives in the next street to us, and his elderly owners often leave him out in the street, in his cage, presumably to get a bit of sunlight. And every time we pass, I cannot help but try to teach the bird to speak a little English. Not the Queen's English. Oh no, salty, earthy, Naval English. I love to hear a parrot swear. 'You will get into trouble one day, cussing at that creature!' Chrissie warned, just a few weeks ago.

'From who?' I replied indignantly, 'nobody round here speaks English. They have no idea what I am saying!' The proof came just a few days before Christmas. There was our feathered friend, basking in the warm sunshine, on his perch. I crept up behind him, until I was about a foot from the cage. 'BILLOCKS!' At that instant, the curtain across the front door of the cottage was swept angrily back, and there stood the old man, glaring accusingly at me. '*Buenas dias!*' I smiled, '*habla Ingles, tu loro?*' Does your parrot speak English? '*Ingles?*' he spluttered, '*no habla puta Espanol!*' He doesn't speak effing Spanish!

So I know what a *loro* is, but why should it be eating chocolate, especially at stupid-o-clock on a Boxing night. And what does this have to do with settling a restaurant bill? 'Have you ever seen a parrot eating Dairy Milk?' I ask my wife.

She sniggers. 'I think you will find eight-out-of-ten parrots prefer Galaxy!'

Teri comes to the rescue. 'Ees what we say here in Espain. The chocolate of the parrot.'

Right, that explains everything. 'But parrots don't usually eat chocolate' explains her new teacher. I bet when Chrissie agreed to conversation classes with this girl she didn't anticipate covering the dietary requirements of a tropical bird with brightly coloured plumage.

'Chicken-feed' confirms Eduardo. 'You say in English 'chicken-feed' for a small amount of money, no? In Spain we say *chocolate del loro*. It has the same significance.

OK. It's late at night, I have had a hard couple of days, and my head just cannot process why feeding confectionery to wildlife has anything to do with a night out. Luckily, Teri recognises my confusion. 'El heffe here is coo-sin of my fathers, so we no need pay for feed here, in *La Cantina.* Ees not much money. Chocolate del loro.'

This is getting ridiculous. I can just about accept a few free glasses of wine, in the bar of old queens, but here in the canteen we have all been tucking in like there's no tomorrow. Surely there must be a bill? I start to protest again, but again Inma prevents me from extracting my wallet. 'Plees, there ees no problem' Terri continues, 'my fathers she work for el heffe here, ees family, no worry!'

I reluctantly relax my grip on my cash. 'Well thank you very, very much for a wonderful evening' I tell the assorted Spaniards, as we all spill out into the street. We all hug and kiss again, the locals all head off towards their apartments in the new part of town, and us Brits head up the hill to the historic part.

We are silent for a minute or so, as we digest the evenings momentous proceedings. Or it could be we are out of breath climbing the steep cobbled street. Chrissie is first to gather her thoughts. 'Was that one of the craziest Boxing Days of your life?'

'No' I puff, 'it was THE craziest Boxing Day of my life! We were offered three jobs, for heaven's sake. What is it about this country? Since we retired people keep offering us work, first Del on his roof, now Teri, the academy and Estefania. I thought we were supposed to be retired? It seems like nobody else is aware of this! But what a lovely evening. And I can't wait to get started at the academy. I knew there was a huge demand for English lessons here.'

'Hmm' my wife ponders, 'I was wondering about that. I hope you have more luck there, than you did with your last pupil.'

I feel slightly offended. 'Who, Miriam, Mohammed's daughter, you mean? I thought I did really well with her, mooing, baaing, ee-awing, barking, meowing, that night in the bar!'

'No, not Miriam' Chrissie replies, a hint of mischief in her voice. 'Think about it, who have you been teaching recently? We were all talking about him tonight.' Nope, not a clue. I am racking my brains, but nothing is happening. She puts me out of my misery. 'That parrot in the next street? The one you have failed completely and utterly to teach any English? One pupil, and one failure, not a good track record is it!'

We have reached the top of the hill and I pause to catch my breath. 'I have only one word to say about that' I wheeze. 'BILLOCKS!'

'I see last week your duck, een Eengland.' A few days later and we are taking our first conversation class at Eduardo's academy in town, our latest adventure. We are now freelance English teachers, which is a lot safer, and more lucrative, than climbing about on rickety roofs, although I am continuing with my occasional 'day job' with Del, at least for the time being. So next time a Spaniard comes up to you and says 'Buenas Dias, proper job me ansome', you will know they were probably one of our pupils!

'Duck?' I enquire of Marta, who is seventeen, and our youngest pupil.

'Yees, thee duck, he have baby' she replies. 'He marry-ed with Cat-ee.' So we have a duck with a baby married to a cat. Hmm... Marta can see I am slightly puzzled. 'How you say, thee duck of Camm-bridge?'

'You mean the Duke of Cambridge? I ask, not quite stifling a laugh. 'Kate had a baby last week, Prince George.'

'Thee dook? She replies.

'No, duke. Du. Not doo.'

She has a bash at it. 'Duuke.' Her sister Sara, and our other pupil Pati join in and we have everyone saying 'Duuke.' Progress I suppose. The class descends into laughter, which it does regularly, so much so that Eduardo has to come into the room and ask us to keep the noise down, as he has a maths class. Clearly the English classes are more fun....

'I am thee black duck' confirms Marta, as we are winding the class up.

'Black duck?' I query.

'Yees, I am thee black duck of the family!'

'I think you mean black sheep' I laugh. In fact we are all laughing again, and if we are not careful Eduardo will be cancelling the English classes!

Sara and Marta are taking their grade 2 English exams next week and have to talk for five minutes about a subject of their choosing. Marta elects to talk about her dog. 'So tell me about your dog' asks Chrissie. 'What is his name and which breed is he?'

'Her name is Tom, and she is a Jock-seer', comes the reply.

'Is he a boy or a girl?' questions Chrissie.

'She is a boy.'

'HE is a boy' Chrissie corrects, 'and what breed is he again?'

'A Jock-seer' confirms Marta. 'A Jock-seer terrierrr.'

My wife looks at me and we all start laughing again. 'Is he a Scottie? I ask.

'Nooo.'

'A Westie?'

'Nooo.'

'What colour is he?'

'She is maroon, and white streeps' comes the reply. I know they have different breeds of canines over here but a maroon and white striped dog I have yet to see. 'One momento plees, I 'ave photo', smiles Marta, delving into her bag for a smart-phone. A few quick flicks later and up comes a picture of a Yorkshire Terrier. 'Thees ees Tom' she announces.

'A Yorkshire Terrier!' states Chrissie.

'Yees, a Jock-seer terrierrr' Marta confirms. She simply cannot pronounce Yorkshire. It's a good job Gaffer is not here.

'Just call him a Yorkie' I tell her. 'The examiner will be fine with that. And he is brown, with white flecks. Just say he is brown.' *Marron* is brown in Spanish so I can see how she got confused. But the image of a maroon and white striped dog will stay with me for a long time.

That evening we go to the theatre with our friends Jose and Cristina. As we are leaving to head home Jose asks me a question. 'Jonneee, do you have sluice in your garden?

Jose has been to our house and was particularly taken with our new patio, so maybe he is enquiring about the underground drainage system I put in. Or perhaps he is referring to the old stone sink, with a corrugated side for washing clothes, which many of these old houses have. We call it the 'rubby-dubby' but perhaps it is known here as a sluice.

'Sluice? I query.

'Yees, leetle animales similar snails' he confirms. 'Sluice.'

'Do you mean slugs?' I giggle.

'Sorree, yees I mean sloogs' he says. We are all laughing again. 'Maybe you ave sloogs tomorrow? he continues. 'It will be doogs.'

Now I am totally confused. 'Doogs?'

'Yees, I see on TV it will perhaps rain tomorrow. Rain like doogs. Hard rain. Like doogs, and cats.'

'In England we say raining cats and dogs!' I tell him, unable to keep a straight face.

A day or so later we are at the library again. 'Jonnee! He come my house. He ring bell. For sex. Yees!'

Around the table is a stunned silence. Jose, the only other man present, has a wolfish grin on his face, but the Spanish women are not laughing. Teri, late-twenties, Rafi, mid-thirties, Maria, late-thirties. And Chrissie. My wife. The Missus. She has a look on her face, which I can read all too well. It says 'wait till I get you home, sunshine, and I will separate you from your testicles. With a rusty knife.'

Alicia ploughs on. 'Jonneee come my house last week, he ring bell, ring for sex. Ha ha ha.' And she leans across and digs me in the ribs. 'Ding ding!'

I glance hurriedly round the table with a 'this is news to me' look on my face, then turn to Alicia. *'Que?'* She has clearly exhausted her English vocabulary so she starts speaking to the others in her native tongue, which I can just about follow. She explains she has a china souvenir bell in her cabinet which bears the legend, in English, 'Ring for sex.' She was given it many years ago. Cue much laughter round the table, and I blow out my cheeks in relief, but that could have turned ugly. I remember now, it was when Del and I went to her house before Christmas to see about her water problem, just after she had asked me to look at the crack in her bedroom wall, she showed me the bell. At the time Del was laughing so much about me looking at her crack that I took little notice of the cursed bell. That will teach me to pay more attention....

'What is this word 'crack' in English, and why you and Jose laughing about Alicia's bedroom wall?' Teri asks. Jose's English is very good, he goes abroad on business regularly and as the common business language worldwide is English, he does pick up a lot of expressions which might not be too polite in a library setting. I explain to Teri that a crack appears in the plaster on a wall or ceiling, usually as a result of settlement. She is an architect, so is naturally keen to learn this English word, but I am simply unwilling and unable to explain why Jose and I are laughing. He clearly knows the alternative meaning of the word, as does Chrissie of course, who is tutting and rolling her eyes at our childish behaviour.

Then, to my amazement, Jose explains in Spanish to the others, why we are laughing. I put my hands across my face and pretend I am not actually present in this conversation, but to my surprise the Spanish women all find this highly amusing. Apart from Alicia, who throws up her hands in horror. 'Oh what I say, what I say, to Jonnee, my crack, in the room of my bed? I show Jonneee my crack, ha ha ha!' and she convulses into a fit of high-pitched cackling. We are all laughing now, and Ana the librarian comes into our meeting room and asks us to try to make a bit less noise. She regularly has to do this, such is the potential for embarrassing and amusing pitfalls when learning a foreign language.

Walking home after the class, my wife seems decidedly un-amused. 'So, Alicia showed you her sex-bell, did she? I don't remember you mentioning this when you and Del went out there. And she invited you into her bedroom, on the pretext of examining her wall. A likely story I have to say. And was she wearing her fishnet stockings that day? Those hooker-heels? That see-through top?'

I have to be careful here. One wrong word and I am toast. And I am a classic blunderer, always dive in with both feet. 'No, don't be silly, she was wearing skin-tight jeans. Actually she has a great figure, for a woman of her age, they really suited her....' Oh no, I've done it again. 'But of course, you look better in your Levi's,' I add, as an afterthought.

My wife snorts with derision. 'Actually I'm not worried about you and her' she confirms. *Whew, it looks like I've got away with it.* 'She would swallow you whole. Chew you up, and spit you out. Mincemeat, sonny Jim. Ding-ding!'

I'm not sure now whether I got away with it, or not. Maybe best just to keep quiet. And pray that Alicia decides to get someone else to fill her crack....

CHAPTER 24. WE THREE KINGS...

A couple of days into the New Year, we are heading into town, and bump into one of the neighbours, Juan, otherwise known as 'The Dustman' on account of his profession. Today he is street-sweeping, equipped with a long-handled brush and dustpan, and a wide-bottomed plastic bucket, which is attached to his belt with a length of Velcro strapping. All absolutely low-tech, but it does the job. As he walks, the bucket drags along behind him, and as he sweeps, he tips the rubbish into the bucket. He usually manages to arrive in our street in time for his morning coffee break, which he conveniently takes at home, thereby ensuring our *barrio* is one of the best-kept in town.

He spots us wending our way down the narrow cobbled steps. 'Neighbour!' he hollers, 'Ray-es-ma-he-co!' Indeed. Juan is a lovely man, always cheerful, always speaks to us, or shouts to us to be more accurate, but we have one big problem. I cannot understand a word he is saying, on account of him having more gaps in his teeth, than actual teeth, and try as I might, I just cannot figure out what he is telling us. Usually I just wing it, utilising a store of stock Spanish answers, including *where, when, what* and *sorry I don't understand.* I raise my eyebrows at this latest nugget, buying a few seconds to figure out my response. I am assuming he is talking about a man, Ray presumably, who is coming to Santa Marta? But is es-ma-he-co his surname? Not a clue. Usually in these circumstances I glance at Mrs Spanish O Level 1969, but with Juan she has the same problem as me. No ruddy idea.

'Donde?' I venture. Where?

'The old fountain, Thursday, half-seven in the afternoon' he bellows.

I smile appreciatively. *'Vamos a ir.'* We are going to go. No idea what we are going to, but be there we will.

Juan exposes his gappy grin, expertly flicks a fugitive dog-end into his dustpan, and disappears up the street. 'So what have we just agreed to? And thanks for your input, by the way! Leaving me struggling, about this Ray fellow!'

My wife is indignant. 'YOU agreed to it, not me! Anyway, I think *ma-he-co* is 'magic'. Magic Ray is coming, for some unknown reason, Heaven knows, but I am sure Maria and the rest of the girls can tell us. Absolutely, where would we be without our Spanish friends? The library is still closed following the Christmas break, so today we are meeting them in a local bar.

'Appy Year New!' cries Juan-Carlos, as we approach the pavement cafe, and draw up a couple of chairs, next to Maria, Rafi and Jose, who curiously for Spaniards, are already waiting. 'Would you like a *cubo?*' and he grabs me round the shoulders, and plants a kiss on each cheek. More 'kissing and flopping', as my mother used to say, ensues, and several minutes pass while everybody greets everybody else. Why these Continentals cannot be satisfied with a stiff British handshake, or better still, a swift 'Good Morning', is beyond me, and kissing another man, even a quick peck on the cheeks, is something completely alien to my entire upbringing. Still, it is New Year, and I should be grateful for small mercies; at least the Dustman didn't give me a quick smacker. Or, given his lack of molars, a quick slobber!

A cube? A cube of what? Suddenly the image of an Oxo slips into my mind, then swiftly slips out again. Obviously not. A Bovril maybe, if we were in Britain in January, watching the rugby in the pouring rain, but here the thought of a hot meaty drink is beyond ridiculous. I am in a short-sleeved shirt, for heaven's sake. 'A cube of what?' I ask the man I have just kissed.

'Beer, of course!' J-C laughs. Beer? BEER? In a cube? OK, the sixth rule of travel is that if someone offers you a beer, in whatever form, you accept with grace, although this is the first time I have ever been offered a three-dimensional alcoholic beverage. I had a cider ice-lolly once, although there was very little actual cider involved, merely the faintest hint of chemically-produced apples. The ladies meanwhile are ordering *tinto de verano*, red wine of summer, consisting of a glass of red, topped up with lemonade, and a *Martini Rosso* thrown in for good measure, even though it's January. The waiter arrives, carrying a metal bucket, filled with ice cubes, into which are shoved five bottles of beer.

'*Ole! Un cubo!*' cries Jose, grabbing a bottle, tossing one each to me and Juan-Carlos. Bottle-openers appear, we crack open our ice-cold refreshments, and chink them together. 'Appy year new!'

Five bottles of beer. I wonder how much this cubo costs? Has to be ten Euros, doesn't it? Two yo-yo's a bottle? 'So how much is this cubo?' I enquire, of no-one in particular.

'Three Euro' replies Jose.

I screw up my face. Three per bottle? Bit steep that, although there is a photo of a Spanish footballer on the label, which probably explains it. The brewery no doubt have to pay a commission to a mufti-millionaire, for the use of his image, although I could have done without it, personally. Who is this brewery anyway? *Cruz-Campo* it says on the label. 'Cross-country' if I am not mistaken. I am immediately transported back in time over forty years, to the school cross-country competition, when Steve 'Killer' King, Chrissy Shepherd and I, the school rugby team front row, would saunter to the off-licence of the Queen's Head, where three bottles of Courage brown ale, and ten Woodbine's, could be procured for about three bob, then leisurely consumed in the trees next to the school gates, before re-joining the runners as they returned. Hell of a team we were too, unbeaten in five years, in both rugby, and punch-ups, particularly against St Brendan's, or *St Bastard's*, as they were affectionately known in my *Alma mater*.

'So fifteen Euros for the cubo?'

Jose almost chokes on his beer. 'NO! Three Euro for el cubo! *Para toda!* For all!'

'Seriously?' I gasp. 'Sixty cents per bottle? Five beers for three Euros?' Unbelievable, although I am guessing there is no tapas provided, at these prices. Wrong! A plate of sliced crusty bread appears, accompanied by beefy tomatoes and *Manchego* cheese, dripping with olive oil. How can they do this, at these prices?

'So who is this magic Ray?' Chrissie enquires. Cue blank faces around the table.

'Can you repeat plees?' Rafi replies.

'Magic Ray. We met our neighbour on the way here, and he told us magic Ray was coming on Thursday evening, the old fountain, seven-thirty.'

All the Spaniards have wide grins on their faces, and Juan-Carlos is actually laughing. 'Plees you tell me what say you neighbour?' he splutters.

Chrissie gathers her thoughts. 'Ray-es-ma-he-co viene la Fuente vieja Juves a las siete-y-media.' Perfect! She sounds just like a native, except that we have clearly misunderstood the Dustman's message.

The locals are almost doubled over with laughter. 'Ees correct you say Toors-day at seven-and-half in fountain old', Maria confirms, 'but ees magic kings who arrive this night. *Los Rayes Magicos*. Magic kings.'

The magic kings. Well that explains everything. So nobody called Ray, then. But who are these kings? And why are they magic? A pop group maybe? The old fountain is one of the main squares in town, a huge public space, palm trees, shady areas, flower gardens, orange trees, a couple of bars, ideal for an open-air concert.

Maria can read the confusion on our faces. 'You no have magic kings, in Eengland?'

Not as far as I am concerned, although I glance at my wife in case she is aware of something which has completely passed me by, which happens more than I am happy to admit. Nope. Reassuringly, she is as confused as me.

'When born Cassoo, in house of coo, appears *Los Rayes Magicos*, the Magic Kings,' Maria patiently explains. *Cassoo?* Jesus? *House of coo?* Cow? A stable?

'THE THREE KINGS!' Chrissie exclaims. 'You mean the Three Wise Men? At Christmas?'

'Yees!' the Spaniards giggle in unison.

Hang on a minute. Christmas is over, it was last week, for heaven's sake. Today is the second of January, Thursday will be the fifth, almost a fortnight late. Where have these kings been? In my junior school Nativity, I met up with Alan Reed and Paul Hayman, on the road to Bethlehem, and we travelled in together, to find the Holy Family, the angels and the shepherds, already there, but nobody said they had been waiting, what, ten days and more, for us to arrive. OK so a school play is not an exact historical re-enactment, but I just don't understand. Chrissie took Confirmation classes when she was a little girl, I will have to ask her later, but in the meantime, I am baffled. 'So these magic kings, are they actual people? Do they dress up? And what do they do, in the old fountain square?'

Jose takes the lead in explaining. 'Ees a procession! Een streets of old town, arrive magic kings. Ees tradition here in Espain, like you have Santa-Clows in Eengland, wises mens bring present for cheeldrens!'

'So how do the Three Kings arrive in Santa Marta?' Chrissie wonders.

'*Camello!*' cries Rafi.

'Tractor!' laughs Juan-Carlos.

Now I really am confused. 'Look, there were no tractors in the Bible! Camels yes, tractors no!'

Maria is laughing. 'Ees no camellos een Santa Marta, ees much shitty! For procession, arrive Three Kings on tractor. But for thees night arrive Los Reyes Magicos een camellos.'

Now I am really, really confused. 'RIGHT! Three men, dress as three kings, and come into town, for a procession on Thursday, on a tractor?'

'Yees!' chuckle our friends.

I narrow my eyes and frown in concentration. 'So three other kings arrive on camels, what, the same night, or a different night?'

'Yees, thee same night, arrive magic kings, they magic!', laughs Maria.

I am none the wiser, but luckily my wife is quicker on the uptake. 'So these magic kings don't actually exist!' she cries, 'I understand now, they are like our father Christmas, or Santa Claus in America, they come with presents for every child!'

'SHHHHH!' cries Rafi, 'the cheeldrens they listen you!'

I am with it now. Eventually. In the rest of the world, one old man, with a sleigh and six reindeer, delivers everyone's presents in one night. But in Spain, there are three of them, on camels. No wonder it takes until the first week of January, to get round. They've probably been gossiping somewhere, or sat in a bar. Drinking a *cubo* probably. 'So Father Christmas comes down the chimney, in Britain. What happens here?'

Jose smiles, 'here in Espain not much houses have chimney! Thee kings they come in door of house.'

'They magic!' Juan-Carlos laughs.

'But not very magic!' I point out, 'they are, after all, ten days late! I'm going to rename them *'the little bit magic but very late Spanish kings!'* And anyone can come through a front door, but only Santa comes down a chimney! And he's sixteen stone!'

'What this sixteen stone, plees?' asks Juan-Carlos.

'About a hundred kilos' I tell him.

'Twelfth Night' Chrissie announces.

I frown at my dearest. 'What about it?'

'Twelfth Night. That's when the kings are coming. Must be something to do with it.'

'What this Twelfth Night, plees?' Maria requests.

Oh yeah, I've just spent about an hour of my life finding out about three blokes on tractors, no way do I have time to explain lords-a-leaping, maids-a-milking, geese-a-laying or a partridge in a pear tree, before one of us dies. 'Twelve days after Christmas' I explain, 'when traditionally all decorations have to be taken down.'

Maria repeats her original question. 'So you no have magic kings, in Eengland?' She is probably thinking the same as me. *How can I have spent an hour getting a yes or no answer to a simple question?*

'Well yes and no!' I explain. 'Yes, they appear in Nativity scenes, they are a big part of the Christmas story, of course. But no, they don't have their own special day, and they don't deliver presents to children.' I think that pretty much sums it up. We got there in the end!

'So what they names in Eengliss, plees?' she wants to know.

'Gold, Frankincense and Myrrh!' I quickly add, keeping a straight face.

Chrissie emits a huge sigh, regarding me disdainfully. 'Don't take any notice of that idiot, Maria. Their names were Gaspar, Balthasar and Melchior. Gold, Frankincense and Myrrh were their gifts to the baby Jesus.'

'The sames as Espain!' cries Juan-Carlos, 'the sames names and sames presents.'

'Maybe, but your Spanish kings were two weeks too late,' I smile. 'By the time they arrived, Christmas was over and everyone had gone home!'

The Spaniards laugh, 'You know we always late here in Espain!' explains Rafi. 'Ees tradition for we! But you must to remember, at the procession on Toors-day, you must to take a bag plastic. The kings they give caramellos to you!'

Caramellos? Caramels? Chocolate-covered caramels? Oooo, I do hope so. I haven't had a chocolate caramel for absolutely years. *Merry Maids* were my all-time favourite, my auntie Rose used to bring me a quarter, every Wednesday, when I was a little boy. Jameson's stopped making them, or went out of business, many years ago, but I can remember the taste, to this day. If we get something similar from the Kings, they will indeed be magic.

On the way home after the class we bump into Gaffer and Diane. 'Hey-oop lad! Summat big 'appenin' in town, no-parking signs everywhere, but we can't read no Spanish, so gawd knows what 'tis. Or when, like!'

'There's a procession on Thursday evening' Chrissie informs him. 'The Three Kings are coming.'

'We Three Kings of Forster Square!' sings Diane.

'Shouldn't that be Leicester Square?' I giggle.

'Tha blooody soft Soothern jessie!' she bellows. 'Course it weren't blooody Leicester blooody Square. It were Forster Square, In Bradford!'

'Get on, tha dafty pie-can!' Gaffer bellows. 'Yon Three Kings weren't from Bradford. They was from Orient Are! 'Tis in the blooody song, like!'

'Where's this Orient Are place then, Keith?' Chrissie asks, just about managing to keep a straight place.

'Ow t'blooody 'ell should I know, lass? China somewhere, weren't it?'

China? No wonder the Kings were late. 'Actually, Orient is in London' I inform our friends, deadpan. 'Leyton way, I believe. Anyway, the Kings give away caramels, we've been told, so do you fancy coming to watch, with us? Half-seven, Thursday evening.'

'Blooody reet!' Gaffer confirms. 'I love caramels, me! Can't eat boiled sweets, cos o' me teeth, can I ower Di?

'S'right' his wife confirms. 'Three 'undred blooody quid 'e spent, 'aving 'is teeth capped, afore we coom 'ere! So 'e definitely ain't eatin' no boiled sweets! '

'OK, so give us a knock about seven-fifteen on Thursday?' says Chrissie.

'Nay lass! Mek it half-six, oos'll sup a couple o' ales, fust! I know a nice little bar in that square, *Tossers* 'tis called, landlord speaks a bit 'o English.'

So we head our different ways, and get on with the rest of our day. Drifting off to sleep that night, I suddenly have a question for my wife. So, do you fancy a few in Tossers, with Gaffer?' There is no reply for a moment or two, then suddenly she starts to sing, very softly.

'On the twelfth day of Christmas, my true love gave to me, three little-bit-magic-but-very-late Spanish kings, plus twelve drummers drumming, eleven pipers piping……….'

Three Kings Day dawns fine and sunny, and after a leisurely breakfast we spend part of the morning dismantling the Nativity village, and taking down the Christmas cards and decorations. From my earliest childhood memories, I always hated this day, and I still feel the same. Although the trimmings are only up for three or four weeks, the house always seemed bare, empty, joyless somehow, with the prospect of a long, cold couple of months to follow, until Spring. At least we won't have that to worry about here. Chrissie places the last of the shepherds in their box, I make us a nice cuppa, and we retire to the terrace, basking in the warm sunshine. We have a procession tonight, and I'm sure another one will be along very shortly.

At six-thirty sharp we hear tuneless singing outside our front door. 'We three Kings from Forster Square, selling knickers tuppence a pair, so fantastic, no elastic, only tuppence a pair!'

I fling open the door. 'Bugger off! We don't encourage vagrants round here, Christmas is officially over, and I told you before, it's Leicester Square! And besides, the Kings have gone to Orient Are, which is near China apparently.'

''Urry oop!' cries Gaffer, 'I just coom across t'dessert, on me camel! Me throat's as dry as a nun's ch...'

'KEITH!' cries his wife, 'shoot tha gert fat mouth! There's ladies present!'

He glances round dramatically. 'What blooody ladies? Booogered if I can see owt! Any-road, we two kings an' two ol' queens is off to *Tossers*!'

Chrissie and I, over the past couple of days, have been puzzling about the location of this establishment, as we simply have no idea where it might be, or why it might have been named in such a peculiar manner. We head downhill to the square of the old fountain, where life seems to be continuing as usual. Families out for their evening *paseo*, strolling around, chatting, laughing, the local shops all open, doing a roaring trade, particularly the bakers, where old ladies laden with sticks of crusty bread are gossiping, people milling around the doors of the church. Just a normal evening. And absolutely no sign of any Kings, magic or otherwise. 'Tha's got t'wrong night, tha blooody soft Soothern jessie!' Diane informs me.

She might have a point there, but at least six Spaniards have confirmed the night, the time and the venue, so I am guessing they might actually know best. 'I am confident of my sources!' I advise her. 'Would you care for a little wager?'

Gaffer takes up the challenge, as I knew he would. 'Bloody reet, lad! Nowt 'appenin' 'ere! Bet thee two pints no blooody kings arrive, this side o' Christmas! Coom on. 'ere's Tossers, look!' and he points the way to a small cafe/bar, tucked away next to the bakers, bearing the legend, in big letters above the door, *'Tostadas y Cafe.'* *Tostada*. Spanish toast. A crusty loaf, sliced in half lengthways, toasted on one side, drizzled with olive oil, and smothered with chopped tomato, pinch of sea-salt and ground pepper. Sunshine on a plate. Add *Jamon Iberico*, cured ham, or cheese, if required. *Tostadas y cafe*. Toast and coffee. Espresso, obviously. Heart-stoppingly strong. Two Euros, all in.

Chrissie and I are doubled over with laughter, as we enter the premises, which are deserted apart from a bewildered-looking Spaniard behind the bar. 'NOW THEN MIGUEL!' cries our friend. ''Ow's it 'anging, like? Four beers quick as you like!'

'Ee speaks reet good English, tha knaws, does ower Miguel' confides Diane. *Which is more than she does….*

I smile at our new acquaintance. 'Hablas Ingles?' I enquire. Do you speak English?

'Not a word' he chuckles, 'although my daughter speaks a little, but she went back to university this week.' He beckons me closer. 'Your friends, they don't speak a word of Spanish.' he whispers.

I grin widely, and gesture him to me. 'They don't speak English very well, either!' He smiles, and we grip hands. Miguel and I have bonded.

'Why the blooody 'ell you gabblin' away in Spanish?' Gaffer puzzles. 'Ee speaks perfect English, tha knaws.'

'Well, just practising what we learned at the library, Keith.'

He grips me round the shoulder. 'I'll tell tha summat, lad, they all speaks English, these blooody Spanish. They pretends not to, like, but they do. They learns it in t'school, tha knaws! So there's naw point tha goin' t'library, like. Waste o' blooody time, lad!'

'*Hay una procession, esta noche?*' I whisper to my new acquaintence. Is there a procession tonight?

'Of course!' he smiles, 'the Magic Kings are coming, in about ten minutes!'

'What tha blooody 'ell ye speakin' t'him aboot now?' Gaffer wonders.

'Oh I was just asking if he'd seen the weather forecast' I reply, straight-faced. 'he says it's going to be lovely for the rest of January!'

'Well tha' knaws nowt!' he cries. 'There's naw blooody kings coomin' tonight. I bet thee four pints, lad!' and he sticks out his paw, to seal the wager.

I wink at Chrissie, who overheard my exchange with Miguel. 'You drive a hard bargain, Keith!' And we clasp hands.

My wife meanwhile has wandered across to the door, and sticks her head out. 'Blimey! Come and see this! Better get your money out, Keith!'

Our friends dash across the bar. 'Blooody 'ell! Where did they all coom from?' gasps Diane. The square is packed, the police have closed the road, balloon sellers are plying their wares, a stall dispensing all manner of fatty snacks has arrived, and old and young are eagerly awaiting the arrival of three blokes dressed up as Biblical characters. I wave my grateful thanks to Miguel, Gaffer is scrabbling for his wallet, and we all pile out into the throng.

From along the street comes a rumbling sound, getting louder by the second, then around the corner come around twenty motorbikes, each ridden by a Santa Claus. Some riders also have a Mrs Claus on the pillion, and one statuesque young lady, displaying an ample acreage of thigh, catches our friend's attention. 'Blooody 'ell! I wouldn't mind filling her stocki....'

'KEITH!' cries his wife, for the second time tonight, 'shoot tha gert fat mouth! There's ladies present!

Before our friend can compose a ribald response, however, the next participants in the procession are upon us. An infant-school dance troupe, accompanied by a four-wheel drive blaring out music at ear-blistering volume. The young ladies are strutting their stuff, ably assisted by the teachers. Following closely behind are more young girls, dressed as fairy-tale characters, Hansel and Gretel, Snow White complete with dwarves, Red Riding Hood and a wolf, all utterly enchanting.

Suddenly, round the bend comes a tractor pulling a huge trailer, on which has been constructed a Santa's grotto style scene, on the top of which, in pride of place, sits a King. No idea which one, Gold, Frankincense or Myrrh, Gaspar, Balthazar or Melchior, but a King he undoubtedly is, surrounded by about a dozen kids, each one scrambling around, throwing cuddly toys, footballs and SWEETS into the crowd.

'Caramellos!' Chrissie cries, as a hail of confectionery rains down upon us. Several hit me on the face, the people next to us are scrabbling around on the road, gathering bonbons like famine-stricken lunatics. The King himself looks half-crazed, cackling loudly as he belts another football into the baying throng, and his helpers are flinging candy in an orgy of largesse, while us mere mortals are groping under the wheels of the vehicle, stuffing pockets and plastic bags with the loot. An old lady near me has brought an umbrella, despite zero rain forecast, and she is using the crook of the handle to scoop up the booty, which she sweeps into a bag-for-life.

Meanwhile Gaffer has gathered a couple of offerings from the pavement, one of which he greedily unwraps and stuffs into his mouth. He chews appreciatively for a second or two then cries out in anguish. 'Oh Christ! Blooody 'ell! Me teeth! This is a boiled sweet, not a caramel, tha blooody useless Soothern twot!' Surely he can't be referring to me? 'Three 'undred blooody quid me teeth cost, an' I just blooody broke me crown off, I told tha' I couldn't eat boiled sweets, ye said 'twas caramels they give oos!'

Diane wades into the fray. 'Tha blooody pie-can! Wot d'ye say it were blooody caramels for? S'all reet for you rich Soothern bastards, but three 'undred blooody quid is a lot t'oos.'

I am beginning to feel somewhat aggrieved. 'Hang on a minute. If they threw out dog-poo, you wouldn't just stuff it in your mouth, would you? You would check first, surely? Anyone can see these are boiled sweets, with cellophane wrappers. Didn't you look?'

Gaffer rapidly calms down, while picking the remains of his semi-masticated sweet from his expensive dental work. 'Ee's right, ower Di. Tis these blooody new glasses, bifocals tha' knaws. Can't see booger-all oop close.'

By this time the first King has moved past, to be replaced in the procession by a musical group of about six blokes in fancy dress, each blowing a trumpet, together with another fellow hitting hell out of a snare drum. The sound from the first King is still audible, and what with the trumpeters, the drummer, and whoever is about to come around the corner, my ear-drums are bursting.

More caramellos are raining down like shrapnel, I have pockets full of the things, which I am passing to Chrissie, to transfer to the plastic bag. Suddenly around the corner appears another huge float, topped by another King, complete with helpers. A stampede ensues, old women shoving aside kids to get to the carpet of sweets landing in the road, whereas my newly-developed technique is to drag them into a pile with my foot, where Chrissie, who is nearer the ground than me, can hoover them up.

Suddenly, through the air, a football is coming my way. I am perfectly placed to reach out and scoop it from the over the heads of the Spaniards around me, like a goalkeeper in the World Cup final. What I fail to notice however is that Gaffer, no doubt assisted by his new spectacles, has also spotted the incoming projectile. It all happens in slow motion. As I raise my arms to effortlessly pluck my prize from the air, Gaffer decides to act like a central defender and head the ball clear of the goalmouth. His face collides with my arm, although he would no doubt claim the opposite, and his expensive eye-wear is knocked clean from his face and disappears into the melee.

'Oh Christ! Blooody 'ell! Me glasses! Tha blooody useless twot! Two 'undred blooody quid they was! Quick, dive down and get 'em.'

Diane meanwhile jumps to the defence of her husband. 'Tha blooody useless Soothern pillock! Why d'ye knock 'is specs off? Two 'undred blooody quid they cost 'im.'

Our Northern friend is scrabbling round on his hands and knees, then with a shout of triumph he emerges from the crowd clutching his intact, but slightly bent, vision-aids. 'Tha blooody, clumsy, lucky booger!

Now I am more than a little upset. Lucky? 'You want to take those glasses back to the shop, Keith. Anyone could see that ball was about three feet above your head. Who do you think you are? Goliath? A giraffe grazing on the Masai Mara? Jack Charlton? You'd have needed a ladder to get that ball. I had it covered, and now it's gone, all thanks to you. We bring you down here to experience this Spanish culture, and all you do is complain. *Tha blooody Northern pie-can jessies*!'

The pair of them burst out laughing. 'Ee's reet, ower Di. These specs is blooody rubbish!'

Another broadside of candy is launched, the third and final King is upon us, and one fugitive bonbon suddenly catches our friend square on the forehead, missing his pricey goggles by a hairs-breadth. 'Didn't see that one coming, did you Keith?' I chortle. 'You're right, those blooody glasses is rubbish!'

The procession is winding up, we are still scraping up the caramellos which haven't been completely squashed by the passing tractors and four-wheel drives, and Chrissie has an impressive haul, easily enough to last us until Easter. We wend our way homewards, but before bidding farewell to our friends, I have something I need to get off my chest. 'Listen, Keith, I'm really sorry about your teeth, and your glasses. I feel really bad about it. I hope you.....'

Diane roars with laughter. 'Nay lad, ee were pullin' yer leg! 'Is glasses were five euros in the Chinese bazaar, an 'ee got 'is teeth done on t' NHS before we come 'ere! Don't believe a blooody word he tells ye!'

Sinking into our patio chairs with a restorative glass of red, after what has been an exhilarating if exhausting evening, I suddenly sit bolt upright in my chair. 'Damn and blast! Curses! Bloody hell!'

Chrissie gazes wearily in my direction. 'What on earth is it now? Haven't you had enough conflict for one evening?'

'You would think so, wouldn't you?' I groan, 'but I've just remembered something about that blooody, Northern, jessie, pillock pie-can.'

'What about Gaffer?' my wife giggles.

I exhale in mock anger. 'He still owes me three pints!'

CHAPTER 25. THE 'RUSSIANS'

'I saw two Russian blokes in our street today!' I am having an evening telephone conversation with Chrissie, who has popped back to the UK for a few days, to look after her mother, who has been unwell recently.

'Russians?' she laughs, 'how do you know they were Russians? Did you speak to them? I mean, I know you're fluent in Russian, but it must be a few years since you had a good old gossip with someone from Siberia!'

This is an occasional source of humour between us, on account of me having studied Russian at school, forty-plus years ago, then promptly forgetting everything apart from 'hello' and 'goodbye'. 'Yeah yeah very funny! They just looked, you know, Russian.'

'Define Russian' she continues, 'come on, give me a clue!'

'OK, they were big, fleshy, grey-coloured skin, looked like they hadn't seen the sun for six months, poorly dressed, smoking their heads off. Does that satisfy you?'

'Cossacks!' she giggles.

'Same to you, cheeky!'

'No, I mean were they dressed like cossacks? You know, leather boots, flappy trousers, big droopy moustaches, that kind of thing.'

'None of those' I confirm. 'They looked like they had been down a salt mine!'

'Balalaikas!'

'You're getting very personal tonight!' I joke.

'No, I mean could you see their balalaikas? Or their Urals?

'No, but I did see one of their bum-cheeks!' I shudder. 'Thanks for reminding me. They look like father and son, the father looks in his sixties, the son late-thirties. The son is huge, about twenty stone, and he bent over so I could see the crack of his backside. Big enough to park a Honda Goldwing!'

'What, you mean he mooned at you?' she splutters, 'how very Soviet!'

It's my turn to laugh, 'No, he was bending over picking something up. They were by that house at the top of the steps, the one that's for sale. If he'd bent over any further, I might have seen his balalaika! Or his Urals!'

The following evening we are having a similar conversation. 'I saw those Russian fellows again this morning, they must have bought the cottage on the steps, they had the front door open, either taking something in, or out. And before you ask, not a Cossack or a balalaika in sight!''

'And did you see their Urals today?' she chuckles.

'Well I wasn't looking that closely, but I'm not actually sure now they are Russians. I spoke to them, in Russian, as I passed by, and they didn't reply.'

My wife is still finding this funny. 'Oh yes, and what part of your extensive vocabulary did you employ? 'hello' or 'goodbye'?'

'I'll have you know' I point out stiffly, 'that I can also say 'yes' and 'no'!'

'Blimey, I wish I'd been there to witness that riveting dialogue!' my troublesome spouse observes. *'Hello! Yes? No? Goodbye!'* Watch out Leo Tolstoy!'

I can't help laughing. 'Yeah yeah yeah, what I actually said was *strass-vu-che*. Hello. And they ignored me.'

'Can't say I blame them! If some English bloke in the middle of Spain came up to me and went *strass-whatsit*, I think I'd ignore him too. Or kick him in the Nabokov!'

The next day I have more news. 'You know those Russian blokes I told you about? Well, they're from Holland!'

'Oh quite close to Vladivostok then, no wonder you were confused!' comes the sarcastic reply. 'Just a quick clog dance from Amsterdam. And the accent is very similar!'

'Well actually they're English, but they both live in Holland at the moment. The one I thought was the father is a property developer in a small way, just does a bit of buying and selling, and his name is Richard.'

My wide dissolves into fits of laughter. 'Oh no, please tell me that's not true! Please tell me you're not going to give him one of your ridiculous nicknames. You are not to call him 'Dutch Dick!'

Now it's my turn to guffaw, 'never gave it a moment's thought! Sounds like something you might catch on a night out in Amsterdam! He says he likes to be called Richie, or Richard. And the one I thought was the son, with the large balalaikas, is called Dominic. He runs a restaurant in a small town south of Rotterdam.'

Chrissie is still in stitches. 'You're not serious! Dick and Dom? Are they buying a bungalow? Tell me you are making this up!'

I have not the slightest clue what she is talking about. 'Who are Dick and Dom, and what does this have to do with a bungalow? Richie and Dominic are two friends, not related at all, who just happen to live in the same town in Holland, Richie has bought the cottage by the steps and is moving here permanently, he is sick of the weather over there. Dom is also buying a house further along the street, that one opposite Auntie Vera, but for holidays only, as he has the restaurant. They both need some sunshine, as you can tell from their complexions. So who are this Dick and Dom when they're at home?'

'They were on children's TV about ten years ago' she confirms. 'Dick and Dom in Da Bungalow.' I doubt you would have seen it.'

'Certainly not!' I splutter, 'I was too busy earning a crust, salting away a few quid into my pension fund to enable us to retire early to the sunshine. Mind you, I always suspected you were sat home watching daytime TV!'

Now it's Chrissie's turn to splutter. 'Oh I think I might have been bringing up our children, actually', she bristles.

But I am on a roll. 'Ten years ago they were at university, I think you will find? Besides, *Dick and Dom in Da House* hardly sounds educational, does it now?'

'Bungalow!' comes the agitated reply. 'Dick and Dom in Da BUNGALOW!'

'Who cares if it was a tower block?' I sniff. 'Anyway, I am going to the Lantern Bar with Dick and Dom, I mean Richie and Dominic, tonight, to discuss a bit of business. Richie needs some help with his house apparently. So lets hope I don't call him 'Dutch Dick', and blow the job! If I do, it will be all your fault!'

The following evening Chrissie announces she will be flying back at the weekend, as her mother is much better. 'Excellent news!' I announce. 'I can brief you about your new job.'

'New job?' she cries. 'New job? Just last night you were bragging about how hard you were working so we could retire to the sunshine, and now you have found me a job? Don't I have enough jobs already? Teri, Estefania, plus the academy. Tell you what, I'll work all night if that helps!'

'Yes but that was before I discovered you were watching daytime TV, while I was out slaving away! Your punishment for viewing 'Dick and Dom in Da House' is to clean Dick's house!' I giggle. 'He has asked us to do a complete house clearance, you know, put everything outside the front door and watch the Spanish come and steal it! Then he would like you to give the place a thorough clean, prior to him arriving back the week after next. I have negotiated an excellent rate on your behalf, minus my commission of course!'

'Be careful' she hisses, 'be very careful. I might just cancel my flight, and stay here with mother.' *Well best of luck with that!*

A week later and I am dismantling an ancient teak-veneer wardrobe on the top floor of Richie's new Spanish house, and anyone who thinks that flat-pack furniture began with MFI and IKEA in the 1970's had better think again, as this stuff easily pre-dates that. The wardrobe is so big, and the old Spanish house so narrow of stairway and hallway, that the beast could only have originally been assembled on-site. It comes apart as a top, bottom, sides, back, and the three front doors, so I begin carefully unscrewing and carrying each piece down two flights of stairs, to leave it outside against the railings where hopefully one of the neighbours will want it and take it away. The jungle drums were beating as I unlocked the house earlier this morning, no doubt the neighbours were wondering what the English would be giving away today, and competition is usually fierce, I can tell you.

As I emerge into the street with the first piece of ancient furniture, the first neighbour I encounter is Pepe, otherwise known as 'Pirate Pete' as he had a cataract operation earlier this year and was wearing a black eye patch for a while. He is a lovely old man and generally gives Chrissie a cuddle, and usually cops a feel of her chest area at the same time, apparently. 'What are you getting rid of that for? he shouts, at usual Andalucian volume which is a nine or ten on the dial.

'My friend doesn't want it' I reply.

'It's a beautiful wardrobe' he continues, 'why are you getting rid of it?'

What can I say? *Oh cos it's a load of old crap?* Not really, I bet he has one the same. 'Do you want it? I ask him.

'No I have got one just the same' he replies.

Up I go for the next bit of wardrobe and when I get back down with it we have exactly the same conversation, word for word. This time a few more neighbours have heard the shouting and have come out for a look, so I have an audience of half a dozen or so. I feel a bit like one of those zebra or antelopes on the David Attenborough wildlife programmes, when they get separated from the herd and look up to see themselves surrounded by lions.

Returning with the third lot I notice that 'Mrs Ferret' has put in an appearance. She lives about four doors up from Richie, and to me resembles a weasel with her narrow face and eyes, but Mrs Ferret she remains. She is closely watching the gradual emergence of the wardrobe pieces, and by the time I have collected the fourth piece she has got her husband outside and he has come down and just casually started taking the bits away. He looks straight at me and does not seem too pleased about something, probably he was planning a lazy Saturday, maybe slip down to the square, have a beer with his mates, and now she has him inside reassembling a damned great wardrobe. Women are the same the world over, aren't they?

Anything left outside in the street is fair game and I am glad the venerable piece of furniture has found a new owner, but this must be a record as I have not even finished putting it all out yet. I collect the final piece and take it up to the Ferrets' house, hand him the collection of bolts, *'gracias'* he says through gritted teeth and he disappears inside.

I get back to Richie's and notice that 'Leopard-skin Woman' has just surfaced. She is a 'woman of a certain age' who dresses in skimpy cotton frocks, often with a leopard print, and flip-flops, but the most remarkable thing about her is her black or dark brown lipstick. Being a man I cannot possibly explain the reason for this but with her dark Spanish complexion and this black lipstick she looks like a photographic negative you used to get in the pre-digital age. She has a wicked sense of humour and we usually have a right laugh when we pass her door on our walks, but today she has a complaint. 'I wanted that wardrobe' she says.

'It was a beautiful wardrobe' chimes in Pirate Pete,' I have one just like it.'

'Yes I wanted it' she continues. What can I say? 'You were too slow?' Hardly. 'Anyway' she brightens up, 'what else have you got? Any kitchen stuff?' Actually there are a few grimy old saucepans left still to chuck away, so almost for a joke I ask if she wants them. They are in Richie's kitchen, and as it is unthinkable for a woman here to enter a house with a strange man, she grabs auntie Vera and in we all go. Honestly you would not use these pots to catch used engine oil, but she grabs them tightly like she has won a prize at a funfair, then turns around and spots the fridge-freezer. 'I want that, can I have it? For me, for me!'

'I don't know' I tell her, 'I will need to check with my friend.' On a fridge scale of one to ten it's about a two, but there is just the chance that Richie might want it until he can get another, although I doubt it. He has told us he wants the whole house cleared, apart from the double bed frame and headboard in the main bedroom. We can ditch the mattress, but he definitely wants the base.

'Please please' Leopard-skin Woman is yelling, 'I only have a small fridge and I want this one, can I have it?' Auntie Vera is laughing but I remain firm, I cannot give Richie's fridge to Leopard-skin woman, even though I secretly believe he fancies her, so I repeat that I will call *mi amigo* tomorrow and let her know. Then Chrissie appears, she has the cleaning gear ready to make a start, when all the rubbishy furniture has been cleared out. 'Cristina!' shouts LSW. 'Can I have the fridge, I want it please, please, I only have a small one.'

'No!' I shout, 'I will call my friend tomorrow.' God this is giving me a headache. 'I promise you can have it if my friend says yes.' With that I usher them out of the house and lock the door, but decide to have a bit of fun with LSW. On the upturned saucepan lid, which she has clamped to her bosom in case it escapes, is a layer of tiny droppings. *'Miras'* I yell,' *caka de rattones.'* Look, mouse shit!

She roars with laughter, like a donkey braying whilst simultaneously firing a machine gun. 'Mouse shit, mouse shit' she roars.

'What mouse shit?' says auntie Vera.

'Who has mouse shit?' says Pirate Pete.

'Look, here is the mouse shit' replies LSW in a voice that can probably be heard in the next province. We have a history of rodent sightings in Richie's house, a rat was spotted in his garden a few days ago, so I bought some poison to put down which LSW saw me doing and every day since she has shouted 'Mind the rat' when she sees me going in there. I am the '*Matador de rata*' apparently, which is marginally safer than being a matador of bulls, I guess. At least I don't have to wear a pink cloak and tight black trousers.

So next day I call Richie about the fridge. 'It is bogging, get rid of it' he confirms, so outside I go in search of LSW, and sure enough the whole group of them are down there gossiping as usual. I decide to do this the Andalucian way, so approaching the group I shout 'My friend says....' and hold out my thumb horizontally like a Roman Emperor condemning the Christians to the lions. I pause a few seconds for dramatic effect. '*Si*' I eventually holler, and my thumb goes up.

LSW jumps up and down like she has scored the winning goal in the cup final. 'I can have the fridge, I can have the fridge' she shouts. Everyone is laughing, although whether it is the sight of a middle-aged woman cavorting in the street about a minging domestic appliance, or the large English idiot with his thumb up, I cannot say. She bellows inside her house and her teenage son appears, and we head to Richie's where her other son is already waiting. Hmmm. I can't work out how he knew. Between us we manhandle the greasy beast out of the door (the fridge not her son) and down the fifty or so yards to her place where we drop it in her sitting room and I beat a hasty retreat, but not before she collars me and asks if her son can come round tomorrow for a look at what else my *amigo* is getting rid of.

'Tomorrow' I smile weakly and retire to the peace of my patio and a cold beer.

The following day Chrissie is cleaning the dog poo from the top floor of Richie's house, which, had I known about previously, I could have used as evidence to extract an extra couple of quid an hour on her wages, and I am cementing some more tiles onto my next terracing job at home, when my phone rings. It is my wife. 'Can you come up here quickly, there is a riot going on. Every woman in the whole street has turned up, mob-handed, it's all kicking off and starting to get ugly.'

I can hear shouting in the background, although at this precise moment I am up to my eyes in cement. 'Why on earth did you let them in?'

'I didn't, they just opened the front door and barged in! Quick, I am inundated with Spaniards, and I cannot get rid of them!' she cries.

'OK, give me two minutes' I reassure her, although what I can do about a baying pack of Andalucian women I really don't know. I clean up and rush to the scene of the crime, to see our neighbours Loli and Isabel just leaving. Loli is clutching a curtain rail, Isabel is empty handed, as it seems the rest of the house has already been stripped bare. LSW and her son are there and a few others have turned up including an old woman in a twin set, pearls and a hump back, who we have never seen before. Everyone is shouting at once trying to claim the remaining furniture, including the kitchen units, which are clearly not bolted down, and the bathroom cabinet. Loli and LSW almost come to blows but a severely harassed Chrissie manages to usher them all outside and peace is restored, but not before the son had bagged himself a bedside cabinet and a chest of drawers, which we have to help him carry, whilst LSW herself, who today was dressed in a lime green nylon tracksuit, is grunting under the strain of carrying six non-matching dinner plates.

Just about the only thing left in the house, apart from a disgusting fat-encrusted gas cooker, is a huge lounge unit with glass doors above and drawers below, as was popular in Britain in about 1976, and that is only because it is simply too big to move. I head back home to resume my tiling and waiting by my front door is Isabel. She beckons me over and in a stage whisper asks 'Can I have the lounge unit?' Getting the bloody thing out the house will be fun. I cannot wait...

The following evening, Isabel, the quiet sister, knocks on the door and asks if her niece Sabrina could have a look at the lounge unit, so we fix a time and Chrissie and I accompany Sabrina, Isabel and the noisy sister Loli up to Richie's place just along the street. It is getting dark so I flip the light switch, but nothing happens. Strange. I check the fuse board, everything seems switched on, but no power. Pirate Pete comes in and starts flicking a lighter which immediately sets off danger signals in my mind, as the gas connection in this house seemed a bit dodgy too, he is sparking away like a madman but then Sabrina walks through to the kitchen and switches on the light there. What the hell is going on? I glance up at the ceiling in the sitting room and notice two bare wires protruding forlornly from the place where a few days ago a perfectly good light fitting hung. Chrissie walks in and I point at the missing appliance, 'some thieving Spanish bastard has stolen the lights!'

She laughs. 'Yes that was the other day when I phoned you to come up and sort out the row that was going on when all the neighbours crowded in here at once. Leopard-skin woman's son took it down and gave it to Auntie Vera. There was nothing I could do as Loli was trying to steal the kitchen units at the time.'

Sabrina looks at the lounge unit but says it is too big for her house. It is about seven feet tall and ten feet feet wide so you would need a big room to fit it in, but none of the neighbours seem to want it. I think it is lovely but we already have something similar, so we will just have to put it out by the bin. Shame, it is a post-modern-Nuevo-Art-Deco masterpiece. Or possibly a hideous piece of chipboard crap, depending on your point of view. Sabrina is however highly taken with the cooker, a filthy grease-encrusted appliance which has clearly seen better days, although you would need a long memory. Can she come back tomorrow with the car? Yes she can.

So the following evening the same cast, accompanied by our other neighbour Fernando in his car, head up to Dutch Dick's, and Fernando and I manoeuvre the cooker into the middle of the kitchen. I am wearing old clothes because the thought of picking up this unspeakable wreck fills me with disgust, we manage to lift it off the ground but it is in danger of sliding out of our grasp because of the generations of congealed lard clinging to every surface. We are just getting it through the kitchen door when there is a loud crash and the bottom falls out, Fernando's eyes are popping and a bead of sweat trickles down his forehead, Chrissie bursts into a fit of uncontrolled laughter, and I am trying to kick the offending bits of cooker out of the way so we can put it down. Finally we wrestle it through the front door and into the rear of Fernando's hatchback, and I go back to collect the fallen bits of metal, which turns out to be a frame with small wheels, meaning we could have wheeled it out instead of getting covered in antique fat. Ah well, you live and learn.

I am just about to lock the house up when Loli appears in the doorway dragging a kitchen base unit. 'Can I have this?'

There are two base units in the kitchen which put a new slant on the term 'free-standing', as they are propped up on bricks. I cannot imagine for one moment that Richie will want them, as they would have been hideous in 1963, but 'no' I tell her, 'I have to check with my friend first.' She persists, but I stand firm. 'If he doesn't want the units you can have them', is my final word, and ushering her towards the front door I can hopefully beat a hasty retreat back to our place and the promise of a cold beer. The problem is that Leopard-skin woman also wanted the kitchen units, so if Richie decides they can go, there could be another mini-riot in the street.....

Loli however has other ideas, and refuses to be shepherded out. The walls in the hallway, and the passage out towards the back door, are clad in tongue-and-groove-effect-plastic-imitation wood, up to about waist-high, the like of which I have never seen before. It is truly horrendous, given that it is actually nailed to the walls, which themselves are clearly un-rendered, so the cladding follows the undulations in the stonework, like some nightmare DIY abomination. Had the perpetrator fixed some wooden battens to the walls, and tacked the cladding to that, it would still have looked unspeakably ugly, but one-thousand percent better than the current image of a drunken rampage in a plastics factory. Our neighbour taps the fake wood, and grins. I screw up my face. 'I know, ugly, isn't it?' I sympathise. That is about the best I can manage, with my limited Spanish.

Once again however it seems I have misjudged the capacity of the local population to covet anything which they think might be about to be given away, regardless of it's apparent value, or aesthetic qualities. Loli fixes me with her best smile. 'Can I have a small piece of this?' I am staggered. She actually likes this stuff? And she doesn't want it all, just a little bit. For what earthly purpose? It's not like it is real wood, so she can't need it for making stuff. I tap the wall with my knuckle, and it rattles, and distorts, and a small puff of dust rises into the air.

'How much do you need?' I enquire, intrigued. This is simply beyond belief.

She holds out her hands, about two feet apart, like a fisherman describing the one that got away, then shrugs. 'Half a metre?'

The thing is, Richie has only tasked us with a house clearance, which we have more-or-less accomplished, followed by a clean-up. He didn't mention stripping vile plastic cladding from the walls, although I am one-thousand percent certain his first job when he eventually arrives will be to get his toolbox out and claw the monstrosity off. 'I will need to ask my friend' I reply. 'This, and the kitchen. I will call him tonight in Holland, and speak to you tomorrow.'

Later that evening, I recount the tale to Richie, who expresses astonishment that someone is interested in his kitchen, and wall cladding. 'You mean that repulsive crap on the walls in the hall? What sort of people are these?'

'Actually, your new neighbours!' I chuckle.

'I just cannot, in my wildest dreams, imagine anyone would want that stuff. Am I moving to the Third World? Strip it off if you have time, then we can see what needs doing to the walls, when I get down there, hopefully in about three weeks time. And those kitchen units. I wouldn't use those as a work bench! Chuck the lot!'

The following morning, Loli is chatting with Jose the Pan, next to his little white van, as I leave home to start my morning's work in Richie's. 'My friend says you can have those things' I inform her. She gives a little cheer, and skips up and down in apparent delight. 'But later this morning, not now!' I continue. I know what Loli is like, she will be waiting outside the door, or worse, barging in to help herself. Chrissie appears with a bucket of bleach, disinfectant, brushes, a mop and various cleaning cloths, and with me bearing the tools I think I will need for ripping the cladding off, we dash to our friend's cottage, firmly closing the front door behind us, hopefully keeping any marauding Spaniards at bay.

My wife disappears upstairs to recommence the cleaning, she has already done the top floor of this three-storey cottage, removing piles of fossilised dog faeces, so today is concentrating on the middle level, containing the main bedroom. In every telephone call with our new friend, he has stressed how much he admires the bed-frame and accompanying built-in headboard, and that we are not to dispose of it, under any circumstances. 'Keep them thieving Spanish off me bed!' he reminded me, only last night. 'You can bin the mattress, obviously, but I like that headboard, and the wardrobe what goes with it.' I cannot imagine why, although it takes all sorts, as they say. But a 1970's MFI-style chipboard laminated headboard, complete with spotlights and a place for your Teasmade? In a two-hundred year-old cottage? I don't think so.

Suddenly, there comes a shout from the floor above. The cleaner needs my assistance with something. 'Come and help me shift this dirty old mattress, will you please, then we can chuck it in the street. See how long it stays there!' I head upstairs as summoned, we position ourselves either side of the bed, and agree that I will lift, and Chrissie will push, to get the frankly unattractively-stained mattress into a vertical position. I reach over and grab the edge of greasy beast, haul it upwards, but am getting no assistance from the other side, as my wife has collapsed in convolutions of laughter. She is sitting on the floor, tears running down her cheeks, whereas I am struggling to hold the filthy refugee from a Chinese brothel in an upright position, unable to see the funny side, as it were. I drag the carcass across the room and prop it against the wall, then turn to see what all the mirth is about. And dissolve into guffaws. Someone has sawn the bed frame in half, tied it up with blue twine, and propped in up on house-bricks. For a second or two my brain is unable to process this information, but there it is, Richie's precious double bed, the victim of a Texas chainsaw-style massacre, although the first thing I can think of is that the bricks will come in handy, for finishing off my new patio in the garden. I am laughing so much I have to sit down, joining Chrissie on the floor, where she is flat on her back, helpless.

We are both laughing so much, and so loudly, that with the bedroom window overlooking the street open, we have attracted the attention of the neighbours. 'Mind the rat!' comes a cry, Leopardskin Woman, obviously. Another shout, 'can I have the kitchen units?' Bloody Loli. They have us surrounded, like a pack of hyenas. But they will have to wait, I am laughing so much at the pathetic spectacle of Richie's sawn-up bed that I am unable to stand, but eventually I am able to fathom out what might be behind the carnage. 'You remember when we bought our new mattress?' I splutter, 'when the chap told us there were two different lengths of bed in Spain, one-eighty and one-ninety? Well I think this frame, which is relatively new, was a one-ninety, but the mattress, of dubious heritage, is a one-eighty. So someone sawed a ten-centimetre piece out of the middle of the frame, to make it fit the mattress. Of course, the frame lost its rigidity, so they had to prop the two halves up on bricks, then tie the two ends together to stop it shifting during the night, and the whole lot going crash, bang wallop. Can you imagine someone having sex in this bed? BANG! 'Did the earth move for you, darling?' 'Yes and I've got a brick up my arse, to prove it!'

'I can't imagine anyone having sex in this dog-shit encrusted, rat infested, HOUSE!' my wife yells. 'Why in God's name did Richard buy this slum? I can't think of a single redeeming feature. Did the vendors pay him to take it off their hands, do you think?'

I am still wiping the tears from my eyes. 'And the bad news is, I have to break the story to Richie! Can you imagine that conversation? 'Sorry mate, some bastard sawed your bed in half, but don't worry, they tied it up with string, and propped it up on bricks!'

'Yes, then some other bastard stole your bricks!' cries Chrissie, doubled-up again. 'Still, you can always blame a Spaniard, can't you!'

'Plenty to choose from!' I giggle, peeping out the window, to see that Pirate Pete and Ferret-Woman have joined the throng in the street below. 'Anyway, let me take a photo on my phone, to text Richie this evening, then we can dump the frame and mattress in the street, so you can actually earn some money cleaning, rather than rolling round on your back, laughing!'

'I am earning, right now!' cries my wife, 'danger money! What with the dog poo upstairs, and whatever infectious bacteria might be lurking in this bed, I am charging top-dollar, don't you worry! I've gone through three pairs of rubber gloves already, and if you think I'm touching this receptacle of bodily fluids with my bare hands, think again! And look over there. Old man's slippers! And his dressing gown. When you promised me early-retirement in the sunshine, you failed to mention I'd be exposed to Bubonic plague!' She narrows her eyes. 'Or was this the plan all along? I succumb to some infectious disease, then you claim my pensions for the next ten years? Maybe that's why Leopard-skin-Woman is hanging around, she is not really after the greasy kitchen units, it's you she has her eyes on. Or maybe Loli? You know, her missing teeth, the way she clears her throat every morning. Or Ferret-Woman? She can run up your trouser legs, give you a playful nip. All these Spanish hotties, I understand now, they are all gagging for a big, strong Englishman to fulfil their fantasies!'

I am still chuckling. 'Yes maybe I'll take the bed frame down to the street myself, offer demonstrations of what can be done with a length of string and a few bricks! You never know, I might get lucky!'

'On your bike, Sonny Jim!' my dearest cries, grabbing one end of the frame. 'if you're taking a bed down to that lot, I'm coming with you!'

The following morning we manage a silent escape from our house, evading the scavenging locals, on our way to Richie's, passing the bin where we dumped the sawn-up bed frame yesterday, which is not there this morning. Large items are collected on the tenth, twentieth and thirtieth of each month, and it is none of those dates now. 'I don't believe it! I simply refuse to accept that someone has taken that piece of rubbish!' my wife exclaims. 'Were they after the string, do you think?'

'Probably the scrap metal' I am guessing, 'although why anyone would go to the trouble, is beyond me. Maybe the wooden slats also had some value, although they were 'bent in the middle, like a one-string fiddle', as we used to sing at the rugby club after about seven pints of draught Bass!'

Chrissie disappears upstairs to continue with the cleaning, while I apply myself to stripping the plastic-wood cladding from the hall walls, which proves easier said than done. I had assumed it was nailed on in panels, but it turns out to be individual 'planks' of tongue and groove plastic, just like the real thing, but a hundred times more hideous. My first instinct is to remove one plank then simply rip the rest from the walls, but it is cracking and splintering and the nails are remaining embedded in the plaster, so I have to use pliers to prise out each and every fixing, and after about half an hour of this I am absolutely raving, ripping and tearing, cursing and swearing, and the floor is strewn with broken lengths of this thrice-damned, cursed, hellish substance. I sincerely hope I never see another plank of this evil Spanish plastic cladding in my lifetime. Sadly however, I have only stripped one wall, there is a whole passageway still to do, so my only option is to call for reinforcements. Who decline to play ball. 'I refuse to get involved in any building work, unless you pay for a manicure, and a pedicure', the cleaning staff advise me.

'A pedicure?' I splutter, 'I'm not asking you to pull the stuff off with your feet! And it's not building, it's un-building, just an easy bit of leisurely pulling off of a few bits of this lovely antique Spanish Art-Deco masterpiece, and recycling it in the direction of Loli.'

'Well that's my price, take it or leave it! And if it's that easy, do it yourself, you agreed to this, it was not my idea, I was not even in the country, I seem to remember.'

She has a point I suppose…. After another hour, against all odds, I have a huge pile of plastic planks lined up by the front door. I have sorted about six of the best lengths, which should cover the half-metre Loli was seeking. I have even dragged the two greasy kitchen base units into the hall, ready for distributing to the neighbours. 'Would your toenails mind awfully assisting me in the removal of these items into the street, please? Just a few yards, shouldn't involve the loss of any nail polish, although I am sure Richie will spring for a tin of gloss paint. From the Chinese bazaar!'

My wife snorts in derision. 'You have absolutely no idea what it is to be a woman, do you? Seven pints of draught Bass. Bends in the middle like a one-string fiddle. When I die, I am coming back as a man! Come on then, let's get it over with!' And she jerks open the front door, then jumps about a foot, as there is Loli, with her face pressed against the glass, waiting for us to emerge. 'MADRE MIA!'

Our neighbour is trying to force her way inside, but I am having none of it. 'Out, out, out' I am shouting, '*fuera*,' waving my arms like I am trying to stop a runaway herd of buffalo. Leopard-skin woman arrives on the scene, Pirate Pete is not far behind her, but I am determined the mass scramble will take place in the street, rather than Richie's hallway. Grabbing a pile of planks, I corral the assorted Spaniards out into the street, drop the offensive items by the bin and return for the next lot.

Pirate Pete shows acute interest in the plastic wood. 'Why are you getting rid of that? I have just the same in my house.'

Next I return for the kitchen units, dragging them both outside, where they receive many admiring glances, despite the fact that one unit only has three legs. For effect, I gather up a couple of bricks and theatrically place them where the missing leg should be. *'Para mi, para mi!'* shout both Loli and LSW, in unison.

'Why are you getting rid of that?' Pirate Pete queries. 'My kitchen is just the same.'

I drag, and push, both kitchen units into the street, return for Loli's six 'good' planks, then lock Richie's front door behind me. Right, we are on the home straight. I can feel a cold one beckoning. Our neighbours meanwhile are still bickering over the division of the spoils. 'OK, it's for you to choose' I tell them. *Elegir*. To Choose. I learned this verb at the library conversation class this week, although little did I think that its first outing would be in connection with the distribution of two repulsive pieces of scrap.

Several rapid-fire bursts of Spanish are exchanged, following which it appears as if peace has broken out. Leopard-skin woman hollers out to her husband, Manuel, who opens their front door to the sound of Elvis, singing 'You Were Always On My Mind.' I was anxious to get home, but now I adopt my best Presley pose, grab an imaginary mike, and start to croon. 'Carrie, tell me that your sweet love hasn't died,' following which Manuel also adjusts his stance, balancing his gut on the waistband of his jeans. 'Geeve me, geeve me onne more chancee to keeep you satisfieeeeed!' Priceless, absolutely priceless. Elvis was , is, and always will be, the King. But me and Manuel? Maybe our act needs a bit of work...

Loli meanwhile is keen to drag her kitchen unit home, although before she does I lay out her six plastic planks on the cobbles. 'There you are, my friend said yes!' I confirm, grinning wildly, feeling I have probably made her day, possibly even her year. What more could any girl ask for? A three-legged collection of every virus known to man, and six floppy lengths of utter hideousness. That will knock her bandy, as Del-Boy Trotter might have said. Apparently not. It appears as if our annoying neighbour is rejecting my generosity, at least as far as the planks go. She doesn't want them, as far as I can tell. What? WHAT? After all that fuss?

Beckoning me to follow, she picks up one end of the kitchen unit, I slap the planks on top, grab the other end of the unit and we stagger back up the street, to her front door. Pausing for breath, she is trying to explain something, which I am struggling to follow, although the gist is that she no longer wants the horrid imitation wood, which I had taken time to carefully select, choosing the six which were least deformed, removing the nails, giving them a wipe down. Good as new, almost, and after all that, she is telling me she doesn't want them. Can't say I blame her, 'they are horrible, not natural wood, complete rubbish!' is the best I can manage, but at least I am agreeing with her, in her native tongue.

Loli shakes her head, grabs one plank, and beckons me to follow her inside, after summoning Isabel with an ear-splitting bawl. She opens the door to her cellar, stands back so I can observe the steps down, and there, in the gloom of a forty-watt bulb, in all its glory, is exactly the same plastic imitation wood, nailed to the wall, undulating in unison with the stonework below, albeit with a damaged section about halfway down. I want the ground to open and swallow me up. After telling her for three days that Richie's cladding was disgusting, she has the brother-and-twin in her own house. With a few broken planks, which is what she was trying to replace. I feel so stupid, and completely embarrassed, but I simply don't have the vocabulary to dig myself out of the hole. I grin awkwardly, but why doesn't she want the planks I have painstakingly selected? 'They are different colours, neighbour' she observes, holding Richie's next to hers. And the penny finally drops. Unbelievably, this hideous concoction comes in different shades of imitation wood. Who knew? Loli's is a teak finish, whereas Richie's is an antique pine, and because it's pre-coloured plastic, there is no possibility of staining it to match.

'Bad luck!' I smile, grabbing the offending plank, and lobbing it into the street with the five others. I wrap my arms around her kitchen unit, making a mental note to be extra liberal with the shower gel, when I eventually get shot of these cursed Spaniards, and heave it through her front door. '*Hasta manana*!' see you tomorrow I cry, and scooping up the planks from the street, I hurry back to the bin and dump them unceremoniously with the others. Turning to finally head home, for that overdue shower, and several cold ones, I hear a voice calling to me. Pirate Pete. 'Why are you getting rid of that? I have exactly the same in my house!'

So does everyone else, Pete, so does everyone else!

CHAPTER 26 DUTCH DICK

It is five days since Dutch Richie arrived, car full of tea towels, but very few tools, and we have been desperately trying to get him to start cooking for himself. He has been eating with us for the last four nights and we need him to start standing on his own two feet, if only for the sake of our sanity. Even his arrival in town was a major drama. The previous weekend we were having a short break in the caravan, when on the Saturday morning I received a call. 'John, Richie here, I am on the road!'

'Which road would that be?' I enquire, somewhat puzzled, given that as far as I am aware, he is in Holland, and coming down to Spain in a few weeks time.

'The road to Santa Marta, of course' he replies, 'should be there in the morning on Monday, probably around six or so, I am driving straight through, sleeping in the car, for a couple of hours off and on.'

'Slight problem there Richie, we are in the caravan on the coast, not coming back until Monday night, but don't worry, we will catch up with you Tuesday morning.'

Silence on the line for a few moments. 'Ah, well, would you mind coming back a bit earlier?' requests our friend. 'The thing is, I am staying in Dominic's cottage, while I do up my place, but I've left his key at home, so I need to borrow yours. He did give you a key didn't he?

'He did, yes' I confirm, slightly annoyed at the turn of events. 'The problem is, our car is in the garage down here at the moment, fuel pump problem and they can't get the part until Monday morning. They tell me it should be ready about six PM, Monday evening, so the very earliest we can be back in Santa Marta is after eight that night , or possibly Tuesday if the car takes longer to fix.'

'Shit.'

'Sorry Richie, but why didn't you let us know you were coming?

'I did, but you didn't answer, so I left you a voice message,' he claims, although where this alleged message is, I have no idea.

'Well how far have you come?'

'About fifty miles.'

'So that's easy then, why don't you turn back, give it a few days, then come down midweek. You might even remember the key!'

'Can't' comes the reply, 'I've turned off the water in the house.'

'What, and they don't have stop-cocks in Holland? Can't you just turn it on again? Or does the water come out of a dyke over there?'

'Nah, I've drained the central heating, it'll be too much of a faff to turn back now.'

I am desperately tying to find a solution to something which is really not my fault, or my problem. 'Right, so why not stop in an hotel on the road Sunday night, get a good night's sleep, have a decent meal, get cleaned up, good breakfast on Monday, arrive nice and refreshed in Santa Marta late afternoon?' Sounds like a perfect plan to me.

'Nah, I'm on the road now, I just wanna get there.'

'Well you're going to be hanging around for fourteen hours, waiting for us, then. Assuming the car is ready. I'll give you a shout late Monday afternoon, as soon as we know.'

Monday morning, we are having a leisurely breakfast in the caravan, when my phone rings again. 'I told you to turn that damn thing off!' complains Chrissie.

'All-right mate?' croaks a jet-lagged sounding Richie. 'I'm here, any news about the car?'

I am not known for my levels of patience, especially during breakfast, and this man is fast exhausting my slim reserves. 'Er, it was Sunday yesterday, and most Spanish garages don't even work Saturdays. I have nothing new to tell you, we will call the garage around half-five this evening, then I will phone you' I tell him, secretly hoping the car isn't ready until about Friday. A few more days in the caravan would be lovely. And between you and me, serve the idiot right.

At half-past five the phone rings again. We are walking to the garage in the village, so I still don't have any news, but I promise to call him when I do. Ten minutes later, he calls again, but I am talking to the mechanic, which is tricky enough deciphering the language, so I pass the phone to Chrissie, who at this stage has not actually met Richie in person. She promises to call him when we have any news, then promptly switches the phone off.

The car is repaired, I offer my thanks to the garage, pay their extremely reasonable bill, and we settle down for the journey home. 'Better switch the back phone on, and tell that Dutch Dick we will be home at around half-eight,' I suggest. 'I'm not bothering to cook when we get back, so invite him down the Chinese with us, if you like. Or not! Give you a chance to get to know him!'

'I feel I've known him half my life already!' she chuckles, turning the phone on. 'Two missed calls!' she cries, 'what is wrong with the bloke?'

And he called twice more on the journey home....

So here I am attempting to persuade Richie to start fending for himself. 'Right, pay attention' I command. 'Your daily bread. Jose the Pan, in his Little White Van, comes along at about 9.15 each morning, gives a little toot, and you can pop down and get your fresh bread.'

'What, that bloody idiot who wakes me up every morning, followed by all that shouting?' cries Richie.

'I wouldn't let Chrissie hear you calling her beloved Jose an idiot' I reply, 'and it's not shouting you can hear, just the neighbours saying good morning to each other.'

'Well it sounds like shouting to me' he says, 'today it sounded like a road-rage incident down there, I almost called the police only I cannot speak Spanish. Anyway, what sort of bread does he sell?'

'Crusty long bread like a French baguette, only fatter,' I inform him.

'Nah, can't eat crusty bread, it gets in me teeth' he says. 'Does he sell white sliced?'

I run my hand across my face and mention that no, an artisan baker does not do white sliced. 'OK, your fruit and veg' I continue. 'There are about a dozen 'fruiteria' shops in town, there is one down in the square which we use, they are very friendly.'

'Christ, I looked in there the other day, it was full of old Spanish women' he protests.

'What the hell did you expect to see in a Spanish fruit shop?' I ask. 'The Hanging Gardens of Babylon? Herds of Wildebeest grazing majestically across the Serengeti?'

'All right Basil' he laughs, 'but you know what I mean, I cannot speak the lingo.'

'Well that's how you learn, listen to what they are saying, get a feel for it' I respond. 'Besides, you can just point to what you want. Uno kilo de este, medio kilo for a half.'

'Nah' he replies, 'can't eat fruit, it gets in me teeth.'

I breathe deeply. 'Right, it's the supermarket then, be here at half six tonight. Oh and by the way, you will need a shopping trolley, they are about eleven Euros in the bazaar.'

'Are we going in the car? he pleads.

'Nope, we are walking' I inform him, with just a hint of malice in my voice.

'Walking?' he splutters.

'Yes, walking, it is only ten minutes. Besides there is nowhere to park and it's all one-way streets. You will enjoy the stroll.'

At half six sharp there is a knock on our door and there stands Richie, with a gleaming new trolley in a fetching shade of red tartan. I burst out laughing, 'Blimey, did you get a pipe and slippers with that thing, Richard?'

'Bollix, it's the only one they had' comes the reply.

'Well, would you mind walking a bit in front of us please? Pretend we're not together?' I ask.

'I will get you for this, matey' he hisses, as we walk gently downhill to the Donna supermarket. By the time we get there he is out of breath, then he causes mayhem in the foyer trying to find a Euro coin to lock up his shopper, and another to unlock a supermarket trolley. In the end I have to lend him the money to prevent a queue of irate Spaniards building up behind him. The first thing we encounter is the bread, rows of lovely crusty loaves of all shapes and sizes. 'Where's the white sliced? he demands. I point it out. 'But it says it's mouldy' he complains.

Chrissie and I burst out laughing. *'Pan de molde'* means it is regular shaped, sliced bread. It doesn't mean that it's mouldy' I giggle, so he suspiciously picks one up, gives it a tentative squeeze, examines it carefully, and puts it in his trolley. Hallelujah!

Next up is the fish counter where two women in rubber aprons and wellingtons are cleaning and preparing fish for the customers. 'Just choose your fish and they will fillet it for you,' I tell him.

'Nah, don't like fish with bones, they get in me teeth' he replies.

'OK what about this, a bag of hake fillets, not a bone in sight. A sprinkle of sea salt, a squeeze of lemon juice, a dusting of flour, olive oil in the pan, two minutes a side, perfection. Or look at this salmon fillet, over a foot long, that will do you two meals. I cook ours in garlic oil, potatoes, veg, sensational.' I am really trying here!

Richie turns up his nose. 'Have they got anything with breadcrumbs on?' he enquires.

'What, like fish-fingers? Over there' I sigh.

He heads over to the boxed fish cabinet and comes back with a breaded something, resembling a giant fish-finger. Delicious.... 'Right, where are the frozen pizzas? he asks. I point the way.

'God, let's hope we don't get an invite to dinner!' Chrissie whispers.

On to the meat counter. 'OK, *cordo* is lamb, *cerdo* is pork, and *ternera* is beef' I tell him. 'Oh yeah, and *caballo* is horse!'

'So what animal is a lomo? he asks picking up a pack of pork loins.

'Wolf!' I reply.

'Jesus!' he shouts, putting it back. 'They eat wolf here?'

'Only joking' I laugh, 'it is pork loin. Look, *lomo de cerdo.'*

'You sure? he asks, suspiciously, putting a pack of *lomo* in his trolley.

On to the wine aisle. 'I only drink *rioja*' he claims.

'Well that's funny, you have been drinking our *tempranillo* all week' I point out, 'and you said it was lovely. Anyway, there's *rioja*, look, 1.45 euros.

'Can't be any good for 1.45' he replies, 'and anyway its mixed with something else. Look, *rioja* and *joven*,' he says pointing to the label. 'They've diluted the *rioja* with that *joven* rubbish. That's why it's only 1.45.

'*Joven* means young' I tell him, grinding my teeth. 'Young Rioja'.

He turns up his nose. 'Too cheap, can't stand cheap wine' he continues.

'Well the wines you were drinking at our place were 1.10 a bottle, and you polished it off, matey, like it was going out of fashion.' I remind him, with just a hint of malice.

He grabs a couple of *Rioja Jovens,* eyeing me suspiciously.

'Blimey, a white sliced, a giant fish-finger, a pork chop and two bottles of wine, and we've been here half an hour already!' Chrissie observes, pointing out our trolley, which she has filled. Didn't you do any shopping in Holland, Richard?

'Not really' he unsurprisingly confirms, 'one of Dominic's shop assistants did our shopping for us, his and mine together. I can't speak a word of Dutch, but they all speak English there, and this girl knew what I liked, so she did it all.'

Indeed. Why am I not surprised? Next up is the fruit and veg. 'Right, listen up!' I instruct, 'here are the basics of many Spanish dishes. Red and green peppers, onions, mushrooms, garlic, tomatoes. Chop that lot up, bit of olive oil in the pan, and away you go.'

'Nah, I don't do chopping, sorry. Can't be bothered chopping stuff up, don't they sell it already chopped?

I really have no idea, and quite frankly I am starting to lose the will to live. 'Well what do you eat then? You've polished off everything I've cooked for you, with gusto, but you don't seem to have any idea what to get for yourself. What about some sausages?'

'Nah, don't like that chorizo stuff. Let's just walk round the rest of the shop, I will know it when I see it.'

Chrissie rolls her eyes. 'There's not much left to see, only the microwave stuff over there, and the cosmetics. Plus the cat food. Fancy some Whiskas, do you?'

But Richie ignores the sarcasm. 'Microwave stuff? Why didn't you take me there first? Which way is it?'

My wife leads the way, as I have no idea. Microwave meals do not feature too highly in my Rick Stein cook-book.

Suddenly we pass a chiller cabinet with what look like bags of rice with chopped vegetables. 'Here we are look', our new friend announces, 'told you I'd know it when I saw it!' He delves inside and comes out with a bag, easily enough for two meals-for-one. 'What does that say, I can't read a word of Spanish!'

'Rice with chopped veg' confirms Chrissie, whose patience is fast running out. 'That one is rice with shrimp, the other rice with fish. Now please, buy something, before our ice cream defrosts, or the sell-by date arrives!'

Richie applies intense concentration to the task of selecting a couple of bags of rice, hefting each one, squeezing and prodding like a judge at Crufts, before finally placing two in his trolley. Right, perhaps we can get out of here, and on with the rest of our lives. Sadly not. 'Hang on' he cries, as we join the check-out queue, 'do these ricey things need to go in a fridge?'

Chrissie regards him with extreme annoyance. 'Er, yes. They came out of one, so obviously they need to go back into one.' She is going to kick him in the balalaikas, at any minute.

He emits an embarrassed laugh. 'The thing is see, I ain't got a fridge, have I? Someone gave it away to the leopard-woman, DIDN'T THEY JOHN?'

'Only as instructed, Richard, only as instructed' I firmly remind him.

Again he gives the problem much thought. 'Right, I need to buy a fridge in the morning, would you come with me, show me where the fridge shops are, please? In the meantime, I need to put this lot back, then come down here again.'

My wife now looks as if she is about to kick him in the balalaikas, the cossacks and the Urals, and for good measure, chop off his Nabokov. 'No don't worry Richard, you can put your stuff in our fridge for tonight, you don't have very much, DO YOU?'

Sounds like a plan to me, although it now looks very much as if we will be three for dinner again tonight. We head to the check-out, which being Spain, is more like a giant social club-come talking shop, rather than a place where you pay for stuff. The contents of our trolley go on the belt, we pay, then transfer it to our shopper, all as per usual. Richie however takes a more unconventional route. He places every single item on the belt, in a perfectly straight line, but for some unknown reason, the check-out lady grabs his items in the reverse order, and fires them into the bagging area, which sets our friend into a complete panic. His agitation is acute, and he flies into a rage, causing the crowd of Spaniards gathered around, chatting away contentedly, to stop and stare at the red-faced Englishman. Somehow he manages to stuff his seven items into his shopper, hands the assistant a fifty-Euro note, snatches the change and the receipt, and muttering 'silly cow', heads for the exit. Astonishing.

Outside the supermarket is a cafe. 'Fancy a coffee?' he asks, 'I need to sort my shopping out.'

'Not really' I reply, 'we are less than ten minutes from home!'

'No come on, I'm buying, all my stuff is in the trolley the wrong way round, because of that silly cow, and I need to sort it all out,' and he barges his way through the door and sits down at the nearest table, then proceeds to remove the entire contents of his shopper, arranging it all over the floor. The waiter strolls over, eyes the shopping, steps around the giant fish-finger and the wolf-steaks, glances suspiciously at me, and asks for our order.

Richie meanwhile is reorganising his seven items in his cavernous tartan trolley, all the while muttering about the cashier. Chrissie has had just about enough. 'Did she put the stuff in your trolley, Richard?' she asks, pointedly.

'No' he confirms, eyeing my wife, 'but I had it all laid out in order, and she messed it up.'

'Right, so you admit you loaded the shopper, but somehow it's that poor girl's fault?'

He looks like he is about to argue further, but wisely judges from the tone of her voice that further discussion is futile. He changes the subject, digging into his pocket and pulling out a crumpled receipt, a handful of Euro notes and some coins. 'So how much was that lot? I can't read that stupid small print!'

I grab the receipt. 'Nine Euros twenty-five.'

Richie bursts out laughing. 'You're not serious? Nine Euros? Christ, it would have been double that in Holland! Twenty-two grand for my house, and nine for my weekly shopping. What a country!'

Chrissie looks him straight in the eye. 'But it's not your weekly shopping, is it? You bought virtually nothing. What about tea, coffee, milk, butter? What are you having with your fish-finger? Or the wolf? You can't just eat them on their own, or dry. What about breakfast, and lunch? Cereal, ham, cheese. Come on man, you really need to get a grip!'

Our friend ponders this for a minute. Suddenly, he is no longer laughing. 'You're right of course, I told you I was rubbish at this. I need to make a list, I can't keep eating with you every night, I know I'm a complete nightmare, it's the AC/DC, see.'

'AC/DC?' I cry, shifting my chair slightly further away.

'Yes, you know, that compulsive wot-sit, AC/DC or whatever it's called.'

Chrissie is doubled over. 'OCD you mean? AC/DC is where you swing both ways!'

'Or maybe you're on the *Highway to Hell?*' I laugh. 'You certainly were last week, driving all the way from Holland in two days!'

'I don't swing any bloody way!' Richie chuckles, having seemingly rediscovered his humour. 'Seen the state of me, have you? They thought I had that asparagus syndrome at one stage, I used to call it hamburger syndrome, 'cos I eat a lot of hamburgers, see, but now I'm just plain old AC/DC.'

Chrissie has her knuckles shoved in her mouth. 'You mean asperger's syndrome?' she splutters, 'sorry I shouldn't laugh as it's extremely serious, but I think you'll find it has nothing to do with asparagus. Or hamburgers.'

'Or *For Those About to Rock*!' I giggle. 'Anyway, is there any chance we might get home with this shopping before one of us dies?'

Richie turns all serious again. 'Tell you the truth, I'm not sure I can get up that damn great hill, with this trolley.'

'You've only got seven items, and it's hardly *Kilimanjaro* my wife reminds him. 'What about us, we have a trolley full! Come on, *benga* and *bamos*, as they say in Spain!'

We head uphill towards home, a gentle slope to begin with, little old ladies bomb up here on a daily basis, but Richie is soon complaining. Although after a couple of hundred yards, he has stopped moaning, mainly because he is unable to speak. He is wheezing and groaning, like a man of ninety, rather than someone just over half that age. Are we ever going to get home tonight? This has been the longest shopping trip of my life, and it's not over. Soon, the cobbled street will rear up like a Spanish Everest. But we're not that far yet. 'How. Much. Bloody. Further?' our new friend gasps. What can we tell him? Presumably he checked out the local area, before he bought the house?

Eventually, we reach the little square below our street, containing a few local shops, a little white chapel, and a cafe/bar. 'Fancy. A. Beer?' he puffs, displaying an acute shortage of breath. 'I. Am. Dying!'

'Be a shame to deny the condemned man his last request!' I giggle. Chrissie rolls her eyes, but she is outvoted. A beer it is, followed by another, accompanied by plates of Spanish ham, and crusty bread.

'Right!' my wife commands, 'come on Richard, last big push. Let's get you up that hill. Got your oxygen?'

'Can't we get a taxi? he protests. It's only another fifty yards or so, but the narrow cobbled street does ascend viciously, although once again, presumably, he knew this before he signed on the dotted line. Up we trudge, pausing every ten yards or so to wait for Richie, eventually reaching the dog-leg marking the half-way point. We can now see our street above, although the gradient appears almost vertical, and our friend has to hang onto the wall to regain his breath. 'I. Can't. Stand. Much. More. Of. These. Bloody. Hills.' he pants. 'Not. Like. This. In. Holland!'

Chrissie has had just about enough. 'So why on earth did you buy a house on the side of a mountain?' she snaps.

'Didn't know there was a mountain' grunts our friend, slowly regaining his breath.

She is incredulous. 'Er, what is that huge, grey mountain-shaped thing towering above us then? Is it a bird? Is it a plane? Nope. Looks like a mountain to me. And it's been there about a million years. It certainly didn't arrive overnight.'

He grits his teeth. 'Yes, well, the estate agent brought us in the car, she dropped us in the street, me and Dom, so we didn't notice any mountains.'

Now it's my turn to be unconvinced. 'But you can see the mountain from about ten miles away, coming along the main road.'

He has the decency to look shame-faced. 'Well it was that Denise, the crafty cow. She saw Dom was about twenty stone, and that I couldn't walk for toffee, so both times we came, she drove up the street. And driving from Granada airport, where she picked us up, we were chatting. So we didn't see any mountains, really. I mean, I knew there was a bit of a slope, like, but nothing like this.'

This is almost beyond belief. 'But Richie, if you seriously can't walk up the hills, how are you going to survive here?'

He grimaces in pain, then heads gradually up the final, steepest part of the climb. Slowly but surely we achieve the summit, where it's just a few yards to our front door. 'Got. A. Moped.' he croaks.

Funny that, I hadn't noticed a moped outside his cottage, and he hasn't mentioned it over the past few days. 'OK, that might be a solution for you' I concede, 'although you will need to be careful on the cobbles when it rains, they are like sheets of glass. So where is this moped then?'

'Holland.'

'HOLLAND? Not much use there, Richie! And best of luck riding it back here, what is it, twelve-hundred miles? Set out now, you might be back by August. Of next year!'

'About fourteen-hundred actually' he chuckles, 'and no, I'm not riding it down! Got a trailer back there, so I will be popping back soon and bringing the bike, and lots of other stuff. In the meantime, I will have to walk up and down the zigzag. I know it's further, and I appreciate you bringing me up the quick way, but I just can't do this. He straightens his spine, adjusts his underwear, then grips the handle of his trolley for support. 'Anyway, I've just remembered, Dom has a fridge in his place, so I don't need to borrow yours tonight! But you are correct, I do need to get a grip on this, I cannot tell you what it means to me, you having me round for dinner every day this week, I am so grateful, but from tonight I am independent! I don't fancy cooking so I think I will pop down that 'Apollo's A Sad Arse' place for a takeaway.

I look at Chrissie. She looks at me. We both look at Richie. 'Apollo's A Sad Arse?' I repeat. I know of no such fast-food establishment.

'Yeah, you know, on the hill down into town, God knows what they sell, but it's definitely a takeaway. I saw it on Monday, when I had all day to kill, waiting for you.'

Chrissie suddenly bursts into uncontrollable laughter. 'You mean *Pollos Asados* I think? Roast chicken.'

'Is that what it means?' he giggles, 'told you I couldn't speak Spanish! Roast chicken, I could kill for roast chicken, especially with a few chips, and doorstep bread and butter! Right, let me dump this lot off in Dom's, and I'm there! Oooo, roast chicken!'

Apollo's a Sad Arse, for heaven's sake, although I suppose it's an easy mistake to make. 'Spit roasted chicken, too, according to Gaffer' I confirm, 'although we've never had it, apparently it comes with chips, and about a yard of crusty bread.' Richie is practically drooling. 'Just one problem though, mate.' I pause for dramatic effect, milking the suspense. 'They're not open tonight, they only open Saturday and Sunday lunchtimes.'

'WHAT?' cries our crestfallen friend. 'A roast chicken place not open Friday nights? You cannot be serious. Every chicken shop, everywhere in the world, opens on a Friday night, it's the law for Chrissake!' He looks as if he is about to cry.

'It's true, Richard,' Chrissie affirms, 'they only open Saturday and Sunday lunchtimes, the Spanish go crazy for it, they queue halfway down the street. But all is not lost!' she quickly adds, 'just down the street a bit further is a hamburger and hot-dog place, and they are open every night.'

Richie perks up considerably. 'Oh yes, I saw that place too, but I thought it was a sandwich bar or something. It didn't say nothing about hot-dogs on the sign, though.'

'*Perritos calientes*' Chrissie states.

'You what?'

'*Perritios calientes*' she repeats. 'Spanish for hot-dogs.'

'You serious?' he queries, 'there's a Spanish word for hot-dogs? I thought hot-dogs was hot-dogs everywhere? This country's doing my head in, the chicken shops don't open Friday nights, and hot dogs are called perry-cally, what was it?'

'*Perritos calientes*'

'Yeah well, whatever, who cares? But do they come with mustard, and fried onions? And the hamburgers, with cheese, onions, ketchup?'

Chrissie indignantly rises up to her full five-foot-nothing. 'Well you've been eating with us all week, Richard, did you notice hamburgers or hot-dogs on the menu? And if you can find a tube of ketchup in our house, I'll let you sleep with me!'

'NO!' I bellow. 'If he can find a tube of ketchup, in our house, he can sleep with ME!'

'Now there's an offer I CAN refuse!' he chuckles. 'Anyway, a voyage of discovery awaits for me tonight! Thank you both so much for everything, I'll see you over the weekend' and off he trudges towards Dominic's cottage, dragging his trolley behind him.

We walk the last few steps back to our place, stow away our rapidly deteriorating food, and slump onto the sofa. After almost a week, we are alone again. Deep joy. 'So what do you fancy to eat tonight? I ask my spouse.

She ponders for a few moments. 'Well, do you know, I feel rather partial to a perry-cally' she giggles.

'And would you like it microwaved, or fried?' I enquire, ' and anything with it?'

She slips off the sofa and pours us both a large glass of wine. 'Well considering we don't possess a microwave, I imagine I am having it fried!' she laughs, 'and I rather fancy fried onions, and ketchup!'

I regard her straight-faced. 'Well Bon-appetit! But please don't think that after eating fried onions, you are sleeping with ME!'

CHAPTER 27. WHO LET THE CATS OUT?

I am standing on Dutch Dick's toilet bowl, in his bathroom, brandishing a screwdriver. When I collected the keys for this house several weeks ago, as he was in Holland at the time, Diego the estate agent warned me there was a water leak 'somewhere at the back of the house.' Now Richie has arrived in Spain, turned on the water, and discovered the location of the leak. This toilet is an old-style one with the cistern at the top of the wall, you rarely see them in England any more, but over here they are fairly common in these old houses. The leak is in the input pipe to the cistern, just a small seepage really, blow-lamp, solder, flux, new bit of pipe, half-hour tops. Even I could manage that, and I am not a plumber.

'Just tap off that tile by the leak' Richie commands.

'What for? I reply.

'Cos that looks like an old cast-iron pipe' he comes back.

'So what? All these old houses are the same' I respond.

'Just tap off the effing tile' comes the reply. OK he is the boss, and more importantly he is paying me, so a few gentle taps and I manage to prise the tile off in one piece, shame to break it, as although the bathroom looks like something out of a Cambodian doss-house, a couple of hours hard graft by the resident cleaner (Chrissie) and it would look as good as new. Well 1971 new, but there are far worse priorities in this house.

Richie climbs up onto the toilet seat and jabs the screwdriver into the wall around the pipe. He swears loudly. 'Just as I thought, cast-iron, it will have to come out.' He traces the imaginary line of the pipe through the wall towards the shower. 'Tap one off there' he commands, so I do. Again he digs at the wall, revealing the pipe buried within, then excitedly removes the screwdriver. 'Copper!' he exclaims. 'Great. I just have that small bit of cast-iron by the cistern to replace. Thank God for that, I didn't want to have to start replacing pipes everywhere.'

How do I break the news to him? He has only been here a day, he is still catching up on his sleep after the long drive from Holland with a car load of clothes and tea towels, having left most of his tools behind. 'That is a new-ish shower, Richie' I point out. 'They just used copper on the new bit. The rest of the house will be cast iron.'

He eyes me suspiciously, as if the pipes are my personal fault. If iron pipes were a problem for him, why didn't he investigate when he bought the place? Probably the same reason he didn't notice the damn great mountain rearing up behind his house.....'Knock off another tile in the corner' he commands, so I do, and again he jabs at the plaster. Again he swears. Loudly. More cast iron.

'What's the problem mate' I ask soothingly. 'There are no other leaks, just braise up that joint and we are out of here.'

'Can't' he replies. 'I left my blow-lamp in Holland.' Little did I know at that time that this would be a continuous refrain over the coming weeks. 'I left my so-and-so tool in Holland.' Still, they were nice tea towels......

However, blow-lamps are fairly cheap, so he can always buy one. But he is still going on about replacing all the pipe work but reckons only this bit of the house will need doing. He disconnects the pipes on the sink and starts knocking tiles off there, again finding iron. The bathroom is starting to look like a demented woodpecker has been let loose in it with tiles off everywhere, and holes on the walls. He starts swearing again. 'I am gonna have to find where the pipes go through the house, and knock holes in the walls to see if it's all iron.' These houses all have solid floors at ground level, on account of being built on solid granite, so the pipes go through the walls here.

'No need mate' I reply. 'Just go out in the street and look in the water meter box, if it's iron there it will be iron throughout.' Most houses here have little trap doors in the front wall of the house containing the water meter, the stop-cock and the incoming pipe from the mains. We go outside to check and guess what? Yep, iron pipes. Richie now has his head in his hands. 'Gawd, I don't need this, replacing all these bloody pipes.'

'Actually it won't be that bad a job to replace the whole lot', I say, an utterance I will have cause to regret in the coming weeks. 'We can channel a new pipe through the walls from the front to the back of the house, easy. Have you got your angle grinder here, or did you leave that in Holland too?' Sarcasm is starting to creep into my conversation.

He checks his tools. 'Yes, all here' he replies.

'OK, no time like the present' I reply, 'You cut the channels, and I will follow with the chisel. Where's your hammer?'

'In Holland' comes the shame-faced response.

I stare at my new friend in disbelief. 'What, you brought a boot-load of bloody tea-towels, and no bloody hammer? I explode. 'What sort of builder are you?' And it's not like he is going to be doing much washing-up for a while, as there is no kitchen to speak of. Leopard-skin Woman stole most of it. So back I go to my house for a hammer, its only fifty yards or so but during the journey I get time to debate whether to knock out a channel in the wall, or to bury the hammer in the back of Richie's head.

When I get back he is standing in the sitting room, where we are going to start channelling the wall. 'Do they sell plastic water pipe here?' he asks.

'No idea' I reply, 'but there's a plumbers merchant down the road. Let's go and find out.'

On the walk down the plumbers I rehearse how to ask for a domestic water system from the meter to the kitchen and bathroom and water heater, in plastic. My Spanish is getting better, three months ago I could only order a beer. 'Follow me' chuckles the guy behind the counter and leads us round the back where a plastic system, complete with joints and fittings, is laid out on a wall board. I get him to jot down the prices and check it's all in stock, and then all Richie has to do is decide if he wants plastic, or the traditional copper. And saying he is indecisive is like saying the Atlantic Ocean is a bit of a lake.

Once back at Richie's place we can make a start cutting out the channels in the walls, so he grabs the angle grinder and I grab my hammer. 'Where's your chisel?' I ask.

He checks his toolbox. He swears. 'I left it in Holland' comes the response.

I still have the hammer in my hand and it takes a supreme effort to stop myself from checking if he has any brain cells, or a pea, inside his thick scull. I drop the hammer on the ground. 'Right, I am off, get yourself down the bloody hardware shop tonight and get the rest of the bloody tools you think we might need to finish this bloody job,' I shout, and out the door I go.

As I stamp off down the street I can just hear my soon-to-be-ex-friend's voice carrying on the breeze ... 'Shame really, I've got loads of lovely tools in Holland.....'

Two days later we are in a builders merchants in Granada looking at toilet bowls. Obviously they sell bogs in Santa Marta, but Richie likes to explore every option before making up his mind.....   'This will do' he confirms. 'Ten Euro's cheaper than at our place'. Even though the fuel cost more than that, plus my time...This is one of those DIY supermarkets where you put the stuff in a trolley and pay at the checkout. The toilets are stacked on pallets, the top one being around six feet up, so I let Dick lift it down as he needs the exercise. As he does so however a puddle of water cascades out of the bowl, all over his head and shirt. Clearly the pallets had been out in the yard at some stage, it is probably only about half a pint but he is covered, and needless to say he is furious and starts swearing at the top of his voice.' It's bloody cats piss!' he is shouting.

How the hell can it be cats? Most of the cats I know go in the garden, after digging a hole. 'It's just rainwater Richie' I tell him, 'the pallets have been outside.'

He is wiping his face with his hands, and sniffing them. 'Here, bloody well smell this' he shouts. 'it's cats piss for sure.' Well, Granada is a World Heritage city, and the Alhambra Palace is the most visited tourist attraction in Spain. Maybe the cats here are posh and do actually pee in porcelain. Seems unlikely. But he is correct. He does smell of cats piss.

A small crowd of Spaniards has gathered to see what all the fuss is about, I catch one old man's eye and declare *'Pee-pee de gato, meeeoww*!' I am assuming that meeeoww in Spanish is actually the same as an English 'meeeoww' so I am relieved when the joke hits home and everyone laughs.

Now, I have been putting up with Richie whining and moaning for the last week or so about a range of subjects, from his aches and pains to thieving Dutch lawyers to the fact that our local bar in Santa Marta does not sell coffee in the evenings. Plus leaving all his tools behind. And sorting out his shopping and daily menus. It is time to get my own back. And I can do a passable Tom Jones impression, so I start to sing. 'Pussycat pussycat I love you, yes I do-o, you and your pussycat eyes!'

The Spaniards are all staring at a large English bloke serenading a wet English bloke, Richie is far from amused and still rubbing his shirt. 'Hey mate' I shout. 'You have two pointy ears sticking out the top of your head. And your coat is looking lovely and glossy. Ginger with a hint of tabby. But your whiskers could do with a bit of a trim, and your claws need clipping!'

'Eff off' comes the reply, but I am flying now and cannot resist.

We get to the checkout and the girl wrinkles her nose. And she is beautiful. 'Hey Felix' I call out, rub yourself against her legs, see if she tickles your tummy!' His reply is unprintable. Across the car park with the trolley, plus urine-smelling toilet. 'Hey Felix, watch you don't catch your tail in the car door!' We load the car and my feline friend drives slowly away. 'Oh damn' I shout, 'you forgot something.'

He hammers on the brakes and provokes a torrent of honking from the car behind us. 'What's that?' he asks, falling into my trap.

The bag of cat litter' I tell him. 'And turn the air-con up, will you? Starting to get a bit ripe in here!'

He is about to explode. 'Just tell me the way back to the main road, or you'll be walking back to effing Santa Marta', he cries.

'Well it's a shame I didn't put butter on your paws' I tell him, 'then you could have found your own way home!'

We drive along in stony silence for a while, but after a few miles I can sense him relaxing, and a wry smile even creeps across his craggy features. 'Is there a bar or a cafe along this road?' he enquires.

'Yes about five miles further' I reply. 'I expect you are dying for a saucer of milk! But do me a favour will you? No licking your arse in the middle of the bar.'

So I get my beer and Richie gets his coffee, then it's back home and I help him unload his purchases in the narrow little street. I have just one last chance for a final dig. 'Hey mate' I call out as I am heading back to my house. 'You have put on a bit of weight lately, watch you don't get stuck in the cat-flap! What time do you want me to come round, and put you out for the night?'

Luckily the stream of abuse is carried away on the breeze.................

CHAPTER 28. WHO LET THE DOGS OUT?

I consider myself to be an animal lover, but right now I hate Del's dogs, or specifically the two out of his pack of about eight who have escaped into the maze of streets and alleyways which typify this part of town. It is a baking afternoon and I am dressed for scaffolding and roofing in jeans and heavy shoes, not for chasing after creatures which, to all intents and purposes, have disappeared from the face of the earth. Del himself is cursing and swearing in a manner unfit for publication here, and all I need right now is a cold drink and an even colder shower. Sweat is running down my sweat and I have had just about enough of these canines and their owner.

The day had started well. I am helping Del with the remainder of his roof, the bit overhanging the front, so we had erected a scaffolding tower in the street and spent a few hours heaving tiles up, and bedding them nicely in place. We were working on a Saturday to avoid the unwelcome attention of the buildings inspector and his extortionate two-Euro building permit, and luckily no cars had attempted to come up or down the street, just a couple of mopeds who were able to squeeze by. We got the tower dismantled and stacked safely away, the street swept as good as new, and Del headed indoors to make us a refreshing cuppa, leaving me waiting on the doorstep. 'Keep the door shut otherwise the dogs will escape,' was his departing instruction, before disappearing inside provoking a cacophony of barking.

Visits to Del's house are always centred around his dogs, which are broadly divided into three categories, males, females and puppies. Due to alleged extreme poverty, none of the creatures are spayed or neutered, one or more of the females are usually in season, which means the groups have to be kept in different parts of the house, and for a dwelling containing virtually no interior doors, this generally proves next to impossible.

Mind you, having to consume my beverage in the street is no bad thing, given that the unruly pack of canines bestow the house with an aroma which could best be described as 'pungent', and that is on a good day.

Sadly, on this occasion, we never got to drink the tea. I am leaning on the wall opposite his house, straightening my spine and picking the remaining fragments of tile from my underwear, when a gust of wind suddenly blows the front door open, and two creatures the size of lions burst out and go galloping off up the street. These are David's Spanish hunting dogs; facially they look like a golden Labrador, only about half as big again as a Labrador, a lot leaner than a Labrador, and much faster than a Labrador. So nothing like a Labrador, really. They reach the end of the street in just a few seconds, one slightly ahead of the other, then turn as if on rails and came hurtling back towards me.

Del then emerges from the house shouting 'Who left the bloody door open, catch them!' Yeah, easier said than done mate! The pair are going so fast that if I get in the way they are going to hit me like the entire All-Blacks front row, with teeth, so I just wave my arms a bit and hope they miss me. I need not have worried. They pass me as if I am not there, the draught of their passing caresses my cheeks, then hurtle off down some stone steps to the street below, round the bend and out of sight, in a manner Usain Bolt would have been proud of.

Del dashes back into the house and emerges with two dog leads, 'quick' he urges, 'we have to catch them. I have to meet Jimmy the Scotsman in half an hour to price up for his window. Grab a lead and let's go.'

Catch them, is he having a laugh? 'Surely they will come back on their own' I plead, hopefully.

'Individually they would' he agrees, 'but Suzie is on heat and Harley is after her of course.'

'Well won't they just head for the nearest bushes, do the dirty deed, then come back?' I suggest.

'No, Suzie is faster than him. He cannot catch her so they just keep running. If they get into town they will cause mayhem'. Into town? The speed they were going they are half way to Madrid by now. Reluctantly I grab a lead and we begin our fruitless search up and down the narrow streets, no one is about of course as it's siesta time, at one stage we reach the edge of town and gaze across the jumbled roofs towards the olive fields beyond. This is hopeless. These canines have vanished into thin air.

Just then round the corner comes Del's neighbour Manolo, he of the plaster in his pants fame. I am guessing he has never read 'Fifty Shades of Grey' but he is clearly wondering why two mad Englishmen are roaming the town carrying leather dog leads, so Del explains his dogs have *escapado*.

'Hombre, no es un problema' he replies. 'The police will catch them, and shoot them for you', and to emphasise the point he makes the classic gun shape with his hand and fires two imaginary shots into two imaginary dogs. Now this seems a bit far-fetched to me, I know the police here carry guns, even the local ones who direct the traffic outside schools and close the roads during fiestas, but the thought of them even drawing their weapons is unimaginable.

Then an image flashes into my mind, what if the dogs also have guns, there would be a massive shoot-out in the town square, like the 'Dogfight at the OK Corral' or a John Wayne movie. Del spots me grinning and I receive a reprimand. 'He is not joking, you know, they do shoot them, or put them down. If they cause havoc in town and the police catch them, they will.' And he puts his head in his hands and seems about to cry. It is an unbelievably poignant moment, I feel so sad for Del, he loves his dogs dearly, even though they are a confounded nuisance, and I want to give him a hug, but am worried that Manolo already thinks we are a couple of perverts, so I refrain. 'The thing is' my friend continues, 'they have been micro-chipped, so if the police catch them they will trace them back to me. I will get fined a hundred Euros. Per dog. That is the whole profit on Jimmy's job gone, I might as well get him to give the bloody money straight to the police.'

Oh well, good job we didn't embrace, then. It was the money, rather than the loss of the hounds, which was causing tears to well in my colleague's eyes. Manolo shuffles off up the street, and we resume our search, but it is hopeless. At least with a needle in a haystack you know the needle is actually there. 'Look' sighs Del, 'I am already late for Jimmy, I need to go now. I will search again afterwards, thanks again for all your help.'

We trudge wearily back up the hill for the last time, climb the stone steps into his street, and who should be waiting patiently by his front door? Yes Suzie and

Harley. Del slips the leads on double quick and breathes a deep sigh of relief that he has saved the two hundred Euros. Suzie has a big soppy, doggy grin on her face, and Harley is looking slightly cross-eyed, his fur is dishevelled, and he has a bit of a limp. If dogs could smoke, this pair would be lying in bed having a post-coital cigarette.

So now it's my turn to get my own back. With interest. I nudge Del in the ribs, 'I reckon Harley has found an extra yard of pace', I giggle. 'You might be hearing the patter of tiny paws in a couple of months.' My business partner clutches his head in his hands for the second time this afternoon. 'Oh God no!' he wails, 'think of the vets bills. That is the whole profit on Jimmy's job gone. I might as well get him to give the money straight to the bloody vet.'

A few days later my phone rings. It is Del. 'Hi mate' he chirps, and immediately I know there is trouble. Usually I am greeted with *All right you old bastard?* 'After all that rain last Saturday my roof is leaking again. I wonder if you could pop up sometime and give me a hand?'

I should at this point make it clear that the bloke who mixed the mortar and carried the tiles should not be blamed for the still-porous roof. That is the fault of the guy who laid the tiles. Del. Besides, these old Spanish houses are like Chinese raincoats. Shower-proof only. They are not designed to cope with heavy rain, so when it does, they leak. At least three other Brits in Santa Marta suffered ingress of water that day. 'I will pop up' I reply, 'but I am not, absolutely not, under no circumstances, chasing your dogs round town again.'

So next day I wander up there and Derek assures me the big dogs Harley and Suzie are locked in the kitchen and cannot escape. Now where have I heard that before? We start mixing mortar, when along comes David's elderly neighbour Maria, carrying a dead rabbit by the ears. It is hunting season here and I have seen several other deceased bunnies being hiked around, and we had rabbit tapas in the bar the other evening. Done in a red wine sauce, lovely it was.... Mind you Maria's rabbit looks like it might have died of old age. 'A present for you!' she shouts and thrusts the greasy corpse into Del's hands. He offers his thanks to her and turns to me. 'Great, I will skin and gut this and have it for supper!' He was in the Navy, but I always thought they ate at

McDonald's. 'Just let me wrap it in a bit of newspaper and bung it in the fridge, then we can get on'.

Up on the roof we climb and he starts rearranging the tiles where the leak was, while I admire the view. Behind his garden is the mountain and immediately above his garden wall is a pen with a huge turkey and a greasy, matted Alsatian. 'See that turkey?' Del laughs,'my dogs hate him! He stands up there, on that scrubby patch of land, gobbling away. last week he escaped and almost ended up in me yard. If he ever gets in there, Harley will eat him. For sure. Have you seen the size of that bird? If he tries to come over the wall he is dead. I would have to try to keep him out. Somehow.'

'How would you do that?' I chuckle.

'Kick him in the nuts!' he replies.

'I didn't know turkeys had nuts!' I snigger, and we both start laughing.

'Yeah, turkey twizzlers!' he chokes, and we are in danger of falling off the roof. Time for a cuppa.

Down we go and Del pops into the house, carefully shutting the door, leaving me on the doorstep again, followed by a prolonged burst of shouting and swearing. Being ex-Navy, Del is highly proficient at both, but this sounds worse than usual so I gingerly follow him inside, to be greeted by a scene of utter devastation. The kitchen is strewn with chewed up newspaper and half-eaten cartons, and the fridge door is wide open. It is an upright fridge-freezer with the fridge bit at the bottom, so clearly one of the dogs has got up on his back legs and opened the door somehow, then consumed the entire bottom and middle layer of the fridge. All that is left is the top shelf containing a piece of mouldy cheese and a carton of UHT milk, presumably the thieving canine could not reach the top shelf, unless they just didn't fancy dairy produce. Probably on a lactose-free diet, I did notice that Suzie was putting on a bit of weight round the backside.... 'Bastards, absolute bastards!' Del is shouting, 'there goes my bloody supper, the rabbit, and they have eaten most of my other stuff as well.'

He rushes out the back and returns with a length of thick nylon cord. I am horrified, 'you are not going to whip the dogs are you?' I shout. I cannot stand animal cruelty.

'No, I am gonna tie the fridge door up!' he replies, and proceeds to knot the cord around the handle then round the back of the fridge, securing it tightly. 'There, that should sort the buggers!' he cries, grabbing a broom and sweeping the mess into a pile. God, I need that cuppa.

I am also in desperate need of a wee, so enquiring where I should go, and how I should get there, am astonished to be told to choose between the kitchen sink, and the mop-bucket, as the route to the bathroom is unavailable due to the various dogs corralled there. I gaze at the filthy water lurking in the mop-bucket, which seems to have been there for months and certainly not a liquid you would wash a floor with. The kitchen sink however is full of dirty, grease-encrusted utensils. Now I consider myself to be a champion piddler, it's one of the few things I am any good at, and I have slashed at some of the world's top tourist spots. Over the edge of the Grand Canyon, at the top of Table Mountain, in the Ganges, over the side of the Sydney Harbour Bridge. In my rugby-playing days, I was known for boldly going where no man has gone before. But I have never piddled on a mate's saucepans, and I don't intend starting now. So it's the mop-bucket then. I perform the dirty deed, sending a foaming spray into the turgid waters, then we both get on with the job.

About an hour later we are inside the house again moving stuff, and Harley escapes from the lounge and comes bounding into the kitchen. Without further ado, he sniffs the mop-bucket and proceeds to drink deeply from the contents, huge laps of the stagnant urine-flavoured liquid. 'OH CHRIST I JUST PISSED IN THAT!' I cry, but it is too late, Harley, fully refreshed, glances up with a huge grin, licks his lips extravagantly, and moves off.

The tabloid press here has been awash with news about Canadian teenage singing sensation Justin Bieber, who allegedly urinated in a mop-bucket in a restaurant kitchen, refusing to go in the toilets like other mere mortals.

So Mr Bieber, you may well of pee'd in a mop-bucket, but I bet, actually stone-cold one-hundred-percent guarantee, that your mate's dog didn't drink it afterwards!

We climb back up on the roof for the finishing touches and again I glance at the turkey, who I swear is laughing at something. I must be me getting light-headed with all the excitement. But he does look amused.... We finish the remaining tiles and descend back to ground level, and again Del goes inside, and once more, incredibly, the shouting and swearing resumes. Oh no, what have they done now? I really do not want to look, but curiosity compels me to enter the house again, to be confronted by the grotesque sight of a kitchen strewn with white polystyrene meat trays, the freezer compartment wide open, and my friend trying to wrestle a frozen steak from Harley's jaws. Suzie is barking encouragement from the sidelines, man and beast seem evenly matched, the contest could go either way, and I feel like shouting 'kick him in the nuts!'. Eventually Del finds a last burst of strength and prises the soggy, saliva-encrusted piece of flesh from the dog's mouth, then proceeds to wipe it on a cloth and chucks it back in the freezer, slamming the door shut.

Trust me on this one. If you come to Andalucía and get an invite to supper Chez-Del, make an excuse. Or maybe choose the vegetarian option. He is effing and blinding about having no food left at all now, apart from the steak presumably, and imagining him eating that is an image too far for me. I do feel sorry for him and consider inviting him to our place tonight, but it's not as if he was paying me for this work, I was only helping a mate. A volunteer. Twenty-five Euros cash might have swung it. I make my excuses and head off home, and as I do I hear the shouting and swearing start up again.....

CHAPTER 29. WHO LET THE SARDENE OUT?

It was during my fifth glass of wine that I notice the sardine winking at me. She is not just any old Sardine either. *La Sardina*, her Spanish title, is beautiful. She is over four feet long, lying on her bed, in a cardboard coffin draped in black crepe, surrounded by flowers and candles, wearing a traditional flamenco dress, with a rose between her teeth. She has lovely dark eyes with long, voluminous eye lashes, and rosy red lips. And as I say, she is winking at me.

After six glasses of wine, I wink at her. I feel there is something building between us, she is there surrounded by people, being carried through the streets and stared at, poked and prodded, which somehow I just know she hates. She deserves better, and she simply longs to be desired.

After seven glasses of wine, we are in love! We are going to run away together from all this madness, find a secluded desert island and maybe raise a family of little *sardinitas.* We just have to be together. For ever.

It gets to you, this wine, and people keep giving it to me, *gratis,* and it would be rude to refuse, wouldn't it? It is the second day of Santa Marta carnival, and we are following *La Sardina* through the streets, accompanied by three male choirs, two dressed in various costumes of stage and screen, the Lion and Tin Man from Wizard of Oz, Aladdin, Pinocchio, Peter Pan, Hook, Prince Charming and Snow White, and another group dressed as widows, in black lace dresses with veils. Each group takes it in turn to sing humorous carnival songs, then the band of drums and cornets take over for rousing upbeat music. And the wine keeps flowing, it is known locally as Ma*laga*, which is where it is produced, and is more like a sweet sherry. Several girls have large containers of the stuff, and plastic glasses, and every time the parade stops, which is about every fifty yards, round they come again. Also being given away are large round biscuits called *rosquillas*, clearly home-made as they vary in shape and size, but absolutely delicious. I could spend the rest of my life eating *rosquillas* and drinking *Malaga*, and at this rate I probably will because any more and I will be flat on my back. But like I say, it would be rude to refuse.....

Every now and again we reach 'neighbours associations' which are like church halls, dotted around the town, where the doors are flung open and everyone invited inside, for guess what? Yes more *rosquillas* and *Malaga*. Progress is slow, but who cares. This has to be one of the best ways to spend a Sunday evening. On the final leg of the parade we spot Declan, the mad Irishman, standing outside a bar, he has heard the commotion and come out to investigate. Actually he looks stranger than usual as he seems to have three heads, and he is madder than usual because England have just beaten Ireland in the rugby. And he has what appears to be a cold sore on his lip, or rather three cold sores on his six lips... 'Nevvvver mihhnd' I commiserate, flinging my arm around his neck, 'graaab a glassh of Malaggaa!' He does, with relish, then there is much clearing of throats among the band, someone shoves another *Malaga* in my hands and we are off again, lurching uphill towards the big finale, the '*Entierra de Sardina*' the burial. As we pass the nearest part of the route to our house, however, we have a big decision to make. Either continue with the procession until the end, and face oblivion, or bail out now and make a run for home. Or a stagger. What the hell, in for a penny, and all that, so we wind our way up the steep cobbled hill, following my fishy lover, to the main square of the town, where a huge bonfire is burning, flames leaping and dancing, the air heavy with the aromatic scent of olive wood. Or it might have been paraffin, who cares?

Our Spanish friend Juan-Carlos suddenly appears, lurching across the square, clutching a half-eaten *rosquilla* and several glasses of *Malaga,* clearly not his first. 'Sooo what issh the bonfire forrr, Juan-Carlosss? I slur, trying, but mainly failing, to focus on his six eyes.

He slides his arm around my shoulder. 'Ees for *La Sardina*, my free-end' he giggles, conspiratorially. 'We burn she, and she go up woooshhh!'

At this time of night, after this much to drink, my brain is struggling to process this information. It takes several seconds to sink in, and when it finally does, confusion still reigns. 'But I thought '*Entierra*' means burial? You know, under the ground?'

'It does' he confirms, breathing *Malaga* fumes into my face, from a distance of about three inches, 'but who is going to dig hole thees time of night? On Sunday too? Everyone here is, how you say in Eengland, drank. No, fire much better, helps the *Malaga* to go down. You teach me thees words in Eengliss, *it warm you cock!*'

'Cockles!' Chrissie chortles, 'it warms your cockles! Although if you get much closer to the fire, you never know!'

So it was never meant to be, *La Sardina* and me. My very own Joan of Arc. Into the fire she go, and she go up woooshhh, as they say in Spain. We could never have found happiness. All I have is a photograph, and the memories of course......

A couple of days later we are at the conversation class in the library, trying to discover why we had pursued a pretend sardine round the streets, accompanied by copious amounts of the local wine. There seems no logical explanation; we are over fifty miles from the coast, so it was not presumably a requiem for a dying fishing industry. Why was the fish deceased, did it pass from old age, or was it done away with, by some dastardly Spaniard? Who were the widows? And what did the Wizard of Oz have to do with it? I need answers to these not unreasonable questions. 'Ees tradition here' giggles Rafi, 'before *Semana Santa* there is four days of *Quaresma*.'

Oh well, that clears it up completely. I don't think. *Semana* is Spanish for 'week', but Santa? Christmas was two months ago, surely there is not another Christmas week to cope with? I wonder if Gaffer knows, and whether he has another turkey tucked away in his camper-van?. And could we cope with another 'reet blooody slap-up Christmas' so soon? I am still getting over the last one.

Luckily Jose comes to the rescue. '*Semana Santa* is how you say, Easter? Before there is Easter, there is forty days where you must to eat nothing *grassa*, fat. **Forty** days Rafi, not four days!'

His compatriot raises her hands to he head. 'HODER! I forget thees, forty, four, ees muy difficult, speaky Eengliss!'

Chrissie has cottoned on to the narrative. 'Lent!' she cries, ' we call the forty days before Easter 'Lent', where it is tradition to give something up, butter, milk, sugar, something like that.'

'I remember from my books in school' laughs Teri, 'in Eengland you make, how you say, cakes of pans, you throw these cakes of pans into the sky, I listen to thees when I was boy!'

'When you were a girl,' my wife gently corrects her pupil, 'you read about English people making pancakes, before the start of Lent. Throwing them into the sky is optional! We call this action *to toss*, tossing the pancake, but you can use a spatula if you prefer!'

Juan-Carlos narrows his eyes, and glances in my direction. 'So person who toss pancakes is *tosser*? I hear you call your free-end from Holland, Richard, a *tosser*. So thees mean they also toss pancakes in Holland, no?'

OK, he has me there bang to rights. 'The word *tosser* has two meanings in English' I carefully explain, avoiding Chrissie's eyes boring into the side of my head. 'To toss is to throw something a short distance. But it is also a rude word for an idiot.' I don't feel I can expand on the definition. There are ladies present, after all. 'So the significance of the sardine' I hastily add, 'is to eat all your luxury food before the start of Lent, very similar to the pancake?' There. I think I might have got away with it.

Walking home after the class, meditating on the new Spanish words we have added to our meagre vocabularies, I turn to my wife. 'Well that went very well today, don't you think?'

She regards me malevolently. 'On the contrary' she hisses, 'my vocabulary has increased. You, on the other hand, are a complete tosser!'

That evening Declan has the floor in the local bar. 'Ah sure, me bathroom sink blocked up the other day', he explains, 'so I got some of that *Agua Fuerte* and poured it down.' This is the acid/ammonia liquid they sell here for unblocking sinks, and removing skin from hands. It has to be dripped, not poured. 'Used half the feckin' bottle I did' he continues, 'took all the feckin' chrome off me taps, and the drain hole, but the sink was still blocked. So I undid the U-bend, put me mouth round the pipe and blew down it. Be Jaysus, I got a mouth full of *Agua Fuerte*, burned all me feckin' mouth it did.'

Which explains the three cold sores on his six lips!

CHAPTER 30. DIA DE ANDALUCIA

'Night of Flamenco' announces the sign, Sellotaped to the lamp-post. '28 February, Club of Flamenco, Santa Marta, 10pm.'

'So where is this flamenco club, do you think?' Chrissie queries. 'There is no address given.'

Well if she doesn't know, neither do I, although I know men, and women, who do. As for just about every query we have regarding life here, the Spaniards at the conversation class are our first port of call. It's like we have our own personal information service.

'You know the centre of ancient peoples, in the street of bars?' asks Jose.

'The old persons' club? I confirm. 'Yes, we were there the other night, following the sardine! They gave me two glasses of *Malaga!*'

'Only two?' our friend giggles. 'So next to here, is club of young peoples, yes?'

'We didn't get any *Malaga* at all in there, but yes, I know where you are.'

'So club of flamenco is next to here.'

I think I know where he means, but I cannot recall anything specific indicating there might be a centre of traditional Spanish music and dance in that area, which is not surprising considering the locals seem highly reluctant to erect signposts. We will check it out personally, in the daylight, after the class.

'So tell me' Chrissie wonders, 'why is the concert on Tuesday night? Surely people have to be up for work, the next day?'

Suddenly, before anyone can answer, there is a commotion at the door and in barges Alicia, dressed in a fur coat, a tight white tee-shirt, a denim mini-skirt, silver sparkly tights and hooker heels. She does this every week, arrives late and causes a massive hullabaloo, then usually plonks herself next to me. The problem is, I am British, and need my personal space. The Spaniards are all grouped together on one side of the table, whereas Chrissie and I have the other side to ourselves, by design. Alicia doesn't appreciate this, she clearly thinks I have thoughtfully saved her a place, although for some reason she rarely sits next to my wife....

The late-comer struggles out of the fur coat, a hideous red-brown foxy thing, thrusts her ample chest in my direction, makes a big play of smoothing down the six inches of denim, then daintily places herself next to me, as always, crossing her legs suggestively. *'Dia de Andalucia'* she cries, presumably having caught the end of the previous conversation. 'Too-ess-dee. Gobby-Enry, he say las dias de puente be Moon-dee.'

Jose, Maria, Rafi and Juan-Carlos are rolling their eyes and sniggering , whereas Chrissie and I, still reeling from the appearance of this fugitive from a Bulgarian brothel, have no idea what she might be trying to tell us. *Dia de Andalucia* is Andalucia Day, whenever that might be, I didn't know there was such a thing, *Moon-dee* and *Tooess-dee* are days of the week presumably, *las dias de puente* are the days of bridges, whenever they might be, but Gobby-Enry? Not a clue. Never heard of him.

Juan-Carlos takes over the narrative. 'Thee day of Andalucia is the next week, Toosday, but el gobierno, how you say gobierno in Eengliss? In house of big bens, in Lon-don?

'The government!' Chrissie giggles.

'Yees, thee goberment he say we have crisees here in Espain, es no moneys, so country cannot to support holee-days Toosday and Wed-nesday, so fiestas of days of saints can be to change to Mondays.

OK, I think we have that, but what about these days of bridges? We have only just learned there is an Andalucia day next week, are there more days celebrating these bridges, and if so, where might these structures be? Given that there are no rivers to speak of, in this arid part of the world.

'Days of bridges are unofficial days, between the weekend, and the day of the saints', Jose confirms. 'So if day of saint is Wed-nesday, the peoples no work, Moonday and Toosday. Days of bridges.'

'So the goberment say we must to work more hard!' Maria complains. 'They are, you tell me thees word last week Jonnee, bastards!'

'Bastardos!' yells Alicia, hoisting her chest fetchingly. 'Gobby-Enry, bastardos!'

'OK, but you said the Andalucia Day was next Tuesday?' Chrissie queries.

'Yees!' comes the chorus from the crowded side of the table.

'So let me get this right' my wife continues 'With the current economic situation looking grave and the country teetering on the edge of bankruptcy, the government in Madrid has decreed that all public holidays and fiestas falling midweek, should be moved to the Monday, to avoid the so-called dias de puente, bridge days, where people take two or three days off work.'

'Yees.'

'But with Andalucía Day on Tuesday, is there a bridge day on Monday?'

'Yees.'

'So this new law? Won't Madrid be, I don't know, a bit cross?'

'Yees.'

Chrissie has run out of questions, but still looks confused. Jose comes to the rescue. 'Andalucia is much distance from Madrid' he confirms, 'and no persons here give toss about they! Jonneee teach me say this word!' he quickly adds, spotting shock on her face.

'Do not worry!' Rafi cries, 'ees no problem, you can to enjoy bridge day Moon-day, sleep long in bed, have breakfast Eengliss, on you terrace, enjoy sunny, siesta, thees Andalucia, no to remember Madrid!' and she waves her arms dismissively.

'Bastardos!' cries Alicia. 'Gobby-Enry, bastardos!'

OK, I think we get the message! Not that it makes one iota of difference to us, of course, our lives here are supposed to be one long days of bridges, although what with the academy, the private students, Dutch Dick's house cleaning and Del-Boy's roof, we seem to be busier than when we were working....

After the class we head past the centre of ancient peoples, and the club of young peoples, in search of this club of flamenco, which proves elusive. It simply isn't there. We discover what appears to be a Great Western Railway signal box, which unless is actually a Tardis, is unlikely to be an entertainment venue. You couldn't fit a guitarist and a singer inside, let alone a couple of women in spotty, frilly dresses.

It is boiling hot, the sun is beating down on my 'solar panel', and I am about to give up, when Chrissie suddenly exclaims with joy. 'Look! There it is, in the corner! The club of flamenco!' Damned if I can see it however, although I am the most unobservant of men, as my darling repeatedly points out. I can however make out what might be the Spanish version of a run-down 1960's holiday camp, the dining room possibly, complete with a small reception in the front. Chrissie is already hurrying across to the down-at-heel structure, so I follow in her wake.

The building is locked of course, but arriving by the front door, and gazing into the interior, we both start to laugh. A small stage is set up on the right, formica-covered tables in the middle, and a bar on the left. 'Maplin's! she cries, 'the Hawaiian Ballroom! Hi-Di-Hi!

'Ho-di-ho!' I giggle. 'Where is Ted Bovis? And Spike Dixon! And what about Peggy Ollerenshaw?

'Cleaning the Olympic-sized swimming pool, I imagine! And Gladys Pugh is getting ready to announce the knobbly knees competition!'

'But what about the dancers?' I continue, 'the ballroom dancers, what were their names? Barry and Yvonne something? We need their help here, to learn flamenco!'

'Barry and Yvonne Stuart-Hargreaves!' cries memory woman, 'but if you think I'm learning flamenco with you, think again! Be easier to train an elephant to dance!'

'A bit uncalled for, that!' I smile, 'don't you remember, down the Locarno, after six pints of McEwen's Export, 'Tiger Feet' by Mud, I was like John Travolta!'

'Like John Deere, you mean' she chuckles, 'you used to dance like a combine harvester!'

Very funny. 'Anyway' I sniff, 'we now know where to come on Tuesday. We just need to be careful who we tell.'

My wife looks puzzled. 'What, don't say anything to Gaffer and Diane, you mean?'

I try to remain straight-faced. 'Tell them if you like, although I doubt they'd be interested. No, I am serious, just don't say anything to Gobby-Enry, OK?!'

So on Dia de Andalucía, at around nine forty-five, we arrive at the club of flamenco to find the place rammed, not a seat left in the house. Every formica-topped table is occupied. A young waiter is rapidly weaving his way towards us at a remarkably un-Spanish pace. 'Blimey, look at Speedy Gonzalez!' Chrissie giggles, but I am too upset to speak. After all that, we are not going to see the concert.

Speedy approaches, grinning widely. 'Mesa para dos?' he enquires. *Table for two?* Well that would be nice, mate, but is he going to magic one out of thin air? Apparently he is. There is a scraping sound behind us, and another chap appears, dragging a table, right down to the front, overlooking the stage. We are in! Speedy produces two chairs, hands us a menu, and I order two beers. Within seconds, plates of crusty bread with chorizo, tomato and anchovies arrive, and the locals appear genuinely pleased that some foreigners have turned up. Everyone seems to be drinking bottles of sherry, so with my first rule of travel being 'do what everyone else is doing' we order one too. Ice cold Manzanilla, a dry pale sherry bearing the legend *La Gitana*, featuring a painting of a dark-eyed gypsy girl on the label, which suits the atmosphere perfectly, although I do pause to wonder what the boys in the rugby club might have thought of old Jonno being a sherry drinker.....

Chrissie leans in towards me. 'How much money did you bring?' she whispers.

'Nothing!' I giggle.

'WHAT?

'I didn't bring any money, you brought it! You have my wallet, presumably.' I am like the Queen, I get someone else to carry my cash.

She delves into her bag, extracts my wallet, and breathes a small sigh of relief. 'Twenty Euros, plus whatever loose cash is in my purse. As Alicia might have said, *you bastardo!*'

'Well who cares? I protest. 'Two beers, three Euros. Bottle of gypsy, five. Tapas, free. Eight yo-yo's, tops.'

My beloved narrows her eyes. 'And what about admission, for the concert?'

'What bloody concert?' I chuckle. 'It's gone half-ten already, can you see any sign of a concert? If this were England, there'd be a riot by now! Anyway, there was no mention of admission on that poster, was there? Forget it. If anyone asks us for money, I will say 'no speaky Spanish!'

Gazing round the Hawaiian ballroom, some familiar personalities and celebrities appear to be in attendance. On the table next to us, the comedian Ernie Wise is in conversation with a woman who is the spitting image of that bloke from the Seventies pop group *Sweet*, the one with the mincing voice, 'We just haven't got a clue, what to do!' Up by the stage, Bernard Manning is chatting to Gerry Adams, behind the bar is Adge Cutler, of *The Wurzels* fame, and next to him is Len, my old boss from the accountants office, who is not famous at all, apart from being runner-up in the 'Tax Personality of the Year' competition once, which is an oxymoron if ever I've heard one. The legendary Italian goalkeeper Gianluigi Buffon is gossiping with the singer-songwriter James Taylor, who is welcome to step onto the stage and do 'Fire and Rain' if this flamenco thing fails to materialise.

'Who was that actor in *Z Cars*, the stern one?' I ask, 'Stratford Johns was his real name, but I can't recall his character. He's sitting behind you, so don't commit any crimes!'

Chrissie turns her head, pretending to look elsewhere. 'Inspector Barlow' she smiles. 'What is it about this place, I've never seen so many doppelgangers all together, they say everyone has a double, but this has to be a record!'

I draw my legs together. 'Well you can't see my doppelgangers!'

Meanwhile Sean Connery is in deep discussions with Foggy from *Last of the Summer Wine*, although of the Maplin's Yellow-coats, Ted Bovis and Spike, there is no sign. Or any flamenco come to that.

Still, no-one seems the remotest bit concerned. A plate of potato salad appears on our table, the gypsy is slipping down a treat, so if the gig is an hour late, who cares? But at this rate, I will need to order another bottle.

Suddenly, Bernard Manning approaches the stage, taps the mike, and starts to speak. It appears something might be about to happen. For one dreadful moment I fear we might be forced to endure half-an-hour of so-called comedy, but thankfully that is not a road we have to go down. Bernard is commendably brief, he introduces the artists, and onto the stage shuffle two men, an older fellow in his sixties, tubby, balding, black suit, open-necked shirt, and a much younger man, probably half his age, thick curly black hair, similarly dressed, clutching a Spanish guitar. Ninety minutes late, we seem about to get under way. The old guy slumps into his chair, leans forward, presses his head in his hands, and rocks gently, backwards and forwards. The guitarist meanwhile begins plucking and strumming, a jumble of notes tumbles out across the stage, entrancing, enchanting, mesmeric, sometimes slow, no obvious rhythm, then speeding to a crescendo. I am trying to follow his finger movements but he is playing with both hands, picking the strings on the fret-board with his left, while his right performs miracles. It might be the sherry, but I am spellbound.

So intently am I concentrating on the guitar that I haven't really noticed the older chap staggering to his feet, clutching his heart. '*Mi corazon, mi corazon!*' he wails, in a plaintive, piercing voice, and immediately I fear for his health. 'Blimey!' Chrissie whispers, 'is he really having a heart attack?' She is a trained first-aider and knows how to administer CPR, which is just as well as my medical knowledge is limited to fitting a triangular bandage in the Wolf-Cubs, in about 1965. Just as she is about to leap on-stage, however, the singer straightens up, and throwing back his head, begins his delivery, a haunting, wailing sound, conjuring up images of baking sunshine, deep blue skies, hilltop castles, whitewashed villages, matadors, dark-eyed senoritas, in a style evoking Spain's north African heritage.

The vocals follow the guitar or the guitar follows the vocals, impossible to tell which, a little of both I suppose, and I am reminded of the axe-heroes of my youth, Hendrix, Clapton, Jeff Beck, Jimmy Page, and wonder how they would compare. Different styles of course, and maybe this guitarist wouldn't fare so well knocking out *All Along the Watchtower*, but I bet he would give them a run for their money. After each number, the duo stand and milk the rapturous applause, and before we know it, two glorious hours have passed and the evening is drawing to an end.

Bernard climbs onto the stage clutching two gallon-sized containers of olive oil which he presents to the now-beaming maestros, who perform one last bow, and depart. Chrissie and I slump back in our seats, shaking our heads in wonder. Did that really happen? The gypsy helped of course, but that was the most magical evening we have spent since we arrived in this country. I must find out more about this club. Bernard is still hanging round so I approach him and enquire, in my best library-class Spanish, when the next concert is. 'Not sure' he smiles, 'we only organise about four each year, so you need to look for the posters.'

I signal Speedy for the bill. 'Eight Euros' he grins, 'sorry, the sherry is very expensive!'

Chrissie and I are still giggling as we wend our way unsteadily up the cobbled street homewards. 'That is the first time someone has apologised for charging us a fiver for a night out!' she laughs. 'What did you think about our first flamenco concert?'

I am silent for a few moments. 'It was OK' I reply, but a bit disappointed they didn't play 'Goodnight Campers. Hi-di-hi-di-hi, ho-di-ho-di-ho, go, go, go, do the holiday rock!'

CHAPTER 31. WHO LET THE RAT OUT?

'Ello mate 'ow ya doin'?'

Oh no, it's Del on the phone. Probably wants me to work on his house, 'just for a hour mate' he will say, which will mysteriously turn into half a day, or longer. He will be skint of course, so payment will be in heaven, there will be no tea and biscuits on offer, due to the dogs being locked in the kitchen, and for the same reason access to the bathroom will be blocked, so that if I need a pee, I will have to use the mop bucket. Sounds like the perfect morning. 'Really busy at the moment' I lie, getting my excuses in early.

Del conveniently ignores this. 'Just for a hour mate, need a little 'and wiv me roof, bit skint at the minute, so maybe I can pay you when we fit Jose's windows?'

Chrissie is wagging her finger at me, mouthing the word 'NO' and making throat-slitting gestures. It's the classic male dilemma, isn't it? Who do I upset, my mate or my missus? 'Like I say, I'm really busy right now' I repeat. 'How about tomorrow afternoon.' My dearest forms a gun shape with her hand, and shoots me between the eyes.

The following day my business partner answers the door, looking particularly dishevelled. Never a vista of beauty, today his eyes are sunken, his skin sallow, his hair greasy and his chin sports about a week's growth. 'Christ what a week I have had!' is his greeting.

'Oh hello John, good of you to come here to help me, without payment, giving up your precious time,' I reply in a sarcastic tone.

Del rubs his hand across his face. 'Sorry mate, but I have had the week from hell. Come and see this.' He leads the way through the house to the kitchen at the back of the house, where there is a surprising absence of dogs, but a cacophony of barking tells me they are not far away.

'Stick the kettle on then' I command, in time-honoured fashion.

'Can't, got no gas' he swiftly counters, 'if you see the gas man on your travels, send him up will ya?'

'Lemonade then, or juice?' I ask.

'Ain't got none' comes the response, 'but I can do you some water' he adds, rummaging through a pile of dirty dishes in the sink, coming up with a tin mug, to which he gives a cursory swill under the tap then fills with water. I glance down at the greasy contents, appalled. Frankly I would rather drink the River Ganges. At that moment the awful prospect of having to use Del's bathroom rears its ugly head. Trust me on this one. If you are ever in his house and need a pee, use the mop bucket. Even if you are a woman.

'Look at this' my friend continues, pointing to three holes at floor level in the back wall of the house, each one big enough for a toddler to crawl into. The house is built of cob, the walls are about three feet thick made from stones and earth, with a plaster render inside and out. It looks as if the Taliban have paid him a visit.

'Jeez, what happened there. Is the wall collapsing?' I ask, stunned at the damage.

'Twas the dogs' he sighs. 'They started about a week ago, biting the plaster, clawing it, then when the plaster was broke they started digging, digging, non-stop. I was going crazy but I couldn't stop them, I put some wood over the hole but they tore it down, so I moved the fridge in front of the hole, so they started digging another. Night and day, digging and clawing, of course they are in the kitchen a lot but there was nothing I could do to stop them, so yesterday I locked them in the garden, then went to bed to try to catch up on some sleep. I was absolutely shattered, I've barely slept all week, I thought the house was gonna fall down if they carried on digging. I had only been asleep a few minutes when there was an almighty commotion, barking, growling, squealing, obviously a massive fight going on. I rushed out the back, and there was Suzy, the big girl, with a massive rat in her mouth. About a foot long it was, not including the tail.'

Regular readers of my ramblings will know I am terrified of rats. My face is contorted into a show of horror, just simply hearing about a foot-long rat will give me nightmares for weeks to come. 'Was it dead?' I ask hopefully.

'Christ I should say so!' he laughs. 'Nothing gets away from my Suzy. Yeah, a huge male it was, biggest rat I have ever seen.'

Hang on a moment. Did he say it was a male? 'What, did you look, actually check it was a male?' I ask in disbelief. The hair on the back of my neck is standing up.

'Didn't need to check' Del grins, 'he had a willy, just like yours, only bigger!' I ignore this slight on my manhood. My mouth has gone dry and I am wishing I had drunk the water while I had the chance. 'Anyway' he continues, 'I went out into the garden and noticed several holes in the back wall of the house. The rat had been digging in from outside, and that's what the dogs could hear, him tunneling away inside the wall.' Now the hairs on the hairs on the back of my neck are shivering. I didn't know rats did that. Truly, this is a living horror story. I swiftly resolve to check the back of our house for holes, although what I would do if I found one I cannot imagine, in case the rat was still inside.

'Anyway mate' Del resumes, 'what I want to do today is mix some sand and cement, nice stiff mix, and throw it in the holes in the kitchen, bit of cement, a few rocks, bit more cement, and so on. What I want you to do is stand outside in the garden, with a spade, and if any rats come running out the holes you whack them with the spade, OK?'

'You can eff right off!' I advise him, forcefully. 'You can eff completely, totally and utterly right off. I would not do that for fifty Euros an hour, let alone the naff-all you are paying.'

'Why ever not? he asks, in disbelief. 'Surely you played 'Bash the Rat' at the village fairs, down there in that Devon?', the last bit in a mock-pirate voice.

'Yes I played Bash the Rat' I confirm, 'but not with a real effing rat. No I'm sorry Del, you will have to get a neighbour to help you. I am off', and I turn towards the front door and blessed relief from this hell-hole.

At this moment my colleague is seized by a massive coughing fit. He is spluttering away like a Romanian asbestos miner and it seems like his life-long twenty-a-day habit has finally caught up with him. Just as I am considering either the kiss of life, or a swift kick in the nuts, the coughing turns to laughter. Uncontrolled laughter. Tears are streaming down his face, he is holding onto the kitchen worktop, his whole body shaking. 'Your face, your face!' he splutters. 'You should've seen your face. Don't worry mate, I have already blocked up the holes in the outside wall. I knew you hated rats so I couldn't resist winding you up, sorry!' My relief is tempered by the fact that I have been well and truly stiffed. *Don't worry however, one day, my time will come......* 'What we are doing today is shifting roof tiles' he continues. 'I have finished fixing the roof, so those tiles stacked on the front terrace need to come down. What I want you to do is carry them through my bedroom out to the back terrace, and hand them down to me in the garden. I can stack them neatly there.' He is still chuckling away as I head upstairs, through his bedroom with the grey satin sheets (or should that be shat-in sheets?) and onto the front terrace. Straight away I can see how revenge will be mine. I will fill his bed with tiles, and cover them with the sheet. Perfect.

Out on the terrace I regard the huge pile of ancient roof tiles. Ever since I have known Del, these tiles have been there, and in that time they have gathered their own thick layer of dust, earth, leaves, paper and various other bits of assorted rubbish. Ideal nest-building material in fact. The perfect place for rodents to make a home. Mice I could just about cope with, but anything larger? I take a step backwards, keeping my eye firmly on the pile. Then I hear rustling. It might have been the breeze, but it certainly sounds like scuffling creatures, to my fevered mind. In a panic I look round for a pole or stick to hit the tiles with, but annoyingly Del has tidied up out here and there is just the pile. I could give them a swift boot but that would leave me exposed to vermin running up my trouser leg. Then out the corner of my eye I spot another pile of tiles against the side wall. I had forgotten those. And I am now trapped between the two piles, with no escape route. Keeping my eye on both piles, I hear more scuffling. There is nothing for it, I will have to call my friend. Maybe get him here on some pretext. 'Del?'. No reply. 'DEL?'. Nothing. He is out in the back garden, clearly he cannot hear me. 'DEL! HELLO!..........HELP!!

There is nothing else to do but make a swift dash for it. Taking a deep breath I sprint forwards into the bedroom, aiming a karate kick at the pile of tiles as I pass. But I lose my footing, bash my shin painfully, and land head first among the shat-in sheets. Del hears the commotion and comes into the bedroom, to find me rolling round in his bed rubbing my shin. 'Blimey' he shouts, 'I know I ain't paying you but I didn't expect you to come here and catch up on your sleep, ya lazy toss!' He narrows his eyes and effects a camp voice. 'Unless you want me to join you in there, honky-tonk!' My humiliation is complete.

'Bashed my bloody leg on your pile of tiles!' I cry, which is strictly true, although not the whole truth. 'Really, Del, I don't know how you can live in these conditions. This place is like the third world, only worse.'

He glances round affectionately, taking in the two piles of roof tiles, the dust, plastic and other assorted debris. His gaze then encompasses the bedroom, with it's broken plaster, the ceiling which has fallen away in places, and the grimy bed-linen. 'Nah, it ain't that bad, really. We got the roof done now, so get rid of these tiles, give it a bit of a sweep, an' it'll be just like the Ritz!' Ever the optimist, my business partner. 'Anyway, I just remembered I gotta couple o' beers in the fridge. Let's shift the tiles, then we can have a bit of a sit-down. Or a lie down, if you're still in the mood!' he leers, suggestively.

We shift the tiles with ease, any vermin which might previously have been lurking behind the piles having long since scarpered. 'Right, beer!' commands Del, 'unless you fancy a quick grope on me bed, that is!' I am tempted, but only because I am exhausted, and could fall asleep on a clothes line, right now.

Thump! 'What the hell was that noise?' We have only been in the sitting room a few minutes when suddenly there is a loud crash from the back of the house, followed by an almighty cacophony of barking. It is surprising the noise that nine dogs can make. Del sits up in his chair, then the thudding starts again. He stands up like a shot, 'there's some bastard on the roof' he shouts, 'quick, let's get out the back.'

In truth I am not that keen, and after all the 'intruder' will not get far, what with nine dogs and all. My friend dashes out the room, showing a turn of speed rarely seen when he needs to climb up a ladder, and I reluctantly follow. His back yard is accessed up a flight of steps, as the house is built on a hill, and as I climb the steps and fend off a river of barking canines. I can hear him laughing like a madman. 'What the hell is it? I ask, breathlessly, reaching the top of the steps. He is unable to speak, and simply nods his head in the direction of the roof. There, perched on the tiles, stands a huge turkey. Nothing so far in my fifty-odd years on this earth has prepared me for this moment, the creature is strutting about as if it belongs there, provoking more barking from the assembled pack. 'How the hell did that get there?'

'Well I expect it pole-vaulted, or maybe swung on a rope like Tarzan,' comes the sarcastic reply. 'How the bloody hell do you think it got there? It used its wings, you know, the things sticking out its back.'

Well I never knew turkeys could fly, they look too ungainly to me, and this one certainly is a monster. I recognise it now, it looks like the one who lives in the pen behind Del's house, along with a matted Alsatian. 'What the hell are you gonna do?' is my next question, but before Del can reply things take a decided turn for the worse. Suzy, the big female dog, springs up the garden wall, from a standing start, just like a cat. Now that wall is seven feet high, I can just reach the top with outstretched arms, and that is some jump for a dog.

'Shit shit shit!' shouts my friend. 'That wall is only a brick wide, she will never balance, maybe fall over, and that bloody great Alsatian is lurking there.' But incredibly, Suzy not only gains her balance, she starts inching along the wall like a four-legged ballet dancer, tail stretched out behind her, and her intentions are now clear. She is trying to walk round the yard wall so she can access the roof, and the turkey. Del is doing his nut, shouting at Suzy, and the others barking their encouragement from below, while the Yuletide feast that never was continues to parade around, pecking at the tiles here and there. Things then take yet another turn downhill, if that were possible. An old bed frame has been placed against the wall on the other side, and as Suzy passes it, she knocks it slightly so that it slips, blocking her return passage. She is trapped. 'Shit shit shit!' repeats Del, 'she will get onto my neighbours patio now, his wife is a Muslim and not allowed dogs in the house or garden. She will put a curse on me, or whatever it is they do.'

'Witchdoctors' I confirm.

'No, she's a Muslim, not a witchdoctor,' he confirms.

'No, it's witchdoctors who put curses on people, not Muslims,' I respond.

'Well whatever it is they do', he gabbles, 'I ain't gonna wait to find out. Quick, grab that ladder and let's get up there, and get her down.'

I look round in vain for the ladder, but only spot a collection of randomly assembled sticks, which might in a previous century have been described as a ladder, although only by a mental patient. 'You are not serious about climbing that thing?' I shout.

'Got no choice' he replies, and once again demonstrating extreme agility, he starts to climb the wall after the fugitive dog. The precarious apparatus creaks and groans under his weight but manages to hold together, and very soon Del is clinging to the wall about five feet behind his dog. I am about to get my phone out to take a sneaky shot when, for the third time, matters deteriorate even further. Harley, the large male, decides he wants a piece of the action and launches himself after his mate, and his master. He is heavier than Suzy however and only succeeds in getting his front paws over the wall, and is left hanging with his back legs scrabbling to get purchase. 'Christ!' he shouts, 'grab him before he falls.'

'Billocks!' I shout back.

'No not his billocks!' he screams, 'get him round the waist, quick.'

'I mean, billocks, I am not going to!' I shout back, 'he has got teeth the other end!' Before the conversation can become even more heated however, gravity takes over and Harley slips back down the wall and rolls ungainly around on his back, before regaining all four legs, then staggers to his feet, and manfully cocks his leg against the foot of the ladder.

So the situation is that a huge turkey is on the roof, Suzy is inching towards him, Del is sat with his legs astride the wall inching towards her, Harley is below licking his balls and the other seven dogs and me are watching intently. For a few seconds, serenity reigns. Then everything happens at once. Del accidentally knocks over the bed frame with his leg and it crashes into the yard, the noise startles the turkey, which launches itself off the roof in a painful-looking belly flop, and somehow part-glides/part-stumbles like a pig with wings back over the wall, Suzy makes a snap with her jaws as the bird passes by, Del grabs Suzy from behind and dangles her towards me shouting 'quick get hold of her, before I drop her!', I step forward into a pile of dog crap and slip against the wall just as the dog is lowered into my arms, Suzy licks my face, I recoil thinking she is about to bite my nose off and stick my other foot in the poo, before dropping the dog the last few feet. Del meanwhile has climbed back down the ladder to be greeted by his faithful pack, and the show is over.

Until the next time.....

CHAPTER 32. PAINTING, SPANISH-STYLE

'Neighbour, what are you doing?' I am in the street outside my house, paintbrush in one hand, paint-pot in the other, and my ladder is standing against the wall of the house. I would have thought it obvious what I am doing, but Loli, our crazy neighbour, always wants to be sure. And it's strange how she always calls me 'neighbour', even though she knows my name. Chrissie is always 'La Cristina', but I am simply 'neighbour'.

'Good morning Loli, I am painting my gutter, navy blue, same as I painted the gutter at the back of the house last week.' *There, that should give her all the information she could possibly need.*

Apparently not. 'Are you painting the front door?'

'No, just the gutter.'

'Are you painting the windows?'

'No just the gutter.'

'Where is La Cristina?'

'She is in the garden, looking after her plants.'

'Ok, off you go' she replies, folding her arms and standing back. *Hmmmm...* Spaniards are fascinated by work. They can stand and watch it for hours, offering advice, criticism, and occasional encouragement. Mind you, they never offer to help. See a bloke digging a hole in the street, there will be half a dozen locals gathered round, each one offering comments, uninvited. The funny thing is, the workmen never seem to mind. In England, a few choice words would send the audience packing, but not here. Personally, I cannot stand being watched. If I had to name a single thing I dislike about this country, it would be having an audience while I am working. But there is nothing I can do, Loli will stand there until she has offered her opinion, even though I can guarantee she has never climbed a ladder and painted a gutter.

So up I climb, carefully avoiding spilling the paint. With my head directly below the gutter, I dip the brush into the pot and gingerly apply the first few brush strokes. I need to take care, as there are no fascia boards here, the gutters are fitted directly to the wall of the house. We have a lovely grey and cream granite facing to our walls and the last thing I need is a blue stripe across it.

'WATCH OUT YOU DON'T GET BLUE PAINT ON THE WALL!' bellows Loli from below, causing me to jump in fright and narrowly avoid a blue stripe on the wall.

I grit my teeth. Count to five. Turn my head and look down at my annoying neighbour, smiling serenely. 'I am a professional' I lie. Loli cackles and exposes her gappy teeth, like some ancient Spanish witch. *Take a deep breath John.* I return to my painting, apply a perfect blue coat to the first couple of feet of gutter, then carefully return to earth.

'Very good, neighbour', Loli comments. 'But you're a bit slow.' Again I take a deep breath.

Before I can formulate a reply however, the door of the next house opens and Isabel, Loli's sister, emerges. 'Neighbour, what are you doing?' *Oh no, not again.*

Before I can repeat my story Loli chimes in. 'Neighbour's painting his gutter, navy blue, same as he did the one at the back last week. But he's not painting the front door, or the windows.'

'Where's Cristina?' asks Isabel.

Again I open my mouth to answer, but Loli beats me to it. 'In the garden, doing her plants,' she informs her sister.

'But this is woman's work' comments Isabel, sweeping her hand in the direction of my handiwork. This is true. In Andalucia, painting is considered woman's work. You very often see women of any and every age groaning under the weight of a bucket of whitewash. And they don't use ladders, preferring to tie a brush to the end of a long pole and lean out of the window. Hence there are a lot of paint splatters in Spain. 'Slap it up and go for a siesta' seems to be the mantra here.

'Cristina is in the garden' I confirm.

'That is your job', Isabel states.

Again, she is correct. Men do the garden, women paint. 'Well Cristina doesn't like climbing ladders', I counter.

'She should get a long pole and tie the brush on, then lean out the window', comes the reply.

'And I don't like gardening' I continue. 'In our house, Cristina does the garden, I do the painting.'

'You are very strange, you English', Isabel comments, although she has a smile on her face. We love Isabel, the quiet sister. Loli is like a volcano, you never know when she is going to erupt. Isabel is completely opposite.

I shift the ladder a few feet and prepare to climb up. Just then the next front door opens, and a stomach emerges, followed several seconds later by a man. Fernando, brother of Loli and Isabel. He is munching a piece of toast. 'Neighbour, what are we doing?' he cries, splattering toast crumbs in my direction.

What are WE doing? Well I am trying to paint, while your ruddy sisters keep interrupting me.

Again, Loli supplies the commentary. Fernando shifts his massive gut towards my handiwork. 'You need to guard the ladder' he informs me.

Is he joking? The chances of anyone creeping up here, with this audience, and nicking my ladder are less than zero. 'Its Sunday morning', I remind him. 'There are no thieves around now.'

'No, you need to guard the ladder' he repeats.

What is wrong with the bloke? 'What, like a robbery?' I laugh.

'No, guard the ladder' he insists, walking over and putting his foot on the bottom rung, then catching hold of the sides. 'Look, guard the ladder!'

Ah, he means HOLD the ladder. That must be what they say here. Another little piece in the jigsaw that is my Spanish vocabulary. A jigsaw with most of the pieces missing.

Just then the door next to Fernando opens and out comes a boy, dressed head to toe in a replica Real Madrid kit, bouncing a football. Manuel, seven years old, he usually stays with his granny at weekends. He skilfully dribbles the ball toward us. 'DON'T COME DOWN HERE WITH THAT FOOTBALL' Loli hollers. 'THE ENGLISHMAN IS PAINTING.' Manuel looks confused. 'HE DOESNT WANT YOU DISTURBING HIM' she continues, without a trace of irony. *Disturbing me? So what have you and your brother and sister been doing the last ten minutes Loli?*

Fernando suddenly turns to his sister and barks a rapid series of instructions, of which all I can catch is 'down below.' He wants her to go down below. Without a word she slinks off down the street.

Right. I need to get on. I shift the ladder down a few feet, but before I can climb up an old lady emerges from the house next to Fernando. Mercedes, Manuel's granny. 'Neighbour, you are painting!'

No actually I am not painting. I am trying to paint. BUT I KEEP GETTING INTERRUPTED. 'While you're up there, can you paint my gutter?' she asks, turning her head and fluttering her eyelashes.

Hmm, a difficult one that. I want to help the neighbours where possible, in fact I translated the instructions for a food steamer from English to Spanish for Mercedes just last week. But I happen to know she has two grown-up children living nearby. Surely if their mother's gutter needs painting, they should come and do it? 'Well, I am a little busy at the moment....' I reply. Then I glance up at her gutter. Or rather, where her gutter should be. 'BUT YOU HAVE NO GUTTER!'

Mercedes, Isabel and Fernando all start laughing. *I remember now, Mercedes' house has no rainwater collection apparatus, so that during inclement weather, any poor unsuspecting soul walking past her house gets a drenching.* 'Ha ha, I have no gutter', giggles Mercedes.

'She has no gutter!' whispers Isabel, as if confiding a secret.

'She got you there!' laughs Fernando, 'but you still need to guard that ladder.'

Right, I really need to get on. Before I can however, Loli comes staggering up the street clutching a large, greasy brown paper bag. 'Churros!' I cry. 'Did you buy any for me?' Churros are a donut-like sweet, but served in a thin coil, deep fried, often with liquid chocolate sauce. Heart attack on a plate. The Spanish go crazy for churros, especially at weekends, for breakfast. And what a coincidence! I learned to say 'did you buy anything for me?' only this week, and this is the first outing for my newly-learned sentence. But will Loli understand, or am I talking gobbledegook? As usual.

'Of course neighbour!' she replies, delving into the bag and breaking off about a foot of churro. Isabel meanwhile has emerged with a roll of kitchen paper, tearing off a couple of sheets for me.

'Got any chocolate sauce?' I enquire, pushing my luck.

'You're getting too fat!' cries Fernando. *Yeah right. Pot. Kettle. Black.*

'Here you are Mercedes' Loli continues, groping around in the bag, again emerging with a foot of the greasy delicacy. 'And what about you, chico?' she shouts at Manuel, who has returned to the scene, having somehow hidden his football. Again she rummages around in the bag, digging out another length.

'OI, STOP GIVING AWAY MY BREAKFAST, WOMAN! Shouts Fernando. *He needn't worry, there must still be about five yards of churro in the bag.* 'Come on, inside' he orders, pushing open Loli's door, and the three of them disappear. Mercedes and Manuel also head back to their house, leaving me suddenly in peace.

Right, I really, really need to get on. I polish off my fatty snack, wipe my sugary hands on my jeans, collect my paint and brush and ascend the ladder for the next section. Hopefully there will be no more interruptions. I chose a Sunday morning thinking it would be quiet.

Wrong. 'Neighbour, nice painting!' *Oh for pity's sake, not again. I'm not sure how much more of this I can stand. In England, I would be finished by now, cleaned the brush, and getting on with the rest of my life.* A front door down the street has opened and Juan and Susanna have come out to see what is going on. Perhaps they smelled the churros. Juan and Susanna are a typical 'comic card' couple, he is short and slim, she is almost twice his size, in height and width. Juan is the local 'Environmental Domestic Waste Redistribution Officer.' Hence our nickname for him, 'The Dustman.' Earlier this year, Juan collected several wooden pallets which had been discarded around the town, then in a frenzy of hammering and sawing over several evenings, constructed a fence, which he proceeded to erect across his garden. The problem was he didn't take into account the undulations in the ground, so the whole drunken structure looked as if it was about to collapse, or already had. He then painted the panels orange and green, as if some colour-blind maniac had been let loose with a paintbrush. Still, it gave us plenty to talk about every time we had friends over.

Meanwhile Susanna has a feather duster in one hand, and is gripping a fluffy white Bichon Frise dog under her other meaty arm. She is dusting the wrought iron round her window, and it looks just as if she is going to polish the glass with the dog. Spanish people love small dogs and you often see the creatures being carried around, as if the owners cannot understand that their canine friends have four perfectly good legs.

'Are you painting my gutter, Jonneee?' shouts Juan.

'I am painting them all, but different colours' I shout back. 'Mine is navy blue, Loli's will be red, Isabel's pink, Fernando's purple…. and yours will be orange and green!'

Juan bursts out laughing, and Susanna's chest is heaving up and down. 'Orange and green, he said' she laughs. The dog is rocking up and down on her ample bosom, and the whole scene resembles a ventriloquist act, as if the dog is supposed to be speaking. 'Orange and green, orange and green.' If so her act needs a bit of polish, as I can see her lips moving. Mind you, even Keith Harris and Orville the Duck had to start somewhere.

'OK, orange and green it is!' laughs Juan, and the pair of them, plus fluffy white dog, disappear back inside.

Right, can I please get on with no more interruptions? Not a chance. Further down the street, Leopard-skin Woman, and her neighbour Auntie Vera come out to join in the fun. Leopard-skin Woman, aka Manuela, is wearing a rather fetching lime green tracksuit top, artfully combined with leopard print leggings, and pink slippers. Auntie Vera meanwhile, aka Antonia, is in the rather more subdued black of the typical Spanish widow. 'Jonneee!' cries Manuela. 'You are painting!' Now Manuela loves her music, particularly Elvis, which she plays at ear-splitting volume while she performs her housework. Her husband 'Campo Pete' is also a fan, and I once had to translate some Elvis song-titles into Spanish for him. 'Heartbreak Hotel' and 'Wooden Heart' were relatively straightforward, but 'Rock-A-Hula-Baby' proved rather tricky.

The most popular song in Spain at the moment is by Enrique Iglesias, called *Bailando*, which translates as 'I am dancing.' The chorus goes *Bailand-o-o-o, bailand-o-o-o,* after which the backing singers chime in with *Contigo,* which means 'with you.' So I decide to tweak the lyrics slightly, to *Pintando,* which means 'I am painting.' So waving my paintbrush up and down in exaggerated fashion, I start to sing. *Pintand-o-o-o, Pintand-o-o-o,* and glancing down the street Manuela and Antonia are dancing, and singing 'Contigo, Contigo.' Manuela is really going for it, her thick, black, wavy Spanish hair flying round her head like a teenager at a Status Quo concert in 1976. Fantastic. I bet no other Englishman in this country has ever got his neighbours singing and dancing in the street to Enrique Iglesias. Which is probably a good thing.

Right, I really, absolutely have to get on with this. I shift the ladder and climb up for the next section of gutter, and manage to paint another couple of feet. Climbing back down, I am concentrating on what I have painted, and what I still have left to do, so I am not really looking as I step down off the ladder, straight into the arms of Cruzojo. He lives opposite Juan and Susanna, and his wife Maria is Susanna's sister. Cruzojo is the street 'nosey parker', he sits in his front room of an evening with the blinds drawn, peeping out at whoever is passing. Consequently, on our evening walks, we often creep up to his window and make animal noises, mooing, barking, meowing, clucking. As you do.

What the hell he is doing standing at the bottom of the ladder? I am so startled to find him there I momentarily lose my balance, stumbling back into him, and he has to grab me round the waist to avoid the pair of us crashing to the ground. For a couple of seconds we stagger round, him gripping me tightly from behind, like a couple of gays on Brighton seafront on a Saturday night. Eventually I recover my balance and untangle my rear end from his grip. Then he starts to sing, something about the 'painting of love', although I imagine the original lyrics were about a portrait of a lover, rather than a fat Englishman slapping up a coat of gloss. Still, it could have been a special moment, apart from three things; firstly, he cannot sing. Secondly, he only has one eye. And finally, he reeks of garlic. So he sounds like a strangled cat, I cannot tell if he is gazing into my eyes, or looking up at the gutter, and he hums like a Frenchman's jock-strap. Ideal.

'What colour are you painting mine, Jonneee' he enquires.

'Red and white spots, like a flamenco dress' I tell him.

Maria is standing behind him, and bizarrely she is gripping a Yorkshire terrier under her arm. What is it about these sisters and their bow-wow's? 'Red and white spots, he said, like a flamenco dress' she laughs, as the dog bounces up and down on her chest, and once again it looks just like a ventriloquist act gone badly wrong. Maybe that's it, the sisters are rehearsing for a double act, for the next series of *Spain's Got Talent.* 'Susanna and Maria and their talking dogs.' Like I say, their act needs a bit of work.

Right, I absolutely, one hundred percent, need to finish this job before I go insane. Or die. I shift the ladder another couple of feet, then-disaster! The sun has now moved round and is starting to shine on the very section of gutter I still need to paint. Hell and damnation, I forgot about the sun, although I wasn't in all honesty planning to take almost two hours to complete the job. They say you shouldn't paint in direct sunlight, although I am blowed if I am stopping now. I only have about six feet left, so providing I have no more interruptions, another ten minutes should see it done. Quarter-hour tops.

I quickly ascend the ladder and start applying the paint, but within thirty seconds in the boiling sunshine I am sweating like a pig. Within a minute I am sweating like a field of pigs outside a bacon factory. And slowly, ever so slowly, my jeans start slipping down. I must have lost a pound or two over the winter, I noticed the jeans were a bit loose this morning when I put them on, I should have fitted a belt but wanted to get on with the job, so didn't bother. A decision I am now regretting, because with the brush in one hand, and the paint in the other, I can do absolutely nothing about it. And still my jeans are sliding down my slippery torso. Gingerly I press my groin against the ladder and try to wriggle my jeans a bit higher, without success. So I transfer the brush to my left hand and with my right I grab the waistband and try to haul it up, but this is really a two-handed job and my efforts make little impression.

Then, as if matters couldn't get any worse, they suddenly do. Loli's door opens and the two sisters emerge, having no doubt eaten their weight in churros, although thankfully Fernando remains inside, polishing off the last few feet of his fatty breakfast. And lo and behold, who should come waddling down the street? You guessed it; Mercedes. 'You still there neighbour? hollers Loli. 'Madre mia, I can see your BUM!' she continues.

Oh God, is this really happening? 'I can see his underpants', confirms Isabel.

'I am going under the ladder' advises Mercedes, 'maybe I will see his cylinder!' Well that is another addition to my Spanish vocabulary, I have never heard a willy referred to as a cylinder before, although quite honestly I cannot think of a worse place to expand my knowledge.

'No, can't see it yet,' Mercedes continues.

'Just wait a minute' leers Loli, 'it won't be long!' *She's not wrong there. In these conditions, 'long' is the last thing it will be.*

I have had just about all I can stand. Just get me off this bloody ladder and get me out the way of these bloody women. I am not sure what the penalty is for indecent exposure in this country, and I am not about to find out. I am coming down, and packing it in, right now.

Just then there is a violent jolt to the ladder and my heart skips a beat, for a split second I feel as if I am falling, but by a miracle I cling on, and by a double miracle I am still holding the brush and the paint pot. But my jeans have passed the point of no return, and suddenly I can feel the hot sun burning my bare arse. *What the hell happened?* Glancing down, heart still going nineteen to the dozen, I spot Cruzojo holding the ladder. 'Ha ha neighbour!' he cries. 'Got you there. Meeooooww!'

The bastard. The utter bastard. I will be howling like a pack of wolves outside his window tonight, that's a fact. Maybe throw in a herd of elephants.

Gingerly, I begin my descent, keeping my groin area as close to the rungs as possible, without bashing my cylinder and causing permanent damage.

Terminado I announce to the assembled throng. 'I have finished.'

'But neighbour' protests Loli, 'you still have a small bit to do.'

Manana' I tell her. 'Tomorrow. Its too hot today.'

'It certainly is!' laughs Mercedes, fanning her face. 'I haven't been so hot for years! I almost saw an English cylinder!'

Loli is cackling, Isabel is grinning, Cruzojo is still singing about the painting of love, Suzanna and Maria are rocking with laughter and their respective dogs are straining in vain against their owners' bosoms. I open my front door, pop my pot and brush down, then lower my ladder and head inside. Just as I am about to disappear into the luxury of some privacy, Loli calls out. ' Neighbour!' I turn to face the crowd.

'Si?' is all I can think to say.

'Neighbour, you have a beautiful bum!'

'Gracias Loli' I reply, and, bowing at my infuriating but lovable neighbours, I gratefully lock my door.

Until tomorrow....

CHAPTER 33. 'I CAN'T GET NO...'

'Foor fockeen queeds for peenta, in Lon-Don.' I am having an after-work beer with Del, and we have been joined by Tony, whose house we are working on. Tony wanders down the bar every afternoon during the week to watch *Bandaleros*, his favourite Spanish soap opera. I glance up at the intrusion and spot a bloke in his mid-thirties, dressed in the casual uniform of the Spanish male of any age, a shiny nylon track suit. He raises his glass. 'Bir. Foor fockeen queeds. I een Lon-Don tree yeers,' he shouts, pointing behind him, a gesture I take to mean three years ago.

The barmaid joins in. 'Eengland ees ver cold yes?' she says. 'Mooch rainings?'

This happens quite a lot. Most young Spaniards have learned a bit of English at school and are keen to try it out.

'What part of London?' shouts Del, a Londoner. Blank look. 'Buckingham Palace, Big Ben, St Paul's?' More blank looks.

'Que barrio?' I shout.

'Yees' our friend replies. Lon-Don. Dart-Foord. Meek Jaguar. Rolleeng Stones. Meek Jaguar he born Dart-Ford, I can get no, satisfac-see-on!', and he grabs his groin, a gesture which will disturb my sleep later that night, jumps down from his bar stool, thrusts his crotch forwards in a lewd fashion, and emits a loud grunt 'uuuhhhh'. Quite. The barmaid turns away in disgust, but us blokes fall about laughing. Thus encouraged, our new friend points to the telly blaring away in the corner. 'Ees sheets' he shouts, making a derogatory gesture at the TV. 'Sheets, lots sheets'.

'Well ah likes it' replies Tony, a Geordie. 'Ganna doon here every day, gets us oot the hoose, like. It's set in the 1880's,' he continues, by way of explanation, 'on the border between Spain and Mexico'.

Del almost chokes on his beer and I burst out laughing. 'What part of Spain is that Tony?' I ask, 'this border with Mexico?'

'Ah dinno' he replies, 'doon South somewhere ah thinks.'

'We are down South' I reply, 'any more South than this you would be in Africa! There's no border with Mexico down here.'

'Well maybe it's up North then', he replies, 'but its on the border somewheres.'

'Failed your geography GCSE mate?' cries Del, tears running down his face.

'Aye, ah did,' he replies' deadpan, 'but ah passed me history, like.'

It is beginning to feel like I have passed into a parallel universe. I am covered in brick dust, and just want a quiet beer. I glance again at the TV and spot the heroine of Bandaleros, a buxom dark-eyed beauty dressed in a long cotton frock, cut at the front to expose acres of ample bosom, which she expertly heaves at every opportunity. 'She is married to that fella there,' explains Tony, pointing to a bloke dressed in cowboy gear standing in front of what appears to be a cardboard cactus, 'but she is having an affair with his brother, him look' he gestures, at a swarthy-looking honcho.

'Teetas', comes another shout from our friend, pointing at the screen. 'Teetas grandes!' Again he makes the lewd groin gesture with his crotch, together with a cupping action with both hands in the breast area. Once more the barmaid shows her disgust, but our friend is correct. The heroine does indeed have teetas grandes.

I glance at Del. 'Your new mate certainly learned some English swear words during his time in Lon-Don' I giggle.

'Well he would do, in bloody Dartford!' he replies. 'Lot of savages down there!'

Tony glances up. 'Where is this Dartford?' he queries. Del and I both glance at each other, we have been working together for a while now and have developed a bit of a double act. 'LON-DON!' we both shout in unison, rolling with laughter, 'for Heaven's sake keep up, you Geordie pillock.'

Another shout comes from the bar. 'Seeeee, Dart-Foord, Meek Jaguar!'

I run my hand across my face. 'Christ, I have had enough of this, just pay the woman and let's get the hell out of here. See you tomorrow Tony.' I escape into the evening sunshine, but as I do the voice follows me out into the street. 'I can get no, satisfac-see-on!'....

CHAPTER 34. THE FAB FOUR

What is it about Londoners and chickens? Almost every one I have ever known (Cockneys that is, not cockerels) has had a few hens scrabbling around in the back garden a few weeks after leaving the Big Smoke. It was the case in Devon, and it is the same over here, with our friend Jackie. My phone rings. 'Ello Johnny me ol' china, can ya come over one day an' fix up me new chicken house? The bits are scattered all acrost me garden, and the instructions are all in bleedin' Spanish.' I am tempted to ask her what bleedin' language she expected Spanish chicken-house instructions to be in, but the thought of a few hours paid work does wonders to curb my sarcasm. 'An while yer 'ere, p'raps you can replaster the chimley, the rain is leakin' in.' There you go, my discretion has been rewarded. A full-day of paid work!

So next day I head over to Jackie and Phil's place, and sure enough the bits of the hen-house are scattered acrost the garden. Four wheels, a base, two sides, a front, a back, a roof and a bag of screws. Who needs instructions, whatever bleedin' language they are in? 'The 'ens is comin' termorra' Jackie informs me. 'Man-well acrost the road is lettin' us have four. Special Spanish 'ens. I can let ya 'ave a few eggs on Friday!'

Over a hundred Euros for the hen-house, plus whatever Manuel is charging for the hens, plus chicken-feed, vets bills and my wages, I am longing to remind her that large brown eggs are just over a Euro a dozen here, but once again the thought of the next pay-day is in my mind. On Friday I just happen to be passing their house, and decide to call in to look at her new 'ens. I love eggs for breakfast at the weekend, fried on toast on Saturday, scrambled on Sunday. Lovely. 'Come an' see me babbies', Phil cries, 'I've gived 'em all names, the big un is Bossy, then there's Flossie, Bessie an' Jessie.'

'Woss 'ee like' laughs Jackie, 'great daft beggar.' Sure enough, four of the largest chickens I have ever seen are pecking away contentedly behind a mesh fence, and I cannot help giving my newly-assembled hen-house an admiring glance. 'Man-well reckons they will lay a coupla eggs a day each, but they ain't laid none yet' laments Jackie. 'Doncha worry Jonny, you'll get yer eggs soon enough!'

A few days later I am passing their place again. I love boiled eggs for breakfast midweek, two rounds of toast cut into soldiers. Lovely. 'D'ya know what?' cries

Jackie. 'I reckon one of them 'ens is a geezer. I swear I could 'ear crowin' last night, although I coulda been dreamin'. Look at that Bossy, 'ow she chases the others round the pen. I reckon she is a geezer. An' they ain't laid no bleedin' eggs yet either!'

'How do you tell the sex of a chicken?' I enquire. 'Do you pick them up and look underneath? Do cocks have, er, cocks? Do they have dangly bits, like blokes?'

'Gawd knows' laughs Jackie, 'but I reckon we will find out termorra. The vet's comin'. Ee's got stuff fer fleas, ticks an all that, plus 'ee 'as some special powder what makes their fevvers all shiny.'

'Yeah me babbies' interrupts Phil, in a voice you would normally use when speaking to children, or puppies. 'Who's gonna 'ave nice shiny coats then?'

'Great daft beggar' laughs Jackie.

I have visions of this vet, with large Euro signs flashing up before his eyes. Someone has told him that Londoners have moved into town. 'Londoners!' he is saying, joyously. 'Where there be Londoners, there be chickens! Money money money!' Actually I am undoubtedly being unfair to the bloke. He is probably a dedicated professional, devoted to the welfare of his patients. But come on. Shiny fevvers? You have to wonder, don't you? Anyway, what do I know about chickens, apart from the fact that they taste great, from the oven? Roast and boiled potatoes, green beans, carrots, gravy. Lovely. But Jackie is correct. Bossy does indeed look like a geezer.

Several days later Chrissie and I are having coffee in town, Jackie and Phil pass the cafe, spot us inside and pop in to join us. 'Watcha fink?' cries Jackie, before she has even sat down. 'All of them 'ens turned out to be geezers! Bleedin Man-well. I ain't 'ad a wink of sleep, crowin' all night they was!'

'Yeah' continues Phil, 'I've 'ad to rename them all. They ain't Bossy, Flossie, Bessie an' Jessie no more. They're John, Paul, George an' Ringo now!'

'Great daft beggar' shouts Jackie, 'we ain't keepin' em. Gawd knows what the neighbours is gonna say, all that bleedin' row all night long.'

'We're keepin' George', insists Phil. 'Ee was always me favourite Beatle.'

'But Man-well is takin' back John, Paul an' Ringo,' Jackie confirms. 'Ee's comin' tonight after 'is siesta. Ee says he will get us a surprise, an' some more 'ens termorra. Well I fink that's what ee said anyway, you know how difficult it is to understand sometimes!'

I am trying to be kind about this, but Jackie's command of English is not that good. Her Spanish is, what's the word I am looking for? Basic? 'Are you sure you asked for hens in the first place?' I ask her.

'I know me Spanish ain't all that great' she confides, reading my mind, 'but I know that a cock is called a *gallo*, and a 'en is a *gallina*. So I says to Man-well *Quiero cuatro gallinas.* I wants four 'ens. That's right, innit?'

'Good job you didn't say 'quiero gallo' wasn't it?' I smile. 'I want cock!'

Chrissie almost chokes on her coffee, Phil bursts out laughing, but Jackie narrows her eyes and fixes me with a stare. 'Cheeky beggar! she cries. 'Man-well is about seventy.' Then her eyes soften and a big sloppy grin appears. 'Mind you, 'is son is drop-dead gorgeous. I could quiero a bit of 'is gallo, any day of the week!'

We are all laughing now, and Phil puts his hand across his mouth. 'Ee's bleedin welcome to 'er' he whispers. The Spanish people in the cafe are looking at us suspiciously, what with all this talk of *quiero gallo*. Strange people, the English.

'Anyway' concludes Jackie, 'call in termorra if yer passin', an' see our new 'ens. Doncha worry Jonny, you'll get yer eggs soon enough!'

The following day I have a few jobs to do so it is early afternoon before I am able to call to see the new 'ens. Jackie answers the door with a sombre look on her face, very far from her usual bubbly self. I step into the sitting room and there is Phil, hunched up on the sofa, wrapped in a fleece blanket. You can cut the atmosphere with a knife. Clearly I have arrived during a major domestic upset. 'Look, sorry' I stammer, hugely embarrassed. 'If this is a bad time I can come back again.'

Phil looks up from the sofa, and for the first time I notice his eyes are red. 'Ringo's dead' he whispers.

'Oh no, poor old Ringo' I reply, almost with relief. 'Blimey, it only seems like yesterday, I can see him on *Top of the Pops,* in about 1965, in black-and-white, grinning away. That's only leaves Paul McCartney left alive now.'

'No not Ringo Starr, ya bladdy idiot,' Phil cries. 'I means Ringo, me chicken, me *gallo.* 'Ees dead, been murdered. Plucked, stuffed, with 'is legs up 'is arse. Out there. I can't even go in me bleedin' kitchen!' And he subsides into his blanket again.

Jackie continues the story. 'Man-well come last night and took away John, Paul and Ringo. I am saying *quiero tres gallinas* he is saying *si si,* then this mornin' there's a knock on the door and it's Maria, Man-well's wife, carrying a huge tray with summat on it covered by a tea towel. She marches straight through to the kitchen, plonks the tray down on the worktop, whips off the tea towel, ta-da, there is Ringo, like Phil says, dead, plucked an' stuffed. Phil almost bursts out cryin', I am speechless. Maria musta thought we was mad. Course, we cannot eat Ringo, 'ee was family, it would be like eatin' the dog. Gawd knows what we are gonna do wiv 'im.'

Well happily I have the perfect solution for them. Jonny comes to the rescue again! A nice fresh chicken would do us three meals this week. First day, in the oven of course, roast and boiled potatoes, pigs in blankets, green beans, carrots, gravy. Lovely. Day two, it's got to be chicken and chips hasn't it? Baked beans, two slices of bread-and-butter for the chip butties. Perfect. Third day, put the remains in a stir-fry, or a paella if there's enough left. I am just about to suggest this happy outcome when I glance through to the kitchen and spot the stricken corpse lying underneath his funeral shroud, or tea-towel, and am overcome with guilt and shame. I too cannot eat Ringo. He was not my family of course but I came to look upon him as a friend. I built his house for God's sake. I can picture him now, clucking around his run, sitting on his little perch in the house. I even knew him when he was a girl, called Jessie. I was with him throughout that unhappy trans-gender period of his life, so I can hardly stick him in a paella, can I? I have to get out of here. I fumble in my pocket for my phone and make a show of getting it out. 'Oh who is this now? Oh look, a message from Chrissie. She has bought ten kilos of fruit and veg, and needs my help carrying it home. I will catch you both in a couple of days.' And I stumble gratefully outside into the warm spring sunshine. Walking home I am overwhelmed by sadness. Sadness for Jackie and Phil, whose dreams of raising poultry among the olive trees of Andalucía now lie in tatters, sadness for John and Paul, who have presumably met a similar grizzly end to Ringo.

But you know what the saddest thing of all is? I still haven't had my bleedin' half-dozen eggs, that's what!

CHAPTER 35. EASTER, SPANISH-STYLE, IS COMING!

Our crazy neighbour Loli must be on drugs. By which I mean prescription medicine obviously, but we are convinced she is, because for about seven days at a time, she is reasonably calm. Then suddenly, for no apparent reason, she 'goes off on one', to coin a phrase, hollering and bawling and throwing wobblies at at her brother, Fernando, and her sister Isabel, often concerning mundane, everyday tasks such as sweeping the garden path. And today is one of those days. 'The medication is wearing off again!' laughs Chrissie, as we lie under the shade of the fig tree, which is bursting into leaf again after the winter.

What I am unable to comprehend is how these domestic chores, which they must have performed countless times over the years, should involve any dialogue whatsoever. Still, as my Mother was fond of pointing out, it wouldn't do if we were all the same, would it?

Suddenly our siesta is shattered by a head popping over the garden wall. 'NEIGHBOUR!' hollers the path-sweeper. '*DOMINGO RAMOS!*'

Si is all I can think to say in reply, against all advice from our Spanish friends, who caution that saying 'yes' to something we don't understand could lead us into big problems, particularly if she is asking me to paint her house, for free. Still, Domingo Ramos sounds like someone's name. I've heard of Placido Domingo, one of the *Three Tenors*, and Sergio Ramos, a footballer with *Real Madrid*. Quite who this *Domingo Ramos* character is I have no idea, but we know plenty of people who will, I assume. Tomorrow morning, at the library group.

I have no time to gather my thoughts further however as Loli is now in full flow, hammering out her staccato delivery. I am assuming this mystery personality is paying a visit some time, so I utilise one of my stock replies, for just these occasions. *'Domingo Ramos? Cuando?'* When? Which seems to have hit the jackpot.

'Two weeks time!' she bellows, cackling like the Wild Witch of the West. Bingo! Result! I'm not saying my system is perfect, but it has served me well, over the past six months.

'Muchas gracias!' I reply, she withdraws her head, and peace reigns once again. Tranquility under the fig tree.

The following morning, Juan-Carlos, Teri, Pati and Jose have made it to the library. *'Domingo Ramos'* Chrissie ventures, hopefully.

'Yees!' Teri smiles, 'ees in two weeks time.' Her English has come on in leaps and bounds, under Chrissie's expert tutelage, although this advances our knowledge not one iota.

'What you do in Eengland, the day of *Domingo Ramos?* Pati queries. Day? Is it a day? We thought it was a bloke! We need to get this nailed down before Alicia arrives and the whole morning descends into complete chaos.

My wife smiles serenely. 'No, tell us first what you do here in Spain?' Hey, clever girl! Wish I'd thought of that!

'Thees day comes *Cassoo* on *burro* to *Herroo-salen'* Jose confirms. Jesus? Donkey? Jerusalem? It has to be Palm Sunday!

I glance across at my wife, who has already made the connection. 'In England we call this day 'Palm Sunday', and at Sunday School, the church for young children, we make palm crosses, to take home.' Indeed we did, my mother always gave my effort pride of place, pinned to the kitchen wall, despite the fact it usually resembled a road accident, rather than a cross.

'So what else happen you countree, this day?' Juan-Carlos wants to know. What else? What does he expect?

'Nothing,' I frown.

'Nothing?'

'Well, Sunday lunch, obviously.' I confirm. 'Roast beef, Yorkshire pudding, roast and boiled potatoes, peas, carrots.'

'Anything else?'

Blimey, what does he want, chapter and verse? Nan usually came round for Sunday tea with a large tin of home-made scones, and a tub of clotted cream, Mum supplied the strawberry jam, then the arguments would start about whether it was cream first, then jam, or vice versa. My Dad, who was Cornish, insisted on one way, I forget which, but the English from the wrong side of the Tamar maintained it was the other. And there is no way I am translating that lot into Spanish.

Chrissie senses my unease. 'So what happens here on Palm Sunday?' she smiles serenely.

'Thees day comes *Cassoo* on *burro* to Her-roo-salen Jose reiterates.

'Yes but that was two-thousand years ago, in the Holy Land', my wife gently points out. 'What happens nowadays, in Spain?'

'Thees day comes *Cassoo* on *burro*!' grins Teri. Oh no, is this another crazy procession, like Three Kings? I have a vision of two blokes dressed up as both ends of a pantomime donkey, and a hail of boiled sweets raining down. And Gaffer breaking his teeth, and his glasses, and blaming me.

'One moment plees!' Teri grins, and she leaves the room, into the main foyer of the library, returning after a few seconds with two glossy booklets, which she presents to Chrissie and me. 'Thees programme for *Semana Santa* here in Santa Marta' she explains, opening one of the publications to the second page, entitled *Domingo de Ramos*, complete with a photo of Jesus riding a donkey, clearly wooden or plaster figures, but seemingly life-size, mounted on a plinth, similar to the one which conveyed Santa Cecilia in November, but bigger, borne by what appears to be around forty young men. Under the photo is a narrative, in Spanish of course, but detailing the start time of eleven in the morning, the departure point, which appears to be a local church, and the route the procession will follow. It even suggests the best viewpoints around the town, and the time the spectacle might be expected to pass by, which seems remarkably un-Spanish to me, but there it is in black-and -white.

Teri turns the page. 'Here ees procession for Monday, at eight o'clock in the evening, from church of Santa Maria.'

'Eefning?' Juan Carlos queries. 'What thees eefning, Teri?'

Chrissie's student glows with pride. 'I have good teacher of Eengliss!' she affirms. 'She tell me that Eengliss peoples they finish they work at five in afternoon, they go to they house and eat at six, after thees is what they say 'evening'. In evening they take they dog for walk to pub!'

'YEES!' cries Jose. 'I learn in school the Eengliss peoples take they dog to pub, drink much beers!'

Sounds pretty much like an evening to me. 'My dog was what you call here a 'Golden' I chuckle, 'in the pub he would stand up against the bar on his back legs, with his front legs on top of the bar, until the manager gave him a treat!' I mean the landlord of course, but I don't know how that translates. Poor old Peter Thomas, it used to cost him a fortune, keeping Nelson supplied with doggy chews!

'Thees ver strange to us!' Pati laughs, 'take dog to pub, ees not allow here in Espain, but I see in books of school, Eenglees dog in pub.'

'It's the law!' I giggle. 'often there is what we call a 'pub-dog', the dog who lives in the pub. My dog 'Nelson' would get very friendly with pub-dogs. Especially lady pub-dogs! Very friendly indeed, on occasions!'

'AHHH!' cries Jose, 'you dog he make fock with dog of pub! You dog, he bastard-dirty! Jonneee tell me thees words' he confides with his compatriots.

Yes, but I didn't tell you to spread it round the library, Jose. But he is correct, Nelson was, occasionally, a right dirty so-and-so, especially with that pretty little collie in the Rose and Crown.

'You have much baby dogs!' Jose continues. *No, not really. He was not big on_ exchanging names and addresses with his canine conquests.* 'Love 'em and leave 'em' was Nelson's motto.

'Right, moving on' Chrissie sighs, rolling her eyes, like that bald bloke in *The Vicar of Dibley*, 'it says here there are processions every day during Easter week, and some days there are two?' We are both flicking through the booklets, each day of Holy Week has a photo of what I presume is the plinth carried that day, bearing various biblical figures, as the week progresses inexorably to the Crucifixion. I feel a shiver of excitement, anticipation of what is to come. These processions clearly mean a great deal to the Spanish, and we are in the privileged position of being able to share these events with the locals.

'So what happen in you countree, *Semana Santa*?' Pati enquires.

Having finished flicking through the booklet, I hang my head in shame. 'Well, nothing like this' I admit, holding up the glossy publication. 'For most people, Easter is two Bank Holidays, and chocolate eggs on Sunday morning. A visit to the garden centre maybe, a trip to the seaside, mayhem on the A30 and long queues at the airport. But nothing like this.'

'I have question for you, Cristina' Juan-Carlos smiles. We both glance up, completely unaware that our life in Spain is about to shift on its axis. 'Would you like to carry a saint in thees procession, on Holy Friday? Ees woman procession, carry Maria Magdalena, but no are sufficient womans carry she. The boss of thees procession friend me, I tell he about you sympathetic Eengliss persons, he say me to ask you help carry Maria Magdalena, no Eengliss womans before do thees, you be first Eengliss peoples do thees. We say here in Espain *la unica costelera Ingles*. Plees say you do thees!'

We both slump back in our chairs. I, for once, am speechless. Chrissie swallows hard. Pati, Teri and Jose meanwhile are overjoyed. '*La unica costelera Ingles*!' Teri cries. 'Ees big honoo for you, and big honoo for they, have Eengliss person carry Maria Magdalena!'

'So what is a costel-thingy?' Chrissie queries, clearly buying some time to think.

'*Costelera* is woman who carry saint' Juan-Carlos confirms, '*costelero* is man who carry. Plees say you be first Eengliss womans be *costelera*!'

My wife glances in my direction. 'What do you think?'

'What do I think? Well it's not my decision, you are carrying the plinth, not me! But it is a huge honoo, sorry honour, to be asked, and to be the unique English costel-thingy is something special. I think you should!'

Chrissie seems very emotional suddenly. 'Juan-Carlos, I would be honoured and privileged to carry Mary Magdalene. Please tell your friend!' and I swear she blinks away a tear.

A huge cheer erupts around the table. 'Can I have you autograph, plees?' giggles Jose, 'la unica costelera Ingles! You famous here in Santa Marta!'

Juan-Carlos meanwhile has left the room, returning a few minutes clutching his phone. 'I call my friend, she name Rosa, she say me you must to go practice of carry saint this afternoon, at seven and half, at *cofradia*, in street of San Jorge.'

'Cough-what?' the unique English carrier enquires.

'*Cofradia*!' Pati laughs, 'ees club of saint, where live she, and where is *el trono*.'

Clear as mud, although a quick flick through the Spanish dictionary reveals the translation of *el trono* as 'the throne', or the plinth on which the figure is mounted. *Cofradia* meanwhile comes out as a 'brotherhood.'

Somewhat shell-shocked, we head home after the class and crash out on the sunbeds under the fig tree, digesting the latest monumental turn of events. We have only a vague idea of what lies in store, but like much of our new lives here, we are on a voyage of discovery. And besides, Chrissie will be doing the hard work, I am simply the spectator...

At seven-and-quarter in the afternoon we leave the house, to be confronted by Loli, who seems to have calmed down since yesterday. 'Where you going, neighbours?'

Chrissie smiles serenely. So much has happened, since our last conversation with the crazy woman. 'To the *cofradia* of *Santa Maria Magdalena*' she smiles. '*Estoy la unica costelera Ingles*!'

For possibly the only time in her life, Loli is rendered speechless. She turns and bangs loudly on her front door. Her sister Isabel emerges, followed several seconds later by the stomach which always precedes brother Fernando. 'La Cristina is the only English costelera, carrying Maria Magdalena!' she bellows, causing yet more front doors to open. Mercedes and the dustman Juan appear, and suddenly my wife is basking in the admiration of the locals, who seem genuinely delighted for her, which is a huge relief as I had wondered if they might be somewhat sniffy about foreigners taking part in their celebrations.

Not a bit of it. 'Are you carrying *San Juan Evangelista*, neighbour?' Fernando asks me.

I lean forward dramatically and clutch my lower torso. 'No, I am very old, and have a bad back!' I giggle, 'and I am carrying the water for Cristina. The weather will be very hot for Holy Week!'

Mercedes embraces Chrissie, 'I think it is wonderful you take part in our traditions!' she whispers. *'Via con Dios.'* Go with God.

We head up to the street of San Jorge, near the top of town, in search of *la cofradia*, but can only find what appears to be a private garage. A very large garage, with a door big enough to drive a coach through, which would be physically impossible as the street is only about ten feet wide, but a garage nevertheless. There is not a soul around, or any signs indicating where a *brotherhood* might be, although we are a few minutes early, being British, and therefore never late. Seven-thirty is seven-thirty, after all, although sadly the Spanish do not recognise punctuality as a virtue. I think they usually set out to on time, it's just that life intervenes, they bump into a friend for example, and all thoughts of where they should be take an instant back seat. You never hear a local saying 'sorry can't stop, I am going to so-and-so.'

I take a stroll up the street, which appears a strange place, seemingly devoid of houses, with several of these huge garages, which are two-storey, with office or commercial premises on the top floors, but no signs whatsoever of what might be within. Ten minutes passes, Chrissie glances at me and shrugs, we know we have the correct address as Juan-Carlos looked it up on his smart-phone, but I am damned if I am waiting here all night, unique English costelera or no unique English costelera. 'Give it until quarter-to, then I'm off.'

Another five minutes tick by, and I am about to bail out, when suddenly two teenage girls come strolling leisurely along, jabbering excitedly whilst tapping away on their phones, a skill I have yet to even contemplate, let alone master. They stop next to us, call out a friendly Hola! and lean on the wall, without even glancing up. 'Looks like two of the brotherhood have arrived, or should that be sisterhood?' Chrissie giggles. 'Excuse me' she addresses the girls, indicating the garage, 'is there a *cofradia* in here?'

They both glance up suddenly, as if seeing us for the first time. 'Yes' replies one, 'inside, Rosa will be here shortly with the key.'

Her friend laughs, holding out her arm, palm facing down, making a rocking gesture with her hand. '*Mas o menos!*' More or less. We have heard this phrase, and seen this gesture, many times here. The Spaniards use it to indicate a time frame spanning several minutes to a couple of weeks. What is the rush, enjoy the sunshine, sit under a parasol, or a tree, and while away the day.

Just then a car pulls up, disgorging several more youngsters, and another group of three are sauntering in our direction, but sadly no-one who looks like she might be in charge. It is now eight PM, and almost dark, and whilst there are a few street lights in the vicinity, presumably the costeleras need to be able to see where they are going? And besides, seven teenagers plus Chrissie will not get very far, from the photos we have seen there are at least thirty carriers of every plinth.

Suddenly a small door within the main garage door opens and an older woman pops her head out. Was she in there all this time? Who knows. She spots Chrissie, 'are you the English woman, friend of Juan-Carlos?' she enquires. 'Welcome, my name is Rosa, come inside please.' We step through the door to find a huge room, maybe thirty feet by forty, ceiling at least twenty high, a set of steps leading to the top floor, a bar along the back wall, around fifteen other women and girls, and there, bang smack in the middle, standing proudly on four legs, wrapped entirely in plastic, *el trono*, the plinth. Up close it looks huge, twenty feet long, at least ten wide, standing over seven feet high, four huge wooden beams running front to back, intricately carved moldings, decorated with silver inlays. Magnificent, even with its protective covering, and seemingly immovable. I for one am glad I am not carrying the beast. Chrissie takes a step back, in sheer awe, and I think for the first time she realises what a huge undertaking this will be, particularly with a bunch of wafer-thin teenage girls.

Rosa produces a strange piece of apparatus, clearly a personal measuring device of some description, only without the flat piece of wood which usually moves up and down and rests on the head. This one has a 'V' shaped slider, and as the first girl steps forward, all becomes clear. The 'V' sits on the shoulders, a measurement Rosa carefully notes on a clipboard, to enable each carrier to be placed in her precise position under the beam, tall ones at the front, shorter at the rear. Then a shout goes up and suddenly everyone is stripping the plastic covering from the *trono*, several of the older women have brought their kids along and before we can say *Real Madrid* an impromptu football match has broken out, balled-up plastic being booted around. Now this is more my style. Stuff humping a ton of wood around the town, but give me a ball of sorts and my inner Pele comes to the fore. I nutmeg a couple of toddlers, round the last defender, and fire what seems like the winning goal into the top corner of an imaginary net. I turn to catch my breath to find around thirty pair of female eyes fixed in my direction. 'GOOOOOAAALLLL!' shouts someone, and suddenly the place is rocking. 'Does your husband want to carry *San Juan Evangelista*, Cristina?' Rosa chuckles, so I do my bit with the injured back again. My wife meanwhile is rolling her eyes, glancing round at her fellow *costeleras* with a 'men, what can you do with them?' expression on her face. Cue more laughter. This carrying business is gonna be a doddle.

Rosa starts arranging each lady to her allotted place under the trono, all the while clutching a silver hammer. Of course, no-one of our generation, when confronted by someone brandishing such an implement, can possibly avoid humming that Beatles song from the *Abbey Road* album, although how *Maxwell* fits into this scenario is unclear. Suddenly, all is revealed. One tap on a little silver bell attached to the front of the plinth calls the ladies to order, two dongs gets them in position, and on three, they lift. The first try is a disaster, the front shoots up ahead of the rear, and the whole thing seems likely to come crashing down to earth, before several of the more experienced hands steady the ship and a tragedy is averted. Chrissie, positioned towards the rear of the right-hand side, looks boggle-eyed, but Rosa has no doubt seen all this before, and after more explanations they try again, and the plinth rises majestically into the air, and settles down, level, onto the shoulders of the carriers. Or almost level, I should say. On the left, the girl bringing up the rear is so short, her shoulder doesn't actually touch the beam, and she has placed a cushion in the gap, whereas at the front there are two girls who are very much taller than the others, which means they are bearing an unfair burden. Nevertheless, we are up and running, the big door into the street is hauled open, and after more clanging, the plinth gradually edges out into the street, now shrouded in complete darkness.

Now the tricky part begins, turning the *trono* so that it faces along the road. The ladies at the back step to the left, those at the front move in the opposite direction, and soon we are aligned. The bell rings for a breather, and there is much feminine laughter and chatter as they ease their collective backs. Chrissie has made friends with the young lady behind her, Carmen, who apparently speaks a little English, and as I approach to check how my wife's spine is holding up, I catch the end of the conversation. 'Cristina plees you speak me in Eengliss, classes conversation, ees good for me!'

Rosa meanwhile is checking her troops, and she joins in with the end of Carmen's question. 'Are you an English teacher? I cannot speak a word of it myself, but my son is learning in school. Can you give him extra lessons, please?' For heaven's sake, here we are trying to join in with some Spanish traditions, and all the locals want are English lessons. Still, nice to feel wanted, I suppose.

Chrissie promises to exchange phone numbers later, Rosa resumes her place by the bell, and we are off again, the plinth making its way slowly down the street. One or two young men have joined in a small group of followers, partners and boyfriends of the ladies I suppose, so I do my best to engage them in conversation. *La unica costelera Ingles!* I tell one, proudly indicating my wife, who seems to be enjoying the occasion, despite the weight on her left shoulder. He looks suitably impressed, I have to say.

More clanging by Rosa indicates we are stopping again, and walking round to the front of the trono, I suddenly realise why. The street descends alarmingly into a valley, surely we are not heading down there? No. Following a verbal command, the ladies simply switch direction, and resume their positions, facing the opposite way. Without a figure mounted on top, the trono can travel in either direction, although now the bell arrangement is at the back. After a quick rest *La Capitana* sounds the alarm again, although a dispute of some sort seems to have broken out at the front, so she has to stroll round to investigate the source of the grievance. Which appears to be focused on us. Blimey, have we trodden on someone's toes? Are the locals objecting on this unique Englishwoman? Then the spotlight is turned to me. Are they complaining about me following along like a faithful puppy-dog? Luckily Carmen comes to the rescue. 'Rosa she say can you hoosband assist carry trono at front, not sufficient womans carry, is much bad for they!' I glance at Rosa, point to myself, then mime lifting the plinth. Twenty-five female nod their heads in agreement, smiling. OK, my moment has arrived. Johnny to the rescue, and all that. I mean, how heavy can this thing be? A bit of varnished plywood. For someone who once lifted the entire front row of the *Old Reds* scrum, admittedly with a little help from a couple of other fat blokes, back in the day when punching your opposition was not only entirely legal, but actively encouraged, this is going to be a doddle. And I bought the Reds a pint afterwards, saint that I was.

I flex my muscles, grinning widely, and take my place at the front, in the middle, in the 'hooker' position. To my left, the 'loose-head' prop is a slim little girl, and to my right is the 'tight-head', an equally diminutive if slightly older lady. I smile at them both, *all right darlings, let me get this*. The bell chimes, we get in position, brace, then on the final bell, lift. And I almost die, on the spot. My neck is bulging, my spine is cracking, and my intestines feel like they are about to spill out over the road. God this thing is heavier than the entire Old Reds pack, plus all the beer we drank after the game. My knees are buckling, my head seems likely to explode and vast beads of perspiration break out just about everywhere. I feel an urgent need to blaspheme loudly, but suddenly remember this is supposed to be a religious procession, so refrain, glancing right and left at my props, who are giggling wildly. Of course, being over six inches taller than any of the ladies, I am bearing the entire weight of the front end. I have been well and truly shafted, but cannot back out now, so after checking surreptitiously that my sweaty testicles are still attached, we step off down the street. This has to be the longest fifty yards of my life, I cannot wait for the torture to end, and I don't even have the option of walloping my opposite number and starting an almighty punch-up. Having seven sacks of excrement kicked out of me would be preferable to this hell. My eyeballs are bulging but I am just about able to make out the doors of the cofradia, when thankfully, merciful, blessed relief, Rosa rings the bell, and with a last whimper I ease my cursed burden onto its feet.

I pat the beam affectionately, glancing round at the assembled females, grinning like a madman, easing my legs apart to allow about a pint of bodily fluids to cascade down my shattered torso, although whether I have any teeth left is open to question. *'Toda esta bien'* I lie. Who am I kidding, everything is good? I am not sure I still have a backside attached, and feel just about ready to collapse into a wet, steaming, gibbering heap. And we still have to put this thing to bed, so to speak. 'You hoosband ver strong!' laughs Carmen, from the back. *He was, Carmen, about forty years ago. Right now, he is feeling his age. About a hundred-and-ten.*

Rosa strikes the bell for the final time and once again, me at the front and twenty-five ladies at the back, we hoist the structure on our shoulders, pivot around so we are facing the open garage, and ease it into place, and with a final clang, lower it gently to terra firma. Deep, blessed joy. I am gingerly rubbing my aching shoulders as Chrissie emerges from the rear, cool as a cucumber, not an ounce of perspiration evident, not a hair out of place, a beaming smile on her face. She regards me with derision, 'tha blooody, soft Soothern Jessie!' she snorts, in a passable impersonation of Diane. 'Come on, let's get you home, before you croak!'

Rosa meanwhile expresses her grateful thanks, but there remains a catch. 'Can you come tomorrow at nine for *el traslado*?' she enquires. Chrissie nods, whereas I shake my head emphatically, having still not regained the power of speech.

Carmen again rides to the rescue. '*El traslado* ees where we take *trono* to chur, where live Santa Maria Magdalena. Ees ver good, all *tronos* be in chur tomorrow. And no worry Jonneee, tomorrow will be womans sufficient to carry *trono*, no need you carry!' Well thank heaven for that!

Walking home, or actually limping in my case, Chrissie has a spring in her step. 'That was fantastic, everything I hoped it would be, and more! I feel so involved, not just a spectator, but actually participating. I cannot wait for Easter to arrive!' I narrow my eyes, and give her a hard stare, rather like Paddington Bear having mislaid his marmalade sandwiches, then break into a wide grin. If she is happy then I am happy, and I am immensely proud of her, although right now I need a couple of glasses of wine, followed by a stiff brandy, followed by about twelve hours sleep….

Next morning we are just finishing breakfast on the terrace, enjoying the sunrise over the olive fields, when our peace is shattered by the ringing of the Spanish mobile. Chrissie answers, on the grounds that I simply refuse to deal with phone calls at that ungodly hour of the morning. It's only just gone nine-o-clock, for pity sake, and I still haven't finished my second mug of strong, black coffee.

'Hello Juan-Carlos' she answers, throwing a withering look in my direction. 'The doctors? When? Ten-o-clock? Today? OK, see you there!' and she rings off. I am just pouring my third mug, after which the day can officially begin. 'Come on, hurry up' she urges, 'we have to go to the doctors, something to do with the *cofradia*. Ten-o-clock, doctors surgery, in the street of pubs, he said, next to the old queens bar.'

It takes me several seconds to digest this information. 'The doctors? What doctors? What for? And you said ten. It's only just nine, sit down, and finish your coffee.' I'm not at my best, at the crack of dawn.

'I don't know why, a medical I am guessing, make sure I don't drop dead carrying Maria Magdalena!' my wife giggles, picking up her mug. 'Juan-Carlos just said to meet him in pub street, next to bar Reina Sofia, and he will take me to see Doctor Have-a-hard.'

'Dr Who?' I splutter, losing half of my third mug-full down my shirt front.

'No, not Dr Who!' comes the somewhat predictable reply, 'Dr Have-a-hard, he said. I don't know, that's what it sounded like anyway.'

'Well I'm not sure I approve of my wife visiting someone called Dr Have-a-hard' I protest, 'what if he wants to examine your chest, what will he use for a stethoscope? Or a thermometer, if he wants to take your temperature?'

'Oh I don't know, it sounds like fun' Chrissie purrs. 'He might be quite dishy, actually! Maybe a Spanish George Clooney!'

'Dishy? Dishy? I haven't heard that expression since about 1976. Anyway, let me finish this, I am coming with you.'

'Oh, there's no need, really, you stay here, I'm just putting on my best underwear, then I'm off to meet the dishy doctor. I should be back before nightfall! On Sunday!'

Like hell she is! I slurp down the remains of my breakfast beverage, lob the mug into the washing-up, and reach for my shoes. Chrissie meanwhile glides downstairs, wearing if not her best dress, then a fairly good one. Certainly much smarter than she would normally choose, for a morning in this dusty old Spanish town. A waft of her favourite perfume caresses my nostrils. 'Blimey, a bit OTT, possibly?' I observe, sourly.

My wife smiles knowingly, 'not a bit of it! My granny always told me to wear my best knickers to the doctors, just in case. Anyway, hurry up, I mustn't keep Dr Dishy Have-a-hard Clooney waiting!'

Juan-Carlos is waiting for us outside bar Reina Sofia, although quite where this medical centre actually is, I am unable to imagine, as there are certainly no signs indicating anything of the sort. After kisses all round, our friend presses a buzzer in an anonymous entrance, the door pops open and we enter, passing a small plaque bearing the legend *Doctor Avellard*. I cannot help sniggering, tapping Chrissie on the shoulder and pointing out her error in translation. She screws up her face, sticks out her tongue in a *sod-off* gesture, and we pass through another door into a small waiting-room, containing around half-a-dozen elderly patients, and a receptionist behind a small desk. Deep joy, we are going to be here all morning, the way these old Spaniards rattle on, we will be lucky to be seen by next Easter. Juan-Carlos announces who we are, but before we can sit down, for what I imagine will be a long wait, the receptionist buzzes through, the consulting-room door is flung open and there stands the white-coated *medico*. George Clooney? More like George-the-Third, if you ask me. Around sixty, and probably the same round the waist, balding, with a noticeable limp, he beams widely and bids us enter. Oh, I am loving this! 'Hope you didn't wear your frilly knickers!' I chuckle, under my breath, earning myself a painful dig in the ribs, and with an apologetic glance at the ancient locals who appear entirely unconcerned by the English queue-jumpers, we file into the surgery.

And perform a double-take. No, a triple-take. There, in front of us, dressed in a crimson cloak, crown of thorns on his head, hands tightly bound, is the life-size figure of Jesus Christ. Standing next to him is another man, clad in Biblical robes, St Peter possibly, and across the room, an older, bearded one dressed entirely in white. God? My senses are reeling, Chrissie gasps in surprise, while Juan-Carlos bows almost to his knees, making the sign of the Cross. Trust me on this one, if you ever visit the GP to be confronted by God, Jesus and St Peter, you'd better be sure your list of lifetime good-deeds exceeds your debits, if you have ambitions of entering the Pearly Gates. And have your last will and testament handy. Nothing in life has prepared me for this moment, the shock is so great that for a split-second it feels like I have died and gone to heaven, the figures are so life-like, so entirely realistic, and so utterly believable.

I take a deep breath, and a step backwards, then glancing towards the door I spot yet more figures, a Roman centurion, and two thieves. Now I understand, these statues are clearly part of the Easter processions, although why they should be stored in a doctor's surgery, and not, say, a church, is beyond me. I tap a speechless Chrissie on the arm and point out the other figures, we glance at each other, then at Juan-Carlos, and finally Dr Avellard. Our Spanish has come on in leaps and bounds during the past seven months or so, but we are totally unequipped for this scenario. 'Son bonito' is all I can think to say, they are beautiful, which seems utterly inadequate in the circumstances, but Avellard beams widely, bids us welcome, entirely in Spanish, and asks us to sit.

Chrissie seems a little nervous, with good reason I suppose, and somewhat disappointed, having been expecting a thorough examination by a George Clooney lookalike. What is this exercise likely to entail? Blood pressure I suppose, given that she will be carrying for around five hours in the heat of the day. Pulse? Possibly. But what else? This all seems completely over the top to me, but with God standing in the corner I am on my best behaviour. Maybe I should have bought the Old Reds pack two pints each, just to be on the safe side, but it is far too late now. Avellard hobbles across the room and throws open the double doors of a huge walk-in wardrobe, revealing over fifty white hospital gowns, ranging in size from kiddies on the left, to extra-large. 'Cristina, you must to choose plees a *tunica*' Juan-Carlos informs her, indicating that she should approach the cupboard. Blimey, it looks like she is getting the full Monty, a thorough going-over as it were. I sense my wife's disappointment. Old Have-a-hard has proved such a let-down, as it were.

Avellard scrutinises her up and down, delves into the collection of tunics and comes out with one which he holds up against her. No, he is not satisfied, he replaces the original, has another rummage and this time produces one slightly longer, not as I first thought a hospital gown, but a full-length heavy cotton cloak, rather like a nun's habit, beautifully tailored, but completely unsuitable for a medical examination. 'Plees you go behind curtain, take off you clothes, wear tunica.' Juan-Carlos commands. Chrissie is open-mouthed, I know what she is thinking as I have the same question, *underwear or commando*? She heads to the curtain and I am certain what she will do. I would go commando, regardless of God watching or not, to hell with it, whereas she will play it safe, and who can blame her. She emerges half a minute later dressed in the tunic, which is skimming the floor. 'Now plees to put on you shoes, on Holy Friday you must to wear *espadrilles* in white, but today you training shoes is OK.'

What idiots we have been, thinking this was a medical examination. No, it is a tunic-fitting session, presumably, unless there is a sting in the tail, which there might actually be as Avellard disappears behind another curtain, this time returning with a long pointed hood, complete with eye-holes. We both stare in disbelief. To anyone raised in American/British culture, this garment screams Klu-Klux-Clan, and I am about to stand and lodge a formal and unmoveable protest, when I suddenly realise that the hateful US organisation has only been in existence for a hundred years or so, whereas these religious processions in Spain clearly pre-date that by many centuries. Still, my wife clearly has huge misgivings as she takes the hood and places it tentatively over her head. And we all fall about laughing, as it is miles too big, the eye-holes are down by her chin, but at least the tension has been broken. Avellard stumps off and returns with a pile of hoods, Chrissie delves in and soon has one she can actually see out of.

She pops the hood over her head, and strikes an extremely uncomfortable pose. 'I know what you think, about koo-koo,' Juan-Carlos apologises, 'I see thees on films Americano, but plees believe me, ees tradition here in Espain. Cristina, you look ver natural, la unica costelera Ingles!' Which is lovely of him to say, and so typical of our dear friend. Avellard meanwhile produces a blue sash with a tassel fastening, which Chrissie attaches, and the ensemble is complete. 'Avellard he say me' Juan-Carlos continues, 'usually to pay ten Euro to join *Cofradia*, but thees year Rosa and ladies and he say ees gratis for *la unica* to be member of she.' Clearly affected, she whips off her hood and everyone embraces, I have a tear in my eye, what an amazing gesture, here we are, strangers in someone else's country, and we have been shown nothing but affection by the locals.

Walking home after what has been a unique experience, to say the least, I cannot help but chuckle. 'Just imagine those old folks, walking into the consulting room, to be confronted by God! Would you have the slightest idea why Avellard keeps the statues there?'

Chrissie is still reeling from the past, monumental twenty-four hours. She shakes her head. 'Too valuable to leave in the Cofradia, maybe? Who knows? Two days ago we had no idea about any of this!' I suddenly have an image in my head of a thief, running down the street, with Jesus tucked under his arm, and I begin to laugh. In my weakened state, tears are running down my cheeks, Chrissie joins in and the pair of us are getting funny looks from passers by, as we lumber up the cobbled street homewards. And we still have *el translado* to look forward to this evening, before which we need to recharge our batteries in the garden. The fig tree is calling.

So confident are we that the transfer of the plinth to the chur will start at least an hour late, we arrive at the *cofradia* around nine-thirty, to find the place a hive of activity. The doors are wide open, every light in the building is blazing, the bar is doing a roaring trade, at least thirty women and girls are milling around, and Rosa is working overtime with her measuring device. Utter chaos, like most things in this country, everyone shouting at once, and as my old mate Paul might have said, there are two chances of this happening before Christmas; no chance, and a dog's chance. We have decided to eat out tonight, after the transfer, and whilst our favourite tapas bar serves food until the early hours, this is going to be touch-and-go. As I say, typical Spain.

Suddenly, and once again typically, everything comes together rapidly. Rosa folds away her height-checker and calls out the revised order, chairs are scraped back, drinks are consumed, handbags are collected from the top of the trono, kids are gathered up by various fathers, and I, scared of getting roped in again, dash to the back of the room and lean nonchalantly against the bar. I am good at this, having been perfecting this art, and truly it is an art, since Killer King, Chrissy Shepherd and I discovered out true vocation in life, aged thirteen, in the *Plough and Windmill*, all those years ago. I needn't have worried however. The ladies fall into line, Carmen grabs Chrissie by the collar and yanks her into position, and we are ready for the off. The bell clangs, backs are braced, and a young lad, who moments ago was engaging his tongue with the tonsils of the tiny girl at the back of the plinth, her of cushion fame, switches on a portable speaker complete with USB stick, and a blast of mournful processional music invades the air. Actually, I recognise the tune, having heard a band practising, most evenings recently, somewhere in the town. Gaffer actually came down to complain about it, one night, as if we were somehow responsible. 'What t'blooody 'ell's that blooody awful noise? Sounds like a cat 'aving 'is guts removed, wi' a rusty nail. Ye can speak blooody Spanish, lad, tell 'em to booger off, we can't hear t'blooody X-Factor!' *Yeah, best of luck with that, Keith, if you can find them, in this maze of narrow streets, on the side of this rocky mountain.* Actually, the music has grown on us, entirely appropriate as it is for this, the saddest time in the Christian calendar, although I imagine something more uplifting will be played on Easter Day. Again, who knows, we still have those delights to come next week, all I know is, right now, the hairs on the back of my neck are standing to attention.

Another round of ringing and we are away, out into the street, a highly professional turn to face the main square of the town, and St Mary's church, the bells of which are already pealing in anticipation. The ladies are striding along, not walking pace but a fair lick nevertheless, until suddenly, without warning, they come to a grinding halt. I am near the back of the plinth, encouraging the unique Englishwoman, so cannot see what the hold-up is. '*Semaforo!*' someone shouts. Semaforo? Semaphore? Seriously? The last time I encountered semaphore was about 1969 in the Scouts, and I have to say I was useless at it, never managing to get past the letter 'J'. So is there someone in short trousers and a woggle, waving two coloured flags about, up ahead? In this country, I wouldn't be surprised.

'How say you *semaforo* in Eengliss?' Carmen calls out. I poke my head round the front of the ensemble to take a look. 'Traffic lights!' I advise her. 'A red traffic light.' We are stuck, of all things, at a red light, which in this narrow cobbled street, with zero traffic, seems like utter lunacy, although I suppose this is strictly a two-way street. About five roads converge on the main square of the town, at least two of which must have been the main road from Malaga to Madrid, in the days of four-legged transport, and before the by-pass was built. Rosa however is unimpressed. 'Eff the traffic lights!' she cries, or something to that effect, and with another bout of clanging, we are off again. *El trono* takes priority, I guess. Now I have been a motorist since 1973, and a cyclist an awful lot longer, and I will admit to running the odd red light, over the years. Not particularly proud of myself, but it happens, doesn't it? St Peter didn't say anything this morning, so maybe I got away with it. But this is the first time I have ever run a red light whilst accompanying a religious procession, and I have to say, it feels good. Eff the traffic lights, as they say in Santa Marta!

We round the bend and approach the main square, and suddenly I regret my recklessness, as the place is crawling with police. *Actually, I am not part of the procession officers, merely an innocent bystander...* St Mary's is on the far side of the square, there are three Bobbies directly ahead of us, and two more lurking outside the church, although a closer examination of these officers reveals them to be the oldest coppers I have ever come across. There was one in the ITV Sunday-evening drama *Heartbeat*, who seemed absolutely ancient, but this lot have about five-hundred years on him. They might conceivably catch a trono, running a red, but a burglar? Forget it. They look as if they were part of the original Spanish Bow-Street Runners, if there was such a thing.

Suddenly, the Boys-in-Blue all start whistling. I don't mean with pursed lips, no, they each produce a police whistle, and start blowing madly, like a referee's away-day to Margate. Who, or what they are hooting at is impossible to say, as not a soul is taking the slightest bit of notice. A few old men are sitting around the square, gossiping, some hard-core drinkers are settled onto tables and chairs outside a bar, and as we pause for breath, a wheezing, rusty Land-Rover shudders to a halt, and the driver, himself wheezing and coughing, stumbles out of the cab and, engine still rattling away, embraces a friend, and the pair of them slump onto a bench beneath a palm tree. To a man, and woman, the entire town is completely ignoring the Old Bill.

Suddenly, a kerfuffle breaks out on another of the approach streets to the square. The whistling intensifies, so I stroll up to the junction to see what all the fuss is about. And there, bathed in the soft white illumination of the street lights, is another *trono*, carried entirely by men. The effect is magical. The palm trees in the middle of the *plaza*, the crescent moon above, the chiming of the church bells, and both *tronos* gliding silently towards the now-open doors of the church, with the ghostly outline of the mountain towering above. Moments to treasure. Even the police have shut up, no doubt realising their efforts are entirely in vain, although they tried their best, bless them. Rosa chimes her bell and we are off again, the men have paused to allow the ladies to lead the way, and slowly but surely we approach the church doors and turn majestically, before disappearing inside.

I follow behind and catch my breath. The church has been completely transformed since our last visit. Most of the pews have been shifted to one side, to be replaced by two other *tronos*, making a total of four, with tonight's arrivals. The other two are massive, much bigger than ours, one even has a canopy, exquisitely embroidered, maybe ten feet high, an awesome sight even though devoid of whichever figures which will eventually be mounted within. Truly, utterly spectacular, I have tears in my eyes, and I cannot wait for Holy Week to begin, on Sunday.

The townsfolk are milling around, plinths are being manoeuvred, bells chiming, the ancient building echoing to the sound of the preparations, and the utter chaos of Spanish life. Chrissie emerges, blowing her cheeks, and I can tell she is moved by the experiences and emotions of this night. The other ladies gather round, embracing, hugging, kissing, and I have a pang of regret that I didn't volunteer to carry John the Evangelist, although there will be other years, no doubt. This time is all about the unique Englishwoman. Rosa approaches, calling out 'manana limpiar!' Cleaning tomorrow? Not me Mrs! I am happy to watch, but catch me with a can of Pledge? No way, Jose!

Carmen plants kisses on both Chrissie's cheeks. 'See you eleffen in morning, for to clean *el trono*, ees ver good, much funny!' That's as maybe, but I have three fat bangers, four slices of bacon, half-a-dozen eggs and a whole Spanish black pudding to deal with. Toast, coffee, and my on-line newspaper. Saturday morning is sorted, as far I am concerned.

And so it transpires. Next morning, my wife chooses a bowl of Cornflakes, and leaves the frying, and the subsequent washing-up, to me, which is entirely as it should be. And what a humdinger of a breakfast it turns out to be. A reet gut-buster, as Gaffer might have said. As a life-long consumer of sausages, of all styles and flavours, I consider myself a connoisseur, from the humble hot-dog, with lashings of fried onions of course, to thick, meaty Cumberland, pork-and-leek, Lincolnshire, hogs pudding in Cornwall, black pudding up north, and every style in between. I cannot pass a butchers window, without feeling a compulsion to delve inside, emerging with a sample of their wares. Again, like many things in my life, this obsession dates from my Boy-Scout days. Truly, sausages fried over an open fire, with copious helpings of dried grass, is the food of the Gods. I should have mentioned it to St Peter while I had the chance the other day, but I tell you this. When my time comes, if there are no bangers up above, I am off down below.

After my blow-out, I have only the strength to ease back in my patio chair, coffee pot to hand, morning paper downloaded, feet up, basking in the warm spring sunshine. Breakfast safely gathered in, I drift off into the slumber of the righteous, to be rudely awakened, some time later, by someone shouting. At me. 'You lazy fat pig! I've been slaving away all morning, been bellowed at by about twenty Spanish women, all at the same time, worn my fingers to the bone, and I come home to find that not only have you not done the washing-up, YOU HAVEN'T EVEN CLEARED THE TABLE!' I open one eye, although for a second or two I am not sure where I am.

Suddenly realisation hits me. Oh no, done it again. Nodded off. My old-man was just the same, 'sleep on a clothes-line, your father!' Mum used to observe. I try to scrabble to my feet, in an attempt to salvage something from the orgy of dirty plates and greasy frying-pans lying around, but my wife gently places her hand on the top of my head. 'Stay there' she commands, 'I have something to tell you.' Blimey, is failing to wash-up grounds for divorce these days? Is she running away with a *costelero* from St John the Evangelist? She does have a strange look on her face, her eyes are glowing somehow, her whole persona has altered, while I've been dozing on a Saturday morning. She pulls up a chair, and flicks a fugitive mushroom off the patio table. *Damn, missed that one!* 'You will never guess what!' she smiles serenely. *Must be the costelero, some swarthy, greasy Spaniard with a tiny bum. Yeah well, bet he can't polish off a full-English, or gargle 'God Save the Queen' whilst downing a pint of Webster's, can he?* 'They let me choose the dress of Maria Magdalena!' Chrissie glows. 'Me! I have chosen her dress for the procession on Good Friday! And the cloak! We polished the plinth for about an hour' she continues, clearly almost overcome with emotion, 'I was doing the silver engravings, when suddenly Rosa asked me to go back to the *cofradia* with her, she took me upstairs, opened up a small wardrobe and inside were about half-a-dozen different dresses, and a similar number of cloaks. Rosa suggested a light-blue dress, and darker cloak, but I chose a white dress, with gold embroidery above the waist, and a two-tone patterned light and dark-blue cloak, with a gold sash. And that is what she will be wearing, chosen by me! Can you believe it?'

Indeed I cannot, and swamped with emotion myself, I stand and give her a huge hug. What an achievement. I am so proud, and to demonstrate I bend my head and plant a wet slobbery kiss on her lips. My wife recoils. 'God, you reek of egg and bacon! Go and have a shower, but before you do, GET IN THE KITCHEN AND CLEAR THE BLOODY WASHING-UP!'

CHAPTER 36. *DOMINGO DE RAMOS*

Domingo de Ramos, Palm Sunday in these parts, is the official start of Holy Week, and we have been gently cautioned by our Spanish friends, all of them, that *British scruffy-casual* will not cut the mustard on this day. No, this is the occasion when the townsfolk get their glad-rags on, apparently. Which presents me with a slight dilemma. Having worn a suit every single moment of my working life, on the day of my retirement I had a cutting-up ceremony, vowing never again to wear a matching jacket and trousers. I still have my trusty Harris Tweed jacket, which originally belonged to my father, and, last time I checked, still just about fitted. Mind you, that was before yesterday's fry-up. I also have a goodly number of high-quality shirts, from a famous tailor in Jermyn Street, in the sure and certain knowledge that a man of a my age should been seen in nothing else, on Palm Sunday anyway. A few pairs of cotton chinos, and one pair of Clark's shoes also survived the move to this southern-European outpost. I think I should therefore, just about, pass muster.

Chrissie of course has no such worries, having a wardrobe full of creations, many of which have never seen the light of day, as far as I am aware. The procession begins at eleven in the morning, and we have arranged to meet Maria from the library group, and her family, outside the church of San Francisco at ten-forty-five, to get a good view of *Cassoo* on *burro* on his way to *Her-roo-salen,* exiting the building. We therefore need to leave home by half-ten, so at around ten-twenty-eight I head upstairs to be confronted by what looks like a dressmaker's window, on Boxing-Day morning. Deftly swerving round the melee, I snatch the first shirt which comes to light, ditto the chinos, on with the shoes, and finally struggle into the jacket, breathing deeply to fasten the strained garment around my middle. Whew knew that Harris Tweed shrank? Must be the heat. 'Right, I am ready!' I announce. 'Come on, you've been up here an hour already! Time to go!'

My wife emerges, gently glowing, from under a pale-blue number. 'Oh. Bully. For. You!' she seethes. 'Mister one-jacket-and-one-pair-of-shoes is ready! Hoo-bloody-ray! I am so pleased for you.' It was ever thus.

'I like that dress!' I flounder, 'never seen that one, it really suits you. Perfect for Palm Sunday!'

Wrong! 'What do you mean, never seen it before?' comes the agitated reply. 'I got it in Peter Jones for Sheila and Mike's wedding, don't you remember?'

Sheila and Mike? Who the hell are they? Did I go to their nuptials? Not a clue. My dearest clearly reads the confusion on my face. 'I'm not surprised you can't remember, you stood up in front of all the guests and sang a vile song about a lobster.' *Sounds about right, I remember the lobster song, of course, but the happy couple?*

Anyway. Who cares. We are late already. 'So, are we ready, because Maria is saving us a space outside the church, and we don't want to keep her waiting.'

Wrong again! My wife flings the blue number into the back of the wardrobe, emerging this time with a floral pink. 'Can't wear that blue, I have no bag to go with it,' she growls.

I smile serenely. *This is going to be good. Very good in fact.* 'Well you do have a bag to go with the pink! Remember, I bought you it for Christmas?' *Who could forget? Having toiled round about a hundred Spanish handbag shops. Cost me an arm and a leg, too.* 'So let's get going, before Mister-one-jacket-and-one-pair-of-shoes starts singing a certain ditty about a crustacean!'.

Chrissie fixes me with a glare, but for once she has no reply. Whatever the handbag cost, it was worth every penny. Or *centimo*, as they say here. Sometimes, occasionally, once in a blue moon, life as a man can be so sweet. But not for long. 'Right, which shoes look best with this dress? The pink flats, or the black?'

Flats? She could wear maisonettes, as far as I'm concerned. Discussion over. 'Oh Mr fisherman, back from the sea, do you have a lobster you could sell to me? Singing aye-diddly-aye, shi....'

'Right I am ready!' she cries, bursting from the second bedroom, home to her collection of shoes and bags. 'Come on! Hurry up!'

We pile out into the street. If we get a move on, we might just make it. *Que guapa, vecina!* Oh hell! Mercedes, Isabel and Loli are waiting for us to emerge. How did they know? Sixth sense? Still, nice of them to say I am looking pretty. I perform a quick twirl, and a bow. 'Not you, neighbour!' Loli cackles, 'Cristina!'

Should have known, words ending in 'a' are usually feminine. 'Soy vecino guapo, no?' I giggle. Mercedes steps forward and plants big wet kisses on both my cheeks. 'You certainly are, neighbour! You make an old woman very happy!' Which is nice to hear, even if she is about seventy-six. As good as it gets, for me, these days.

We make our escape, and head off down the cobbles. If we really, really hurry, we might possibly, just about, if we are lucky, make it on time. Into our little square, past the Lantern Bar and the *Ferry-Terry*, then plunging downhill again, before Chrissie suddenly places her hand in front of my eyes. 'Oh. My. God! Don't look!' Which is of course a red rag to a bull. Jerking my head backwards, my eyes focus on a backside. A female backside, encased in the tightest, teeny-weeniest pair of shorts ever seen this side of Copacabana. Below, a pair of long, slim legs stretch endlessly down to a pair of vertiginous heels, which are clip-clopping along the street at quite a pace, all things considered. 'Could you wind your tongue back in, please, you dirty old man?

I almost choke. 'I wathn't awarthe myth toungth wath outth! And leth of theth oldth! Suddenly, as we round the corner we espy three more young ladies, dressed almost identically, only one has the miniest of mini-skirts. 'Quick, we must catch them up!' I tell my wife, 'in case one of them trips up on the cobbles, then maybe I can save her!'

Chrissie grabs my arm, and hauls me back. 'You are much too slow, Grandad. Besides, here are their boyfriends, look. Now that's more like it!' Half a dozen young men, in dark suits, white shirts and perfectly knotted ties appear, much hugging and kissing ensues, and the noisy group heads off down the street, in the direction, presumably, of the church. Unless a Russian lap-dancing club has suddenly opened it's doors in Santa Marta. Unlikely, although I have to say the girls in particular seem inappropriately dressed for a religious procession. Midnight Mass on Christmas Eve was bad enough, but this is far worse. Or better, depending on your point of view, and whether one's wife is present....

Rounding the final corner, we see a small crowd has assembled outside the church door, and it becomes clear that, for the ladies of the town, baring ones thighs is the order of the day. A number of old ladies have gone with a more discreet look, but for the rest, including some women of a certain age, who probably should have known better, hemlines are well north of the knee. There is no sign of Maria so we stake a place opposite the door and soak up the atmosphere of our first Spanish Palm Sunday. And as the library crowd warned us, everyone has made an effort to dress up. First procession of the Spring I suppose. 'Do you have a pair of scissors in your bag?' I ask.

'Scissors? No of course not! Why do you want scissors here?'

'Well' I chuckle, 'I thought I would cut about a foot off the bottom of your dress!' Just at that moment, Maria comes around the corner. 'Do you have any scissors, Maria?' I smile, after the usual double-kisses all round, although her husband Jose has to make do with a firm British handshake.

'Scissors? What this scissors plees?' I make a snipping gesture with my two fingers. 'Ahh, scissors. Why need you scissors this day?'

'Don't listen to him, Maria' Chrissie warns. 'He wants to cut the bottom of my dress, so I look like everyone else' and she sweeps her hand around the assembled ladies.

Maria swiftly translates for Jose, and the pair of them burst out laughing. He grabs my arm and makes a lewd gesture towards a group of mini-skirted girls, which I do my best to ignore, what with it being Palm Sunday and all that. 'Ees normal here in Espain, day of Domingo de Ramos!' Maria laughs. 'The peoples like, how you say in Eengliss, to flash?' Now it's our turn to guffaw, but there is no time to explain further as an expectant hush falls over the crowd. A priest, clad in white robes and bearing a ceremonial cross, emerges from the church, followed by two small boys, again all in white, swinging a huge incense burner. 'My cheeldrens!' Maria proudly announces. 'Luis and Manuel. Hola chicos!' The pair grin sheepishly as they pass, followed by more children bearing palm leaves, not folded into crosses but left in their natural state, four-to-five feet in length, and as they pass they peel off single fronds and hand them out to the spectators.

More followers are pouring out of the church, adults now, each wearing the same white gown Chrissie was given just a few days ago, only these have conical stiffeners inside their hoods, so that the headgear stands up in a perfect point. Many are barefoot, silently gliding by, unlike anything we have ever seen. Enchanting, uplifting somehow. Holy week has begun.

Suddenly a collective gasp emits from the crowd, as from the darkened interior of the building appears the *trono*, four rows of black-suited young men, backs straining, as slowly, slowly, into the daylight, emerges the plinth, entirely covered in pink carnations. The life-size figure of Christ, right hand raised, left hand bearing a palm leaf, is seated sideways on a donkey. Standing either side are a boy and a girl, clad in Biblical robes, and at the back of the trono, a full-size olive tree. There is one big problem however. Although the arched doorway of the church is massive, easily twenty feet high, the tableau is higher, and the figures are not going to clear the stonework. The bell-captain is at the front, he chimes once and the lads crouch down, still inching forwards. The suspense is unbearable, are they going to make it? If they do, it will be a miracle, and I find myself breathing in, urging them onwards. After what seems an age, the top of the olive tree clips the arch, and they are through. The crowd bursts into a massive round of applause, I breathe out and wipe a tear, or is it a bead of sweat, from my eye. Another chime of the bell and the *costeleros* lower their burden onto its legs and stand up straight, huge grins on their faces, uncurling their spines, stretching arms, massaging shoulders.

Suddenly, from further down the street, a silver band strikes up, a strident, jaunty tune, which is surprise to me as I was expecting a more sombre tone. I convey this to the one who attended Confirmation classes, all those years ago. 'No, initially Jesus was attending the Passover in Jerusalem' she confirms. 'The sad part came later that week. So this music is entirely appropriate.' More bell-ringing indicates we are off again, the lads hoist their burden and slowly, the whole procession wends its way up the street, silver band bringing up the rear, resplendent in their black uniforms, trimmed with red and gold.

'We are go to take beer' Maria confirms, 'we must to wait four hours for Luis and Manuel to return, with procession! You like take beer with we?'

We both smile warmly. Such lovely people, and what is more, nobody has called me a blooody soft Soothern jessie yet. Maybe there's still time? Somehow I doubt it. 'Thank you so much, but as this is our first Easter procession, we had planned to follow the *trono* around, at least for a while.' Chrissie confirms, 'but don't forget to come and see me on Holy Friday!'

They certainly will, another round of hugging, kissing and hand-shaking follows, and we cut around the block to get to the square of the old fountain, to watch the whole procession pass by again. Second time around, we are able to take in so much more, from the white-hooded *Nazerenos*, the little palm girls, Luis and Manuel still swinging the incense, and the trono itself, the wooden carvings, the silver engravings, the flowers, immaculately arranged, and finally the pure theatre of the figures. How anyone could fail to be moved by this spectacle, whether religious or not, is beyond me. Although we knew nothing of these processions before we came to Spain, I feel somehow I have been guided, drawn to this moment in my life. And Chrissie clearly feels the same.

The band pass slowly by, and we head homewards, thoughts of lunch in the garden uppermost in our minds. Crusty bread delivered this very morn by Jose the Pan, drizzled with olive oil, strong cheese, a slice or two of *Jamon Iberico,* washed down with a good old-fashioned cuppa. Best of both worlds. Into our little square, and who should be sat at a pavement table outside the Lantern Bar, but Gaffer and Diane. In truth, over the past couple of months we have been seeing less and less of them. Our classes at the library of course, our academy work, our private students, my jobs with Del-Boy, and the onset of Spring and spending our afternoons in the garden, have all contributed to us drifting further from their orbit. The eternal Ex-pat dilemma I suppose. We arrive in a foreign country, meet a few compatriots, and a 'honeymoon period' ensues, for a few weeks or months, until a natural balance is restored, and we find our own interests, activities, either immersing ourselves in the local culture, learning the language, or standing outside, retaining our British ways, customs, diets and lifestyle. We have chosen our Spanish path here, for better or worse, and with the exception of Del who mixes and converses freely with the locals, we seem to be the exception to the rule.

'Now then lad' Gaffer cries, 'where'sta been? An' why'sta done oop like a dog's dinner?'

'Palm Sunday?' Chrissie replies. 'The procession. It was beautiful, so moving. Didn't you want to see it?'

'Nay lass,' chimes in Diane, 'seen one procession, seen 'em all.'

I take a deep breath before replying. 'But you told us you had never been here for Easter. The flights were too expensive, you said. And every procession this week is different, look, I have a booklet here in my pocket. I got you a copy. In fact, we put your names down to help out with the carrying! Keith on Wednesday, and Diane on Thursday!'

Gaffer takes the publication, glances down, and hands it swiftly back. 'No blooody good to oos lad, 'tis all in Spanish. An' bloody forget oos carryin' owt, unless there is a throne on a mobility-scooter, wi' an engine an' wheels!'

'OK, I understand, but it is easy to follow. Look, ninth of April, 19.00h, tenth April, 20.00h, etc, and it tells you which church the processions are leaving from.'

'What time is that, in England, 20.00h?' Diane enquires.

For a moment I am not sure how to reply. England? What does it have to do with England? 'Well, 20.00h is 8pm, here, and we are an hour ahead of the UK, so 7pm in Britain.' I suspect she is taking the mickey, but I cannot quite work out how.

'No blooody good to oos, lad' Gaffer laughs, 'seven-o-clock is when Emmerdale's on.'

'We're not missin' Emmerdale' joost t'see some blooody procession!' Diane confirms.

Ah yes. I had forgotten. British television, the number-one topic of conversation whenever Ex-pats get together over here. We briefly toyed with the idea, when we first arrived at the camp-site, attended a demonstration involving a huge six-foot satellite dish and a set-top box, then we bought the house here with the kitchen terrace where we spend our evenings, the views of the olive-fields, the ever-changing town below, and most of all the sunsets, and promptly forgot all about it. Classic FM on the laptop, our Kindles, a few glasses of wine and a nightly Rick Stein special, and that is the evening taken care of. Besides, fitting a six-foot satellite dish to a rickety old Spanish cottage? One gust of wind and you'd have no wall.

I smile widely. 'OK, Monday, Tuesday and Wednesday processions are in the evenings, but Thursday and Friday are in the mornings. Thursday, half-nine, Good Friday, Chrissie's procession, nine sharp. Oh yes, and the mobility-scooter procession is Sunday lunchtime, between the bars! I will get you both changed to that one, if you prefer!'

'Ooh I didn't tell you did I?' Chrissie smiles, 'I was invited to carry Mary Magdalene on Good Friday morning, it all happened in the last couple of days, but I am the only British person ever to do this.'

'What, dress oop like t'blooody Koo Kuc Klan wi' a pointy 'at? Lug that blooody gert thing round t'town? Tha's blooody mad, lass! Coom in the pensioners procession, wi oos!'

'An' she were a blooody prossie!' Diane confirms, deadpan. 'Every booger knaws Mary Magde-wassname were a prossie! Why tha' wanna carry a blooody prossie round t'town?'

Chrissie chuckles 'I think it shows how everyone is welcome, saint and sinner, rich or poor. Anyway, are you coming with us, Thursday morning? Half-nine at St John's? Look, here are the photos in the booklet, Jesus with the Cross, Mary and John the Evangelist.'

Gaffer snatches the pamphlet back, and studies the page Chrissie is indicating. 'Half-nine?!' he cries. 'That's half-eight in England, we can watch the procession, Di, Thursday mornin' then get back for the Jeremy Kyle Show!'

Easter week unfolds for us like a moving, ever-changing tableau. A different church every evening, two tronos each time, always Jesus of course, in various stages leading towards the Crucifixion, accompanied by other Biblical figures on the second plinth. Each brotherhood interprets the story in its own way, accompanied by bands from various towns and villages around Andalucia. Every evening we arrange ourselves outside the church doors to see the departure, usually an event in itself as the crowds are huge, then as the figures wend their way down the narrow streets we head home to eat, and after an hour or so relaxing on the patio, we head out again to a different point on the route, usually the square of the Old Fountain, to re-live the experience.

Thursday morning dawns fine and sunny and at nine-sharp comes the knock on the front door. We are ready of course so the four of us head off towards St John's, a bright, modern church in the new part of the town, where they boast such things as wide streets, and pavements. Such luxury. The crowd seems smaller today, maybe due to the hour or possibly more space, but there is a subdued air and most people are speaking in whispers, highly unusual for Spain where shouting is considered normal volume. Gaffer is also behaving strangely, although for a different reason. 'Me an' Di got summat t'ask tha', lad' he confides. 'In the pamphlet, which I forgot to bring, it said about a homo in today's procession. What's all that about, like?'

In the corner of my eye I can see Chrissie with her hand tightly across her mouth, and it almost sets me off too, taking supreme self-control not to burst out laughing. She recovers her poise while I take a huge, deep breath. 'Ecce Homo' she confirms, 'it's Latin. They were the words spoken by Pontius Pilate as he delivered Jesus for sentencing. It means 'here is the man', not sure exactly, but that is the gist of it.'

'Behold the Man' I whisper, 'that is the literal translation, I think. So the figures on the plinth today will reflect that scene, maybe Jesus with the Cross, we won't have long to wait, look, the church doors are opening.'

Gaffer is staring at me, and for once his repertoire of corny one-liners has deserted him. 'Can tha' speak Latin, lad?'

'I didn't study it as such' I confirm, keeping an eye firmly on the church door. 'But I studied English Literature, and Latin phrases crop up in that quite often.'

'What country do they speak Latin in, then?' Di enquires. 'They tried to learn me French, in school, blooody useless I was!'

I am just about to frame a suitable reply when gaffer butts in. 'Italy somewhere, lass, down that way, any-road.' And he favours me with a sly wink. Before anything further is said however the first of the white-hooded *Nazerenos* are upon us, moving silently, eerily along the street. Three to a row, clearly women by their stature, mostly barefoot. Not a whisper is coming from the crowd, who like us are spellbound.

Suddenly, a much larger figure is moving through the ranks, clad head to toe in the same ensemble, but with an extra robe covering his tunic. He draws level with us and comes over, placing his hand in Chrissie's, then doing the same with me, before moving silently off. 'Avellard' Chrissie whispers, beaming widely. Indeed it is, old Dr Have-A-Hard Clooney, and suddenly all becomes clear, as the first trono emerges from the church doors, bearing Jesus, nailed to the cross, behind him the Roman centurion, and the two beggars. The figures from Avellard's surgery, although of God and St Peter there is no sign.

At that moment a single drum beat rings out, echoing round the silent street. Ten seconds pass, then another beat, followed by three stark notes on a bugle. The first *trono* draws almost level with us and stops, and for the first time I notice the *costeleros* are entirely enclosed within a richly-embroidered fabric cover, so that only their feet are visible. Meanwhile the second plinth has exited, featuring a female figure, clad in a dark-blue cloak, head bowed, surrounded by a bank of candles. Mary clearly, flanked by the other two statues from the surgery, which a quick glance at the leaflet reveals to be St John the Evangelist, and John of the Forest. So not God and St Peter then.

Just then an old man approaches from the opposite direction, shuffling purposefully down the middle of the road, an intense, staring look on his face. Curiously, he is puffing on a big fat cigar, drawing vast clouds of pungent smoke into his lungs. He gets to within about six feet of the leading *Nazareno*, and stops dead, looking up as if seeing the procession for the first time. I imagine he has escaped from a day-centre somewhere, although whether he knew it was Holy Thursday or not is impossible to say as the appearance of the procession seems to have taken him entirely by surprise. Then again, he is only able to walk down the middle of the road because the police have closed it to traffic. Perhaps we will never know, and I am sure he doesn't.

Suddenly, after another draw on his cheroot, he hawks, an evil, disgusting drawing of a lungful of phlegm from the very depths of his windpipe, reverberating from his nasal passages, rattling his tonsils in a fusillade of mucous. Truly, a world-class effort, and if this were a rugby pitch, deserving of a huge round of applause, a chorus of Eskimo Nell and free drinks all night. I would have bought him a pint, for sure. Sadly however this is a religious procession and his performance has not gone down too well, to say the very least. The *Nazerenos* are leaning forwards, although because their faces are covered it is impossible to determine if they are splitting their sides laughing or being sick, although I suspect the latter. Old ladies on both sides of the street are cringing, Gaffer is shaking with silent laughter, and the whole street is gripped by a feeling of utter, horrified revulsion.

The entire parade is gripped by the dreadful prospect of what will happen next. Truly, if Senor Snot ejects the contents of his diaphragm onto the pavement, there will be mayhem. Most of us are just about keeping our breakfasts down, but if he starts flobbing and gobbing, I will almost certainly be reunited with a bowl of Weetabix, two rounds of toast, and three black coffees. And I have a stomach of iron. Glancing round, I am not sure my fellow spectators share my robust constitution. An image of dark clouds gathering above, and a huge bolt of lightning piercing the sky and spearing the old man through the chest flashes through my mind, just as a ghostly-white, if somewhat rotund figure drifts to the front of the parade. Avellard to the rescue! He inclines his head and speaks softly to the old man, who turns slowly on his heels and shuffles off back down the street. A collective sigh of relief passes through the crowd, an old woman next to me shakes her head, '*Madre Mia!*' she whispers. Indeed.

Drama over, another single drumbeat rents the air, followed by a second, the same three notes from the bugle, and silently the whole procession moves slowly along the road. The *costeleros* carrying the plinth of Mary are similarly entirely shielded from view, so that she seems to be floating, gliding, candles flickering in the morning breeze. I am utterly transfixed, desperately trying to take in as much of the scene as possible, the stunning floral arrangements covering the base of the plinth, and her exquisitely embroidered cloak particularly, although of a certainty we will be catching up with the procession later in the morning.

Visibly moved, I blow out my cheeks and smile at Chrissie, who is similarly effected. Moments like these are why we came here, surely. I glance at Gaffer and Diane, raising my eyebrows in a *wasn't that unbelievable* type expression. Sadly, it seems they do not share our enthusiasm. 'Didn't think much t'that, lad' he complains, 'reet blooody mournful it were, like a blooody funeral. Could o' done wi' a bit o' tuneful music, like. Liven it up a bit.'

'A funeral?' I splutter. 'A funeral? Did you happen to see that bloke nailed to a cross? That is exactly what it was, a funeral.'

Chrissie is similarly enraged. 'What sort of music did you expect? The Bee Gees? Ah ah ah ah stayin' alive, stayin' alive?'

'Aye, summat like that, wi' a bit o' beat to it, any-road' Diane asserts.

Gaffer turns to us, 'thanks lad, but please don't invite oos t'no more bloooody parades', and the pair of them trundle off, arm in arm.

'I guess that means they will not be turning out tomorrow morning, to see you?' I giggle.

Chrissie however has still not cooled down. 'A funeral, can you believe that?'

'Don't worry about it,' I tell her, 'we enjoyed it, that's all that matters. But didn't Avellard do a wonderful job with that old man! Can you imagine what would have happened if he'd gob.....'

'All right all right!' she cries, 'my stomach is still recovering!' And we both burst out laughing. 'Tell you what,' she continues, wiping tears from her eyes, 'let's hope old Senor Snot doesn't make it to the New Fountain! My nerves couldn't stand it!'

CHAPTER 37. GOOD FRIDAY

Viernes Santo. Good Friday. The big one. Chrissie's debut as *la unica costelera Ingles*. Four *tronos* are scheduled to leave St Mary's at nine in the morning, for what promises to be a memorable day for my understandably nervous wife. I am the self-appointed carrier of water, and a big bag of boiled sweets, gathered off the road during the Three Kings procession in January, which we are still ploughing our way through. With the unique one in full regalia, but carrying the hood, and me in my usual Harris tweed/shirt/chino combination, we depart the house at around eight-fifteen to be assailed by a full complement of neighbours. I still haven't worked out how they do that. Are there secret cameras, or pressure sensors buried in the floor, to alert them we are leaving? Are they psychic? 'LA COSTELERA!' Loli bellows, alerting the entire neighbourhood. More heads pop out of doors, including Fernando, preceded by his stomach of course. The ladies all gather round Chrissie, poking, prodding, adjusting, and I have to say she looks magnificent, whereas I look like an Englishman.

'What are you doing, neighbour?' Mercedes enquires.

'*Yo tengo los caramellos!*' I announce. I have the sweets.

'*Caramellos?*' Fernando echoes. 'Give me some *caramellos*! Chrissie gives the assorted spectators a twirl, but old fat guts is not getting a sweet.

'Sorry, for *costeleras* only!' I smile, and we head off up the street, towards the square, which is bustling, crowded already, people milling around, band members smoking, *costeleros* and *nazerenos* in different coloured tunics, standing around chatting, a priest hurrying past, several octogenarian policemen doing absolutely nothing, and three Toby jugs. Not the ceramic or pottery kind often found hanging above the fireplace in Elizabethan coaching inns, but living, breathing life-size Toby jugs, big blokes too, each one eighteen stone easily, like a Spanish Pontypool front-row, in identical high-collared, long-tailed navy-blue jackets. What on earth could they be? Town criers? I lean towards my wife, 'how do you say **'Oh Yea!'** in Spanish?' I giggle.

She sniggers. 'No idea! *Oye* possibly? Anyway, never mind that, I have to get inside the church, wish me luck!'

'I will be outside the church door, on your side of the *trono*, and I will follow around the town. I am so proud of you, unique one!' and I give her a quick hug. She disappears inside and I continue my tour of the square, shaking hands with Spanish friends and neighbours, all the while keeping an eye out for any more Toby jugs, but they appear to have vanished.

The town clock chimes nine, and right on cue the church doors are thrown open, bells pealing, and the town band, who have hastily assembled in formation, break into the National anthem. A bell chimes from within the church and the priest slowly leads the *nazerenos*, all men, clad in purple cloaks and hoods, into the cobbled street, followed by the *trono*, covered in red carnations, slowly but surely, revealing the life-sized figure of Christ, clad in the same purple robes, bearing the Cross on His shoulder, the crouching figure of the beggar behind. The spectators break into respectful applause as the *costeleros* inch their way through the door into the bright sunshine, before heading slowly off across the square.

Another band is lining up and the mystery of the town criers suddenly becomes clear. The Toby jugs are a band! What an amazing uniform, and straight away I decide these are my favourites. They might actually sound like an out-of-tune cats choir, but as far as I am concerned, they are the champions. Most of the band, young and old, male and female, are normal-sized Spaniards, but through the crowd I can just make out the three huge Toby jugs lining up at the back, one with a bass drum, another with a tuba, and the third with a side-drum. The rhythm section, clearly! And according to the programme, Maria Magdalena is next. The *nazerenas,* all ladies of course, begin to emerge, wearing the same white tunics as Chrissie, but with a blue cloak on top, each one holding a palm leaf. A bell chimes inside the church, and I can picture Rosa with her silver hammer. And here she comes!

I do not of course have any idea what the decorated *trono* will look like, having only seen it in its 'naked' form, devoid of embellishments. I find myself holding my breath as the girls edge the plinth through the door, into the daylight, and on Rosa's command, pause to rest. And the reaction from the crowd is ecstatic, far more animated than the previous trono, several women near me are in floods of tears, many others visibly affected, and no wonder. There is Maria, alone on her throne, palms outstretched, face raised to the heavens, surrounded by a simply stunning garden of flowers, pink and white roses, gladioli, carnations and orchids. On her head is an exquisitely decorated silver crown, and she is dressed in the white tunic, embroidered with gold thread, gold sash around her waist and the dark-and light-blue cloak, all as chosen by Chrissie.

The whole scenario is almost too much to take in. Were we simply spectators, this would be an incredible sight. But to actually be involved is, as Teri mentioned just last week, a huge honoo. I have a lump in my throat as Rosa, I assume it is her as she has her face covered of course, chimes the bell, and

Maria Magdalena rises majestically, in perfect unison, onto the shoulders of the carriers. The Toby jugs fire up, and instantly it is clear they are a hugely professional outfit, another level above the Santa Marta band, who themselves are no slouches in the genre.

The plinth edges round the square, and I get my first official glimpse of the only Englishwoman ever to do this. On first glance of course she looks identical to her hooded sisters, but I can tell it is her, particularly as she gives me an imperceptible wave of her white-gloved hand as she passes. A momentous day, in both our lives.

I now have a small dilemma to resolve. I can either follow along behind, or wait to see the exit of the final two *tronos*, St John the Evangelist, and Mary, mother of Christ. Judging by the speed the first two are travelling, I can easily catch up, so decide on the latter. And here is St John now, followers and carriers dressed in olive-green tunics with red sashes, intricately carved wooden plinth, adorned with red roses and lilies, and deep blue iris. Dressed in a red and gold tunic, right arm pointing the way, left hand holding a giant palm frond, and bearing a more-than-striking resemblance to Jon Anderson, lead singer in the seventies prog-rock band 'Yes', St John makes his stately way across the square in pursuit of the others.

Have they saved the best till last? Quite possibly. The most ornate *trono*, certainly. Covered by a velvet canopy, laced with gold thread, standing in a field of white roses and orchids, behind a bank of candles, on a plinth of ornate silver carvings and engravings, wearing a black cape stretching out behind her, gold head-dress featuring star-bursts, lace coif wrapped around her face, down which several tears are coursing, Mary stands regally above us. A poignant, moving sight, her followers and carriers in black tunics with crimson trimmings, her captain tolls the bell and the *trono* rises with military timing, despite which the canopy swings alarmingly from side to side, before steadying itself to a huge round of applause from the crowd. The third and final band, dressed in Naval-style uniforms, strike up a haunting piece of music, the one Gaffer was complaining about the other day, but which is entirely appropriate for the occasion. Mary glides past, the church doors are hauled shut, and the audience start to disperse, some heading homewards but many following behind.

And now I have my work cut out catching up with Chrissie, as the street down which the procession is heading is so narrow, I will be simply unable to pass. I either have to remain at the back until the street widens in the little square at the bottom of the hill, or nip down one of the side streets and zigzag my way to the front, or rather *trono* number two. Reluctant to neglect my duties as bearer of refreshments, I decide on the latter so embark on a breathless dash along tiny cobbled lanes, some little more than footpaths, before I spot the figure of Maria Magdalena resting peacefully on the hillside, having travelled maybe only three hundred yards from the church doors. It is going to be a long, hot day for the *costeleras*.

The girls have all emerged from underneath the plinth, stretching, whispering to one another, keeping their hoods across their faces. Carmen is practising her English with Chrissie so I simply wave the water bottle in her direction, which she declines. Suddenly, from further back up the street, comes a sound exactly like someone dropping a sack of cement from a great height. All heads turn of course, and I am horrified to be confronted by the stricken form of a young girl, one of St John's followers as she is wearing the green cloak, spread-eagled across the cobbles. About twenty people rush to her aid, which is probably the last thing she needs, and I want to shout 'give her some air' but my Spanish vocabulary has deserted me. The casualty is breathing thankfully, and after a few seconds she staggers painfully to her feet, pride rather than body damaged, I imagine. But a lesson for everyone to keep hydrated, and maintain sugar levels. I again wave my supplies but again *la unica* declines. Rosa is enquiring after her oldest team member, then approaches me and whispers 'after the next two stops we would all love a *caramelo*, thank you!' *Unless I have eaten them all myself, by that time, Rosa…*

Off we go again, and after the somewhat nervous beginning to the day, not really knowing what to expect, I really start to enjoy myself, sometimes forging ahead, past the plinth of Jesus, sometimes dropping back, past St John, to Mary. Due to the twisting nature of the tiny streets, at no time are all the plinths visible at once, and it is truly magical to round a bend to be presented with another trono, as if seeing everything afresh. Each tableau is maintaining a healthy distance from the one in front, and even the sounds of the individual bands are not competing. All along the route, people are gathered, some leaning out of their windows, others standing on balconies, rose petals are thrown occasionally, and it seems the whole town, young and old alike, have turned out. I have spotted several locals we know, even though we have not yet arrived at our part of town, where I imagine the majority of the neighbours will be gathered.

Soon, we approach the Old Fountain part of the route, where the programme indicates there will be a *beso*, a kiss, although who might be kissing whom, and what it has to do with Good Friday, is not clear. The square is packed, both the gardens in the middle, and round the edge, where a VIP area has been set up, with seating. Everyone else has to stand, and as Jesus rounds the corner I notice they are four or five deep, kids running in and out, under the legs of the adults, pushing, jostling as kids do. I, of course, do not have to worry about the crowds, following the *tronos* along the roadway, feeling ever-so-slightly involved, even though my wife is doing all the work, and I am only carrying a rapidly diminishing bag of sweets, after the last fuelling stop.

This being abroad, where they drive on the 'wrong' side of the road, Jesus' plinth traverses the garden in the middle of the square to the right, the way normal traffic would go, if the roads were open. Maria Magdalena and St John then follow, but as Mary approaches it becomes clear she is heading to the left, which means she eventually ends up face-to-face with her son. Both tronos pause to rest, then following a blessing from the priest, Jesus and Mary are raised up, and begin to move forwards and backwards together, accompanied by sombre, heart-rending music. The whole scene is incredibly moving, people are openly weeping, as mother and son part for the final time. The 'kiss' of course.

'OK, final push, all uphill from here! Big effort now! Fancy a sweet?' I urge *la unica*. Even though I can only see her eyes, I can tell she is cursing me, by her body language, and accompanying hand gestures. But it is true. All uphill from here, to St Mary's. But maybe the best bit, as many of the neighbours are lining the route, and I am fully occupied pointing out where Chrissie is, third from the back. Leopard-skin Woman, Auntie Vera, Ferret Woman, Cruzojo, the Dustman and Mercedes, among others, waving as we pass. Our friends Cristina and Rosa walk alongside for the final few hundred yards, and all-too-soon, or none-too-soon according to whether you were carrying or not, we arrive outside the church, to find the doors locked. It seems we have to wait for the final two plinths to arrive, before all four line up in unison, and move together, in time with the music, before disappearing inside, one by one.

I am dog tired, heaven knows how Chrissie must be feeling, so am supremely keen to forget all about Good Friday, and slump on the sunbeds in the garden. No such luck, sadly. Each *trono* has to be half-dragged half-carried into the far corner of the church, and chaos reigns. People have crowded inside, many trying to steal the flowers from the exquisite displays on the plinths, a sign of good luck apparently, although personally I would have them shot. Eventually, each plinth is safely stowed away, and the officially-sanctioned stripping of the flowers can begin. Carmen actually climbs aboard and starts throwing blooms down, Chrissie catches a few, promising to hand them out to the neighbours, and we are finally free to go. As we leave the church, the clock is striking two; five hours to traverse a few streets of the old town, which a reasonably fit person could easily have done in thirty minutes. But what a momentous five hours they were.

Heading across the square, we pass a bar with outside seating, and there, with their backs to us, are Gaffer and Diane, talking to another British couple whom we have not yet met. 'One of our English friends is one o' these carriers, wi' the pointy 'ats.' Gaffer is explaining. 'She's t'only Brit ever to do it. We're reet proud of her, ain't we Di?'

I squeeze Chrissie's hand as we slip silently up behind them, she throws her arms around his neck and kisses him on the side of his head. 'That's why we love you, Keith' she smiles broadly. 'Now I need to lie down. Garden. Sun-bed. Wake me up on Easter Sunday!'

CHAPTER 38. EASTER SUNDAY

We awake on Easter morning to the depressing sound of rain. Not just a light drizzle, but hard, steady rain. After weeks of warm, unbroken sunshine, the final day of Semana Santa, the joyous day, has been ruined by the weather. Spaniards are frightened by the rain, are reluctant to leave the house at the merest hint of the wet stuff, and if they do, are always togged up with coats and umbrellas. Even teenage boys on the school bus carry brollies, action which would surely earn them a stiff kicking in the UK. So there is no way today's procession will take place. Chrissie is utterly distraught. 'I was so looking forward to this morning. You know that all week I have been a bit keyed up about Maria Magdalena, so now the pressure is off, and I can enjoy the end of Holy Week, we have this cursed rain.'

'Well maybe we might be lucky' I venture, scooping two boiled eggs out of the pan, and placing them carefully in my Volkswagen camper-van egg cups. When I was a little boy, it was always boiled eggs for breakfast on Easter Sunday, with toast cut into soldiers, a tradition I have carried on to this day.

'No chance' my wife sighs, 'you know what the Spanish are like, and there is no way this rain will stop before ten-o-clock.'

I smile serenely, but am concentrating on tapping the top of the first egg, and peeling off the shell. I have always been a 'tapper', rather than a 'slicer', having once put my fingers through the entire egg, attempting a slice. 'If I can get you into the Easter Sunday procession, what will you give me?' I grin, cutting the first round of toast into soldiers.

'An Easter bunny!' she cries. 'A chocolate Easter bunny!'

No, that's not fair!' I complain, dipping the first soldier, always a delicate operation. 'The shops are closed, so you must already have the bunny. In fact, I'm willing to bet a million quid there is an Easter bunny, right now, in your wardrobe!'

'Well that is a million you owe me then!' she laughs. 'He is in the dressing table!'

'No, still not fair. You already bought me the bunny. If you want to see the procession, you must get me something extra. Those are the rules.'

But somehow, Chrissie always manages to have the last word. 'Who says the bunny was for you anyway. For all you know, I might have been planning to eat the entire thing, in secret. But get me to the procession, and you can have the whole rabbit. Although you might like to let me have the ears!'

'Show me the bunny!' I cry, scraping out the first egg. 'Then I will tell you my cunning plan!'

She leaves the table, dashes upstairs, returning with a huge Lindt rabbit, around a foot high, by which time I am tapping off the second egg. I hold out my hand, but she keeps the gift behind her back. 'Come on, cunning plan first! Let's hear it!'

'Rabbit on the table!' I demand, slicing up the second round of toast. 'In the middle!' Down goes the bunny, but on her side, next to her coffee. She cups her hand to her ear, indicating she needs to hear the plan, which actually is more of a giant bluff, or a complete guess, given that we have never seen an Easter Sunday procession, here, or anywhere else. 'OK,' I begin, 'two *tronos* this morning, Jesus, and Mary, from San Raphael church?'

'Correct.'

'So the plinths will already be made up, figures mounted, flowers in place, everything ready for the off?'

'Yes, but look out the window, you idiot!' she groans, pulling her alleged gift off the table.

I am momentarily occupied with my final two soldiers, but manage to tap the table firmly. 'Back with the bunny, now!' This is going to be good. Very good. 'So everyone will be at the church, the *costeleros*, the band, the *nazerenos*, all milling around, nobody knowing what is happening, the typical chaotic, Spanish lash-up, in fact. So we go to the church, blag our way inside, the *tronos* will be in there, so we get to see them, they can hardly kick us out, can they? OK, so it won't be like a real procession, but better than nothing!'

A wide grin spreads across her face, and leaving the confectionery unguarded, she dodges round the table and tries to plant a kiss on me somewhere. I am too quick for her however and reach across the table and grab my prize. Too late, she realises her error and makes a desperate lunge, getting a couple of fingers on Mr Rabbit, crushing him into a hundred pieces. I place the shattered creature on the table, and carefully peel back the gold foil, revealing, as expected, a chocolate jigsaw. 'What sort of Easter present is this?' I complain, 'all smashed to pieces!'

'Oh stop complaining, you have to break him up to eat!' she giggles, diving into the foil and stealing the ears, popping them into her mouth before I can even blink. Like I say, she usually gets the final word....or in this case, the best bit.

By nine-thirty the rain has almost stopped, so donning light jackets we head down to San Raphael, where, as predicted, chaos reigns. The band, the carriers and followers, a dozen or so spectators, even the priest, are simply standing around, chatting, par for the course. We slip inside the church unnoticed, and the doors close behind us. We have gate-crashed a church lock-in. Pride of place is taken by the two plinths, fully decorated, ready to roll as it were. Jesus, naked from the waist up, red and gold cloak slung over one arm and draped over his lower torso. And Mary, resplendent in a cloak of green velvet embroidered with gold, stretching out behind her, face uplifted to the heavens. No tears, today.

The pews have been pushed back to make a bit more space, but it is still impossibly crowded inside. Suddenly, the priest stands up in front of the band, who have assembled near the altar, apologises that the procession is cancelled due to the weather, but to compensate there will be dancing. Dancing? Is he serious? There is barely room to swing the proverbial cat, the old lady in front of me keeps treading on my toes, a walking frame belonging to an old man is sticking into my back, and a fugitive umbrella keeps prodding me in the leg. Nevertheless, dancing there will be, and big applause for *los capitanos*. Two men step forward, the first one barely five-feet tall, eighty if he is a day, like a miniature Marlon Brando, dressed in a crimson robe. The second fellow is maybe half that age, slightly taller, clad all in white, with a bandanna tied to his head, a Silvio Berlusconi lookalike with a manic grin on his face, like he is on his way home from a *bunga-bunga* party. Or on his way to one, possibly. Maybe that is what is happening now? Dancing, followed by geriatric intercourse?

The band suddenly fire up, and in this confined space my ear drums almost burst, I step back and the walking frame shifts from my back to my back passage, the old woman is pressed against my groin, and it takes a supreme effort to stop myself crashing to the ground, bringing down the entire band in a domino effect. Bells clang, the *tronos* are hoisted, Marlon directs his boys towards the far side of the church, whereas Silvio urges his troops in pursuit, like some wild-eyed matador. Indoor bullfighting, on an Easter Sunday. The music continues at ear-splitting volume as the two plinths chase each other across the nave, missing by inches as they come together, Jesus and Mary rocking like two ships tossed on a summer storm, *costeleros* grinning like maniacs, Marlon headed for a certain cardiac arrest, with Silvio hanging on to his coat-tails like some demented devil.

The bells chime again, the tronos are lowered, the band falls silent, and tumultuous applause breaks out. Unbelievable. Completely and utterly unbelievable, the best ten minutes I have ever spent inside a church. Apart from our wedding, of course... And it is not over yet. The musicians have clearly caught the bug, belting out another strident, rousing tune, Marlon steals a march on his rival, whipping his men into a frenzy, taunting Silvio like Ali Versus Frazier, the Rumble in San Raphael. Bandanna-man is not to be outdone, his team hoisting Mary aloft, arms outstretched, and in a blistering sweat-soaked finale, both figures are paraded round at a frenetic pace before a final crescendo of drums and woodwind bring the dance to a close, *tronos* are brought crashing down to earth, and Marlon, Silvio and both teams embrace amid an orgy of hugging and back-slapping. There is barely a dry eye in the place, although in my case that could be more to do with the position of the walking frame. Somehow, however, I doubt it.

The procession, or rather the dance, is over. Easter is over, and with heavy hearts we begin the trek homewards, reflecting on a momentous week in our lives. Twenty-one processions, each and every one different, the same basic format admittedly, but for the figures, the decorated plinths, the carriers, the followers, the costumes, the accompanying bands, the atmosphere and the entire presentations, completely unique. One of them even had an Englishwoman carrying, apparently.....

CHAPTER 39. DANCING ON THE HILLSIDE.

It is past one o'clock in the morning when the old woman stands on my toes, but as I have no shoes on, it is possibly my own fault. I am dancing barefoot in a narrow cobbled street, along with about a dozen other people, and am having trouble staying upright, not I hasten to add due to the amount of *cervezas* I have drunk, but because the 'dance-floor' is also a steep hill. You try dancing on a cobbled hill and see how you get on! Still, life is all about new experiences they say, and this certainly is one. On a rare flat bit of street, a four piece band are belting out what sounds like a complete re-run of the 1972 Euro-Vision Song Contest, and looking around me there are no signs that the last forty years have actually happened. Perhaps I have been beamed back in time somehow. Their favourite song, and the one the crowd seem to love best, goes something like 'Granny smokes, Granny drinks, Granny dances'.... and the dancers are making smoking, drinking and dancing gestures along with the music, like some crazy Spanish version of 'Agadoo', or heaven forbid, the 'Birdy Song'. How has my life come to this....

Further along the street, at its narrowest point, a temporary bar has been set up, and Little Paco, who is about five feet tall, and his wife Louisa who is the same size around, are dispensing drinks and tapas respectively at record speed, Paco shouting above the music in his high-pitched voice and Louisa cackling away like a demented dwarf. Paco greets me as a long lost friend even though I have only been to his real bar about three times, and he will apparently keep on serving us until we tell him to stop.

Next to the bar, tables and chairs have been set up, almost touching the cottages in the narrow street, so that the occupants can barely get out through their doors, although one house in particular has many people coming and going, who I presume are relatives who have returned for the fiesta. We are invited to sit in a large group consisting of a few Brits, a Moroccan, and some locals, and soon plates of tapas start to appear and are passed round, Spanish style. Feeling an urgent call of nature, I ask one of the locals where I can have a pi-pi, and he tells me to go into the house where all the people are. 'But that's a private house,' I point out, doubtfully.

'Sure, no problem, follow me!' he replies and off we go into the hallway of someone's house, past an old man watching the bullfighting on TV, past the kitchen where about half a dozen women are chatting excitedly, out into the courtyard and the bathroom. Imagine throwing your own house open to an entire fiesta? Thought not! On my return the matador narrowly avoids getting his man-bits removed by the bull's horns, and the old fella shouts a stream of abuse at the TV, but whether it is directed at the matador, or the bull, I cannot tell.

So back to the old woman standing on my foot. She cackles loudly and carries on bopping, as do I, and we continue, and mostly fail, to dance in a respectable fashion on this crazy slope. Then the old lady starts on about chocolate, 'where's my chocolate, I want chocolate, come on let's have chocolate.' OK but it's getting on for 2am and I am guessing the village shop has shut, but then everyone starts vacating the 'dance-floor' leaving the band playing valiantly alone, and sure enough large jugs of liquid chocolate start to appear from the house in question, followed by women bearing plates of cakes and pastries. We each get a plastic cup of chocolate and some cake to dip in it and suddenly people are slurping and gulping like a nursery of toddlers learning to spoon-feed. I am wearing white chino's and feel certain to get some down the front, especially when the fruit salad appears and I pour it in the chocolate and drink the whole concoction, but by some miracle my clothing remains unscathed. Until that is we return to the dance-floor. 'Have you cakked yourself?' Chrissie giggles, 'you have suspicious-looking marks on the back of your trousers. Not a good look!' Apparently, I have brown stains on my bum, some unsteady Spaniard has clearly spilled some chocolate down behind me, but what the heck.

We dance away until the band finish, after a reprise of 'Granny Smokes', but the night is not over by a long way as the disco immediately starts up. We have clearly moved on a decade to the 1980's now, but I am feeling the effects of the tapas, the beer and the chocolate, not to mention the thought of the matador's tackle, so we gracefully retire for the night. Paco is slumped in a chair near our table so we ask him how much we owe. 'No idea' he laughs. 'How many drinks have you had?' As bar tabs go this is one of the craziest, but our last visit to his bar was the same, and one Sunday lunch he couldn't remember how many plates of food he had served us. We toddle off to Tony and Jo's place, where we are crashing for the night, and drift off to sleep to the distant sound of Rick Astley, who was very big in Spain apparently, which is not something I wish to contemplate at silly-o-clock in the morning.

Next day it all begins again, the women of the village have been asked to provide a plate of food for Sunday lunch and said plates have to be delivered at 12 noon to the 'bull-fight' house, and sure enough the old man is still there in front of the TV. It seems like a different bull today and the matador has changed his trousers..... Paco is still standing behind the bar, whether he made it to bed is impossible to say but two bottles of beer appear as if by magic and off we go again. Sunday lunch in Spain is all about large family groups and different plates of food, which are shared around, and behind us two giant paellas are on the go. We are asked to help stir them, which according to Jo is a great honour, but to me seems like cheap labour, but I do make a mean paella myself, courtesy of Rick Stein of course, so maybe I can teach these Spaniards a thing or two....

Soon all the tables are packed with families, then the food appears and a huge stampede ensues, I am being very British and not pushing in but most of the locals, especially the older ones, are able to duck underneath me as they are so short, so I have to move fast to get any grub whatsoever. 'Madre mia' cries the woman handing out the paper plates as she is almost trampled in the rush, and very soon all the platters have been picked clean like a meeting of a flock of seagulls, a pack of wolves and a couple of lone hyenas. Likewise the paella, even though an Englishman helped to make it, or maybe because of that, impossible to tell really.

A couple of hours, or possibly a couple of days later, I turn to Tony. 'I cannot stand much more of this, I am thinking of going back to England'. I inform him.

He regards at me with a strange grin, and slips his arm around my shoulder 'What, all the free food and cheap beer and the heat and the sunshine, you mean? I was just thinking the same myself..........'

'*La Romeria!* Thee weekend! Booey! Carroza! Rebelhito! Ees ver good! Much peoples. Wicky! Comidas! Jam! Ben! Brax! You come! Take brax plees!' We have run into Alicia, of conversation group fame, on our way to the Santa Marta Saturday morning market. Never one to hide her light under a bushel, or whatever the metric equivalent of a bushel might be, today she is dressed in an extreme of *hooker-chic,* black ankle boots, fishnet tights, a red leather mini-skirt, tight white blouse which I am trying, and spectacularly failing, to ignore, topped off by a red beret. And she has me firmly by the hand. I glance desperately behind to check that nobody I know has witnessed the capture, and more importantly, that Chrissie has not abandoned me to a fate worse than death. Luckily, my wife seems to be tagging along, so I grab her arm and the three of us, Alicia tottering, and us stumbling, make our unsteady way to a pavement cafe, where we are commanded to sit. 'Brax is good for me thees day, ees good for you?' Before I have time to enquire what a brax might be, and whether we might actually want one, a waiter has appeared, and Alicia places an order, although whether we are sharing one, or have one each on the way, is unclear.

Suddenly, mercifully, around the corner comes Chrissie's star pupil, Teri. She spots us waving frantically and starts to come over, then recoils as her eyes come to rest on the vision of overt sexuality that is Alicia. It is too late for Teri of course, she has to sit down to avoid giving offence, and I stand gallantly and offer her my chair, thereby ensuring a decent gap between me and the Spanish cougar. 'Brax, Teri?' enquires fishnet legs.

Our saviour shakes her head, 'cafe solo' she confirms. *Espresso.*

'Alicia was just telling us something, before you arrived.' Chrissie explains, and all eyes turn to the older woman, who repeats, more or less word-for-word, her original narrative. Before Teri has time to translate however, the waiter returns, bearing three long plates, each one containing about a foot of crusty bread, toasted, smothered in chopped tomato, and four espressos. Brax. Breakfast, in Alicia-speak. Actually, I am not sure I want this brax, having already polished off egg, bacon sausage and fried bread, not an hour since, plus my usual coffee ration, but hey, I am British. I have standards to maintain. If Alicia can eat one, so can I, although somehow I doubt she put away a full-Monty, before leaving home.

'Next weekend is the *Romeria* here in Santa Marta' Teri helpfully explains, 'how do you say *Romeria* in English?'

I am fully occupied sawing up this huge loaf, which is actually big enough to go to work, as my mother might have said, and trying to avoid getting tomato pips over my trousers. Besides, Teri is Chrissie's student. Let her explain we have not the slightest clue what a *Romeria* might be.

My wife however cleverly turns the tables. 'Why don't you explain, in English, what a *Romeria* is, Teri?' she smiles.

Her pupil puffs out her cheeks, 'I will try!' she giggles. 'OK, is weekend party, of flamenco dresses. Origin of gipsy people, horses, guitar music. Saint of labradors. Do you have flamenco dress, Cristina?'

She does actually, bought a few months ago in a church charity-shop in Nerja, a resort on the coast about thirty miles east of Malaga. A bit of a tug-o-war with a Spanish woman, who had tried to seize it, even though Chrissie had tried it on, and was in the process of taking it to the counter, to pay. My wife might only be little, but can be fierce when roused, and she certainly was that morning. And said dress has sat in her wardrobe to this very day, all spots and frills, weighs a ton too, and personally I had doubted it would ever be worn. I mean, it's not the sort of thing for a trip to the shops, although now there seems the possibility it might get an airing. But what is this saint of labradors? And if there is, what about the golden retrievers, or alsatians?

Chrissie smiles, 'yes I do have a flamenco dress, it is green, with pink spots, a deep frill round the neckline, short puffy sleeves, and two deep, wired frills around the hem. And I absolutely love it, cannot wait to wear it!' I am still ploughing through the last few inches of bread and tomatoes, which is taking a bit of doing, I can tell you. *But never mind the frilly wires, what about the labradors?* My wife usually knows what I am thinking, often before I have even thought it. 'Saint of labradors?' she enquires.

'Yees, labradors. Santa Victoria, she is saint of they. How you say labradors in Eengliss?'

I am mopping up the last few toast crumbs, 'woof woof!' I splutter.

Teri looks confused. 'Dog? Labrador is dog?'

'Woof woof!' chuckles Alicia, who I have to say is doing extremely well with her brax, although I imagine she has a few crumbs lodged in her fish-nets, not that I dare look, of course.

'Yes, a labrador is a breed of dog, in English' explains the teacher, 'tell me what the word means, In Spanish.'

Our pupil frowns in concentration. 'OK, ees person who work, outside the city, in, how you say, side of country?'

'A farm labourer, working in the countryside' confirms *la profesora*. 'Victoria is the patron saint of labourers. So what else happens in this fiesta?'

Teri is really laughing now, having confused a farm worker with a breed of hound. 'OK, so evening of Friday, Santa Victoria come out of *la ermita*, and womans in flamenco dress follow she round the town. Eventually, in middle-night arrive she at Church of Santa Maria, and sleep here this night. On Saturday, in morning, come out Santa Victoria with booey. How you say booey in Eengliss?'

I cannot help it. I put my thumbs in my ears, waggle my toasty fingers, and cry 'Booey!' Ever the kid. I mean, come on, how else do you say booey in English?

Alicia is rocking with laughter, but Teri is clearly struggling. Complicated language, this Eengliss. 'Big animal, for milk, you say *coo*? Moooo!'

A cow? A booey is a cow? 'A cow?' Chrissie ventures.

Teri is clearly wishing she'd stayed in bed this morning. 'Coo is woman coo, no? Booey is man coo.'

A bull? Surely a bull is a toro? Everyone knows that.

Alicia, having cleared her plate, pushes back her chair, parts her thighs and dangles her entire arm between her legs, swinging it from side to side. Chrissie has tears running down her face, and the waiter, who at that moment was approaching to clear the table, steps back in utter bewilderment. Not often you see a woman in boots and fishnets, clearly mimicking a male appendage, in the middle of a cafe. A first for me, certainly. But surely a bull is a *toro*. So what other bovine creature, with large dangly bits, is there?

'An ox?' Chrissie sniffs, wiping her eyes on a tissue. 'A big bull?'

Teri meanwhile has been tapping away on her phone. 'Och!' she cries, 'booey is och!'

'Ox' Chrissie giggles. 'OXXXXX!'

But Spaniards cannot pronounce the letter 'X'. Probably explains why, when I enquired after a pair of shorts in the local menswear shop, the manager apologised they didn't have *ekky-ekky-elly*. XXL. *Cheeky swine. Surely I am only XL?*

'Och, moooooo!' laughs Alicia.

Teri is continuing her story, which at this rate could take until after this Romeria. 'OK, so are two och, pull caravan of Santa Victoria, to the old fountain, where appear much caravans, we call them *carrozas* in Espanees. In caravan is food, cheese, jam, chorizo, and much drinkings, *rebelhito.* How you say *rebelhito* in Eengliss?

Not a clue, obviously. 'What type of drink is this?' Chrissie enquires.

Teri grimaces again. 'Is vine, vine white, with lemon gassy-oso.' Sounds like white wine with lemonade, to me. Very refreshing, no doubt, if served chilled. Could do with one now, actually, wash down the bread mountain, and all that tomato. But it appears there is another ingredient. 'And wicky' Teri confirms.

Nope, me neither. 'Wicky?'

'Yees, wicky, how you say wicky in Eengliss? NO! Wicky ees Eengliss! From Scott-land. Yees!'

'Whisky!' we both exclaim. Is she serious, or is this another 'lost in translation' episode. Never mix the grape with the grain, my mother always warned me, especially not in the same glass, as this rebel-whatsit concoction appears to be. 'So white wine, lemonade, and whisky, all together?' I enquire, doubtfully. Whatever will they make of this, in Scott-land?

'Yees, ees delicioso!' Alicia cries. 'Salut!'

Indeed. 'Right, to recap' Chrissie smiles, 'on Friday evening, everyone dresses in their flamenco, and we follow St Victoria around the town. She stays the night in St Mary's church, then on Saturday morning, two oxen pull her in a caravan, we meet more caravans, then start eating cheese, ham and chorizo, and drinking white wine with lemonade, and whisky. Is that correct, and then what happens?'

'Yees!' Teri cries, 'ees perfect! You sure you no have *Romeria* in you countree?' *No, I am sure we would have remembered, although after mixing whisky and wine, maybe not....* 'So caravans, booey, sorry och, Santa Victoria and peoples go through town, then up mountain to ermita of Santa Victoria', she continues. 'In afternoon, is siesta, peoples sleeps, and at the night is big party. Party until Sunday.' And she slumps back in her chair, exhausted, fanning her face, grinning widely.

'Well done Teri!' Chrissie smiles, swallowing hard. Her pupil has progressed impressively in the last few months, and this *Romeria* was not the easiest subject in the world to describe. 'So do you have a flamenco dress, and will you be going on Friday evening? And you, Alicia?'

'Yees!' both women exclaim. OK, sounds like we have next weekend covered. All I need to do now is pay for the braxes. Three huge toasty, tomatoey things, and four espressos. Has to be best part of twenty, doesn't it? I think I have one, in my wallet. The waiter approaches, trying his best not to look up Alicia's skirt. 'Six Euros' he winces, having either caught a glimpse, or cricked his neck. Six Euros? Unbelievable, like much of this country.

Walking home after the brax, having abandoned the market, I cannot help an ironic chuckle. 'Looks like your famous dress will get an outing, sooner than expected. Better get it out, give it an iron, make sure it still fits!'

My wife narrows her eyes. 'Are you daring to suggest I might have put on weight recently?' she hisses.

'Not at all, if anything, you have lost a few pounds, actually. It is I who might have bulked up with muscle, you know, mixing cement for Del, carrying bricks up the ladder, that kind of thing.'

'Yeah right' comes the predictable reply, 'massive breakfasts, more like. Two massive breakfasts, in fact! Anyway, yes, I need to get the dress out, to see the exact colour of the new shoes I need to buy, for Friday night, then I need a silk flower for my hair, and speaking of which, I must get my hair done, remind me to call Lola, when we get home. Oh, and by the way, what are you wearing on Friday night?'

'Me? Who cares what I am wearing? That old white cotton shirt, those old chino shorts. It certainly won't involve a haircut, or new shoes, or a silk flower, will it?' For which I earn a swift dig in the ribs. Cannot win, can I? Besides, what is so special about dressing up to watch a few caravans? Taunton Deane services, on the M5, any Friday night in August, there are about a billion, clogging up the inside lane. Although to be fair, I have never seen an och, or even an ox, outside Costa Coffee.......

Friday evening it takes me less than thirty seconds to change, whereas Chrissie has been ensconced in the bedroom for about an hour. The procession is due to commence at seven-thirty, so we need to leave by seven at the latest, due not to the distance involved, as *la ermita*, the little white chapel, is only in the next street up. No, we have to run the gauntlet of the neighbours. Word has spread that *la Inglesa* is dressing up, and a large crowd is predicted. 'I can hear them out in the street!' Chrissie laughs, 'it sounds like there are hundreds out there! Just come and tie this string, and we can be off.'

String? Is she serious? Do dresses in Spain fasten with string? Surely not, although having said that, they are complete bodgers when it comes to building houses, so maybe it's true. Here she comes, rustling and swishing downstairs, like a scene from *Gone With The Wind*, spotty frills billowing all around her, pink silk rose in her hair, matching fan in her hand. And I have to say, with her dark complexion, looking every inch the gypsy girl. She gives me a twirl, and there it is. String. Dangling from the neckline. Unbelievable. These dresses cost over two-hundred Euros, new, often much more. Surely, for that money, they could have bunged on a few of those hookey things they attach to bras? Maybe this is why this garment was in the charity shop in the first place. A Friday-afternoon flamenco dress. No time to stitch on the hooks, whack in a bit of string, and let's all go for a massive sleep. Wouldn't surprise me, to be honest. And they have hardly been over-generous with the twine, leaving about an inch either side for me to work with. All fingers and thumbs at the best of times, my eyes are popping and sweat is breaking out just about everywhere, as I struggle in vain with this miserable length of cord. Give me a decent bit of rope, thick as your thumb, and I could rustle up a *sheep-shank* quicker than you could say 'Wolf-Cub.' But this is like trying to poke butter up a porcupine's back-side, with a red-hot knitting needle, as my old mate 'Killer' King used to say.

Utterly defeated, I tuck the ends into the neckline. No-one is going to notice anyway, with her hair covering the collar, or whatever you call this bit at the back. I fling open the front door, Chrissie steps though, and a massive cheer breaks out, followed by clapping, and shouting, and I remain inside to allow my wife to bask in the limelight, fluttering her fan, twirling for her audience. Suddenly, however, a dispute breaks out. 'NEIGHBOUR, WHAT IS THIS?' Loli, of course, who unceremoniously yanks up a fist-full of hair, revealing my pathetic attempt at knotting. 'YOU ARE AN IDIOT, NEIGHBOUR!' she announces to those viewers in Madrid who might be watching by satellite. I stand, arms outstretched, mouth open, milking the laughter, but clearly I have committed some unforgivable sin, as the women are gathered round, poking and prodding my beloved gypsy like some prize exhibit at the Devon County Show. Loli stands behind the frilly Englishwoman, hefts up her entire chest area like someone performing the Heimlich manoeuvre on one of those rubber dummies they used to provide at St John's Ambulance Brigade first-aid classes, and Isabel steps in and pulls about a foot of string from either side of the neck-hem, and ties off a neat little bow.

The problem is, Chrissie is unable to breathe. She is, after all, a northern-European woman, attempting to squeeze into a garment designed for one of her Mediterranean sisters, who, in my limited experience, seem to be rather broader in the beam, and generally less well endowed, up-top. Whereas my wife, and I am sure she will forgive me for announcing this, or possibly not, but what the hell, is the opposite. And rapidly turning red. More prodding ensues, then Mercedes saves the day, and a call to the ambulance service, by grabbing the entire neckline and hiking it upwards. And breathe! Chrissie is fanning vigorously and sucking in lung-fulls of air, her face returning to its normal shade, all the while spluttering with laughter. A few more minor adjustments, and we are free to move off up the street, round the zigzag bend, following a veritable procession of spottily-clad ladies, until we arrive outside *la ermita*, where multicoloured chaos reigns. A full spectrum of shades, a plethora of spots, many of which would not normally be seen in close proximity. I must admit, when I first saw Chrissie's dress in the charity shop, that Lincoln green and dark pink would not have been my first choice, wouldn't have been my last choice come to that. And some of the colour combinations on display here this evening likewise. They just don't, to my mind, go together. Having said that, for a time during the late sixties/early seventies I could be found in an apple green cheesecloth shirt, and purple loons, so what do I know?

Outside the chapel is a small plaza, so we weave our way through the milling crowd, past the band tuning up and smoking simultaneously, and crane our heads above the throng to discover what, if anything, is happening. About a hundred colourful souls have crammed their way into the building, which seems like it should comfortably hold about fifty, and there, at the far end, is the virgin, Santa Victoria, maybe half life-size, dressed in a blue cloak embroidered richly in silver, surrounded by a sea of white lilies, mounted on her plinth and covered by a domed canopy. In her arms is a baby, the size of a child's doll, dressed identically. The priest appears to be winding up the service so we decide to place ourselves outside to get the best view of the *trono* emerging, when suddenly from the crowd comes a loud cry. 'Cristina! Heeeey!' Oh blimey. Alicia. I can hear her voice, but cannot yet pick her out from the assembled gathering. All I can see are spots There could be leopards and cheetahs hidden amongst this lot, and no-one would be any the wiser. Suddenly a vision of yellow breaks free, actually an extremely tasteful-looking lemon yellow, trimmed with grey polka-dots, and flashes of white. And there was me expecting fishnets again. Usually, Alicia stands out from the crowd, but tonight she blends in perfectly, and somehow it doesn't suit her. Her dress is beautiful, clearly very expensive, expertly tailored, and we are told that each one is subtly different, that no two are ever exactly the same. But they all follow the same basic pattern; frills and spots. Big spots, little spots, flappy frills running diagonally or horizontally, long sleeves, short sleeves, some dresses actually stop at the knee, some slit up the side. But to me, all basically the same design. Then again, as someone who once wore a floppy, black felt 'bippety-boppety' hat to a Deep Purple concert, I am not best placed to comment.

The three of us move to the side of the street, as a chiming bell from inside the chapel tells us the whole show is about to get under-way, and suddenly we are joined by Teri, who in turn has linked up with Ana and Maria, from the academy. The Spanish girls all express themselves delighted that Chrissie has made the effort to dress up, and her ensemble receives many admiring glances. 'Cristina, you are Espanees now!' cries Ana, in amazement. And quite honestly, she does look the part.

The band strikes up, a jaunty, happy tune, such a contrast to the Easter processions, and following a barrage of rockets from somewhere on the side of the mountain, which does my digestion no good whatsoever, we are off. The plinth, carried entirely by ladies, emerges from the little white chapel, the single bell of which is clanging crazily, and the cavalcade moves slowly away down the narrow cobbled street. The girls all shift to the centre of the road, naturally hogging the limelight, whereas I stay at the side, sometimes moving slightly ahead, sometimes dropping back. I pass several other acquaintances, and have to point out where my wife actually is, not that anyone could actually pick her out, from a distance, so well camouflaged as she is.

As the cavalcade wends its way slowly, with frequent pauses, towards the new part of town, flamenco-clad women join the procession, until it is impossible to see the beginning, or the end. The whole event seems like a giant social occasion, with a virgin and a band thrown in for good measure, and by the time we reach the first hairpin bend, the entire parade has descended into good-natured anarchy. At one point, the *trono* has completely disappeared from view, and many ladies are actually walking up the street, against the flow. Being almost mid-summer, it is still daylight, but a quick glance at my phone reveals it to be past nine-thirty. Has it really taken two hours to walk what amounts to less than about five hundred yards? Sounds impossible, but true.

My back is aching from walking so slowly, and my stomach is rumbling, a sure sign that we need to enact the second part of our plan for the evening, and bail out for something to eat in our favourite restaurant. Easier said than done, as my wife and her friends are nowhere in sight, having completely vanished. Are they in front, or behind? So intently have I been watching the proceedings I have completely forgotten, so trusting my instinct I head back up the hill to discover the British flamenco-wearer amid a group of around ten *Espaniolas*, all laughing and joking. I am reluctant to break up the party but manage to catch Chrissie's eye, she rubs her tummy and grins, the cue that she is ready to quit. Much hugging and kissing ensues, with promises to meet up again in the morning, for the caravan section of the weekend. As we weave our way down the slope Alicia's voice calls out from the crowd. 'Tomorrow! Booey!'

Saturday morning and another day of discovery in this crazy country. Chrissie has forgone her heavy flamenco dress in favour of a light cotton, navy-blue-and-white, polka-dot, knee-length number, which she cleverly knocked up a few weeks ago, ready for the summer. A woman of many talents. We assemble outside St Mary's just before eleven, presumably Santa Victoria made it back last night, if the round of explosions at two in the morning was anything to go by, unless, on the other hand, a small war broke out somewhere. The usual milling around of assorted Spaniards is taking place, although of the alleged caravans and oxen, there is no sign. Surely they are not inside the church? Who knows, although presumably we are about to find out, as from across the square comes the sound of wheels trundling, big, wooden cartwheels, by the sound of it. And there they are, the *booeys*, a pair of oxen, huge, magnificent beasts, brown and white, brass bells dangling from yokes around their necks, several feet of vicious-looking horn protruding from beneath their blue head-dresses, pulling a four-wheeled open wooden cart, decked with flowers. The majestic creatures, with their driver, come to rest outside the church door, then behind them come another pair, darker brown these, identical cart, who pull up behind their fellows. We edge closer to get a better view of these docile, placid animals, their dark, liquid eyes regarding the comings and goings with apparent disinterest. Just another day, in the lives of Spanish *booeys*.

The church doors creak open, the band bursts into life, and from inside comes a large silver cross bearing an embroidered pennant, followed by the figure of Santa Victoria, as seen last night. The flag is then mounted onto the first cart, Victoria onto the second, and after a few last-minute adjustments, and a quiet word from the drivers, the man-coo's plod serenely across the square, followed by the band and the remainder of the entourage. And us, of course. The direction they are heading seems impossible, descending as it does into a steep-sided valley, uneven cobbles waiting to catch the unwary, I myself having come a cropper just a few months ago. Our four-legged friends have no such worries however, coping easily with the gradient, bells tinkling, wheels crunching, as we pick our way down the hill, to the little square at the bottom, where the caravans, plus cheese, ham and rebelhito, are allegedly waiting. Personally I cannot wait to get stuck into a white wine and lemonade, with a whisky thrown in for good measure, having lined my stomach with a goodly layer of bacon and eggs this very morn, so as to be prepared, like the good Boy Scout I was.

And we start to laugh, for there, stretched out along the valley, as far as the eye can see, is a wagon train. Covered, miniature wagons, reminiscent of a scene from a John Wayne movie, only with more colour, and music. Blaring music, each 'caravan' competing with his fellow in both volume, and the number of different coloured spots on the canvas covers. A flamenco wagon train, if you will. We both take a step back, in utter amazement, and to give our ears chance to adjust to the assault. Sensory overload. Complete and utter Spanish madness. Some of the wagons seem to contain only children, half-a-dozen little ones chattering away loudly, passing round bags of vomit-inducing orange-coloured corn snacks, and bottles of cola. Other carts are bearing plates of food, Spanish hams, cheeses, crusty bread, *chorizo* of every shape and size, tortillas, plus crates of beer, and plastic barrels of who-knows-what, this *rebelhito* stuff hopefully. All we need now is for someone to offer us some.

And we don't have to wait very long. We decide to stroll towards the back of the wagon train, wherever that might be, stretching as it does around the bend. There could be twenty carts, or a hundred, who knows, but we are about to find out. Or maybe not. From the third wagon in line comes a shout, 'goood morning, you are Eengliss yes? Plees to share with us *comidas*, and beer!' A large man, late-thirties maybe, with a wide grin and bone-crushing handshake, I feel I have seen him before, but cannot place where. 'My name Jose, my woman she Veronica' he confirms, indicating a lady approaching with a tray of food. 'You take, plees!' and before I can protest a plate of ham and cheese is placed in one hand, a beer in the other. 'I see you, in acca-demmy of Eduardo' our new friend continues. 'I learn Eengliss, ver bad, in class basico', but I come to you class in Julie.'

Julie? As far as I am aware, there is no-one in the academy called Julie. 'Julie?'

'Yees, Julie! Abril, Mayo, Junio, Julie, Augusto...'

'July!' I smile, trying not to laugh at our new pupil, particularly as he has just provided us with lunch. 'April, May, June, July, August...'

'Ahh, I say you my Eengliss ver bad! Eduardo at acca-demmy he say me, must to Speak to Jonny and Cristina, natives of Eengliss! In Julie! Sorree, July! *Hoder!*' Jose places his arm around my neck, and for the first time I notice his eyes are not completely focused, and he is swaying slightly. Must have been a long night. 'Now plees we take *rebelhito*, ees tradition here in Espain, in *Romeria.*' I start to protest, mainly as both hands are occupied with food and beer, but resistance is futile. Jose rummages around in the back of his wagon, producing a suede-leather drinking vessel, maybe the size of a small dinner plate. He undoes the stopper, throws his head back, squeezes the skin and directs a jet of foaming fluid expertly down his throat. He screws up his eyes, wipes his mouth with the back of his hand, and passes the receptacle to me, Veronica meantime having relieved me of my burdens. The *cantina* is floppy, I can feel the liquid sloshing around inside, and straight away I know the chances of me repeating Jose's feat are next to zero, and that most of the *rebelhito* will end up down my front. Also, I am not sure what to expect. Wine and lemonade I can cope with, but exactly how much whisky is mixed in with it? Is it wine, lots of lemonade, and just a hint of whisky? Or wine, whisky and just a splash of lemonade? Only one way to find out, and I can sense a glint of a challenge in Jose's eyes. Chrissie and Veronica are giggling away, and a small crowd has formed, clearly expecting the Englishman to make a mess of his shirt. What they may not realise however is that they are looking at someone who once downed a pint of Old Peculier, whilst chewing a Mars Bar. I grab the floppy bottle and adopt a comic pose, rather like Tommy Cooper performing one of his famous tricks, milking the crowd. Tilting my head back, I wink at Chrissie, steady my aim, squeeze, and allowing for wind direction, the curvature of the earth, atmospheric pressure and the phase of the moon, a satisfying spray hits the back of my tonsils in perfect alignment. *Just like that!*

A huge roar erupts. 'OLE!' cries our new student, although my throat is burning, assaulted by what must have been almost neat whisky, with the merest dribble of wine, and a sniff of lemonade. Rot-gut whisky too, I've seen it in the supermarket, three Euros a litre. Single-malt it ain't. I pass the concoction to Chrissie, who clearly doesn't want to get any of this paint-stripper down her new dress, and who can blame her? She makes a good fist of waving the skin around, however, like a matador teasing a bull, then simply squeezes a few drops into her plastic wine-glass, and daintily sips. She receives another round of applause, and a hug from Veronica. 'Tu eres lista!' You are clever. Indeed she is.

I indicate to Jose that we are heading off to look at some of the other caravans. 'Plees, when start procession, you walk with we?' he pleads.

Sounds like a plan, but when is this thing actually getting under-way? Everyone is eating and drinking like crazy, and nobody seems the slightest bit concerned that nothing is actually happening. Presumably someone is in charge of this shindig, but who they are, and where they might be, is beyond me. The complete lack of urgency, or organisation, in this country is unbelievable, in the UK a huge row would have broken out by now, but glancing around at the spotty-dressed ladies dancing next to their caravans, their menfolk sloshing drinks and stuffing tortilla into their faces, I know where I'd rather be. And the sun is out, which always helps.

Moving off down the street, after promising our new friends to catch up with them somewhere on the route, we are enthralled by the sounds, colours and sheer variety of the covered wagons. Most are of the hooped canvas variety, but a number have been left open, one decorated with giant multicoloured wings, another shaped like a caterpillar with legs, and butterflies hovering above. Even the towing vehicles, mostly four-by-fours, with the odd tractor thrown in, are festooned with silk flowers, so much so that the drivers, when the time eventually comes to move off, will barely be able to see where they are going. Suddenly, as we turn the final corner and the last caravans of the procession appear, comes a shout from deep within a particularly large group of flamenco ladies. I have spots before my eyes, literally, so am unable to discern who might be trying to attract our attention, although I am prepared to admit the *rebelhito* and beer might have something to do with it, and the egg and bacon are also taking their toll. 'Cristina! I here!' My wife, having moderated her whisky-infused wine-beverage intake, soon spots another friend. Laura, occasional pupil, clarinettist in the marching band, and her woodwind colleagues, Victoria and Elena. Late teens/early twenties, lovely girls. I screw up my eyes, breathe deeply, and yes, there they are, a vision in spots, both large and small, in front of a cart decorated with balloons, and paper flowers.

'Jonnee! Come here plees! And Cristina, We have drink for you! Ver tradition! *Rebelhito!' Oh no, I am about to be plied with more drinks. Life can be an absolute bugger at times, can't it?* We cross the street, and after the obligatory hugging and kissing, a wine skin is produced, the girls expertly fire dainty little slooshes into their open mouths, lick their lips, and pass the leathery pouch to the teacher of Eengliss. This time, of course, Chrissie has no glass, so she tips her head back, places the skin directly above her open mouth, and gravity takes over, directing a tiny dribble on to her tongue. The girls, and several other ladies who might, or might not, be something to do with this caravan, burst into raucous applause. The honour of *la profesora* has been upheld. Then of course, the baton is passed to me. Feeling somewhat like a performing seal, I again strike the pose, but this time overconfidence is the order of the day, or maybe I have consumed one too many, as the resulting jet sprays across my face, hitting my left ear, and cascades down my shirt.

The ladies are creased up with laughter as I wipe the sticky concoction from my eyes, but before I can have another go a shout goes up, the drivers all stagger to their cabs, engines fire into life, and we are off. Amid choking clouds of diesel fumes, with more than a hint of whisky, the caravans lurch forwards, and the entire drunken procession is under way. Elena manages to grab a plate of tortilla before it disappears up the street, although we have nothing to worry about, as the whole thing comes to a shuddering halt. Fifty yards in about two hours. Remind me to phone the Guinness Book of Records, when we eventually get home. If we ever get there, before Christmas. Still, there is plenty to eat, the tortilla does the rounds, and someone spotty hands me a beer.

The hold-up is only temporary, however, as by the time we have leisurely strolled up to Laura's cart, the whole shooting-match is off again. 'Plees you walk with us?' Laura smiles. 'I passed my exam, thees week, so I have much thank-you, Cristina!' Cue lumps in throats, another success, one-hundred per-cent, so far, and we both give Laura a huge hug. She is clearly overjoyed, and so are we, bless her. So much so, that my throat is getting dry, and I feel the urgent need of a lemonade, and if it happens to contain the essence of Scotch, what the hell?

'We are also walking with some other students' Chrissie explains, 'so we will go to see them now, then come back, is that OK?'

'Of course!' Laura grins, 'but plees be quickly, I am much celebrating!'

We weave our way towards the front of the procession, past the wings and the caterpillar, avoiding as far as possible the engine fumes with a hint of whisky, to which has been added the pungent fragrance of burning clutches, to find that Jose and Veronica have vanished. Still, at this rate they cannot have gone far, so following the route, which is basically the same as Good Friday, we soon catch up with their caravan. But of our new student, there is no sign. Typical Spanish lightweight, cannot hold their booze, this lot. Crashed out in the back of the wagon, no doubt. Mind you, he was about six sheets to the wind, last time we saw him. Veronica greets us with a round of beers, and a plate of drumsticks, which I am hoping are chicken. 'Where is Jose?' Chrissie enquires, expecting to find this bear of a man snoring his head off, comatose, among the plates of *Jamon*.

'Driving,' his wife smiles, indicating a figure sitting in the cab of the *Santana*, essentially a Spanish Land-Rover.

Driving? The last time we saw him, he could barely speak, let alone stand. But there he is, perched on the tiny vinyl seat, wide grin across his features, eyes attempting, but failing spectacularly, to focus. 'Jonneee!' he cries, as I poke my head through the driver's window, so close that we could kiss, were we that way inclined. 'Plees, you take!' unhooking a wine-skin from the rear-view mirror. A different wine-skin than the one we sampled earlier, and glancing into the back seat I spy four of the things, whether empty or full it is impossible to say, or indeed whether they contain this vicious cocktail, but clearly he is determined not to go thirsty, on the journey.

And so the day passes. We alternate between Jose's cart, and that of Laura, along the crowded streets, until we reach the parting of the ways, where one road leads up the side of the mountain, the other towards the new part of town. I am boiling hot, and in need of a good lie down. 'Jose, we are heading home, have a siesta, thank you so much for everything, we will see you in July, at the academy.'

The big man frowns in concentration. 'No! We see you thees night, plees. You come to top of mountain, ees *feria*, big party, much drinkings!' *OK, if you insist, if we have any strength left, that is.* We promise to meet up later, digestion permitting, and with a wave of the hand and a cloud of diesel, he disappears up the hill, with Veronica sitting in the back of the *carroza*, still holding a plate of cheese.

We stroll back to Laura, again offer our grateful thanks, and congratulations on her exam results, and arrange to meet up the following week for a celebratory beer. Arriving home, I fling myself on the bed, fully clothed, and am asleep in ten seconds, or less.

Several hours later, suitably refreshed, we are ready for the off again, up the mountain, big party, much drinkings. And this *feria* thing, which I am assuming is a fair. Sounds like one anyway, although we have been wrong before... The only problem with going to a party up a mountain is getting there of course, and as much drinkings are on the cards, plus my intake already today, means one mode of transport only. Walking. And even though it is half-ten in the evening, and almost dark, it is still over thirty degrees, I imagine. Still, coming down will be easier, hopefully. The chapel where Santa Victoria is supposed to be resting is a white-painted building offering spectacular views over the olive groves and mountains behind, and is known to us as the 'White Church.' Heading out of the town, up the snaking, narrow country lane, we are joined by a few other walkers, and quite a few cheats, in cars. 'Could do with a bus service up here!' Chrissie pants. *Yeah right, a bus service to the middle of nowhere!* For the top of a mountain, or as near the top as makes no difference, is a strange place for a religious building, in my opinion, although you do see these places dotted over this part of Spain. Hermitages, I suppose, hence the Spanish name *ermita*. And the other curious aspect is the huge car-park cum rest-area outside, far larger that a tiny chapel would possibly need. This route is one of our regular walks, or it was in the winter and spring before it became simply too hot to stroll up mountains, but with stone picnic benches and space for hundreds of people, it never ceases to amaze us, as we have never seen a single soul up here, and the chapel is certainly never open.

As we near, the top, we are not really sure what to expect. There were over one hundred caravans at the start this morning, are they all going to be up here? If so, that will be over twenty tractors, four times that number of four-by-fours, plus all the carts, at least five hundred people, plus the ones who have made their way up independently, like us. And four oxen. And what will they all be doing? Chatting, obviously, much drinkings and a big party, according to Jose. But where? Certainly not in the picnic area. And everywhere else is mountainside, surely? And so far, I have to say, we cannot hear a thing.

Just then we are passed by a bus, chugging purposefully up the hillside, packed with party-goers, all shouting and waving, as Spaniards are occasionally known to do, particularly at British idiots, walking. Chrissie turns to face me. 'What fool said there was no bus service?' Guilty as charged, although in my defence, this must be a one-off *Romeria* bus, a Spanish park-and-party, if you will.

Cresting the ridge we are suddenly hit for six by a wall of sound, a sensory assault, a heaving, thumping cacophony of noise, dozens of competing sound systems at maximum volume, which stops us dead in our tracks. The picnic area outside our peaceful little white church is now a giant collection of sideshows, shooting galleries, hoopla, hot-dogs, candy-floss, pony rides, shove-halfpenny, a soccer penalty-shoot-out and a shady collection of dubious-looking traders selling knock-off handbags, DVD's and Nike trainers. A pop-up bar has been erected outside the church door, and there, in the far corner, shoved against the wall, are the two ox-carts. Of the beasts themselves, there is no sign. Cars are parked at crazy angles on the steeply sloping hillside, tents have been pitched optimistically at ludicrous angles although the possibility of getting even a wink of sleep in this bedlam is unthinkable.

The bulk of the noise appears to be coming from a patch of scrub-land behind the church, so before checking out the sideshows I gesture to Chrissie, as speaking to her is simply not an option, that we explore that area. We have to attempt to find Jose and Veronica, a notion beyond ridiculous, given this lunacy. We stumble off the tarmac, and suddenly there they are, the caravans, spread out randomly across a precipitous rocky gradient, some almost touching, huge gazebos and family sized frame-tents squeezed into impossible gaps, flashing lights and lasers piercing the night sky, and each one with huge speakers turned up to skull-splitting volume. We have to get out of here before our heads explode.

Returning to the picnic area, where shouting is at least possible, we explore the sideshows. I have always loved these end-of-the-pier attractions, and quite fancy myself as a sharp-shooter. We study the prizes and I have a real taking for a pair of cute-looking cuddly bulls. The rest of the prizes are rubbish, Real Madrid key-rings and other tat, but these *toros* would look good on the dresser. 'GOT A EURO?' I bellow.

'WHY?' Chrissie mouths, 'WE. DON'T. WANT. ANY. OF. THIS. CRAP!' but laughing, she pulls out a coin nevertheless. I hand it to the stall-holder, and get three corks in return, plus a rifle of dubious vintage, which might have featured in the gunfight at the OK Corral. The original one, not the movie. Right, first shot as a range-finder, then two kills. Primeval. Man and battered pop-gun versus a cuddly toy. I place the first cork in the barrel, crank back the trigger mechanism, sight and squeeze. Bang! A direct hit, straight between the eyes. And my target doesn't move. Not a millimetre. The stall-holder is impassive, and Chrissie is in stitches. 'BLOODY GLUED DOWN!' I reckon she is right, but try to look nonchalant. Second shot, I need to get lower, so I am firing in an upward trajectory, catch the blighter on the chin. And I could do the same with the bull, come to that. Repeating the action, but lowering my torso, I catch the grinning man-coo in the throat, lifting him off his feet, and onto the ground. I cheer loudly, attracting the attention of some onlookers, and the less-than-pleased showman. Two shots down, one to go, and I want that second bull. I need that second bull. This is war. My very status as a man is at stake. Failure is not an option. Chambering my final round, breathing deeply, lowering my pulse, sniffing the air, and crouching, the cork catches the fluffy beast in the neck, and down he goes, to a huge shout from the audience, which for a few blissful seconds, drowns out the blaring music. Joy, sheer, utter joy. Gripping my prizes, like some ten-year-old schoolboy, I turn to Chrissie. 'HERE YOU ARE, TWO BOOEYS, FOR YOU!'

Foregoing the hoopla and hot-dogs, we arrive at a stall where there are boxes of sweets laid out on the ground, the object being to throw a twenty-cent coin to land on top, to win. I have a suitable coin in my pocket, so, gesturing to Chrissie that she should have a go, I then run through my suggested strategy. I am of course a champion marksman. Crouching low, like Jonny Wilkinson lining up a World Cup-winning penalty, I lick the back of the coin, to provide a bit of friction, bearing in mind the box is wrapped in cellophane, curl my index finger round the front, to give suitable back-spin, and mimic a gentle lob. I pass the money to my wife, she grabs it angrily and hurls it it the general direction of the prizes. What a girly shot! I mean, it is the twenty-first century, where there is no place for gender stereotyping, but that was a complete and utter waste of four-bob. Turning away in disgust, I have visions of the coin zooming past the stall, landing in the dust, being trampled in and lying, undetected for several millennia, perhaps until the year twenty-five twenty-five, if man is still alive, and if there are still metal-detectorists. So imagine my total amazement as another shout goes up, and my wife emerges from the crowd, clutching her box of sweets. Score one for the girlies!

Chrissie is dancing around, waving her prize, when along comes Mohammed, he of Paolo's cottage and the huge pile of bricks fame. 'Hey Cristina!' he cries, 'you are a winner!' and he digs into his pocket and retrieves two twenty-cent coins, which he insists she 'invests' on more boxes of sweets. Beginners luck, of course. She could surely not replicate her victory? Mohammed and I embrace, as is the norm here, but I also am keen to shield his eyes from stray coins, which based on the last effort, could go anywhere. We are still thumping each others backs when another shout pierces the air, I turn to see the aggrieved purveyor of choccies-to-win handing over another box, and my wife performing her second victory jog. Mohammed is beaming widely, whereas I am speechless. One more coin left, she is on a hat-trick, surely an impossibility? Although stranger things have happened, and surely worth a wager? Why is there never a branch of Ladbroke's around, when you need one?

Without further ado, or preparation of any sort, the marks-woman lobs her final coin in the general direction of the sweets, it bounces off one, slides tantalisingly across another, then, almost in slow motion, drops onto a third, and comes to rest. She has done it! Almost too embarrassed to collect her prize, she nevertheless whoops with delight, then presents one to Mohammed, who smilingly declines. 'Not halal, can't eat that!' he chuckles, a prohibition which never seems to trouble his conscience when he is having a beer.

It is time to go, been a long day, and we are not really in need of anything more to drink, until next Wednesday, at the very earliest. Strolling back down the mountain, hearing gradually returning, Chrissie gently squeezes my hand. 'What an amazing day that was!'

'It certainly was' I giggle, 'two bulls and three boxes of toffees! We are the champions!'

'Not the crappy bulls, you plonker!' she bridles, but she knows I am only joking. It was a truly memorable day, weekend in fact, all the better for us being on the inside, so to speak. Not simply spectators, but actually invited to join in the processions, not once, but twice. Hugely gratifying, testament to her in particular, getting us started with the private pupils, building a network of not just Spanish contacts, but lasting friends. A real skill, whereas my dubious talents lie solely in mixing a bit of cement for a Cockney wide-boy.

'It was a spectacular weekend actually,' I confirm, 'and all thanks to you.' We have reached our front door, and I am ready to drop. 'There was just one fly in the ointment, however. Spoiled it a little bit, for me.'

Chrissie, as is her nature, is at once full of concern. 'What is it, what was wrong, for you?'

I take my time answering, pondering, drawing out the suspense. 'Well,' I sigh, 'do you really think the bulls I won you are a load of crap?'

Two weeks later, as dusk is falling, we are back at the 'White Church', to celebrate the end of Santa Victoria's sojourn on the mountain, her first night was presumably a bit rowdy, to say the least, although I imagine it settled down after that. So now, she is returning to her home, the little white chapel in the old part of town, where the Romeria started that Friday evening, known to us as the 'White Church Near Mohammed's Mother.' Not terribly inventive names, but it is hardly our fault if most of the chapels and churches here are painted white. Apart from the 'Pink Church' that is. In stark contrast to our last visit, tonight everything is calm, peaceful, tranquil, and no-one would ever suspect that a fortnight ago, the mother of all parties was taking place right here. Well, apart from the entire population of Santa Marta, and the surrounding villages, that is.

Suddenly, annoyingly, a bus comes creaking round the bend. For a country lane with no bus services, I am getting sick to death of seeing the damned things, particularly as they always arrive when we have already reached the top. The door is flung open and out scramble the town band. Actually, it is only a small bus, containing about half the band, the drums and cornets by the look of it, with no sign of Laura, Victoria or Elena. Got the night off, by the look of it. We stroll across the picnic area towards the chapel, and I grab Chrissie by the arm. 'Look, it was about here that I won you those two booeys!'

'As if I could ever forget' she sighs. The bulls lasted one day in the sitting room, being consigned to the spare room on day two, and despite my best efforts to sneak them back, there they have remained.

For the first time since we arrived here in this crazy town, the White Church is open, so we sneak inside, where Santa Victoria is lined up on her plinth, amid a bed of flowers, similar to her 'upward' journey, ready for the off. A few people are standing around taking selfies with the Saint, which seems somewhat disrespectful to me, but no-one seems the slightest bit put-out, even the two old ladies by the door manning the chapel shop, which comes as an even bigger shock. I mean, Westminster Abbey has a retail outlet, catering for countless millions of visitors, but this place? Only open for two days a year? And the souvenirs are specific, bearing the legend 'Santa Victoria, patron saint of Labradors.' Mugs, key-rings, medallions, candle-holders, all they need are a few tea-towels and sticks of rock, and this could be Torquay. Our younger daughter has a labrador, and I consider getting her a mug, but decide it might not be in the best possible taste, so we smile at the 'shopkeepers' and make our way outside, ready for the 'downward' journey.

The band have formed up, the chapel bell is chiming, the incense is lit, and the all-male carriers are ready. 'Typical!' Chrissie hisses, 'the women carried her around the town, and up the hill to St Mary's that Friday night, and now the men get the easy ride, all downhill!'

I suck in my teeth. 'Not so sure about that,' I venture 'I bet coming downhill is harder, as gravity will start to take over, and they will struggle to hold the plinth back. Remember when you went downhill on Good Friday, was that harder than going back up?'

My wife screws up her eyes. 'You know what, Mister Know It All, I am going to throw those cursed bulls out the minute we get home. In the bin with the damned things!' Looks like I might actually have won an argument, for once, although the night is still young. She will get me back, for sure, but for now there is no time for domestic bickering as the *trono* is being hoisted onto the manly shoulders, the small bell on the front is being tinkled, and we are off on our first rural procession. The drums and cornets strike up, the priest and incense boys lead the way, and we tag along behind with the rest of the spectators. And what a spectacular route it is. The town, laid out below us, street lights starting to twinkle, and the mountain, towering above, glowing gold in the setting sun.

After negotiating the tricky, stony hairpin bends, we approach the town, where huge crowds await. The remainder of the band are spread out across the street, then round the corner come half a dozen pure white Andalucian thoroughbred horses, each one ridden by a man in tight jeans, white open-neck shirt with a red sash, and a black felt sombrero. My wife perks up noticeably, having seemed to be flagging on the last part of the descent. 'Oooo, that makes a nice change' she purrs, completely ignoring a group of ladies in spotty dresses performing a flamenco dance on the other side of the road. 'Quickly, let's follow the horses, never mind Santa Victoria!' She needn't worry. Horses, dancers, the remainder of the band, the *trono* and the *costeleros* all funnel into the tight narrow streets of the old town, then come to a grinding halt. We have managed to edge ahead of the chaotic parade, but still within sight of the tight jeans, and soon the reason for the delay becomes apparent. A refreshment stop. From out of the little cottages, a small army of women appear, each bearing a tray of home-made cakes, closely followed by yet more ladies with huge jugs of what appears to be wine, and plastic glasses. A tray is shoved under my nose. *Pest-in-yo? Tomas!* Take a pestin-yo. Looks like a sugar-coated deep-fried pastry to me, which is just what I need having just walked up and down a mountain. I take a bite, then a deep breath. Blimey, it has alcohol in it, a lot of alcohol, too, a spirit by the taste of it.

Chrissie is also sampling the delights of the pest-in-yo, but getting a running commentary into the bargain. 'Pest-in-yo con wicky, con anneee, con ron, con Malaga' explains the cook, pointing to the different sugary offerings on her tray. With whisky, anise, rum and Malaga wine. *Don't they have a rebelhito version?*

She chooses the anise variety, her favourite spirit since moving to this country, takes a bite, then her eyes almost cross. 'Mucho anneee!' she grins. Another lady slaps a plastic glass into my other hand, and sloshes about half a pint of this ruby-coloured liquid, some into my glass but a goodly measure over my toes, which quite frankly could do with a bit of a swill, having just conveyed me down the dusty hillside. Lucky I am wearing sandals, although I am fearful of this heady concoction taking the colour out of the leather. But not for long, what the hell, they were only a few Euros. Complete strangers are plying me with food and drink, what do a few spillages matter?

After half-an-hour of this largesse, everyone seems to have completely forgotten about the procession. Sadly however the trays are empty, the pitchers drained, so it is time to move on. Actually, we are only around a hundred yards from home, but such are the crowds pressed into this tiny, narrow street, that we are unable to squeeze by, and simply have to wait until the parade passes our hairpin.

Finally escaping, we head homewards, reflecting on another momentous evening. 'Tell you what,' Chrissie smiles, 'forget cooking tonight, let's go down Manuel's tapas bar.'

And why not. We are repeatedly given free food in this ridiculous country. So let us head down to Manuel's, and make a night of it.....

CHAPTER 41. 'IF WE ARE STILL HERE NEXT YEAR...'

We are in the foothills of the Pyrenees, parked at the side of the road, staring down, in the gathering gloom, at a camp-site. On our way back to the UK, almost a year to the day since we left, we have some things to discuss. Big things. Like, are we staying in Spain? Is it what we want to do with the rest of our lives? Or the next few, years, at any rate. Ever since we arrived in this country, every discussion about the future has been prefaced by the sentence 'if we are still here next year...' Not for any particular reason, simply that we have the choice. Nothing is set in stone. This is our first joint return visit since we left the UK at the end of last August. I went back before Christmas, following a change of tenant in our bungalow, to redecorate, and Chrissie was there for a week or so in the New Year, when her mother was ill, but now we are having a holiday, and I have to say, we are looking forward to it, despite a phenomenally successful year in Spain. Still miss the old place, I guess. Looking forward to seeing the girls too, of course.

'So are we going into this camp-site, or are we just going to sit here all night?' It has been a long day, travelling almost the entire width of the country, from bottom left to top right, along back-roads, from the dry, dusty olive groves of Andalucia, through the vineyards of Rioja and Navarra, the ancient kingdom of Aragon, towards the brooding, majestic mountains separating Spain from France. And Chrissie is keen to get there. 'You said we were going camping in the Pyrenees, the last time I checked there was a tent, two sleeping bags, and two pillows in the boot. Those mountains there, are the Pyrenees, I saw the sign, and I have the map. That is a camp-site. SO COME ON!'

She has a point, but I have reservations. So I adopt a man-pose. Suck in my teeth, rub my chin. 'Yes, I admit it's a camp-site, but look at the size of the place. Has to be twenty-five Euros a night!'

'So what?' she cries. 'I will lend you the money, if that is all you are worrying about!'

'Yes, but think about it,' I sigh. It's gone eight now, by the time we get booked in it will be past nine, and all the facilities will be closed. The pool. The ping-pong tables. The crazy golf. The Tiger Club for the kiddies. Rory the Tiger will be long gone. The bingo will be finished, the knobbly-knees contest and glamorous-granny, over. The disco will be churning out eighties crap, Rick-bloody-Astley, Duran-Du-bloody-ran. The beer will be five quid a glass, for that watery French rubbish. And look at all those damn kids, running around. We won't get a wink.'

My wife stares in disbelief. 'I wonder about your sanity, sometimes, I really do. Is this what my life has become? Am I condemned to spend the rest of my days listening to this nonsense? Rory the Tiger? How many years ago was that? Our kids are grown women, now! And I can remember you dancing to Rick-Du-bloody-ran, as it happens!'

Surely not? I will admit to many things, some of them not too savoury, in the harsh light of day. But dancing to Rick-Du-bloody ran? Over my dead body. Not my era. 'Tiger Feet,' by Mud. Cockney Rebel. Sweet, 'Ballroom Blitz'. The Rubettes. I even went to a Showaddywaddy gig once, free tickets mind you. And whisper this, I saw David Essex at Pontin's, in Paignton. 'Old me close, don't let me go!' Classics, all.

'SO WHAT ARE WE DOING, THE FERRY LEAVES ON SUNDAY!'

It does indeed, but I was a Boy Scout, so I am looking for somewhere a bit more, er, rustic, and free. Whip out my penknife, and whittle up a bivouac, covered with ferns. Gather some sticks, rub a couple of cubs together, get a fire going, sausages, and baked beans. Potatoes in the embers, charred to a crisp on the outside, raw in the middle. Roast a chicken in a biscuit-tin, covered in mud. Milk a cow in the morning, instant coffee, in a tin mug. The food of the

Gods. I turn the ignition, and the ancient Volvo coughs reluctantly into life. 'Trust me,' I smile serenely, 'I will find us somewhere better than this!'

My wife racks her seat back, holds her head in both hands, and begins to count. 'One, two, three.....'

Five miles up the road, and another thousand feet in elevation, I spot the perfect resting place, in the last glow of the sunset. A green lane, surrounded by fields on either side. Completely shielded from the road, tinkling mountain stream, for ablutions. Ideal. I slide out of the car, stretch my back, breathe the fresh mountain air. Bit parky, mind you, good job we brought the sleeping bags. Still, we are about seven-thousand feet above sea-level. Last night, in Santa Marta, it was over thirty degrees. Here, I wouldn't be surprised to find a frost on the tent, in the morning. Chrissie joins me, then jumps rapidly back in the car. 'YOU. CANNOT. BE. SERIOUS? The tent is in the boot. The mallet is under the back seat. The pegs are God knows where. Let me know when the tent is pitched, then fetch me my fleecy pyjamas!'

I love doing this. Laying out the tent, finding a flat piece of ground, in with the poles, untying the guy-lines, tapping in the pegs, tying the door-flap back, open the car boot, sleeping bags, pillows laid out. I tap on the car window, 'your chamber awaits, your majesty!'

My wife regards the basic, two-person structure. 'When I promised to marry you, almost forty years ago, for richer or poorer, I never envisaged, in my wildest dreams, that we would still be doing this, when we were retired, or that we would still be this poor. Surely to God we could have afforded an hotel?'

I smile sweetly. 'Of course we could, but some impersonal hotel? Where's the fun in that? It would be forgotten, in a few weeks. This night, you will remember all your life! Back to nature, and all that!'

She snorts derisively. 'No, I will never forget this, that is what you should have said! I will never forget you were too mean to spring for a guest-house, and had me, a woman approaching sixty, in a cheap, crappy Chinese tent, not enough room to change my underwear, in some boggy field next to a mosquito-infested swamp.'

'Ahh, where's your sense of adventure!' I giggle, 'come on, get the ham rolls out the boot, we'll sit outside the tent, watch the stars, then cuddle up inside, warm and snug!'

'Yes and that's another thing! You are too mean to buy a girl dinner. Cheese and ham rolls, which have been gently steaming away in the boot all day. And for breakfast tomorrow too. I should have married Alan Summers! Even he wasn't as tight as you!' She is not happy, but I think it will be all-right. Or maybe not. 'And you can forget all about a cuddle, sunshine!'

Suddenly the mention of my some-time love-rival jolts me from my Boy Scout reverie. 'Alan Summers? That lanky, Local-Government-employed pillock? In your semi-detached suburban, Mrs James? Do me a favour!'

She storms to the car boot, snatches the sweaty crusty rolls, ham for me, cheese for her, slings the bag in my direction, then slumps, cross-legged, outside the Oriental two-person shelter. Oh yes, it is definitely going to be all-right!

It must have been around two in the morning when the bells started up. Cow-bells. Alpine cow-bells, that dull, clanking, metallic sound, reminiscent of Switzerland, Heidi, St Bernard dogs, and cuckoo-clocks, that chocolate with the light-blue wrapper. That cheese full of holes. Lake Geneva, where Deep Purple had their *Smoke on the Water* moment. Suddenly I am wide-awake. Cows? Bells? There were no cattle in sight when I pitched the tent, and surely we are safe here, outside the field. Unless the creatures have escaped, and are about to come galloping down the lane, sticking their wet, bovine faces through the tent flap, or worse, stampeding over the top of us in the darkness. It is pitch black, both inside the tent, and outside, as I poke my head through for an exploratory peep, and freezing cold, I am wearing only shorts and a tee-shirt, and groping around for my plimsolls, I stagger to my feet then crash headlong into the undergrowth, catching my foot on a guy-line, and stubbing my toe on a tent-peg. Swearing loudly, I suddenly realise Chrissie is nowhere in sight. She has vanished, together with her sleeping-bag and pillow. Has she driven away and found an hotel somewhere? No, she would not have taken her sleeping gear, in that case. And if she has just popped out to *powder her nose*, likewise. My eyes are gradually adjusting to the blackness and I can just about make out the silver shape of the Volvo, so shuffling my way towards it I need to switch on the headlights, and find out what the hell is going on. Grasping the door handle, I am just about to yank it open when I spot the sleeping form of my wife, curled up in the back seat, head on the pillow, tucked up warm and snug in her bag.

I back stealthily away from the car. One problem solved. Now, what about these cursed cows? The bells are not getting any louder, farther away if anything, and quite honestly I am so tired, and so cold, it's decision made. Chrissie is safe and sound in the tank, so crawling inside the tent, flopping back into my bag, I am asleep in seconds.

'WAKEY WAKEY, RISE AND SHINE!' Daylight is creeping into the tent as my wife's voice, like some sadistic sargent-major, invades my peaceful reverie. Through half-closed eyes I see her yank open the zip of the tent, and poke her freshly-made-up face through. 'Well, what a wonderful restful night I had!' she grins. 'Lovely and comfy I was, snuggled up in the back seat. I thought I might have to run the heated seats if it got a bit nippy, but I was so warm and toasty. But what is this white on the tent? Frost? Ooh, I hope you were warm enough in here! I love these mountains, you must bring me here again! So calm, so silent. Breakfast will be slightly delayed, while it thaws out, so I have been down feeding the horses!'

I am still half-asleep. 'Horses? What horses?'

'Down there in the meadow, there are two of them, in a paddock, with bells tied round their necks, Alpine bells, such a pretty sound, don't you think, tinkling away. I have been feeding them.'

'Feeding them? What with? Not my breakfast rolls, I hope!'

'No, I told you, the rolls are stiff. Polo's, I gave them, I know you shouldn't, but they looked so adorable!'

I sit bolt upright, now fully awake. 'POLO'S? MY POLO'S? You know very well we don't have many left. I told you we need to buy another stock, in England. And you're giving them away to bloody horses, the same damned ones I suspect of waking me up in the middle of the night! And start the car, will you, the rolls are wrapped in tinfoil, I can put them on the engine, thaw them out a bit, because I am absolutely STARVING!'

My wife dissolves into laughter, and flops onto the grass, kicking her legs in the air. 'Beautiful, absolutely beautiful. Got you back, Sonny Jim!' She regains her feet, grabs the front of my tee-shirt, and pulls it tight around my throat. 'So listen here, sunshine.' she hisses. The change is astounding. 'Don't you ever, ever, suggest we go wild camping again. Or. I. Will. Kill. You. Maybe not that night, maybe when you are least expecting it. But I will do away with you. UNDERSTOOD?' I nod furiously, half choking. 'So pack away that pathetic excuse of a tent and get me out of these cursed ruddy mountains, over the top and down into France, where you will stop in the first village we come across, and buy me the biggest breakfast they have. *Comprendo?*'

That was Saturday morning. It is now Sunday evening, and we are on a beach near Calais, waiting for the midnight ferry to Dover, the full turning of the circle, twelve months on. Saturday evening we spent in a lovely little rural camp-site in the middle of France, no Tiger-Club, no glamorous granny, just a shower block, and peace and quiet. Eight Euros. Perfect. 'OK, so let's have a walk on the beach, then grab a bite to eat in a restaurant somewhere. Maybe we can find that little place we went last year, with the pensioners discount!' And I quickly scrabble out of the car, to avoid any chance of being done away with. Then quickly scrabble back inside, as it's absolutely freezing. Grey clouds, howling gale. The English channel, at the end of August. 'Quick, open the boot, get the coats out!' A real shock to the system, gone are the tee-shirts, shorts and flip-flops, back are the fleeces, long trousers, and walking shoes. This is what living in the sunshine does for you. Makes you forget the weather, in northern Europe.

Suitably attired, we begin our walk on the flat, sandy beach. The coast of Kent is just visible on the horizon, and in just a few hours we will be there, back in Blighty. So are we staying in Spain? 'Right, discussion time!' I smile. 'What do you think?'

Chrissie hunches her coat round her neck, pulling up the zip as far as it will go. 'I think I haven't been this cold, since we were here last year! she grimaces. 'I'd forgotten how bad it was up here!'

'So chalk one up for staying in Spain then!' I giggle. 'Anything else?'

'Well you know my answer, because we have talked about it before. We have gorgeous weather, a fantastic standard of living, a lovely house which can only get better, as we terrace more of the garden, and we are so fortunate to have made so many wonderful Spanish friends, and been accepted into local society, far quicker than I would ever have thought possible. We have fresh food and decent wine every day for what, forty quid a week? It is a wonderful life, all told. A huge success. But my big problem is that I miss having a good old girly chat with a few British women. It is hopeless in Santa Marta. Lucy is fine but everything she does she has to check with Paul first, or she has to wait around for him to come home. How many times have the pair of us actually been out for coffee, in twelve months? Twice? And Diane? Gaffer doesn't let her out of his sight. Remember that one time she managed to escape for half an hour, and he followed us down the cafe? Of course, the British women who have holiday homes here, Maggie with Colin, Ros with Jake, and Janie with Nigel in our street, are fantastic, but they are only here a couple of weeks a year. They have all said they are coming in September or October, but after that, nothing until the New Year.'

I do feel so sorry for Chrissie, we have talked about this problem endlessly, I have racked my brains for a solution, but we simply cannot magic some female company out of thin air.

'Marie from the library group is almost fluent,' she continues, 'and she is great company, but she has Luis and the kids, and with the long three-month school summer holiday, she cannot get away in June, July or August. I haven't seen her since the end of May. Teri will be fluent very soon, the way she is progressing, but she has her architect job so is only able to get out of the office from time to time. Anyway, there is nothing we can do about it. So what about you?'

'Well' I sigh, 'the biggest problem for me, or potential problem, is the bungalow in the UK. The change of tenants.'

'Why?' Chrissie ponders. 'I thought Steve, the new tenant, was settled there? We have management now by the agents, so what is the problem?'

'I am sure you are right,' I continue, 'we blundered at first by not having management, but Greg next door was supposed to be keeping an eye out, and doing any handyman jobs which cropped up. Then he moved away, left us in the lurch a bit, but we have management now, so that is fine. No, what I didn't take into account, when I dreamed up this plan, was changing tenants, because for every void period, we are losing money, and that is the bulk of our income of course. We are still learning this business, we knew nothing about letting, and I am sure it will be OK long-term, but if we get changes in tenants every six months, we might have to rethink. Who knows? But again, there is little we can do about it.'

Chrissie takes a deep breath. 'Well, not looking good, is it? Two big negatives. And both things which are out of our hands, to a large extent.'

We have reached the end of the beach. Time to turn back, and try to hunt down that pensioners menu. I glance across the murky waters of the channel at the grey, forbidding outline of the English coast. Are we seriously talking about returning? There will be no spectacular sunset here tonight, that's for sure. And we haven't seen an olive tree for two days, either. 'So, anything else?'

Chrissie shrugs. 'Well just little things, really. I did miss the autumn last year. We didn't really get one, in Santa Marta, did we? You know I used to love kicking through crisp autumn leaves.'

I start to laugh, a huge release of tension. 'Yes, well, for autumn leaves, you need trees! Deciduous trees, which shed their leaves. And you know very well that olives are evergreen. And the only other trees we have are those Mediterranean pines. So no, we didn't get an autumn. But we didn't get a winter, either, did we? Remember winter, do you? Bare trees, grey skies, freezing cold? A bit like today, really! Remember Christmas Day walking Gaffer's dogs round the mountain? We were sweating! And how much did we spend on gas bottles, for that portable gas heater? How much was our total winter fuel bill? Thirty Euros? Not much more. Forty tops. I used to spend twenty quid a week on anthracite, in the bungalow. Anyway, we did have an autumn in our own garden. The fig tree shed all its leaves, remember? Huge leaves, big crunchy ones!'

'Yes, but in January!' she giggles. 'You cannot have an autumn in January!'

'OK, I know what you mean about autumn, but think of the places in Spain we came through on Friday, once we had left Andalucia. They had trees there, we could easily have a weekend away in the autumn, do a bit of wild camping...NO! I mean find a small hotel, do a bit more exploring, a bit further afield.'

My wife squeezes my arm. 'Sounds good to me! And look, over there in the village, there is that restaurant with the pensioners menu. Last one there pays!' And for once, she lost....

Rolling off the ferry in Dover in the early hours, I need my wits about me, driving on the left again, in this cavalcade of lorries, coaches, caravans and cars, but it comes back naturally, just like we've never been away. We are heading for Bristol to stay for a few days with Chrissie's mother, so I want if possible to get along the M4 heading west, and grab five hours kip in the car in the first services after the M25, then head down to Bristol in the daylight. I had forty winks on the boat, so I should be good for three hours driving, but if I start to feel sleepy we will have to pull over earlier. Soon, the traffic thins out and we are rolling along, and before long we are past Heathrow, and pull into the next services. To be confronted by a rather unpleasant shock, to say the least. 'Two hours free parking only,' reads the sign, 'after which you pay £8. Failure to pay the £8 will result in a penalty of £90, and we have your registration number on our plate recognition cameras.' Or words to that effect.

'The swine!' I cry, in my best Victor Meldrew voice. 'The filthy swine! Two hours only? This is a joke, right? Is this supposed to be a motorway services, where people can rest up? I don't believe this. I am not paying those bastards £8. Since when have you had to pay in a services. Why? It's not like an airport, or Wembley Stadium!'

'OK OK' Chrissie soothes. 'I will set the phone, we can grab an hour and fifty minutes here, then we go on to the next services. It's probably because this one is near London. I am sure the next one will be different.'

So back goes my seat, I drift away, but after what seems like about five minutes, Chrissie is tapping me on the arm. 'Come on, time to move.' Ridiculous. Absolutely ridiculous. I feel like mooning at the number plate recognition camera, if only I knew where it was. So on another twenty miles or so to the next services, and this time I am rendered speechless, as there, at the entrance, is exactly the same sign.

Or almost speechless. 'What sort of country is this? What must foreign visitors think? Compare this to Spain, where the services have huge expanses of land with no restrictions whatsoever!'

So another hour-fifty, and we are off again. 'What time does your Mum get up?' I ask. 'Because I reckon we should press on to Bristol, stop in her apartment-block car park, and get a couple of hours there.'

'She is not usually up and about until around nine, I think' she replies. Perfect, another couple of hours kip there, then catch the mother-in-law just as she is getting the egg and bacon on! Result!

Sadly not. We pull into the parking area, to discover yet more restrictions. Visitors need a permit. 'Not to worry,' Chrissie sighs. 'Mum has a permit, my brother uses it, I remember now, she told me they had introduced this system. We don't have the permit yet, but it's only six o'clock, no wardens are around at this hour, so come on, back with the seats!'

After the broken, restless night, I am shattered, but at least we are here now. 'Right, heads down until nine, into your Mum's, then later this morning I will pop down the butchers, get her some of that ham off the bone she loves, one of his cheese pasties for you, and a home-made pork pie for me. Then tonight, down the pub, fish n chips! OK?'

Chrissie smiles in the affirmative, I crank back my seat, and am away to the land of nod. Thirty seconds later, although it might have been half an hour, comes a tapping on the car window. I half open one eye, and spy a parking warden. For pity's sake, can't a man get a decent nap in this country? Where we live, sleeping is a national obsession. Stuff him! I decide to ignore the officious little oaf. No such luck. He taps again, so I snap bolt upright, conjuring up my best venomous angry face, and roll down the window. 'WHAT?'

'You cannot park here,' he whines. Residents, and visitors, only.' Well technically, we are both, as we kept mother-in-law's address as our UK abode for official communications, and we have correspondence to prove it, in the suitcase, in the boot, but I am damned if I am rummaging around for it, at seven in the morning. And, of course, we are visitors.

Chrissie is well aware of my intense dislike of petty officialdom. I usually react badly, to jobsworths. 'It's OK,' she smiles, we are visiting my mother, in number twenty-six, but she is not up yet. We have driven from Spain, you see, but we are a bit early!'

Anyone with half a brain would have wished us a good morning, with a smile, and gone about his business. Not this idiot, who clearly has less than half. Which is why he has this job. 'I don't care if you have driven from Timbuktu. You need the permit. Anyone can say they are a visitor. No permit, you are getting a ticket.'

I crank the seat back up, start the engine, and flash him my best smile. 'Right, we are off to the newsagents, to buy a lottery ticket, and if we win, I will give you some money, so that your parents can get married.' And rolling the window back up, we glide serenely away, leaving our friend, open mouthed, uncomprehending.

What is happening to me? We have only been back in this country a matter of hours, and already I am turning into an ogre. OK, lack of sleep is a factor, but if I don't calm down I am going to get myself arrested, or worse, have my bum pictured on a number-plate recognition camera.

A few minutes down the road is a park, so I pull over, and we get out for a walk. A fine drizzle is falling. I am too angry to sleep now. 'Can you believe, for just one millisecond, that we were even remotely considering coming back to this country?'

Chrissie smiles sweetly, remarkable self-control, after the night we have had. 'I wonder what is happening right now, back home?' she ponders. 'I bet Isabel will be out sweeping the street. Loli will be on her patio, clearing her throat. Fernando will be blowing his nose, like the Queen Mary leaving Southampton. The Dustman will be towing his rubber bin up the hill. Cruzojo will be peeping through his blinds. Susanna will be polishing her windows with that white dog. Campo Pete will have his Elvis records on, Leopard-skin woman and auntie Vera will be gossiping, and sexy-eyes Jose The Pan will be missing me, I hope! And, of course, the sun will be out.'

Home? Did she say home? She *did* say home! Our Spanish home, of course, in the land of sunsets, and olives!

Made in the USA
Middletown, DE
18 June 2019